# Beat Your Drum Loudly

## The Revolutionary War Patriots
## of the Raines and Painter Family

Minuteman illustration courtesy of the Smithsonian Institution Research Information System: Stephens, Ann S. *Pictorial History of the War for the Union*. New York: Benjamin W. Hitchcock, 1866. Public Domain.

Cover painting: Joseph Christian Leyendecker (1874-1951). Public Domain.

Compass
Flower
Press

Published by
Compass Flower Press

Columbia, Missouri
compassflowerpress.com

Library of Congress Control Number: 2025916208
ISBN: 978-1-951960-72-8

# Beat Your Drum Loudly
## The Revolutionary War Patriots
## of The Raines and Painter Family

## Virgil E. Raines

Compass Flower Press
Columbia, Missouri

**"Stand your ground,
don't fire unless
fired upon,
but if they mean
to have a war,
let it begin here!"**

*—Militia Captain John Parker, Lexington Green, 19 April 1775*

# Table of Contents

# About the Author

Colonel (U.S. Army Retired) Virgil E. (Sonny) Raines Jr. was born in Jackson County (North Kansas City) to V. Elwood Raines and Ruby Nadine Adams/Raines. He was raised on a farm in Shelby County, Missouri, attended school there, and graduated from Paris High School in Paris, Missouri. He enlisted in the army during the Vietnam war and obtained a commission as a second lieutenant. He became an army aviator, served in several overseas assignments, and commanded from captain to colonel level during his nearly thirty-year military career. He graduated from Park University and the University of Pennsylvania with multiple degrees. He is a graduate of the Army Command and General Staff College and the Army War College. He has served on several college faculties as well as a professor of military science at the U.S. Naval War College. He has written several articles and books: "Criteria for Military Success in the War on Drugs," *Horse Sense—William Rains and the Missouri Seventh Volunteer Cavalry, Footprints of the Painter and Scott Families of Missouri,* and *The Problem of the Perrigo Patriots of Pownal.* He has also written several short articles on family members who served in the Second World War, as well as technical aviation articles. Virgil is a member of the Sons of the American Revolution and teaches genealogy research to potential DAR and SAR members as well as to patients at veterans' homes. He is also a board member of the Monroe County (Missouri) Historical Society.

He is married to Emma Jo Painter, also of Paris, Missouri. The Raineses live on a farm in Boone County, Missouri, and have three children and seven grandchildren.

## Preface

Storytelling is a traditional tool used by many cultures for passing on historical knowledge in a way it will be remembered by subsequent generations. That is how I learned some important information about my family, around the kitchen table or in the living room after a family meal. Other family members—uncles, grandparents, and distant relatives—would also pass along these treasures I still remember. Maybe these stories were not 100 percent fact, maybe they were a little embellished or maybe my memory is now playing tricks on the facts I heard. Nonetheless, stories like these are an important part of the fabric of our lives. I maintain that these stories even help us understand events in the future when they occur. I wouldn't say they predict the future, but perhaps these stories help us understand and react to events as they happen. Does history repeat itself?

I believe that modern American society has become structured to the point that this "storytelling hour" often does not take place. It is easy to say we are simply too busy, but I'll leave that up to the readers. I am, however, certain that young people today know far less about their ancestors than my parents and I did when we were younger.

I cannot say this book is a "storytelling effort," as I am unfortunately not an adept storyteller. Neither is it an historical novel, but it is my effort to pass along family history in a way it will be remembered. I believe I have done that.

# Acknowledgements

A project of this magnitude was a major undertaking that required assistance from a variety of sources. It involved searching for Patriots hidden within at least 512 family groups—from both Emma Jo's and my own family lines—seven or eight generations in the past. Then there was the task of separating myth from fact, sometimes wondering if that was necessary. I had a lot of help, and I owe recognition to numerous individuals, and I certainly will miss some.

My wife Emma Jo has supported this multi-year undertaking with ideas, criticism, and patience. It would not have been possible without her knowledge of the finer points of DAR and of history in general.

I must recognize the late Richard Scott, a first cousin of Emma Jo who did fruitful research on the Murphy and Scott lines of their family in the late 1980s BC (Before Computers). Those records were left to Emma Jo, and our review of them forty years later allowed me to reopen those lines that I had frankly set aside as "roadblocks." Thanks to Ricard, I am now telling their stories.

Gary David Ashby, a modern-day descendant of Patriot David Ashby, has collected a trove of primary sources he obtained the hard way—from libraries and other institutions—and made these sources available to others. I owe him deep gratitude for helping me tell the "Ashby Story." Gary, I sincerely hope I have presented this great American family in the best light.

The late professor Don Bishop, a descendant of the Perrigo family, produced a Perrigo family newsletter forty-five years ago. This served as a basis for my research of that family and was instrumental for writing the book *The Problem of the Perrigo Patriots of Pownal* and for some of the Perrigo stories contained in this book. I respect but do not always agree with Don's facts and proposals, but I suspect he might not have agreed with some of my ideas. Thanks, Don, your work from last century was a big assistance in my telling the Perrigo story.

The late Robert Jerome "Bob" Younger has served as an inspiration to me in my pursuit of family stories over the years. A gifted author, publisher, and uncle, his knowledge of family and military history, and the ability to put all that together in an inspirational package, has been the model for much of my work. His book *The Younger and Plummer Families of Missouri* seems to continue where this book ends. Bob, I wish I had known you longer, maybe I'd shoot a little straighter. (Hint: that's in a country-western song.)

**"Every post is honorable in which a man can serve his country."**

—*George Washington's letter to Benedict Arnold, 14 September 1775*

## Chapter One: Lest We Forget

Early in my life, I found it difficult to embrace the study of history. I noticed people kept making the same mistakes by failing to grasp the lessons left us, and that discouraged me. As I matured I came to realize that I could play a role in passing on some of the lessons of my forefathers through study of their lives and acccomplishments. That gave me some perspective on the value of the lessons of history. We need to listen to these lessons, for there is so much to be gleaned from them and applied to our lives in the modern world. Also, I found it both interesting and rewarding to know where I came from. I often find it hard to live up to the examples set by my many grandfathers and grandmothers. They were made of the right stuff!

One of my pastimes is researching my family history. My mother was active in this endeavor, as is my brother Gary. He is much more accomplished at this than I, but I saw an opportunity to delve into my family's military contributions to this nation. This soon led me to research the American Revolution to discover if any of my or Emma Jo's family had been involved in this war. Most of our family lines have lived in this nation for hundreds of years, so I expected to find maybe two or three Patriots in the bunch. I was pleasantly supprised by the number of Patriots we found, and we may never complete this project, as my ancestors have so much to tell us. One only needs to know where to look and what questions to ask. My great uncle, a professional historian and publisher, once told me that his ancestors talked to him. At that stage of my life, that seemed a bit "fringe" to me, and it made me a little uncomfortable. Bob Younger was a respected writer, publisher, and reseacher, so I merely said, "That's nice, Bob," and changed the subject. That was a lesson that took some time to be fully appreciated by me. Our ancestors do talk to us! Bob is long gone, but I will always treasure the wisdom he passed on to me.

I am in awe of Patriots. I have met only a few modern patriots, but I hold those men and women in high regard. I place those who fought for and supported this nation in its fight for independence in a special category. I am humbled by their vision, commitment, and bravery. If you are a member of my or Emma Jo's family lines, the Revolutionary War Patriots I have researched are first family, and secondly, they did something very significant. Their service to this new nation influenced history in no small way, and their lives were influenced to the extent that it shaped future generations, even to this day. **They placed their lives, sacred honor, and fortunes at great risk for their family's freedom and the freedoms we enjoy today.** Their lives are worthy of recognition, and we would do well to listen to what they have to tell us. This book is my attempt to gather their stories and present them in a useful and interesting way. I have researched these stories mainly for our children and grandchildren, but there is something for everyone, family or not. Here are some notable accomplishments or activities of featured Patriots to watch for in this book.

- A great-grandfather knew and did business with Thomas Jefferson and George Washington.
- A featured Patriot was the second great-grandfather of one of the most well-known outlaws of the nineteenth century.
- Several great-grandfathers fought in some of the most decisive battles of the Revolution and were wounded multiple times. Several were taken prisoner of war by the British, Tories, and Native Americans.
- Four great-grandfathers fought in the first battle of the Revolution and probably heard the "shot that was heard around the world."
- Three or four of these Patriots were first-generation Americans. They came to the colonies and soon took up arms to protect their new-found freedom.
- A featured Patriot's uncle signed the Declaration of Independence and was a major financier of the Revolution and a close confidant of George Washington.
- A great-grandfather fought with Ethan Allen and the Green Mountain Boys. Remember studying those guys in school?
- A great-grandfather was a personal bodyguard for General George Washington. The father of this man served with then Colonel Washington in the French and Indian War. This man's father and uncles also served as chain bearers for George Washington while he served in the western parts of Virginia prior to the French and Indian War.
- Four featured Patriots served all or part of the first winter of the war at Valley Forge.
- A Patriot great-grandfather's son became one of the Civil War's most well-known generals and later a presidential candidate.

The following Patriots are included in the main body of this project, and Emma Jo Raines and I are direct descendants of them. While there are other Patriots in the family tree, and many discussed in this book, there is a direct dependency line established with the first forty-five historical figures. Others are just related. Several of these individuals are recognized by both the Daughters of the American Revolution (DAR) and the Sons of the American Revolution (SAR) as Patriots, and this is noted in their stories. Here is a synopsis of their relationship to our family. Their complete stories follow in chapter four.

**1. Joshua Logan Younger**—Fifth great-grandfather on the Raines side. My grandmother Raines was a Younger.
**2. Major Joseph Gist**—Fifth great-grandfather on the Raines side. My great-grandmother Younger's mother was a Plummer, and her grandmother was a Gist and a granddaughter of Joseph.

3. **William Gist**—Sixth great-grandfather on the Raines side. Father of Major Joseph Gist above. He was awarded Patriot status by the Daughters of the American Revolution for patriotic service, as he signed the Maryland Oath of Allegiance.

4. **Samuel Adams**—Fifth great-grandfather on my mother's side. Adams all the way down.

5. **Captain Casper Reinecker**—Fifth great-grandfather on the Raines line. Casper's daughter married the son of Major Joseph Gist, so is related from the Younger family line.

6. **Paulus Reinecker**—Brother to Captain Casper Reinecker, number 5 above. Paulus's great-grandson was Hiram Renaker, my great-grandfather on the Adams line. This makes Paulus my fifth great-grandfather. Two sides of our family lines (Adams/Younger) link with the Reineckers.

7. **Johann Peter Wise (Weiss) Sr.**—Fifth great-grandfather on the Adams line. His son John's daughter Susannah married Hiram Rennaker, and their daughter Doretha married Walter Grant Adams. Their son Walter Raymond Adams was the father of my mother, Ruby Nadine Adams Raines.

8. **Johann Adam Christopher Wise (Weiss)**—Sixth great-grandfather on the Adams line. He was the father of Johannes Peter Wise, above.

9. **Jacob Painter**—Fourth great-grandfather on Emma Jo's side. Painters all the way down.

10. **Sergeant Fielding Ashby**—Fourth great-grandfather on Emma Jo's side. His daughter married John Lewis Murphy. Jo's grandmother Scott was a Murphy and granddaughter of John Lewis Murphy.

11. **David Ashby**—Fifth great-grandfather on Emma Jo's side. His son Fielding above also served.

12. **Captain Robert R. Ashby**—Sixth great-grandfather on Emma Jo's side. David, number 11 above, was his son. Emma Jo is descended from three generations of Ashby Patriots.

13. **Richard Lee**—Fourth great-grandfather on the Raines line. His granddaughter married Robert Fowler, and Robert's daughter Louvisa Raines was my great-grandmother.

14. **John Whipple III**—Sixth great-grandfather on the Adams line. His daughter Jemima Whipple married Patriot Samuel Adams, number 4 above. His father was John Adams, his son John Quincy Adams, his son Walter Grant Adams, his son Walter Raymond Adams, and his daughter Nadine Adams/Raines is my mother.

15. **Captain William Scott**—Fifth great-grandfather on the Raines line. His daughter married Patriot Richard Lee, number 13 above.

16. **Ensign Henry Carmen**—Fourth great-grandfather on the Painter line. His granddaughter married John Thomas Painter, and his son was Frank Painter, Jo's grandfather.

17. **Martin Johnston**—Fifth great-grandfather on the Painter line. His son John Johnston's daughter Betsy Johnston/Jaquess married William Carmen, son of Patriot Henry Carmen, above.

18. **Lieutenant Joseph H. Wright**—Sixth great-grandfather on the Painter line. He was the father of Patriot Martin Johnston's wife above.

19. **Sergeant Joshua Pearce Sr.**—Fourth great-grandfather on the Adams line. Joshua Pearce Jr.'s daughter Catherine married John Quincy Adams, the father of Walter Grant Adams, my great-grandfather.

20. **Nehemiah Patch**—Fifth great-grandfather on the Adams line. His daughter Mary married John Adams, son of Patriot Samuel Adams, number 4 above.

21. **John Patch III**—Sixth great-grandfather on the Adams line. His son is Nehemiah above.

**22. Nathaniel Wells**—Sixth great-grandfather on the Adams line. His daughter Hepzibah married Nehemiah Patch, above.

**23. Ellis Jones**—Fourth great-grandfather on the Younger family line. Ellis Jones's son Lewis Reice Jones married Elizabeth Gist, the granddaughter of Joseph Gist, number 2 above. Their daughter Eliza Pamela Jones married Franklin Plummer, my great-great-grandfather. Their daughter Sarah (Sallie) married Coleman Younger, my great-grandfather, thus Ellis Jones is my fourth great-grandfather.

**24. Captain Alexander Wells**—Fifth great-grandfather on the Younger family line. Son Richard's daughter Leah married George Gilbert Plummer, who was father of Franklin Plummer, noted above.

**25. Lawrence Abraham Woolery**—Fourth great-grandfather on the Younger family line. Son Lawrence George's daughter Jane married Charles Lee Younger Jr., who was the father of my great-grandfather Coleman Washington Younger. This Charles Lee Younger Jr. is the son of the more well-known Charles Lee Younger, discussed elsewhere in this book.

**26. George Lee**—Fourth great-grandfather on the Raines/Younger line. His daughter Ann Matilda married Lawrence George Woolery, son of Lawrence Abraham Woolery above. Their daughter Jane married Charles Lee Younger, whose son Milton Toney Younger was the father of my great-grandfather Coleman Washington Younger.

**27. Lewis Murphy**—Fifth great-grandfather on the Painter/Scott line. His son was John Murphy Sr., who married Elizabeth Ashby, daughter of Fielding Ashby, number 10 above.

**28. John Murphy Sr.**—Fourth great-grandfather on the Painter/Scott line. He married Elizabeth "Betsy" Ashby, and his son was Fielding Murphy, father of Joseph Roney Murphy, Jo's great-grandfather.

**29. Jesse Oglesby**—Fourth great-grandfather on the Painter/Scott/Murphy line. His daughter Maria married Ellis Roney, and his daughter Elizabeth Roney married Fielding Murphy, whose son Joseph Roney Murphy was the father of Bessie Pauline Murphy/Scott, Jo's grandmother.

**30. Jacob Oglesby Jr.**—Fifth great-grandfather on the Painter/Scott/Murphy line. He is the father of Jesse Oglesby above.

**31. David Witt Sr.**—Sixth great-grandfather in the Painter/Scott line. Son David Jr.'s daughter Celia married Patriot Jesse Oglesby above.

**32. Henry Myers**—Fourth great-grandfather on the Painter/Scott line. His daughter Barbara "Barbary" married George Allen. Their daughter Melinda married Joseph M. Crooks, and their daughter Fannie Braden married DeMarcus Scott, Emma Jo's great-grandfather.

**33. Sergeant Joseph Roberts**—Fourth great-grandfather on the Adams line. His grandson John Samuel Robert's daughter Stella Catherine Roberts married Andrew Jackson Perrigo. Their daughter Stella Francis Perrigo/Adams was my grandmother.

**34. Benjamin Roberts Sr.**—Fifth great-grandfather on the Adams line. Benjamin was the father of Sergeant Joseph Roberts above.

**35. Thomas Triplett**—Fifth great-grandfather on the Adams line. His daughter Francis married Sergeant Joseph Roberts above.

**36. Hugh Glenn Sr.**—Fifth great-grandfather on the Raines line. His son was Martin Glenn, and Martin's daughter was Mary Ann Polly Ann Glenn, wife of Grissom R. Lee, who was the son of Richard Lee, Patriot number thirteen above.

**37. Hercules Roney II**—Fourth great-grandfather on the Painter/Murphy line. His daughter Elizabeth married Fielding Murphy; their son Joseph Roney Murphy was the father of Bessie Scott, Jo's grandmother.

**38. John Duncan Sr.**—Sixth great-grandfather in the Scott/Painter line. His son was John Duron Duncan Jr., and John Jr.'s son was Joseph Duncan Sr., whose daughter Elizabeth married Thomas Burris Embree. Thomas's daughter Nancy Ann married Davis Scott, Jo's second great-grandfather.

**39. Sergeant John Duron Duncan Jr.**—Fifth great-grandfather of Emma Jo and the son of John Duncan shown above.

**40. Joseph Duncan Sr.**—Fourth great-grandfather of Emma Jo and the son of Sergeant John Duron Duncan above. They represent three generations of Patriots.

**41. William Webb III**—Fourth great-grandfather in the Painter/Dilts line. His daughter Mary Polly married Alexander Cooper Baker. See the next Patriot.

**42. Maurice Baker**—Fourth great-grandfather in the Painter/Dilts line. His son Alexander Cooper Baker's daughter Anne Elizabeth married Henry Boren. Their daughter Louise married Albert G. Dilts Jr. His daughter Stella married William Franklin Painter, Emma Jo's grandfather.

**43. Ishmael Rains**—Fifth great-grandfather in the Rains/Raines line. His son was Ambrose, his son was Charles, his son was John Washington Marshall, his son was William Pleas, and his son was my father V. Elwood Sr. Raineses all the way down.

**44. David Perrigo**—Fifth great-grandfather on the Adams line. His son was Justice, his son was Justice Jr., his son was Martin Van Buren, his son was Andrew Jackson Perrigo, and his daughter was Blanche Perrigo/Adams, my grandmother.

**45. James Perrigo Sr.**—Sixth great-grandfather on the Adams line. He was the father of David Perrigo above.

**"To be prepared for war is one of the most effectual means of preserving peace."**

*—George Washington in the first annual address to both houses of Congress,*
*Friday, 8 January 1790*

## Chapter Two: How They Organized and Fought

I should first take a short side-trip to explain how military units were organized for the Revolution. You will see various organizational terms used throughout the book, and it is important to recognize how the colonial military was organized and how our ancestors fit into those units. That is a part of the history and story of these Patriots.

The basic military organization was the "regiment." It was commanded by a colonel and consisted of 4–7 companies, which were each commanded by a captain. Each colony and some counties and cities organized regiments for local protection, and then the Continental Congress directed that some of the regiments be assigned to federal control, which created the "Continental Line." General Washington commanded nearly all the Continental forces. The Continental Line forces were identified as colony units and were paid by the Continental Congress. The county and city units were usually classified as militias. You might see a regiment identified as, for example, the Fourth Virginia Regiment. There may have been more than one such unit. One may have remained in the control of the colony, one in the control of the Continental Line, and then one organized and controlled by a city or county. It is important to make this distinction when researching these units, as these factors can contribute to confusion in research, and each unit has its history.

As the war progressed, unit strength changed drastically because of illness, discharges, and casualties. This required consolidation of units to maintain combat-effective units. Thus, you might notice a Patriot serving in several units. This may be due either to unit consolidations or reenlistment in another unit. Soldiers enlisted for various lengths of service. Some regiments—especially those of city, county, or state control—allowed almost any length of enlistment, from thirty days to several months. Some state-controlled regiments, especially those destined for Continental control, encouraged enlistment for the duration of the war.

Regiments, especially the Continental Line units, were identified numerically: third, fifth, etc. Most written records identified the regiment as Colonel Smith's Regiment, etc., and gave the numerical designation if it had such a designation. Some regiments elected their company commanders, as with the Green Mountain Boys, which also elected their regimental commander.

I do not want to overlook the fact that there were fighting organizations not organized as regiments, although the regiment was the basic organization. The Pennsylvania colony organized some of their militia as battalions consisting of any number of companies. They were smaller organizations than a regiment that were commanded by a lieutenant colonel. You will see "dragoons" or cavalry units, as with Lightfoot Lee's horse cavalry. I will discuss the Guilford Courthouse Battle in which this type of unit was very important to the regimental soldiers in shaping the battlefield. You will see "ranger" units that served as an intelligence source and as tripwires for the fighting forces. The artillery units were essential supporters of the fighting regiments. They were often assigned in direct support of a regiment, although controlled by a higher headquarter. Artillery was always in short supply, therefore tightly controlled.

Units did their own recruiting. A soldier enlisted with a company, and its parent regiment maintained and paid that soldier. Promotions were at the will of the regimental commander. Often, soldiers received inducements to serve in the form of land warrants or bounties. After serving honorably and being discharged, the soldier could apply for the warrant and use that warrant to obtain a land patent from their state of enlistment. The rewards for service varied greatly from colony to colony. Some did not offer any such rewards. Some soldiers would sell their warrant rather than move to the west to obtain unsettled land in Indian country. Later, in 1818, the federal government offered pensions to Revolutionary War veterans. The application was an involved process requiring county court action. During this request process, the Patriot would make a verbal statement accounting for his service and recall the names of his officers and commanders. They would sometimes account for their lives following the war. These statements are of tremendous value toward understanding their stories. These pensions have the appearance of being need-based. Those applying were required to establish a need for a pension. Men of means usually would not make such a statement and would not apply. Sometimes the wife would apply after the death of the Patriot. It is useful to know that a Patriot's wife was not eligible for a pension unless they were married during the war. This is sometimes useful to settle the marriage date range for a Patriot and his wife.

To be historically correct, there were more Pension Acts than the 1818 act that provided for Continental Line soldiers and officers. A 1780 act provided for widows and orphans. An 1832 act provided for all officers and soldiers and who served in the various militias not covered by the 1818 act. The 1832 act did not provide a pension for surviving wives who were not married during the war. These widows were not included for several years, at which time few of them remained alive.

After the war, most regimental records were sent to the National Archives, and those records were cleaned up and checked for errors and missing documents. Some regimental records remained at the colony/state level. This fact offers possible sources for research and multiple possibilities for mistakes. My research has used all available sources, at both the national and the state level, as well as books, manuscripts, and family records. Research will continue of our family Patriots; therefore, this version is a first edition subject to future update and correction as may be necessary over time.

An important part of these stories is that several of the relatives discussed in this book never served in the military during the Revolutionary War, yet I am calling them Patriots. How is that possible? Both the Daughters of the American Revolution and the Sons of the American

Revolution assign Patriot status to those who performed other important duties, otherwise identified as "patriotic service," and I follow those guidelines. Some of those individuals were:

1. Elected officials who supported the Revolution at city, county, colony, and national level.
2. Members of the various Committees for Safety. These organizations supervised the city and county militias. They put themselves at risk by performing these important duties and were vulnerable to activities of Loyalists and other misfits. Remember, this was as much a civil war as a revolution. Many would have been hung had they lost the war. They were not military, thusly they would have received much different treatment than former military.
3. Those individuals signing loyalty oaths required by many towns and counties. These records are available for the most part and would have surely been used by the British to exact retribution had they won the war.
4. Individuals who sold or gave material support to the military organizations. This included food for individuals or animals as well as boarding soldiers or providing them health care. Following the war, procedures were instituted to reimburse these individuals for this support at the county and state level. My second great-grandfather lost a musket to a local militia and later claimed that loss and was reimbursed. He would have been maybe ten or twelve years old. He did not serve in the military, and I believe his musket served in the Battle of Guilford Courthouse, but that is another story. Another group of people falling into this group is women. Their contributions to the Revolution often go untold. Some sold supplies to local militias, or these supplies were just taken while their spouses were away with their units. Again, they placed themselves at risk of retribution from Loyalists for these acts. I have records of my sixth great-grandmother selling supplies, later making a claim and being reimbursed following the war. Some women followed their husbands and units and performed important functions such as laundering and cooking. Few records exist reporting those activities, and these Patriots go unrecognized. I believe such a Patriot may be unrecognized in the Perrigo family, and I will discuss that question later.
5. Those families that suffered deprivation. I have found one such example in Emma Jo's family line.

I explain in each Patriot's story if they served in a military organization and the designation of that unit as well as where they served and the battles they fought in, if possible. The same standard applies for patriotic service claims. Records exist for those who served in appointed or elected positions that materially supported the Revolution. Records also exist for claims for providing material support, such as rations, livestock, or other materials. I document those claims with appropriate notes and references.

**"A people unused to restraint must be led, they will not be drove."**

*—George Washington to Major General Stirling, Sunday, 19 January 1777*

### Chapter Three: Family Connections

I discovered at least ten father-and-son groups (total twenty Patriots) serving in the Revolution. I was surprised to discover this level of family commitment to the Revolution. Even more surprising was the fact that in several families there was a three-generation commitment: father, son, and grandson Patriots. The Ashby family is notable. Grandfather Robert, son David, and then grandson Fielding all served not only in the Revolution, but during the French and Indian War. In fact, this family, including uncles and cousins, produced more than twenty Patriots. A later chapter in this book will recount their stories. William Gist and son Major Joseph Gist are a further example of fathers and sons serving. The extended Gist family also produced more than twenty Patriots, and their contributions are worth telling, so a later chapter in this book will be devoted to the Gist family of Baltimore, Maryland.

The Perrigo family of New England produced at least fifteen Patriots. My fifth and sixth great-grandfathers David and James Perrigo Sr. of Pownal, Vermont, are featured in this book. The mother of David, Lydia Hayward, is a *Mayflower* Descendant, and I will devote a chapter to this family later in the book as I believe harsh treatment encountered by the family based on state and religious policies might have motivated them to prove their worth. This family line produced some incredible stories that I will relate. In fact, I have published a book about the Perrigo Family.

There were father/son-in-law connections as well—for example, the John Whipple III/Samuel Adams relationship. Samuel married John's daughter. The Whipples were a very well-known and prosperous family, and Samuel, although not a poor man, was of common origins. John and Samuel fought in the same unit and were neighbors. Both family lines had lived in the Ipswich, Massachusetts, area for at least four generations by the time of the Revolution.

The second father/son-in-law example is the Captain William Scott/Richard Lee connection. This was not discovered in my early research but became evident during the development of the Revolution story. William's daughter Elizabeth married Richard Lee prior to the Revolution. These were old Virginia families that made history.

The Reinecker/Gist relationship was like the Scott/Lee relationship. Both families owned businesses and were involved in agriculture. Captain Reinecker's daughter Maria married a grandson of Major Joseph Gist. The Gists were from Maryland, with the Reineckers being from Pennsylvania. Both families later settled in the same West Virginia county. The Reineckers are connected to the Raines family in more than one way.

The Sergeant Joshua Pearce/Adams connection further adds to the father-in-law to son-in-law element of this project. Joshua's son, Joshua Jr., had a daughter that married into the John Quincy Adams line. John Quincy was a grandson of Samuel Adams.

These relationships are likely confusing to most people without family tree diagrams, but the intent of presenting these relationships was to suggest that the Revolution was a family affair. It influenced family development, as did the Civil War seventy-five years later. I am not sure that the later great wars can make a similar claim. As with the Civil War, I discovered brothers sometimes facing brothers in several instances. That should have been of little surprise, as Benjamin Franklin and his son took opposite sides during the Revolution. There are numerous other family relationships revealed throughout the book that support the contention that the Revolutionary War was a family affair.

As research for the project matured, it became obvious that more than fathers and sons, brothers and sons-in-law contributed to the success of the Revolution. There was much more to the story that I seemed to be glossing over. I was overlooking the stories of the wives of these Patriots. They contributed in no small way but in many ways I had simply overlooked. Many of these forty-five Patriots were married when their service began.

Consider the fact that several of these families had children and that the father was absent for at least ninety days, and in some cases, the entire duration of the war. Consider that the man probably took the one rifle in the family and left perhaps a shotgun. Crops were in the field, and the livestock still needed to be cared for. Consider the fact that this war was as much a civil war as a revolution. The Tories presented a real threat to remaining family members, as did certain tribes of Native Americans. See the Gist and Ashby chapters later in the book to gain an understanding of the threats faced by the families who were missing a source of protection.

The various local and state militias, and especially the Continental Line units, had tremendous logistical needs. Some of these needs were met by foraging. Families would often be asked to sell livestock, food, or services to the military. They received no reimbursement at the time of purchase but sometimes received an IOU from a commissioned officer. These receipts were to be later presented to the various county courts for reimbursement. These activities became a part of history that I utilized for research. More importantly, some families suffered deprivation because of these activities. I believe I will ultimately discover women Patriots using these documents, but that is a future activity.

It is important to consider the spelling of the family names of our Patriots. I encountered many ways to spell the same name. I devoted a chapter in my book *Horse Sense—William Rains and the Missouri Seventh Volunteer Cavalry* to tracing the spelling of that family name. The same fact applies here: if you are unable to read and write, you are at the mercy of whomever records your name. Many of our Patriots could not read or write very well, if at all. Consequently, I found military records using different spellings than later census records and sometimes even different spellings for marriage and probate records.

I encountered different spellings of several Patriot names. This fact does not detract from their stories but presented some potential for mistakes and missed evidence. Considerable research time was devoted to rooting out such distractions to ensure I got it right, and I believe I did that. The Patriot stories below discuss activities involved with the Adams line, for example. There were a bunch of Samuel Adams of that era, all from Massachusetts, but I have the right Patriot here.

Identification of the right Patriot and his family line was an objective of top priority in this book. I have few doubts about the success of this endeavor. First, these men are well-documented Patriots, and second, I have the right family line connected to that Patriot. I have addressed some questions about two descendants, and that research will go on. I've applied the standard of "preponderance of evidence" and left it for future evidence to totally resolve these questions. I was particularly careful and diligent with the three Virginia "Lee" lines connected with these stories. I do not lightly claim these connections; I have researched those lines for several years and collaborated with other researchers. As I will note later, I elected to not include descendancy from a Lee line Patriot in this book since I could not prove the relationship.

The documentation of lineage was an important effort with all the Patriots presented. I elected not to include several family Patriots for the simple reason that I could not prove the lineage, and I will continue the effort to tell their stories in later editions. More on this subject in a later chapter in this book.

I included names of descendants of these forty-five Patriots at the expense of making the book a more difficult read, but it was an important undertaking from a historical viewpoint. For example, I thought it useful to mention that outlaw Cole Younger was a descendant of Patriot Joshua Logan Younger. It is interesting that sons or grandsons of these Patriots also distinguished themselves in later wars or political leadership. It is a part of the story.

**"It is infinitely better to have a few good Men, than many different ones."**

*—George Washington's letter to James McHenry, Friday, 10 August 1798*

## Chapter Four: Our Patriot Stories

**Joshua Logan Younger**
Born: 11 May 1755, Hampshire County, Virginia (now West Virginia)
Died: 2 Aug 1834
Burial: Bedford, Lawrence, Indiana Leatherwood Cemetery
Service: Twelfth and Eighth Virginia Regiments, Continental Line
Rank: Private
Service Dates: 28 Jan 1777–11 April 1779
Wife: (1) Elizabeth Lee and (2) Catherine Yoter
Lineage: Son Charles Lee Younger, Milton Toney Younger, Charles Lee Younger, Coleman Younger, Blanche Younger, V. Elwood Raines Sr., my father
DAR: A130307
SAR: P-326473

Joshua was the son of John Younger (1707–1770) and Sarah Kennard (1714–1772) of Shrewsbury Parish, Kent, Maryland, later of Goochland County, Virginia. This is not a proven relationship, but several of his possible siblings settled in Hampshire County, Virginia, and I have seen DNA evidence linking John Younger to Joshua, Joshua's son Richard Lee Younger, and the well-known outlaw grandchildren.[1]

His birth date was found in an Indiana DAR book documenting his burial location.[2] His birthplace of Hampshire County, Virginia, now West Virginia, was given in his pension statement in which he stated he lived in that county until he moved to Nicholas County, Kentucky, in 1779. I have a copy of his lengthy pension request. Hampshire County was established in 1754 from parts of Frederick County, Virginia. It is interesting that Hampshire County was initially surveyed by George Washington with the assistance of a survey crew from the Ashby family of Frederick County in the 1740s. Patriot David Ashby, discussed later in the book, was accompanied by his father and brothers on this project authorized by Lord Fairfax. The Ashby Patriots and this survey will be discussed at length later in the book.

Joshua first married Elizabeth Virginia Lee (1755–1784), whose family heritage is elusive. This marriage may have occurred in Hampshire County in July 1770, but those details remain unproven. Some researchers claim she is the daughter of Senator William Henry Lee, thus being closely related to Robert E. Lee, but that is merely a claim and not supported by evidence. Coleman Younger the outlaw made this statement in his book late in his life when he said she was the

---

[1] The Younger Family DNA Surname Project, December 2007. This study utilized the results of five participants and seems to link the Missouri Younger family with John Younger and Sara Kannard of Maryland. While there were exceptions to the linkages to some of the Missouri Youngers, the link between Joshua Logan Younger and John Younger is a solid relationship. Source: Genealogy by Genetics Ltd., Houston, Texas.
[2] *Soldiers and Patriots of the American Revolution Buried in Indiana.* Compiled and edited by Mrs. Roscoe C. O'Byrene, Chairman. Originally published by the Indiana Daughters of the American Revolution, 1938, and reprinted by the Clearfield Company, Inc., 1994. 1999. Page 394.

sister of General Lee.[3] I have researched this topic for years and can say neither I nor other serious researchers have produced evidence supporting that claim. The William Henry Lee line is well researched and documented, and Elizabeth Virginia's birth date is about one year prior to the marriage of Senator William Henry Lee and Ann Aylet, and Elizabeth is not reflected in any of the family records I have reviewed. Elizabeth's death date and location and those facts remain a mystery. She died a young woman and probably moved to Kentucky with Joshua and their six children that were born prior to the move, with four more children being born in Kentucky after about fourteen years of marriage. The Raines line is descended from Elizabeth.

Joshua married Catherine Yoter (1766–1858) after the death of Elizabeth. Catherine was possibly born in Alsace, Lorraine, France, but most likely in Hampshire County, Virginia. The marriage date of 15 September 1787 was given by him at the time of his 1818 pension application. Joshua and his ten children were living in Nicholas County, Kentucky, but the marriage was in Hampshire County, a fact he provided in his pension statement. Other researchers have given her birthplace as France, but Catherine stated in the 1850 census that she was born in Virginia.

Records show more than one unit of service, but as combat losses mounted and enlistments expired, it was necessary to combine units. This was unpopular with the soldiers who had enlisted in a specific unit, but it became necessary to maintain combat-effective units. He is recorded in the "List of Revolutionary War Soldiers of Virginia."[4]

He applied for a pension on 18 June 1818 and stated that he served from January 1777 until May 1779, when he was discharged due to injuries he had received in battle at Winchester, Virginia. His former regimental commander, Colonel James Wood, certified that Joshua had been a good soldier and had in fact been wounded several times and that the last wound required he be discharged. He lived in Kentucky at the time of the application for pension. His pension number was W-1009.[5]

The Sons of the American Revolution records show that he enlisted on 28 January 1777 in Captain William Vance's Company of the Twelfth Virginia Regiment of Foot commanded by Colonel James Wood for the period of the war. He fought at the Battle of Boston, the Battle of Quebec, the Battle of Germantown, and the surrender of Burgoyne. He was with Washington at Valley Forge, and at the Battles of Monmouth, Brandywine, and Germantown. He is a documented survivor of Valley Forge, where he wintered in Jan–May 1777. An April 1778 muster reports his presence at Valley Forge. His regiment was taken prisoner at Charleston, South Carolina, in 1780, and these soldiers served the remainder of the war as prisoners of war, but fortunately Joshua had been discharged in 1779 before the campaign to Charleston.

Several other Patriots discussed in this book also served in the Twelfth Virginia Regiment. That regiment was consolidated with two other Virginia regiments (Fourth and Eighth) by the time of their capture at Charleston.

---

[3] *The Story of Cole Younger.* Cole Younger. Triton Press. 1988.
[4] "List of Revolutionary War Soldiers of Virginia." Special Report of the Department of Archives and History for 1912. H.J. Eckendorf, Archivist. David Bottom, Superintendent of Public Printing, 1913. Page 335 lists Joshua as a Virginia soldier.
[5] "Revolutionary Pensioners of 1818." A Report of the Secretary of War. 28 March 1818. Page 156.

Joshua received a six-hundred-acre land grant in Nelson County, Kentucky. This was grant number 6001.[6] The 1810, 1820, and 1830 Federal Census Reports show he lived in Nicholas County, Kentucky. He farmed for a living in Kentucky as he reported in his pension hearings, and I believe that his farming activities involved owning and selling fine racehorses. His son Charles Lee Younger owned racehorses as a young man and was known to race and bet on local horse races. He no doubt obtained some of those skills from his dad, Joshua. The Younger family's association with fine and fast horses is the stuff of legends.

In a pension application, he claimed few assets and no land. Records have been found showing earlier land ownership in Kentucky, so further research is needed to determine what happened to the land. He likely transferred the land to his sons well prior to his death. I have Joshua's National Archives military records including his pension request and associated documents. His service is also recorded by the state of Virginia.[7]

He is buried in Indiana, and that location is just across the border from the state of Kentucky. He and Catherine lived with his son Stever (Steven) at the time of his death, and most of his children from his second marriage lived near them. He is buried in the Leatherwood Cemetery in Bedford, Lawrence County, Indiana. His family requested and received a military tombstone in 1928.

The DAR has recognized his gravestone with a plaque, and I have a copy of the presentation by the chapter registrar. She stated that Joshua and his wife had lived with their son Stever in Bedford for about two years prior to his death.

The children of Joshua and Elizabeth Lee are difficult to trace, but I believe they had the following ten children:

- Elizabeth Lee Lewis, 1772–1859. Married and lived in Orange County, Indiana.
- Peter Logan, 1772–1841. Remained in Grant County, Kentucky.
- Isaac, 1775–1847. Lived in Bullitt County, Kentucky.
- Henry, 1775–1830. Served as a soldier in Kentucky in 1793 and settled in Bullitt County, Kentucky.
- David, 1776–1865. Lived in Jessamine County, Kentucky.
- Joshua Logan Jr., 1776–1858. Lived in Shelby County, Kentucky.
- Rachel Ward, 1782–1811. Married and lived in Knott County, Kentucky.
- Charles Lee, 1783–1854. Charles Lee is my fourth great-grandfather.
- Amelia Ann Hardin, 1783–1839. Married and lived in Perry County, Indiana.
- Littleton, 1784–1862. Traveled by wagon train to Yamhill County, Oregon, in 1847.

---

[6] *Revolutionary War Bounty Land Grants Awarded by State Governments*, Lloyd De Witt Bockstruck. Genealogical Publishing Co. Inc., Baltimore, MD, 1997, 1998, p. 595. 16 March 1822.

[7] *Historical Register of Virginians in the Revolution: Soldiers, Sailors, Marines, 1775–1783*, John H. Gwathmey, Abingdon, Virginia, 1938, renewed 1966. Reprinted by Genealogical Publishing Company, Baltimore, MD, 1973, 1979, p. 868.

Six of Joshua and Elizabeth's children were probably born in Hampshire County, Virginia (now West Virginia). Charles Lee Younger claimed Virginia as his birth state in the 1850 census, but his 1783 birth date brings that claim into question, given their stated relocation year to Kentucky as 1779. We are uncertain of where his first wife Elizabeth died and the location of her burial in 1787, but it was likely in Kentucky in Nicholas County.

I have been challenged by other researchers who were unable to prove that Charles Lee Younger is the son of Joshua, as they have found no birth records. I have Kentucky court records showing that Joshua signed for his son Charles Lee's first marriage to Nancy Toney.[8] This marriage occurred in April 1798, and this fact seems to prove that relationship. I have a copy of those marriage records. Recently published DNA evidence also seems to support the claim of relationship of the Missouri Younger line to the father of Joshua. Charles Lee's middle name seems to support his mother's maiden name of Lee. A quick review of the names of Charles's children seems to link him to his siblings' names. It is important to remember that the Younger DNA project cited above supports this father/son relationship and the connection to the Younger outlaw part of the family two generations later.

It is interesting that Joshua does not mention his first wife or family resulting from that marriage in his pension request.

Joshua and Catherine Yoter had the following eight children who were documented with his probate records and newspaper articles. They were a well-known and respected family. Several of Joshua and Catherine's children moved a few miles to Indiana from Kentucky in search of land, and Joshua and Catherine later followed. Their son Stephen (Stever) later became a state representative in Indiana in the first legislature.[9]

- Nimrod, 1790–1860. Settled in Saline County, Illinois.
- Poly Rayburn, 1792–1883. Married and lived in Lawrence, Indiana.
- Majory Welborn, 1793–1880. Married and lived in Lawrence, Indiana.
- Sarah (Sally), 1795–1873
- John, 1795–1820. Lived in Nicholas County, Kentucky.
- Stephen (Stever), 1799–1893. Lived in Bedford, Lawrence County, Indiana.
- Lewis, 1802–1890. Lived in Bedford, Lawrence County, Indiana.
- Garrett, 1806–1872. Lived in Bedford, Lawrence County, Indiana.

Much has been written of Joshua's son Charles Lee Younger with these papers also disclosing important information about his father. History professor Becky Carlson in a *Missouri Historical Review* article links Joshua to his son as well as documenting Joshua's military service.[10]

The details of the lineage shown above from Joshua Logan to my family group are as follows:

---

[8] Kentucky Pioneer and Court Records Abstracts of Early Wills, Deeds and Marriages from Court Houses and Records of Old Bibles, Churches, Graveyards, and Cemeteries. Copied by American War Mothers. Compiled and published by Mrs. Harry Kennett McAdams. The Keystone Printery, Lexington, Kentucky, 1929, p. 99. Joshua is listed as father to Charles Lee for his marriage to Nancy Tony on 13 April 1798.
[9] Stever's December 26, 1893, obituary in the *Indiana Times* newspaper.
[10] "Manumitted and Forever Set Free. The Children of Charles Lee Younger and Elizabeth, a Woman of Color." Becky Carlson. *Missouri Historical Review*, The State Historical Society, Columbia, Missouri. Vol. XCVI, no. 1, October 2001.

- Charles Lee Younger, 1783–1854. Son of Joshua Logan Younger.
- Milton Toney Younger, 1802–1852. My third great-grandfather. Son of Charles Lee and Nancy Toney, first wife of Charles Lee and born in Kentucky. Milton married Mildred (Millie) Taylor in 1824 and died in Clay County, Missouri. Milton's mother was the first wife of Charles, Nancy Tony. Milton is mentioned in his father's 1853 Missouri will in which he left the sum of $1 to Milton because he had already provided for his inheritance.
- Charles Lee Younger, 1827–1907. My second great-grandfather. Son of Milton and Mildred Taylor, born in Howard County, Missouri, married Jane Woolery and is buried in Saline County, Missouri. Their photo is shown in figure 4-1 below and was taken in Parkville, Missouri, circa 1900. Jane is the granddaughter of Patriot Lawrence Abraham Woolery (1739–1839), who will be discussed later in the book.
- Coleman Washington Younger, 1848–1913. My great-grandfather. Son of Charles Lee and Jane Woolery. Married Sarah "Sallie" Virginia Plummer on 12 August 1871 in Saline County, Missouri. Coleman is shown in his father's 1850 census at the age of three in his father's home. I will present multiple Patriot direct ancestors of Sallie Plummer later in this book.
- Blanche Betrand Younger, 1887–1957. My grandmother. Daughter of Coleman and Sallie Younger. Married William Pleasant Raines on 16 October 1907 in Pettis County, Missouri. Blanche is shown in her father's 1900 census at the age of thirteen.
- V. Elwood (Pat) Raines, 1915–1998. Son of William P. and Blanche Raines. He married Ruby Nadine Adams (1917–1991) in Shelby County, Missouri, on 2 June 1940. They are my father and mother. His birth certificate lists his mother as Blanche. They are both listed on my birth certificate.

This lineage will be referred to multiple times throughout this book as the various Younger-related Patriot stories are developed, starting with the next Patriot, Major Joseph Gist.

Figure 4-1 Charles and Jane Woolery Younger

## Major Joseph Gist

Born: 30 Sep 1738, Baltimore, Maryland
Died: 22 Jan 1803
Burial: Franklin, Brooke County, West Virginia
Service: Baltimore County Maryland Militia, Soldiers Delight Battalion
Rank: Major
Service Dates: 25 May 1776–November 1781
Wife: Elizabeth Elder (1742–1814)
Lineage: Son Cornelius H. Gist, his daughter Elizabeth P. Gist/Jones, Eliza Pamela Jones/Plummer, Sarah (Sally) V. Plummer/Younger, Blanche Betrand Younger/Raines (my grandmother)
DAR: A045407
SAR: P-166751. He is my approved Patriot for membership in the SAR.

Joseph is my fifth great-grandfather and was the son of William Gist and Violetta Howard of Baltimore, Maryland. William is a Patriot, with his life story following Joseph's story. Joseph's birth is recorded at the St. Thomas Parish in Baltimore.[11]

He married Elizabeth Elder (1742–1814), daughter of John Elder and Jemima Dorsey. I have several documents supporting this marriage in addition to the *Colonial Families of the USA* shown below. Elizabeth also submitted a pension claim based on Joseph's service following his death, and I have this document.

SAR/DAR Patriot Joseph Gist secured a commission in the Soldiers Delight Battalion as a quartermaster of the Militia of Baltimore, Maryland, on 25 May 1776. He was promoted to first lieutenant on 6 June 1776, and to major on 10 September 1777. He resigned from Colonel Isaac Hammond's battalion in November 1781. After his death, his wife applied for a pension based on his service. It was approved, and the pension number is W.7517. A further description of Baltimore County and the Soldiers Delight units is given later in the Ellis Jones story and a later chapter on the Gists of Baltimore. I have copies of Joseph's National Archives military records to include his pension request.

About 1796, he and some of his family moved to Ohio County, Virginia (now Brooke County). He paid taxes in 1797 in Brooke County, the first year it was legally organized. On 24 March, he purchased four hundred additional acres of land on Buffalo Creek, Brooke County, from George McCullock. He died soon after moving to Brooke County in 1803. There is no evidence that he received a land grant for his service.

He and his wife were buried on their plantation in Brooke County about three miles east of Wellsburg. Their burial site was plowed over around 1929, and their tombstones were laid against a wall inside the old spring house. Their family removed the tombstones in the fall of 1946 to Franklin Cemetery east of Wellsburg, where many of their descendants are buried. [12] He

---

[11] *Colonial Families of the USA 1607–1775.* A Seven-Volume Set. Mackenzie, George Norbury, and Nelson Osgood Rhodes editors. Reprinted by Baltimore Genealogical Publishing Co. Inc. 1966, 1995. Vol. IV, p. 4. Gives birth, marriage, and death dates for Joseph Gist. Also shows father William and wife Elizabeth Elder.

[12] Wiki-Tree Ancestral File Number CDQ-KB.

and his wife remain buried at an unknown location on their former plantation. He has two tomb-stones at the Franklin Cemetery, one being the original in poor condition, and the other being a new one erected by family and researchers—this one was dedicated to his service on 21 August 2010. Joseph originally owned over one thousand acres of land in Brooke County located on what is now Genteel Ridge Road in that county. Part of the land is now part of the Brooke County Park.

Joseph and Elizabeth had the following children who were documented from DAR records:

- John Elder, 1761–1785
- Cecilia Cole, 1762–1847. She married Patriot Abraham Cole.
- Joseph, 1764–1786
- Jemima Dorsey, 1766–1834
- Joshua Howard, 1768–1830
- Cornelius Howard, 1770–1830. Cornelius married Maria Clara Reinecker, the daughter of Patriot Captain Casper Reinecker. Cornelius is my fourth great-grandfather.
- Violetta, 1772–1773
- William, 1772–1855
- Elizabeth King, 1774–1827
- Owen, 1778–1801
- Samuel, 1779–1848
- Nancy Ann Haney, 1781–1827
- George, 1783–1857

We know that Cornelius was the son of Joseph from the *Colonial Families of the USA*[13] and from a 1913 article in the *Maryland Historical Magazine*, as well as several DAR-published Maryland historical references.[14] The daughter of Cornelius Howard Gist and Maria Clara Reinecker, Elizabeth Pamela, married Lewis Reice Jones, also of Baltimore. Lewis was the son of Patriot Ellis Jones Sr., whose story is later in this book. Their daughter Eliza Pamelia married Franklin Plummer, whose daughter Sarah "Sallie" was my great-grandmother and the wife of Coleman Washington Younger. It is a bit complicated, but you might be able to see the intersection of the Gist, Reinecker, Jones, and Younger Patriot families. To add to the complexity, you will see later in this book the stories of Patriots Lawrence Abraham Woolery and George Lee, whose children also married into the Younger families. You will see the documentation of these births and marriages as the story unfolds.

Joseph's father, William, was also a Patriot, and his story follows.

---

[13] *Colonial Families of the USA 1607–1775*. A Seven-Volume Set. Mackenzie, George Norbury, and Nelson Osgood Rhodes, editors. Reprinted by Baltimore Genealogical Publishing Co. Inc. 1966–1995. Vol. IV, pp. 236 and 237 give birth, marriage, and death dates for Joseph Gist and the birth dates and names of his children.
[14] *North American Family Histories 1500–2000*. Lineage Book for the Daughters of the American Revolution. Vol. 055, p. 422 gives birth and death information for Joseph Gist and son Cornelius Howard Gist and their wives.

## William Gist

Born: September 1711, St. Thomas Parrish, Baltimore, Maryland
Died: 19 November 1794, Baltimore, Maryland
Burial: St. Thomas Episcopal Church Cemetery
Service: Patriotic service
Rank: None
Service Dates: None
Wife: Violetta Howard (1716–1783)
Lineage: His son Joseph Gist is discussed above.
DAR: A045459
SAR: No

William Gist was the son of Captain Richard Christopher Gist (1683–1741) and Zipporah Murray (1685–1760), also of Baltimore, Maryland.[15] While William did not serve in the military, he is recognized by the Daughters of the American Revolution for patriotic service, having signed the Maryland Oath of Allegiance in 1778.[16] As I have discussed throughout this book, this does not constitute military service, but it was a risky act likely leading to serious retribution had the colonies lost the war. Furthermore, this public act could—and did in some instances—lead to hostile acts against signees and their families during the war. I believe that William spent his entire life in Baltimore and Baltimore County, Maryland. We see him there for the first U.S. Census of 1790.

The Gist family is an old and interesting family with roots in Baltimore from the earliest history of that colony. William had four brothers, all Revolutionary War Patriots with notable leadership and combat achievements worthy of further examination. I will explore that family line in some detail in a later chapter of this book entitled "A Story of Leadership, Exploration, and Tragedy—The Gists of Baltimore." When I used William's son Joseph as my Patriot for membership in the Sons of the American Revolution many years ago, I was not aware of the deep history of the Gist family with respect to the Revolution and early American history. It's time to fill that gap. Several relatives in my family have used son Joseph as their Patriot for membership in the Daughters of the American Revolution.

William and Violetta had nine children:

- Joseph, 1738–1803. Patriot discussed above.
- William Jr., 1743–1802
- Anne Calhoon, 1745–1799
- Sarah McCune, 1747–1819
- Thomas, 1750–1808
- Elizabeth McGee, 1750–1794
- John, 1752–1782

---

[15] *Colonial Families of the USA 1607–1775*. A Seven-Volume Set. Mackenzie, George Norbury, and Nelson Osgood Rhodes, editors. Reprinted by Baltimore Genealogical Publishing Co. Inc. 1966–1995. Vol. IV, p. 4 gives birth, marriage, and death dates for Joseph Gist. Also shows father William and his father Richard.
[16] DAR Patriot number A045459. Recorded as signing the Maryland Oath of Allegiance in 1778.

- Violetta Lewis, 1755–1783
- Ellen, 1757–1799

We know that Joseph was the son of William from several sources footnoted above in his son's story.

**Sergeant Samuel Adams III**
Born: 16 May 1742, Hamilton, Essex, Massachusetts (baptism date)
Died: 18 Nov 1835
Burial: Hamilton, Essex, Massachusetts
Service: Minutemen, Captain Whitney's Company of Ipswich
Rank: Sergeant
Service Dates: 19 April 1775–1776
Wife: Jemima Whipple (1746–1832)
Lineage: Son John Adams, John Quincy Adams, Walter Grant Adams, Walter Raymond Adams, Ruby Nadine Adams/Raines (my mother).
DAR: No
SAR: P-101566

Samuel was the son of Samuel Adams Jr. and Sarah Tredwell of Hamilton, Essex County, Massachusetts.[17] He was born in Hamilton and married Jemima Whipple, also of Hamilton, on 6 December 1766. Jemima was the daughter of John Whipple III and Dorothy Moulton.[18] John Whipple III was also a Patriot and is discussed later in this book. Samuel and Jemima had the following five children.[19] The birth and death information of their children is recorded in the Ipswich/Hamilton city records.

- Hannah Dodge, 1767–1849. Married and remained in Ipswich.
- Samuel IV, 1769–1849. Remained in Ipswich.
- Martha, 1771–1772. Died in infancy.
- John, 1775–1863. My third great-grandfather, remained in Ipswich.
- Betsey, 1779–1796. Died at age seventeen, never married.

Records pertaining to Samuel and his extended family reflect both the towns of Hamilton and Ipswich, Massachusetts. They did not move, but Hamilton was originally a hamlet of Ipswich until it was incorporated in 1793 (Wikipedia and noted references). The town of Ipswich maintained the vital records pertaining to the family for over one hundred years.

He joined Captain Whitney's minuteman company at the age of thirty-two on 19 April 1775 and was discharged in 1776 when the minutemen were disbanded. April 19 is a significant date in pre-war history, as there was a call-up of minutemen to go to Lexington, Concord, and Mystic on that date, and his home was only a few miles from Lexington. He fought in the battle of

---

[17] "Massachusetts Town and Vital Records," Ipswich, Essex County, gives his birth, marriage, and death dates, as well as the name of his father, p. 184, and Hamilton deaths, p. 81.
[18] Ibid., p. 453.
[19] Ibid.

Lexington on 19 April, **which was the first battle of the Revolutionary War!** That battle lasted only a few minutes, but he was present on that historical occasion. He served for four days on that call-up and later for sixteen days for a call to Cambridge. He was paid for his mileage on those trips. I have found records associated with a request to the army for a tombstone for the un-marked grave site of Samuel Adams in 1839 in Hamilton, Essex, Massachusetts, and it was approved. His service is documented in *Massachusetts Soldiers and Sailors of the Revolutionary War*.[20] I have found records of Captain Whitney—his minuteman company commander—as a militia regimental commander from Massachusetts after the war began, but no further records of Samuel's service, so he likely did not join a militia or the Continental Army after the minutemen were disbanded in 1777. He married Jemima Whipple, whose father was Patriot John Whipple III, who also served in the same minuteman company. John's service is well documented. There were many Samuel Adams from this era, most from Massachusetts and several from Ipswich. I am confident that this Samuel is our family member and have well documented the family history to Shelby County, Missouri. He was a Massachusetts landowner and married into one of the wealthiest families in the colonies, although he himself was not a wealthy man. I have seen the term "yeoman" associated with Samuel, and that was an old English term for non-slaveholding farmers who owned their land.

As there were so many Samuel Adams of the colonial era, it was challenging to determine which one was my great-grandfather. I narrowed the search by researching all the other Samuels of that period and their burial locations. All the other Samuel Adams of Massachusetts were buried in locations other than Essex County, in which Ipswich is located. The excellent Ipswich city records of births, deaths, and marriages also support this family connection. He is buried in the Hamilton Cemetery opposite the First Congregational Cemetery in Essex County on 924 Bay Road.

His son John married Mary Patch, whose father and grandfather also served in the Revolution and are discussed later in the book. They were Nehemiah Patch and John Patch III. His grandson John Quincy is said to have fought in the Civil War and is buried in Clarence, Missouri. John Quincy's grandson Clifford fought in World War II and is buried in Omaha, Nebraska.

Then there is a "dog gone" story shared by D.M. Morris in 2014 about two severe weather incidents experienced by the Samuel Adams family. In March 1781, lightning descended the chimney of his home, struck down his wife (who was resuscitated), killed a dog near the andiron, from which his daughter had just risen, and killed two sheep at the end of the barn. About ten years later, in June 1791, he and his two sons rushed to an oak tree to avoid a sudden shower. Their dog preceded them and reached the tree before they did. It was instantly killed when lightning struck and destroyed the tree, and one of his sons was knocked senseless by the lightning bolt but was revived.

The relationship of Samuel Adams to either of the President Adams' is distant, if it exists at all, and we can trace this Adams line to England to the twelfth century. The first Adams of our line to settle in the colonies was William Adams, who immigrated from England in 1628, and the

---

[20] *Massachusetts Soldiers and Sailors of the Revolutionary War: A Compilation from the Archives.* Wright and Potter Printing. Vol. 1, p. 71.

family had lived in Ipswich for four generations by the time of the Revolution.[21] This Adams line is very well researched and documented to the current family. The birth, marriage, and death records of Ipswich are excellent and provide many of the records we needed to document all the Adams, Whipple, and Patch families for this book. The Patch Patriot stories will follow later in the book.

**Captain Casper Johauan Reinecker**
Born: 30 July 1733, Heilbronn, Baden-Wurttemberg, Germany
Died: 30 July 1790
Burial: Hanover, Pennsylvania
Service: Sixth Battery of the York County Pennsylvania Militia and the York County Committee of Public Safety
Rank: Captain
Service Dates: 1774–1778
Wife: Anna Maria Carle
Lineage: Daughter, Maria Clara Reinecker/Gist, Elizabeth Gist/Jones, Eliza Pamelia Jones/Plummer, Sarah Plummer/Younger, Blanche Bertrand Younger/Raines (my grandmother)
DAR: A095182
SAR: P-277215

Casper, my fifth great-grandfather, arrived in Philadelphia, Pennsylvania, on 15 August 1750 aboard the ship *Royal Union* from Germany.[22] The family bible records state he came to Pennsylvania with his father, George Adam, and brothers George, Adam, and Paulis.[23] Records show Casper owned 260 acres in Manheim Township and in Heidelberg Township, as well as slaves.[24] The 1789 tax list reflects his total amount of taxable land.[25] He also owned the Sign of the Horse Inn in Hanover. It is well documented that Thomas Jefferson stayed in the inn on his way to Philadelphia to write the Declaration of Independence on April 12, and again in September 1776 upon his return to Virginia.[26] He later stayed at the inn when traveling with his daughter upon his return to Virginia. George Washington also stayed in that inn, but probably after Casper's son took over the inn in 1790. I believe that inn remains standing in Hanover.

Casper owned some key property in York County, and his sons George and Conrad added to that list of historical properties. They owned a hotel adjacent to the courthouse that housed the Continental Congress. It was Casper's son-in-law Jack Fite, who married Anna Dorthea, who built and decorated the Congress Hall which was used by the Continental Congress during the Revolution.[27]

---

[21] *Some Descendants of William Adams of Ipswich, Massachusetts.* W.S. Appleton. Boston, David Clapp and son.

[22] Renicker History 2. Shared by Carl Renicker on 16 March 2009. Take by work by Gail Renicker in 1978.

[23] Volume I, pages 431–32 and Volume II, page 497, *Pennsylvania German Pioneers*

[24] "Pennsylvania, U.S. Land Warrants and Applications 1733–1952," Harrisburg, Pennsylvania, State Archives. Warrant 138, 10 August 1774. York County.

[25] "Provincial Papers: Returns of Taxables of the County of York for the years 1779,1780,1781,1782 and 1789," Series 3, Vol. XXI, p. 791. This list reflects 250 taxable acres of land belonging to Casper Reinecker.

[26] "Thomas Jefferson Encyclopedia," based on J.R. McGrew, Monticello Research Report, May 1991. Hanover, Pennsylvania. Gives the account of Thomas Jefferson's visit to Hanover, Pennsylvania, at the Sign of the Horse Inn on 12 April 1776.

[27] *The Old Congress Hall Tavern, Baltimore, Maryland.* Forsythe, Tim, 2009 ID: N108
Linked to: Alexander Forsyth (1746–1829). Contains the story of the Baltimore Tavern owned by Henry Fite, the father of Elizabeth Reinecker, the wife of George Reinecker, the son of Casper.

He served in the Sixth Battery of the Second Company of the York County Militia as a captain for four years. I did not find evidence of a warrant or a pension from this service. He also served on the York County, Pennsylvania, Committee of Safety prior to and during the Revolution.[28] The Committees for Safety were the governing bodies for the various militias organized within the county. Pennsylvania was tasked by the Continental Congress to raise 16 regiments. They were very effective in that task and raised over 134 regiments. Was Casper his own boss? As we discuss throughout this book, being a member of a public safety committee was not without its risks. We encountered several stories of these members from different colonies who were taken prisoner or harassed by British soldiers or Tory leadership. It was not a safe job.

He is buried in the Mount Olivet Cemetery in Penn Township of York County, Pennsylvania. His grave is marked with a tombstone.[29]

Casper and Anna Marie had the following ten children who are named in his will of 13 November 1789 that was probated in 1790 in York County:

- Anna Maria Eichelberger, 1752–1837
- Johann George, 1754–1838
- Maria Catherina Kuhn, 1757–1832
- Eva Margaretha Meyer, 1762–1790
- Susanna, 1764–1781
- Conrad, 1766–1810
- Johan Adam Reinecker, 1768–1852
- Elizabeth Scherman, 1771–1855
- Anna Dorthea Fite, 1773–1819
- Maria Clara Gist, 1776–1868. My fourth great-grandmother.

Their daughter Maria Clara married Cornelius Howard Gist—the son of Patriot Joseph Gist discussed earlier in this book—in 1792. Cornelius was upper sheriff of Baltimore in 1797. He and his family moved to Brooke County, West Virginia, around 1804, as his father had moved there several years earlier. I have their marriage records and the Cornelius Howard Gist will that names their children.

Cornelius and Maria Clara had twelve children. Their oldest daughter, Elizabeth Pamelia (1798–1824), married Lewis Reice Jones (1798–1877). Lewis Reice and Pamelia had a daughter named Eliza Pamelia who married Franklin Plummer in Brooke County in 1849. Franklin is my second great-grandfather and father to my great-grandmother Sarah "Sallie" Virginia Younger. The father of Lewis Reice Jones is Patriot Ellis Jones Sr., discussed later in this book.

Franklin Plummer's mother, Leah Wells, was the granddaughter of Patriot Captain Alexander Wells, who is also discussed later in this book.

---

[28] *North American Family Histories 1500–2000.* Lineage Book for the Daughters of the American Revolution. Gives birth date and location, death date, marriage date, and wife, as well as military service including the Committee of Public Safety.
[29] Pennsylvania U.S. Veterans Burial Cards 1777–1812 for Casper Reinecker.

Casper's brother George Martin (1739–1822) was a Patriot serving in the Pennsylvania Continental Line as a lieutenant. His second brother Paulus is also a Patriot, and his story follows as I am also descended from him:

## Paulus Reinecker
Born: 3 January 1745, Heilbronn, Baden-Wurttemberg, Germany
Died: 3 June 1799, Silver Run, Frederick, Maryland
Burial: St. Mary's Cemetery, Frederick, Maryland
Service: Patriotic service recognition by the DAR
Rank: None
Service Dates: 1776–1782
Wife: Ann Margaret Gibler (1751–1826)
Lineage: Son George Michael Reinecker, Michael Angel Reinecker, Hiram Rennaker, daughter Doretha M. Adams, Walter Raymond Adams (my grandfather)
DAR: A204911
SAR: No

It is important to consider that the colonists and the Reinecker family used multiple ways to spell this family name. I documented more than ten variations but have used the correct English spelling of this German name. I discovered that some records of Paulus's line may have used the Renecker spelling, or perhaps other recorders used this variation starting in Maryland. Paulus was the younger brother of Patriot Casper Reinecker discussed above. They were both born in Germany and immigrated to the United States with their father, George. Both Casper and his father settled in York County, Pennsylvania, while Paulus settled in the neighboring Frederick, Maryland area. Paulus was a plantation owner and an influential community leader. He also served on the area Committee of Safety and as juror for the "Oath of Allegiance" for the state of Maryland.

The DAR has recognized his service on the Committee of Safety.[30] While this may appear to be a low-risk responsibility, it was far from that. Community leaders who publicly supported the Revolution, such as Paulus, were under the watchful eye of British military leadership, and had the colonists lost the war, he would have certainly been hung and his family's belongings confiscated.

He married Ann Margaret Gibler in 1750, and they had several children, including George Michael, my ancestor.[31] While I was unable to locate their marriage records, the referenced Lutheran Church records have records of the baptism of their children with their mother being named.

Paulus lived the remainder of his life in the Frederick area and is buried in the cemetery of St. Mary's Lutheran Church. His tombstone still stands in that cemetery.

---

[30] *North American Family Histories 1500–2000.* Lineage Book for the Daughters of the American Revolution. Gives birth date and location, death date, marriage date, and wife, as well as public service while serving on the Committee of Public Safety.
[31] Baptism records for St. Mary's Evangelical Lutheran Church, Silver Run, Maryland. Years 1783–1784.

At first it may seem confusing that I came claim direct decadency from brothers, but it is a true statement in this instance. The Paulus Reinecker line traces through the Adams family line. The Casper Reinecker line traces through the Younger family line. Paulus is my fifth great-grandfather, as is Casper.

Three of Paulus's sons—Johannes, Peter, and Daniel—moved to Harrison County, Ohio, and then to Tuscarawas County in that state.

George Michael Reinecker, third son of Paulus, and my fourth great-grandfather, was born in Frederick County on 18 April 1773 and died on 23 January 1852 in, Franklin County, Pennsylvania.[32] Records reflect that he married Eva Ann Wilsdain (1759–1849) in 1800 and that he might have had a previous marriage.[33] We believe that he had a child with Julia Ann Angel (1771–1851) and this child was named Michael Angel Reinecker (1800–1885). While the name indicates his father was a Reinecker, little other evidence has been found attributing him to George Martin. The father of Julia Ann, Charles Angel Sr. (1740–1811), recognized Michael Angel Reinecker as a son of Julia with an inheritance in his will probated on 7 January 1811.[34] There has been speculation by other researchers that there was a marriage prior to 1800 and that Julia Ann did not convert to the Lutheran Church, thus leading to an annulment. However, Julia's birth is recorded with a Lutheran Church, therefore her conversion was not necessary. This was possibly an out-of-wedlock birth. Whatever the situation, she was an independent lady with enough resources to remain independent, and Michael Angel is certainly a proven son. Her father, who was somewhat wealthy, left her a large inheritance in that will also.

Julia Ann moved to Carol County, Ohio, soon after 1800 and did not marry until 1845, where she owned several tracts of land. On 21 February 1824 she deeded land to her son Michael Angel under written terms concerning required support of her for the remainder of her life, and she lived with Michael until her marriage. She died in 1851 at the age of eighty. In that agreement, his name was spelled as Rennecker.

Michael Angel Reinecker (Rennecker) was born on 17 March 1800 in Frederick, Maryland, and died in Grant County, Indiana, on 11 November 1855.[35] He married Margaret Steffey (1804–1885), and they had eighteen children, of which Hiram Renecker was the seventh. Hiram was my great-great-grandfather and was born in Indiana.[36] His daughter Dorthea married my great-grandfather Walter Grant Adams. Hiram fought in the Civil War and moved to Missouri following the war. He lived near Clarence, Missouri, at the time of his death, had been a farmer his entire life, and is buried in the old Clarence Cemetery. We have a family photo of Michael Angel, and I believe that to be the oldest family photo in our collection.

You may have noticed that Hiram spelled his name differently. I had sometimes wondered if there was a connection with the Casper Reinecker line, until recently. This connection was easy

---

[32] Maryland U.S. Births and Christening Index 1662–1911. Recorded in Saint Mary's Lutheran Church, Silver Run, Carroll County, Maryland.

[33] U.S. International Marriage Records 1560–1900. These records show that his wife, Julia Ann Angel, was born in Maryland and that George was born in 1770.

[34] Register of Wills for Frederick County, Maryland, in Will Book RB1, p. 149, and probated on 7 January 1811.

[35] A certified copy of the marriage record of the Probate Court of Harrison County Ohio documents the marriage of Michael Renicker and Peggy Steffy on 22 August 1821 in Harrison County.

[36] U.S. Civil War Draft Registration Records, 1863–1865, Eleventh Congressional District, State of Ohio, June 1863, shows his place of birth as Ohio and that he was married.

to document, as the Germans and their churches kept excellent records. All the early Reineckers prepared wills, owned property, belonged to the Lutheran Church, and were very visible citizens. Records abound.

The Reinecker line is linked with seven lines of the forty-five Patriots discussed in this book. There were several other Reinecker Revolutionary War Patriots, but the Raines family has directly descended from these lines. They all contributed to our heritage.

> Captain Casper Reinecker
> Paulis Reinecker
> Joseph Gist and his father William
> Ellis Jones
> Joshua Logan Younger
> Captain Alexander Wells
> Johannes Peter Wise and his father. His story follows:

**Johann Peter Wise Sr.**
Born: 12 March 1758, Frederick, Frederick County, Maryland
Died: 4 October 1821, Stark County, Ohio
Burial: Marlboro Cemetery, Marlboro, Ohio
Service: Washington County Pennsylvania Militia
Rank: Private
Service Dates: Discharged in 1782
Wife: Mary Magdalene Miller (1765–1821)
Lineage: Son Peter Jr., his son John, his daughter Susannah "Susan," who married Hiram Reinecker. Their daughter Doretha married Walter Grant Adams, my great-grandfather.
DAR: A126819
SAR: P-322851

Peter was the son of Johann Adam Christopher Wise (Weiss) and Maria Juliana Gerhard of Carroll County, Maryland.[37] His father was born in Hesse, Darmstadt, Germany, in about 1718 and came to Maryland about 1748. Peter lived in Carroll County, Maryland, and moved to Washington County, Pennsylvania, with his father in 1770. He married Mary Magdalene Miller (1765–1821) in 1782. She was the daughter of Christian Ludwig Miller and Catherine Weisman. The Greene County Historical Society of Waynesburg, Pennsylvania, has published a book with the Wise Family History that documents the family of Peter and his father Adam.[38]

We know Peter is the son of Adam as he is listed in his father's Pennsylvania will dated 13 April 1781, as are his brothers. We also have his baptismal records from the Lutheran Church in Maryland listing both his father and mother.[39] He served in the Revolutionary War with his brother

---

[37] Maryland Births and Christening Index 1600–1995. Index. Family Search, Salt Lake City, Utah. 2009, 2010. Film Number 13931.
[38] *The Tenmile Country and Its Pioneer Families.* A Genealogical History of the Upper Monongahela Valley. Howard L. Leckey. Sponsored by the Greene County Historical Society, Waynesburg, Pennsylvania. Gives the account of the Adam Weiss (Wise) family and sons, including Johan and Peter Sr.
[39] "Lutheran and Reformed Congregation." Manchester, Carroll County, Maryland, 1760–1836. Page 6 gives the names of Peter's parents and his birth date.

Adam Jr., who is also listed in that will. He also owned land adjacent to his father's land in Pennsylvania. Peter was born on Big Pipe Creek in Frederick, Carroll County, Maryland, and his father owned land there. Peter is my fifth great-grandfather on the Adams family line.

Prior to moving from Maryland to Pennsylvania, Peter took the Maryland Fidelity Oath, which would qualify him for Patriot status.[40] He served in the fifth battalion of the Washington County Militia under the command of Lieutenant Colonel Thomas Crooke and Captain Ezekiel Rose. These companies were raised in West Bethlehem township, which was Peter's home township. As we discussed earlier, Pennsylvania organized battalions at the militia level and was successful in attracting many German-heritage citizens to defend their newly earned religious freedoms. These Pennsylvania militia units consisted of volunteers, as nearly every able man joined one of these local units in the event that they might be needed to protect their home townships from Tories, Indians, and British soldiers. There was plenty of unrest in Washington County, as attested to by the stories of other Patriots of Washington County discussed elsewhere in this book. It was the "Wild West" of the colonies. The unit remained under the control of the county and was not assigned to the state or Continental Line.

It is important to note that there were at least two other persons of the same name from the colony of Pennsylvania who also served in the Revolution. The wives of both men received pensions after the pension act was passed in 1830; however, this Peter Wise died in 1821, as did his wife. One of these Patriots' wives applied for a pension in Montgomery County, Ohio, in 1830, so it is easy to confuse these three men's service. This Peter Wise and his wife Mary Magdalene did not receive such a pension. He is, however, listed in an official record of Ohio soldiers who fought in the Revolution.[41] I could not determine the date of his enlistment; however, with the Pennsylvania conscription laws, it is safe to assume his enlistment term or terms were for ninety days each. His records reflect he served on at least three call-ups for a few weeks each between 1776 and 1782.

He married Mary Magdalene Miller in Washington, Pennsylvania, in 1782 after his service in the militia. He was a farmer and is listed in the West Bethlehem Township tax roles for 1781 as having two horses, two cows, eight sheep, and two hundred acres of land. They had the following thirteen children:

- *Daniel Miller, 1784–1818. Born in Washington County, West Bethlehem Township in Pennsylvania and died in Canton, Stark County, Ohio. Mentioned in his father's 1821 will.
- *Jacob, 1785–1786. Died as infant.
- Andrew, 1785–1844. Born in Washington County, West Bethlehem Township, Pennsylvania and died in Adams County, Indiana.
- Catherine Shidler, 1788–1875. Born in West Bethlehem Township and died in West Bethlehem Township.

---

[40] Maryland Compiled Census and Census Substitute Index 1772–1890. He took the Fidelity Oath in 1780.
[41] "The Official Roster of the Soldiers of the Revolution Buried in the State of Ohio," p. 827. This shows his birth date, wife's name, and unit of service. It shows him living in Starke County, Ohio.

- Hannah Zollars, 1791–1841. Born in West Bethlehem Township and died in West Bethlehem Township.
- *Peter Miller Jr., 1791–1870. Peter Jr. is my fourth great-grandfather. Born in West Bethlehem Township and died in Cadiz, Henry County, Indiana. Mentioned in his father's 1821 will.
- Susannah Peterson, 1792–1864. Born in West Bethlehem Township and died in Stark, Ohio.
- *Mary Molly Bricker, 1794–1889. Born in West Bethlehem Township and died in Brandon, Knox County, Ohio.
- *Adam, 1797–1865. Born in West Bethlehem Township and died in Canton, Stark County, Ohio. Mentioned in his father's 1821 will.
- Elizabeth Smith, 1801–1891
- Jacob, 1803–1845. Listed in his father's 1821 will.
- Abraham, 1804–1855. Mentioned in his father's 1821 will.
- Rebecca Carper/Briton, 1805–1830. Born in West Bethlehem Township and died in Canton, Stark County, Ohio.

The children's names marked with a (*) are listed with the DAR as Peter and Mary's children. While this is not proof of relationship, there are strong, well-documented connections established by this listing. Multiple families have used these children to apply for membership in the DAR, and these applications were approved.

Not all Peter and Mary's proposed children were listed in his will. Seven were not listed, and they were: Andrew, Catherine, Hannah, Susannah, Mary, Elizabeth, and Rebecca. I will assume they were either their children or the children of Peter Sr.'s brother, Adam Jr., who also lived in West Bethlehem Township of Washington County, Pennsylvania.

Son Peter Jr., my fourth great-grandfather, was born in Washington County, Pennsylvania, in 1791 and married Susanna Miller in 1826 in Stark County, Ohio. Stark County is only one county away from the western Pennsylvania line, so it was not a long move from Washington County. Stark County was first settled after the Revolution by German immigrants, such as the Wises.

We know Peter Jr. is the son of Peter Sr., as he is listed as a son in his father's 1820 will and probate papers.[42] He also lived on his father's land at the time. He and his wife Susanna Miller (1800–1882) had the following ten children:

- John, 1819–1887. John is my third great-grandfather.
- Daniel, 1827–1911. His Indiana death certificate lists his father and mother.
- Catherine Kircher, 1828–1884
- Peter W. III, 1830–1913
- Sally, 1834–1844

---

[42] Pennsylvania Wills and Probate Records 1683–1993. Will Books Volumes 001–002, 1781–1814, p. 8 of 568. Contains the will of Johann Peter Weise (Wise).

- Eliza, 1836–1844
- Joseph, 1837–1904
- Eli E., 1839–1923. His Indiana death certificate lists his father and mother.
- Henry, 1840–1920
- David, 1842–1925

His oldest son, John, was born in Plain Township, Stark County, Ohio, and married Margaret Peggy Lotteridge in 1841 in Henry County, Indiana. He lived in Henry County until about 1849, when he moved to Grant County, Indiana. I have Grant County records of a land transaction on 19 May 1882 in which John and his wife Margaret purchased land owned by his siblings Daniel, Catherine, and Henry. This further strengthens the proof of his family connections to the Peter Wise Jr. line. John is also listed as a son in his father's will of 1870. He died on 20 December 1887, and his wife Margaret died about three months later. John and Margaret had ten children:

- Mary Jane Monroe, 1846–1931
- Susanah Susan Alzeta Rennaker, 1849–1934. My second great-grandmother.
- Peter Edward, 1850–1815
- Sarah Ann Withrow, 1851–1918
- John William, 1853–1939
- William Henry, 1857–1923
- Amanda Wilcutts, 1859–1942
- Rebecca, 1863–Unknown death date
- Daniel, 1866–Unknown death date
- Sarah, 1868–Unknown death date

His daughter Susanah Susan Alzeta was born in Grant County in 1849. We see her in the John Wise home for the 1860 Grant County census at the age of ten. She married Hiram Rennaker on 18 April 1869 in Grant County. We know she is the daughter of John, first because of the 1860 census records, and second because her father is shown on her 1934 Missouri death certificate. Hiram is the son of George Michael Rennaker, who was the son of George Paulis Reinecker discussed above. Note the spelling change with the last name.

Hiram had recently served in the Civil War in an Indiana Union regiment and had a previous marriage of ten years with at least seven children from that marriage, three of which were surviving at the time of his second marriage. His first wife died after the birth of a son. Susan had seventeen children by their marriage. She and Hiram moved to Clarence, Missouri, around 1888, with their farm being about five miles northwest of Clarence. Hiram died on 5 November 1907 and is buried in the old Clarence Cemetery. Susan lived another twenty-four years and died at the age of eighty-five while living with a daughter in Holts Summit, Missouri. She is buried along with Hiram in the Clarence Cemetery. It is my belief that their tombstones no longer stand in that cemetery due to damage. Hiram's stone was a military headstone, but I am unsure if there was a headstone for Susan.

I am compelled and proud to feature this tough lady, Susan. She married a man with three children, with at least seventeen children being added to the household over the next twenty-two years. She raised at least twenty children and outlived many of them. Times were probably tough, as they lost their Shelby County farm in 1903 prior to Hiram's death. I wish we could award her Patriot status.

Figure 4-2 Susan Alzeta Wise Rennaker
1849–1934

Their daughter Doretha married Walter Grant Adams in Shelby County, Missouri. They are my great-grandparents. He is buried in the Shelbyville Cemetery, and she outlived him by twenty-two years and is buried near Omaha, Nebraska, where she had been living with her children.

Hiram Rennaker was mentioned earlier in this book because of his Patriot connections to the Paulus "Paul" Reinecker and Captain Casper Reinecker lines. My family is connected to those lines through both my mother and father.

The story of Johannes Peter Sr.'s Patriot father, Johann Adam Wise, follows:

**Johann Adam Christopher Wise (Weiss)**
Born: 24 January 1718, Gross-Winterheim, Rhein Essen, Germany
Died: 9 June 1781, West Bethlehem Township, Washington County, Pennsylvania
Burial: Wise family burial plot in West Bethlehem Township in Washington County
Service: Patriotic service. Suffered deprivation and took the Oath of Allegiance.
Rank: None
Service Dates: None
Wife: (1) Maria Grafin and (2) Catherine Bradford
Lineage: Son Johannes Peter, his son Peter Jr., and his son John, and his daughter Susannah Alzeta Rennaker, their daughter Doretha Adams, their son Walter Grant Adams, their son Walter Raymond Adams, and their daughter Ruby Nadine Raines (my mother)

DAR: A 126803. Suffered deprivation in 1781
SAR: P 328704. Oath of Allegiance

Johann Adam Wise (Weis) was the son of Abraham Weiss and Maria Juliana Gerhard of Darmstadt, present-day Germany, formerly Prussia. Johann is my sixth great-grandfather. He married Maria Elizabetha Grafin in Germany before departure for the British colonies. They sailed on the ship *Hampshire*, arriving in Baltimore, Maryland, in July 1748 and remaining on board until the ship arrived in Philadelphia on 7 September.[43] They settled near Pipe Creek, Maryland, near the present city of Frederick, and lived there for about twenty-two years.[44] They were engaged in the business of milling, distilling, and farming, and he was a prosperous businessman. His wife Maria died in 1763 after the birth of their daughter Maria Elizabeth. The spelling of this name is probably an Americanization of the name Weis. I have seen American records spelled both ways, but their official records soon reflected the Wise spelling.

Around 1770, he and some of his family moved by wagon to Washington County, Pennsylvania, located in the southwestern part of the colony, where he settled in West Bethlehem Township. The first colonial settlers had arrived in that area just four years prior. (See the Gist chapter in this book about early Washington County). He erected mills and a distillery. This was the first of such enterprises in that area, and it was very successful, although they faced tough times during and following the Revolutionary War. The family business consisted of milling local grain, moving it down the Monongahela River to the Ohio River, and on to the Mississippi River and New Orleans. The war greatly disrupted that prosperous trade.[45] Elsewhere in this book we discuss the Whiskey Rebellion following the Revolutionary War, and this rebellion was centered in Washington County area. Some of the Wise family produced grain that was likely used to produce whiskey, and the federal tax on whiskey resulted in the rebellion. Adam became somewhat wealthy from grain and whiskey production.

Adam is recognized as a Patriot by both the DAR and SAR for patriotic service. Even if he did not serve in the military, his activities and importance to his community earned him this recognition. His patriotic service is based on two facts: first, he and his family suffered extreme deprivation, and second, he took the Oath of Fidelity in Washington County. I have a copy of County records reflecting he oath he took voluntarily. The deprivation claim is not difficult to understand when you consider the recent history of the county as experienced by explorer Christopher Gist just a few years prior to the Wise family's arrival. Additionally, you will see that another Washington County Patriot family mentioned later in the book also suffered greatly. The DAR recognizes both the fidelity oath and the deprivation.

Adam had eight children by first wife Maria and then seven children with Catherine Bradford, whom he married in Maryland before setting out for Pennsylvania. Several of his sons fought in the Revolutionary War, including his third son, Johannes Peter Wise (discussed above), and

---

[43] "Annotations to Strassburger and Hinke's Pennsylvania German Pioneers." Friedreich Krebs, *Pennsylvania Genealogical Magazine*, vol. 21:3 (1960), pp. 235–248.

[44] *Settlers of Maryland, 1679–1783. Consolidated Edition.* Coldham, Peter Wilson. Baltimore, Maryland: Genealogical Publishing Co., 2002. Page 736 lists the counties and tracts owned by Adam.

[45] *The Tenmile Country and Its Pioneer Families.* A Genealogical History of the Upper Monongahela Valley. Howard L. Leckey. Sponsored by the Greene County Historical Society, Waynesburg, Pennsylvania. Gives the account of the Adam Weiss (Wise) family and sons, including Johan Peter Sr.

Adam Jr. Twelve of his children were listed in his will of 16 August 1781. I have listed the two children not named in his will and provided the reason I assigned them to this family group.

- Adam Jr., 1748–1840. Revolutionary War Patriot listed in the will.
- Catherine Horn, 1750–1803. Not listed in the will. Born in Maryland, married, moved to Kentucky, and had likely lost touch with her family.
- Frederick, 1753–1802. Listed in the will. Served in the Revolutionary War as a major.
- Johannes Peter Sr., 1758–1821. Listed in the will. Revolutionary War Patriot. Discussed above and is my fifth great-grandfather.
- Anna Marie, 1761–1761. Died as an infant prior to the writing of Adam's will.
- John Adam Christopher, 1763–1842. Listed in the will. Revolutionary War Patriot.
- Henry Adam, 1763–1810. Listed in the will. Revolutionary War Patriot.
- Maria Elizabeth, 1764–1841. Listed in the will, and I have birth records.

The mother of these children was Catherine Bradford:

- Mary Ann, 1766–1856. Listed in the will.
- Jacob, 1767–1825. Listed in the will. Revolutionary War Patriot.
- Daniel, 1769–1834. Listed in the will. Revolutionary War Patriot.
- Julian, 1773–1880. Listed in the will.
- Abraham, 1775–1844. Listed in the will.
- Tobias, 1777–1856. Listed in the will.
- Judith, 1779–1821. Listed in the will.

Adam died in 1781 in West Bethlehem Township and is buried in the family cemetery on what was then his plantation. I have several photos of that cemetery with his well-worn stone and a picture of his house at that location. The location of the plantation and cemetery is on the Ten Mile Creek about five miles from its junction with the Monongahela River.

This is a well-researched family, with current family members who continue to research his family lines. I found discrepancies, as is to be expected in such a large family. First, the DAR has awarded memberships based on son Peter's service. Some of the family lines used for these memberships are connected to a different Peter Wise of Lancaster County, Pennsylvania, which is in the southeast corner of the state. The incorrect Peter Wise eventually settled in Montgomery County, Ohio. The correct Peter Wise settled in Stark County, Ohio. They were different men, although both Patriots. The DAR has recently corrected most of these application conflicts. Several historical references I used and cited are incomplete and seem to confuse the various family connections. My research focused on the Wise line that lived in these locations:

-Pipe Creek, Frederick, and Carroll County, Maryland, until about 1770 and 1778
-West Bethlehem Township of Washington County, Pennsylvania, until about 1818
-Stark County, Ohio, until about 1837
-Liberty Township, Henry County, Indiana, until about 1840
-Pleasant and Sims Townships, Grant County, Indiana
-Shelby County, Missouri, around 1888

### Jacob Painter
Born: 1743, York, Pennsylvania
Died: 5 June 1824, Martinsburg, Berkeley County, West Virginia
Burial: Old German Lutheran Cemetery in Martinsburg, Berkeley County, West Virginia
Service: Pennsylvania Line. First Company of the Fourth Battalion later identified as the Fifth Pennsylvania Regiment.
Rank: Private
Service Dates: 19 November 1778–1783
Wife: Eve Catherine Seibert, married in 1773
Lineage: Fifth great-grandfather, son George Washington Painter, John Amos, John Thomas, Frank. Oliver Painter to Emma Jo Painter/Raines.
DAR: A086243
SAR: P-264771

Jacob was the son of Hans George "Bender" Painter (1712–1784) and Mary Magdalena Reinhart (1720–1784) of York, Pennsylvania. He is Emma Jo's fourth great-grandfather. The name Painter is probably an American pronouncement of Bender. His father was born in Mosbach, Baden, Germany. He came to America in 1738 after marrying Mary Magdalena Reinhart in England in 1738.[46] George and Mary had five children mentioned in Mary's 1784 will: Andrew, George, Jacob, John, and Christina. George had died a few months prior to Mary writing the will. She died the same year. A son Valentine was not mentioned as he had died prior to the writing of the will. Jacob then married Eve Catherine Seibert (1755–1827) in York, Pennsylvania, in 1773.

Jacob took the Oath of Allegiance to the colony of Pennsylvania in 1779. This act alone would qualify him for Patriot status with both the DAR and SAR.[47]

He enlisted in the First Company of the Fourth Battalion of the Pennsylvania Line on November 19, 1778. Later, he served in the Fifth Company of the same battalion commanded by Lieutenant Colonel Caleb Davis in 1782. He may have served until 1783. This unit was made up of Chester County men.

His home, Chester County, was adjacent to Philadelphia, and history has it that the county was comprised primarily of German immigrants who were quick to demand that the county secede from the thirteen colonies prior to the war. The British method of dealing with this attitude was to assign a German Hessian regiment within the county. That was the regiment that George Washington attacked on Christmas Day early in the war by crossing the Delaware River (Battle of Trenton). Jacob was probably not in the army at that point of the war, but it was in his home county.

---

[46] "Pennsylvania German Pioneers: A Publication of the Original Lists of Arrivals in the Port of Philadelphia from 1727 to 1808." Ralph Beaver Strasburger. Edited by William John Hinke. Norristown [PA]: Pennsylvania German Society, 1934. 3 vols. Vols. 1 and 3 reprinted by Genealogical Publishing Co., Baltimore, 1964. Repr. 1983. Vol. 1. 1727–1775, p. 776.

[47] *Names of Persons Who Took the Oath of Allegiance to the State of Pennsylvania.* John B. Linn and William H. Egle. Willow Bend Books. Westminster, Maryland. Page 118. Jacob Painter took the Oath of Allegiance to the state of Pennsylvania.

The battalion was established in December 1775 and fought in the Philadelphia, Brandywine, and Germantown battles in September and October 1777, and spent the winter of 1777 to 1778 at Valley Forge, Pennsylvania. Their uniforms were blue with white lapels. Jacob did not join until November 1778, so he did not participate in these events. In 1779, a company of the battalion was responsible for storming the British fortifications at Stony Point, New York, in July, and then they spent the remainder of the year at West Point and wintered at Morristown. The next year, they took part in several small engagements in New Jersey and again wintered in Morristown. On New Year's Day 1781, members of the battalion joined in the mutiny of the Pennsylvania regiments then quartered at Morristown, as they had not been paid for a long time. General Washington became involved, and a settlement was reached, and they were paid. His regiment was furloughed at Trenton on January 17, and the unit was disbanded in January 1783, but it is uncertain if Jacob was still in the unit. Soldiers in the unit in January 1781 were reassigned to other units that participated in the Yorktown final battle. Records indicate that he may have been transferred to the First Company of the Fourth Battalion and that he did serve out his enlistment until 1783. More research is needed here.[48] The mutiny is well documented, and there were several other units involved. General Washington was masterful in resolving this conflict without having to execute any of his valuable soldiers at this critical point in the war. It is worthy of note that most of Washington's Continental Line units were then guests of the British army as POWs in Charleston. He could ill afford to lose several regiments due to mutiny, especially given the fact that it was over not being paid.

I found it interesting that there are present-day organizations that conduct reenactments of this regiment's battles and wear correct uniforms. These associations also recognize the role of those Patriots' wives who were present during battles and assisted with water, ammunition, and medical treatment as needed. As Jacob was married prior to entering the regiment, it would be very interesting to know of his wife's activities during the battles he fought in, such as the Stony Point battle and battles later in New Jersey. If we can prove Eve Catherine's participation in these activities, she can be considered a Patriot.

After the war and prior to 1800, he moved to Berkeley County, Virginia, now West Virginia, purchased land (probably a land grant for service), and resided there until his death in 1824. His will is recorded in the Berkeley County records.

His move to Berkeley County, Virginia, was not a particularly long move, as the county is located just south of the Pennsylvania state line and just north of the Maryland line and is one of two Virginia counties in the northern neck of Virginia. He lived near Martinsburg, the county seat of the county. Martinsburg is considered the northern gate to the Shenandoah Valley of Virginia. Berkeley County settlers were mainly colonists of German descent from Pennsylvania. Many of the early settlers there were Revolutionary War Patriots, including General Gates and other officers.

Jacob had nine children. Eve Catherine was not the mother of Jacob Jr., as she would have been too young, being born in 1755. I did not find marriage records for Jacob's first marriage.

- Jacob Jr., 1759–1816. Named in Jacob's will.

---

[48] Volume I, pages 431–32 and Volume II, page 497, *Pennsylvania German Pioneers.*

- Margaret Mong, 1776–1852. Named in Jacob's will and remained in Berkeley County, West Virginia.
- Margaret Ox, 1776–1856. Named in Jacob's will.
- Catherine Walters, 1776–1855. Named in Jacob's will and remained in Berkeley County, West Virginia.
- George Washington, 1784–1853. Not named in his father's will. Moved to Florida, Missouri, and is Emma Jo's third great-grandfather.
- Ela Catherine Swartz, 1789–1861. Named in Jacob's will.
- Elizabeth Helferstay, 1792–1838. Named in Jacob's will.
- Sarah Sally Neff, 1793–1838. Named in Jacob's will.
- John L., 1796–1879. Named in Jacob's will.

The fact that his son George Washington Painter was not named in his father's will is not especially problematic, as he mentioned in his will that not all his children were listed. He apparently held notes for some of them, which he had sold prior to his death in 1824. The following facts justify his inclusion as a son:

- George is listed by the DAR as a son with several memberships being approved because of this relationship. While not proof of relationship, these memberships have stood the test of time.
- George and his father are shown as next-door neighbors in the Virginia 1810 census in Martinsburg, Berkeley County.
- Jacob's father's name was George.
- I think it was likely that Jacob held a note for George and that he considered that note as part of his estate. This was common practice if a family member was indebted to another at the time of probate, and this practice is still common.

Jacob was a first-generation German American. Jacob's son Jacob Jr. remained in Pennsylvania and ran for state representative in Pennsylvania and held that office until he ran for Congress and lost by only seventeen votes. Jacob Jr. then served as a judge for the remainder of his life and died in 1816.[49] Another son, George Washington Painter, was a War of 1812 veteran.

He wrote his will on 10 September 1823 and left all his possessions to his wife Eve, with instructions that after her death the remaining land and possessions be divided between sons John and Jacob and proceeds from the eventual sale be distributed to his other children. Now, Jacob Jr. was dead by 1816. A mystery surrounds his instructions: I found divorce records in which he divorced Eve in 1800, even though they appeared to still be married in 1823. Jacob died in 1824 in Berkeley County and is buried in the German Lutheran Reformed Cemetery in Martinsburg, Berkeley County, now West Virginia. I believe that Eve was his second wife, as she was too young to be the mother of Jacob Jr., who was only four years younger than Eve. Eve Catherine was surely the mother of their last eight children.

His son George Washington Painter, born in 1784 in Berkeley County, West Virginia, moved his family to near Florida, Missouri, in the mid-1830s and farmed near there for the remainder of his

---

[49] "North American Histories 1500–2000. Pennsylvania Genealogies—Index of Surnames". Ancestry.com. Page 600 gives the political history of Jacob Painter Jr.

life. He is buried in the Florida cemetery, and we visit his grave site each year. George Washington Painter is Jo's third great-grandfather. His son John M. (Amos) Painter fathered John Thomas Painter, who fathered William Franklin Painter, who fathered Oliver Forrest Painter, Jo's father. All the Painters from George Washington to Emma Jo lived in Monroe County, Missouri. We have marriage records for this entire family line, as well as probate documents that support these family relationships. My book *Footprints of the Painter and Scott Families of Missouri* has extensive documentation for this line.

The family name prior to immigration from Germany was "Bender." It was not unusual for European names to be mispronounced and misspelled and thus changed forever, or for them to be intentionally changed.

**The Ashby Family**

Sergeant Fielding Ashby, his father David Ashby, and his father Robert Ashby represent three generations of the Ashby family serving in the Revolution. Emma Jo is a direct descendant of this line. Their stories begin with David, followed by father David and his father Robert.

**Sergeant Fielding Ashby**
Born: 1762, Frederick County, Virginia
Died: 17 October 1842, Floyds Fork, Oldham County, Kentucky
Burial: Oldham County, Kentucky, in the Ashby Cemetery
Service: Virginia Line, Colonel Edward's Regiment
Rank: Sergeant
Service Dates: 1779 for eight months and fifteen days
Wife: (1) Rebeca Earickson (1762–1830), married 3 Feb 1790 and
    (2) Francis Bohannon, married 21 March 1831
Lineage: Daughter Elizabeth Ashby/Murphy, Joseph Roney Murphy,
    Bessie Pauline Murphy/Scott, Leta Blanche Scott/Painter (Emma Jo's mother)
DAR: A003410. This is Emma Jo's DAR Patriot
SAR: P-109921

Fielding was born in Frederick County, Virginia, in 1762. His military pension records as well as the Kentucky Pension Roll supports this date. His father was David Ashby, and his mother was Jane Issacs. I have no family documents proving this relationship; however, the civil court case mentioned below seems to prove the claim that he is David's son. The Ashby family was well known for their exploration of the Shenandoah Valley prior to the Revolution. His father, grandfather, uncles, and other family members are credited for serving as chain and rod bearers for George Washington when he surveyed that region prior to the French and Indian War. One early explorer, as he headed west over the mountains, asked someone what was west of the Appalachians, and the answer he received was, "Just Indians and Ashbys." His grandfather Robert served as a company commander for the Virginia colony during the French and Indian War. In fact, his father David and all six of his Ashby uncles either served in the Revolution or are recognized by the DAR for patriotic service. A later chapter in this book is dedicated to the Ashby family and their service during both the French and Indian War and the Revolution. Figure 4-3 below depicts the Ashbys who served in Virginia during the Revolutionary War.[50]

---

[50] *Historical Register of Virginians in the Revolution: Soldiers, Sailors, Marines, 1775–1783.* John H. Gwathmey, 1938. Richmond, Virginia. Reprinted by Genealogical Publishing Company Inc., Baltimore, Maryland, p. 24.

24     VIRGINIANS IN THE REVOLUTION

Ash, Francis, 2nd Lieut., Fauquier Mil., oath 1779.
Ash, Francis, Capt. Benjamin Harrison's Co., Va. Volunteers.
Ash, Gim, E.
Ash, James, 11 CL.
Ash, Jesse, Inf., nbll.
Ash, John, Lieut. at Ft. Nelson in 1782. T-EV2P966.
Ash, John, Clark's Ill. Reg.
Ash, John, 9 CL.
Ash, John, 13 CL, also 9 CL.
Ash, John, 13 CL.
Ash, John Jr., E.
Ash, Mathias, 8 CL.
Ash, Uriel, Capt. Benjamin Harrison's Co., Va. Volunteers.
Ashberry, George, E.
Ashbey, Benjamin (Ashby) Lieut., 7 CL.
Ashbey, Bladen (Ashby) 9 CL.
Ashbey, Stephen (Ashby) Captain, 12 CL.
Ashbey, Thomas, 2 CL.
Ashbrock, Joseph (Ashbrook) 15 CL.
Ashbrook, Aron, 12 CL.
Ashbrook, Joseph, 11 and 15 CL.
Ashbrook, Joseph, 15 CL, also 11 and 15 CL.
Ashbrook, Stephen (Ashbrook, Joseph) 15 CL.
Ashbrook, Thomas, Owen Co., Ind., mpl.
Ashbrooke, Aaron, 12 CL.
Ashburn, Lott, Seaman, Navy.
Ashburn, Luke, Navy, E.
Ashburn, Thomas, Seaman State Navy, nbll.
Ashburn, Wm, Graves, Caroline 1778.
Ashbury, George (Asbury) 5 CL.
Ashby, Bailey, E.
Ashby, Benjamin, Ensign 11 CL Nov. 30, 1776; Regimental Quartermaster Jan. 1, 1777; 1st Lieut. 7 CL Sept. 14, 1778; 3 CL Jan. 1, 1781; retired Jan. 1, 1783.
Ashby, Benjamin, Capt., 3 CL.
Ashby, Benjamin, 11 CL, also 7 CL.
Ashby, Benjamin, Midshipman, Navy, 2666 acres.
Ashby, Bladen, 9 CL.
Ashby, Bladen, 13 CL, also 9 CL.
Ashby, David, 9 CL.
Ashby, David, Commander in Chief's Guard, E.

Ashby, Enoch, Capt. Benjamin Harrison's Co.
Ashby, Enoch, Q. M., Orange 1782.
Ashby, Fielding, Ky. pensioner, E.
Ashby, George, 1st Lieut., Accomac 1777.
Ashby, George, 8 CL.
Ashby, Henkerson, IP.
Ashby, James, Sgt., 9 CL .
Ashby, Jesse, E.
Ashby, Joel, E.
Ashby, John, Culpeper Mil., in Oct., 1775. AB.
Ashby, John, 1 Va. State Reg.
Ashby, John, 2 CL.
Ashby, John, Captain 3 CL March 18, 1776; wounded at Germantown; resigned Oct. 30, 1777; Major Mil. 1780-81; residence Fauquier.
Ashby, John, 6 CL.
Ashby, Lewis, Fauquier, rec. as Ensign 1778.
Ashby, Lewis, Capt. Benjamin Harrison's Co., Va. Volunteers.
Ashby, Nathaniel, Ensign 3 CL. Mch. 18, 1776; 2nd Lieut. Oct. 8, 1776; resigned Nov. 14, 1777.
Ashby, Stephen, Captain 12 CL Sept. 9, 1776; 8 CL Sept. 14, 1778; retired Jan. 1, 1781. Of Hampshire, E. 4000 acres.
Ashby, Thomas (Ashbey) 2 Va. State Reg.
Ashby, William, Navy, E.
Ashcraft, Amos, Capt. Gaddis' Co., Mil.
Ashcraft, Amos, Howard Co., Mo., mpl.
Ashcroft, Daniel, Ky. pensioner, E.
Ashcroft, John, Harrison, mpl.
Ashebrooke, Joseph (Ashbrook) 15 CL.
Ashenbright, Augustin, Capt. Smith's Co., Augusta 1779.
Asher, Anthony, 10 CL.
Asher, Anthony, 14 CL, also 10 CL.
Asher, Bartlett, Clark's Ill. Reg.
Asher, Charles, Clark's Ill. Reg. in 1782. T-EV1P447.
Asher, Charles, E.
Asher, George, 2 Va. Brigade.
Asher, John, E.
Asher, Leroy, E.
Asher, Levi, 3 and 7 CL, also 5 and 11 CL.
Asher, Levi, 5 CL, also 5 and 11 CL.
Asher, Levi, 7 CL, also 5 and 11 CL.

Figure 4-3 Ashbys who served in the Revolutionary War
Source: *Historical Register of Virginians in the Revolution*

Ashby joined the Virginia Line commanded by Colonel Edmund in the fall of 1779, in Captain John Smith's Company, and served two months. He then enlisted in the spring of 1780 in Captain Gill's Company and served four months until September 1780. In September 1781, he enlisted in Captain Gill Bell's Company for two months and fourteen days. I have his written account of his service written when he was seventy years old. One of his company commanders stated that he had been a good soldier when responding to his pension request. His records show that he was at the Siege of Yorktown. After the war, on 12 March 1784, he received 804 acres of farmland in Fayette County, Kentucky, as a grant for his service. This is a large grant, so something in his military history must have indicated he deserved that grant for less than 1½ years' service. Sergeants would have received only a 400-acre warrant for land; perhaps the reenlistment was justification for an added grant. I have a copy of the survey for that grant: Survey Warrant 1762 on Howard's Upper Creek dated 12 March 1784 in Fayette County. I have a portion of his National Archives military records, including the full pension request. His pension number was S 302249. He filed for pension 19 August 1833 in Oldham County. He received $28.33 per year for his service. This account of his service was obtained from a typed letter sent by the National Archives in response to an inquiry for his service records. The handwritten statements from his pension application are difficult to read.

Recent research has uncovered a story of his service written by a modern descendent of Fielding, Gary David Ashby. Gary's research has shown that, after enlistment, he marched with Captain Bell down the James River to the country around Jamestown in company with the Virginia Regiment of Major Charles Magill of Winchester. They returned after being in the Jamestown area for a short time and crossed the James River at Cabin Point in Surry County, and they remained there for some time. He was discharged by General Steuben after having served two months. In the spring of 1780, he served as a volunteer for six months under Captain Erasmus Gill in Frederick County, Virginia. He was in the continental light horse company, and the horses were pressed for the use of the army, and a uniform was furnished by the army. They quickly marched against some Tories, dispersed them, and returned to Francis Stribling's house in Frederick County. They remained there in the camp until Colonel Bland's Regiment of light horses appeared, and Fielding volunteered to join that unit. Captain Bell directed him to take some men and deliver some horses to Colonel Bland. After delivering the horses, he was discharged before his term of service had ended. In September 1781, he was hired by Colonel David Canaday and was authorized to hire men to fight in the place of Quakers. He served with Captain Henry Catlett and Lieutenant Richard Briley. They marched from near Winchester through Fredericksburg via Williamsburg to York, where he remained until Cornwallis surrendered. He received no discharge papers but was in the service of the United States for eight months and fifteen days. This information was taken from Fielding's pension request, which we have, but we were unable to read it in its entirety. I am grateful that Gary David Ashby was successful in reading this set of documents and making them available. This account varies somewhat from the pension request letter mentioned above, but only in minor details.

I found court records showing that, following the war in August 1783, he served as a witness for the sale of twenty-five pounds of tobacco from Robert Ashby (his grandfather) to Argyle Taylor. This was in Frederick County, Virginia.

He said in his pension hearing that he left Virginia in September 1784 for Jefferson County, Kentucky. However, tax records indicate that he lived in Fayette County, Kentucky, in 1798. He received an 804-acre land grant in Fayette County on Howard's Upper Creek in that county in 1784. I have a copy of that Survey Warrant 17612. He remained in that county until 1802, when he appears on that county's tax list. He then moved to Shelby/Oldham County in the northern-most part of the state by 1810, and he is shown on the census as living there also for the 1820 and 1830 censuses. The Fayette County confusion can be explained by the fact that Jefferson County was formed from part of Fayette County in 1780 by the Virginia General Assembly. His first Kentucky land was in the portion of Fayette County that was assigned to the new Jefferson County. I believe his land was in what was to become Jefferson County. The Shelby and Oldham County confusion also stems from Oldham County being formed from Shelby, Jefferson, and Henry Counties in 1832. He merely lived in the part of Shelby County that became Oldham County. His family remained in Oldham County for several years after his death. Louisville is in Oldham County, today one of the richest counties in the state. The Kentucky county formation information was obtained from Wikipedia and its references.

In his pension request, he stated that he had few resources and made a list of possessions which included a twenty-seven-year-old horse. He was living with his children and was about seventy years old. On 23 March 1831, he had conveyed his estate to all his children as he was about to enter matrimony for the second time. Rebecca had died in 1830, and he married Francis Bohannon on 21 March 1831.

Some 1821 civil court records from Oldham County, Kentucky (Taylor vs. Ashby), show he was sued by a person that had sold 150 acres of his 1,000-acre farm in Jefferson County to Fielding's father, David Ashby.[51] David had since conveyed that land to Fielding on 20 July 1801. That person stated that more land had been transferred than originally intended, and that Fielding owed him $43 an acre for the 36 extra acres. Fielding won that case and did not have to pay. It is an interesting court case, as the judge gave incorrect instructions to the jury, and they voted as instructed. Ashby probably should have been made to pay the requested amount. Kentucky law schools use this case when discussing poor jury instructions. After study of the court case, I believe that David gave Fielding that land, further strengthening the claimed father/son relationship. I am indebted to Gary David Ashby for making this story available.

I also discovered a 6 April 1791 Jefferson County probate case for John Hawks in which Fielding and David Ashby were instructed to perform an inventory of a neighbor's estate. This seems to establish the Fielding and David relationship in Jefferson County.

Fielding and Rebecca had eight children who are mentioned in his August 1842 will:

- Elizabeth Betsy, 1792–1855. Betsy is Emma Jo's third great-grandmother.
- Jane, 1794–1860. Lived in Oldham County, Kentucky.
- James E., 1796–1851. Lived in Oldham County, Kentucky.
- John, 1796–1844. Lived in Oldham County, Kentucky.
- Matilda Robertson, 1797–1855. Lived in Oldham County, Kentucky.

---

[51] Oldham County Circuit Court Case 117, Taylor v. Ashby. October 27, 1829, Judge Covenant presiding. In this case Fielding Ashby stated land sold to him by his father, David Ashby, contained surplus land that he now lives on. This seems to establish Fielding as the son of David Ashby.

- Francis "Fanny" Willis, 1798–1852. Lived in Oldham County, Kentucky.
- Sydney Ann, 1802–1853. Lived in Oldham County, Kentucky.
- Rebecca Ann Ellis, 1804–1864. Buried in Pleasant Hill Cemetery, Monroe County, Missouri.

Fielding and Rebecca's daughter Betsy married John Lewis Murphy, a son of Patriot Lewis Murphy (Murphey) discussed later in this book.[52] John Lewis and Betsy's son Fielding Murphy married Elizabeth Roney, granddaughter of Patriot Hercules Roney II, also discussed later in this book.[53] Their son Fielding Murphy is Emma Jo's second great-grandfather. These relationships are first documented in the Missouri Scotts' family bible, and various census reports and marriage and death records are also in our possession. Fielding is Emma Jo's Patriot used to establish her membership in the DAR. His father's story follows:

**David Ashby**
Born: 1737, Frederick County, Virginia
Died: 1803, Oldham County, Kentucky
Burial: Ashby family cemetery, Floydsburg, Oldham County, Kentucky
Service: Continental Army, Virginia Line, Ninth Regiment
Rank: Private
Service Dates: November 1776–August 1777
Wife: Jane Isaacs (1740–1815)
Lineage: Son Fielding discussed above
DAR: No
SAR: P-33601

David was born in Frederick County, Virginia, to Captain Robert Ashby and Dorthy Baylis. His family was well known by George Washington, as Robert and David's brothers had served as chain bearers and recorders for Washington when he surveyed the Shenandoah Valley prior to the French and Indian War. Washington served as a major and colonel for the colony during this war, and his personal notes—before, during, and after the French and Indian War and the Revolution—include many mentions of his work and visits with various Ashby family members. The Ashbys were well-known explorers of that region, with his uncle Nimrod being killed by Indians during the French and Indian War.

David joined the Ninth Virginia Regiment of the Continental Army in November 1776 and served at least until August 1777. In June of 1777, he was appointed to General Washington's personal bodyguard unit. This was a position of great honor and responsibility. Any soldier appointed to this position would require the personal approval of the commander. The general clearly knew his family and probably knew David personally. The Ninth Regiment was commanded by Colonel George Mathews until he was transferred to the general's guard. His commander was Captain Smith Snead while serving as a guard. His National Archives records reflect this important assignment.

---

[52] Kentucky Marriage Records 1792–1830. Records the marriage of John Murphy to Betsy Ashby on February 12, 1816.
[53] Kentucky Marriage Records 1783–1965. Records the marriage of Fielding Murphy to Elizabeth Roney on September 11, 1851.

The Ninth Regiment fought in the Battles of Brandywine and Germantown in late 1777, but it is likely that David had been discharged prior to the regiment's capture during the battle of Germantown in October 1777. The regiment was also captured at Charleston in 1780, but David had been discharged two years prior to that event. I have David's National Archives military records.

There is a recorded pension number for his service: S30249. He received a Kentucky land grant for his service, and he settled in Jefferson County soon after the war. He owned several tracts of land, of which one was sold to his son Fielding as related in the above story. He later moved to Oldham County, where he lived the remainder of his life.

David is buried in the Ashby Cemetery in Oldham, Kentucky. His son Fielding is also buried there.

David and Jane's children are:

- Fielding, 1762–1842, He is Emma Jo's fourth great-grandfather. His Patriot story is above.
- Charlotte Bartlett, 1764–1824
- Lavinia "Vina," 1766–1818
- Mary Ann "Polly" Hyatt, 1770–1853
- Louisa, 1772–1818
- Washington, 1774–1836
- Willis, 1776–1830
- Landon Edward, 1780–1826

The names of their children are found in the Shelby County land records related to their father's estate. These children are also listed in the Shelby County 1815 tax records. These records were listed in David Gary Ashby's family records. His son Willis was listed as caring for his mother Jane's estate in 1815, her death year.

The story of David's father, Captain Robert Ashby, follows:

**Captain Robert R. Ashby**
Born: 1710, Stafford County, Virginia
Died: 27 February 1792, Delaplane, Fauquier County, Virginia
Burial: Ashby Cemetery near Delaplane in Fauquier County, Virginia
Service: French and Indian War and patriotic service as recognized by the DAR for the Revolutionary War
Rank: Captain during the French and Indian War
Service Dates: 1759–1760
Wife: (1) Dorothy Baylis and (2) Catherine Combs
Lineage: Son David Ashby above, son Fielding Ashby, daughter Elizabeth Ashby/Murphy, Joseph Murphy, daughter Bessie Murphy/Scott, daughter Lita Scott/Painter
DAR: A003422
SAR: 95787

Robert was born to Captain Thomas Edward Ashby Sr. in Stafford County, Virginia. His mother was Rosanna (Rose) Berry. Thomas Sr. was born in Leicestershire, England, and immigrated to Virginia in the 1690s. Robert had five brothers and four sisters and spent his entire adult life in and around Frederick and Fauquier Counties in Virginia.[54] He was a farmer and was successful in acquiring good farmland and retaining it. Possibly some of this success can be attributed to his serving on several surveying crews and then acquiring land following those projects for Lord Fairfax of Virginia. George Washington headed some of those crews, and Robert and his family are mentioned often in Washington's personal notes pertaining to those surveys.[55] I am unsure of his middle name, but I noticed he used the initial "R" when he signed a 1783 indenture involving his second wife Catherine Combs.

Robert served as a marker in the survey project conducted by George Washington for Lord Fairfax on 15 March 1748. Washington's notes reflect that he stayed at the Ashby home during that expedition. During this survey, he surveyed a tract of land for himself adjoining Curtis land, which consisted of 346 acres on 27 October 1750. I assume that was payment for his work.

Robert served in the French and Indian War in the Fauquier County Militia as a captain, joining on 27 September 1759, and received a land grant for his service.[56] He married Dorothy Baylis in 1735. She passed away in 1774, and Robert married Catherine Combs (1742–1791) shortly after his first wife's passing.[57] David Ashby discussed above was his first son. Most of his sons, including David, served in the Revolution. One son, Nimrod, was killed by Indians during the French and Indian War.

A sad tale surrounds the death of Nimrod. As a company commander during the French and Indian War in Virginia, he traveled to Richmond to pick up funds to pay his troops. During his return, he was killed by Indians, and the funds were stolen. The Colony of Virginia held his estate liable for that money, which was collected from his estate. No excuses were accepted. His father was greatly upset over the treatment but was not able to settle his account to his family's favor. Robert later provided for Nimrod's children in his estate.

Robert had extensive land holdings of as much as twelve thousand acres in the Shenandoah Valley, with tobacco being the primary crop. He was a slaveholder, with slaves being given to grandchildren in his will. He also operated an inn at Yew Hill originally known as Shackletts and Watts Tavern, which George Washington visited more than once.[58] The inn still stands and is on the National Historic Landmarks Register of Historic Places. His home at Yew Hill also still stands.

---

[54] *Encyclopedia of Virginia Biography,* **Vol V**. Edited by Lyon Tyler L.L.D. Lewis Historical Publishing Company. New York. Reprinted by the Genealogical Publishing Co. Inc., Baltimore, Maryland. Pages 1124–1125 give the early history of the Ashby family from first-generation Thomas to the third generation.

[55] *Diaries of George Washington,* **Vol. I, 1748–1765**. Edited by Donald Jackson and Dorothy Twohig. University Press of Virginia, Charlottesville.

[56] *Colonial Soldiers of the South, 1732–1774*. June Clark Murtie. Clearfield Co. Second Edition. January 1983. Page 513 lists Captain Robert Ashby's service in the Virginia militia.

[57] *Register of Maryland's Heraldic Families.* **Vol 1**. Alice Norris. Page 85 gives Robert's vital information, including the name of his wife.

[58] *Diaries of George Washington,* Volume II, 1766–1770. Edited by Donald Jackson and Dorothy Twohig. University Press of Virginia, Charlottesville, p. 133. George Washington stayed with Robert Ashby at Yew Hill on 9 March 1769.

In his later years, Robert and Catherine moved to Deleplane and built a home, which also still stands, and he is buried in the cemetery there. We have visited Deleplane, which is about seven miles east of Paris, Virginia, on Federal Highway 50. Paris is located adjacent to the Ashby Gap, which was founded by brother John (Jack). Yew Hill is located across the Ashby Gap about eight miles west and south of Paris, also on Highway 50. There is an Ashby Inn in Paris that dates to prior to the Civil War, and this is still open. I am uncertain if any of the Ashby family has ever owned that inn, but the Ashby Gap is in clear view from the front of the inn. Deleplane is historically significant in that Generals Stonewall Jackson and Johnson loaded a large corps-sized unit at that train station, which still stands, for a quick trip to nearby Washington D.C. for the First Battle of Manassas (Bull Run) on 21 July 1861. It is said that General Jackson slept on the steps of that inn in Paris on the evening of 20 July prior to the train trip to Manassas. We were fortunate enough to obtain a room there for our recent visit. History abounds in Paris, and we were treated to a tour of a local resident's historic home and received a long visit from the unofficial mayor of the town.

His final will and testament, filed on 27 February 1792—and filed in the Fauquier County Will Book, page 216—contains good accounting of his family and wealth. He did own slaves, with several of them being willed to children and grandchildren. He provided for the children of Nimrod, the son that was killed during the French and Indian War. Interestingly, Robert did not mention his son David in his will. He did mention someone had been omitted, but no name was given. He mentioned a son that had received all he was due prior to the writing of the will. I worked nearly a year researching court records to establish this relationship with David. I was partially successful. David's birth date is consistent with the birth of his brothers and sisters. Also, David served on survey crews with his proposed father and uncles, as George Washington's notes support that claim.[59] I found more than one court case in which they both gave testimony and served as witnesses to various cases. As discussed above, I found a court case in which David's son Fielding also served as a witness in one of Robert's court cases. They clearly knew each other and worked closely together on family matters. I also found part of a court document pertaining to some financial problems encountered by David. The final test was to eliminate the possibility that David was the son of one of Robert's brothers, and I was successful in that attempt. None of Robert's brothers were the father of David, as their marriages and the births of their children do not support this conjecture. Given that there was only one Ashby family line in Virginia during that period, David is clearly the son of Robert. I will discuss this issue later in the Ashby chapter.

Robert did not serve in the military during the Revolutionary War but was recognized for patriotic service by both the DAR and SAR. He provided supplies to the militia.

These are the known children of Robert and Dorthey Bayless:

- David, 1732–1803. Discussed above and not mentioned in his father's will. Revolutionary War Patriot.

---

[59] *Diaries of George Washington*, Volume I, 1748-1765. Edited by Donald Jackson and Dorothy Twohig. University Press of Virginia, Charlottesville. George Washington recounts his survey projects in northern Virginia.

- William, 1734–1722. Married Mary Tebbs and had two children. Died before his father's will was written.
- Nimrod, 1736–1754. Married Francis Wright and had six children. He was killed in the French and Indian War. Mentioned in his father's will.
- Robert, 1738–1780. Married Mary Harding and had six children. Died before his father's will was written.
- Captain John, 1740–1815. Married Mary Elizabeth Turner and had seven children. Mentioned in his father's will. Revolutionary War Patriot.
- Winfred (Winney) Piper, 1741–1790. Married James Piper. Mentioned in her father's will.
- Mary (Molly), 1743–1799. Mentioned in her father's will.
- Ann Farrow/Smith, 1745–1807. Mentioned in her father's will.
- Thomas Enoch, 1747–1790. Married Sarah Henley and had ten children. Mentioned in his father's will. Revolutionary War Patriot.
- Benjamin, 1747–1823. Married Jane Ash and had six children. Mentioned in his father's will. He was a Revolutionary War Patriot.

The service of the Ashby family (Fielding, David, Robert, and their sons) does not on the surface appear to be particularly noteworthy. They honorably served their colony and their fledgling nation in several ways. They were indeed Patriots. However, when I studied the entire Ashby family of that era, a vastly different story emerged: the "family story." It is a story of service, dedication, and heroism over six generations of this nation's history. The stories of Fielding, David, and Robert cannot be told in isolation. I will tell a more compelling story in a later chapter in this book: "Nothing There but Indians and Ashbys." This family produced twenty-three Revolutionary War Patriots and were probably instrumental in George Washington's success as a regimental commander during the French and Indian War. They made history.

**Sergeant John Whipple III**
Born: 25 June 1717, Ipswich, Essex County, Massachusetts
Died: 27 December 1794
Burial: Hamilton, Essex County, Massachusetts
Service: Minutemen of Ipswich, Massachusetts
Rank: Private and later sergeant
Service Dates: 19 April 1776
Wife: Dorothy Molten (1718–1766)
Lineage: John's daughter Jemima married Samuel Adams, my fourth great-grandfather. See the Samuel Adams lineage above.
DAR: No
SAR: P-317716

John was a third-generation American and the son of Captain John Whipple II and Hannah Whipple of Ipswich. His birth, as well as the names of his parents, is recorded in the City of Ipswich records. His mother's maiden name was also Whipple, and she was a third cousin of her husband.[60] His uncle William Whipple (1732–1785) was a general and a signer of the Declaration of Independence. William was a wealthy seafaring businessman and was a friend of George Washington. He probably was a major financier of the war, and he had only one child who died in infancy.[61] Several Whipples held titles of military rank, but that was a stylized rank rather than a military or seafaring rank. John's death records reflect the rank of captain, as did his father's death records. Uncle William left property to John III in his estate just a few years prior to John III's death.

He married Dorothy Moulton on 18 August 1737 in Ipswich. That marriage is recorded in the City of Ipswich vital records.

John served with the minutemen of Ipswich under the command of Captain Elisha Whitney. The company marched on call on 19 April 1775 from Ipswich hamlet and fought in the battles of Lexington and Concord, where he served for a total of eighteen days for two call-ups.[62] These are recognized as the first battles of the Revolution, even though the Declaration of Independence had not yet been signed. He was allowed 108 miles of travel for both call-ups. He served in the same unit with his son-in-law, Samuel Adams, another Raines/Painter Patriot discussed earlier in this book. The city of Hamilton, Massachusetts, requested and received a tombstone for him 140 years after his death. He is buried in the Old Hamilton Cemetery in Hamilton, near his son-in-law Samuel Adams. The website Find a Grave has a photo of that stone.

John was not a young man by the time of the Revolution, being fifty-eight years old at the time of the Battle of Lexington. His wife was dead, and his children grown and away from home. He and his family were community leaders, and his presence at this historical event would have sent a strong message about the importance of the coming Revolution.

The Whipple family home is owned by the Ipswich Historical Society, still stands in Ipswich, and can be toured as a national monument. This home was built by John's father or perhaps his grandfather, with John III adding to it.

John and Dorthey's children were:

- Hannah Dodge, 1738–1824
- Martha Lamson, 1740–1824
- John IV, 1741–1808. Also served in the Revolution
- Jemima Adams. Wife of Samuel Adams and my fourth great-grandmother.

The births of his children are recorded in the Ipswich, Essex County, vital records. Jemima is also recorded in *History and Genealogy of "Elder" John Whipple of Ipswich, Massachusetts*, listed in the below footnotes. The inventory of John's estate following his death reveled a large and complex estate. He had several relatively small debts or notes amounting to over 215

---

[60] *History and Genealogy of "Elder" John Whipple of Ipswich, Massachusetts. His English Ancestors and American Descendants.* Blaine Whipple. Whipple Development Corporation. Victoria, British Columbia, 2003. Birthdate and marriage for John Whipple III shown on page 348.
[61] Ibid., p. 90.
[62] *Massachusetts Soldiers and Sailors of the Revolutionary War,* Volumes 1–17. Massachusetts Secretary of the Commonwealth, Wright & Potter Printing, 1896–1908. Volume 17, page 13 shows John Whipple's service in the minutemen.

pounds, but he owned several tracts of land, as well as livestock. It appears that these debts required the sale of one or more tracts of land in order that the estate be settled to the satisfaction of the Ipswich city leaders. This was a normal probate resolution, as few people held cash early in our nation's history. His estate inventory is interesting and points to the fact that his farm was a working farm and that he had an extensive list of possessions but little cash. The property descriptions often included the term "marsh." John was described as a "country gentleman" when mentioned in the probate proceedings.


### Richard Lee

Born: 31 July 1753, Warrenton, Prince William County (now Fauquier County), Virginia
Died: 21 October 1820, Madison County, Kentucky
Burial: James Barnett Cemetery, Silver Creek, Madison County, Kentucky
Service: Continental Army, Virginia Line, Third, Fourth, and Seventh Regiments
Rank: Private
Service Dates: October 1777–November 1783
Wife: Elizabeth Scott (1761–1838), daughter of Patriot Captain William Scott discussed later in the book. Married in 1771.
Lineage: Son Grissom Lee, his daughter Emeline married Robert Fowler, their daughter was Louvisa Fowler/Raines, who was my great-grandmother.
DAR: No
SAR: P-82373


Richard is my fourth great-grandfather and was born to Hancock Lee II (1709–1762) and Mary Willis (1716–1766) in Warrenton, Fauquier County, Virginia.[63] Another source of the Hancock/Richard Lee relationship is the Henry Willis family bible, which establishes Richard as a son of Hancock II. Henry Willis was the father of Mary Willis, the mother of this Richard.[64]

Some researchers report that Hancock's will gives his wife Mary guardianship authority for Richard, who was nine years of age at the time of his father's death, but I have not located that document, though I believe it does exist. The suffix of II has historically been used with his father's name in several sources, but he is the son of Hancock Lee Sr., son of Richard Lee, therefore a Jr. by today's genealogy standards.[65][66] I question the middle name of Bland sometimes attributed to this Richard, as there are several notable men of the Virginia colonial period with that name. One of these men signed the Declaration of Independence, and another was also a member of the First Continental Congress, therefore it is easy to confuse these well-known men. This Richard Lee was neither of those two men, and I found no evidence that he used that middle

---

[63] *The Brewster Genealogy 1566–1907*. A Record of the Descendants of William Brewster of the *Mayflower*. Ruling Elder of the Pilgrim Church Which Founded Plymouth Colony in 1620. Volume III. Compiled and edited by Emma C. Brewster Jones of Cincinnati, Ohio. The Grafton Press—Genealogical Publishers. New York. Lists Hancock Lee's father and son Richard Lee (Ditchley Lees).

[64] *The William and Mary Quarterly*, Volume 6. 1898-04-01. Omohundro Institute of Early American History and Culture (William and Mary University). This journal contains information from the Henry Willis family bible (Henry was the father of Mary Willis, the mother of Richard Lee) and documents the father-son relationship of Hancock Lee II and Richard Lee.

[65] *Colonial Families of the USA 1607–1775*. Edited by Mackenzie George and Nelson Osgood Rhoades. Boston Genealogical Publishing Company, Boston. Page 490 lists the sister of Hancock Lee II (Elizabeth) and her parents.

[66] *Married Well and Married Often: Marriages of the Northern Neck of Virginia 1649–1800*. Headley, Robert K. Genealogical Publishing Company, 2003, Baltimore, Maryland. Page 224 gives the marriage date and location for Hancock Lee II and his wife Mary Kendal Willis, as well as the names of their parents.

name. There are kinship connections with these men, but distant. Richard is my fourth great-grandfather on the Raines family line.

Before continuing, it is essential that I firmly link him with the correct line of Virginia Lees. Hancock Lee II's grandfather was Richard Lee (1617–1664), and his grandmother was Anne Owen Constable (1622–1706), and they immigrated from England. This Richard's line is often referred to as the "Ditchley Line," with the Ditchley Plantation being the home place of Hancock Lee Sr. his grandfather. The *Encyclopedia of Virginia Biography* accurately describes these relationships.[67] I will also add that Sarah Elizabeth Allerton, the wife of Hancock Sr., is a *Mayflower* Descendant, and I'll discuss those connections later in this chapter.

Hancock Lee III (brother of Richard) was a civil engineer and one of the earliest explorers in Kentucky; he claimed that he preceded Daniel Boone in exploring the state. He was involved in surveying Madison County in 1776, and in fact his brother Willis and a cousin were killed by Indians in that county that year. They received patents for Madison County property after the war. That was his home. [68] I believe that brother Hancock Lee's well-documented activities in Madison County, Kentucky, prior to the Revolution influenced Richard to later obtain two land grants there.

Richard married Elizabeth Scott, also of Virginia and daughter of Captain William Scott, a Patriot of the Raines/Painter family line discussed following this story. His son Grissom fought in the War of 1812 and later settled in Pettis County, Missouri. Grissom's daughter Emeline Jane Fowler is the mother of my great-grandmother Louvisa Fowler Raines. Richard and Elizabeth had eighteen children.

As with his father, I have seen genealogies that attribute Grissom's family to the Senator Richard Henry Lee line of Virginia because his given name of Grissom is found in that line. That link is not fact, even though there are some Grissoms found in the Richard Henry Lee line. That Lee line generated Revolutionary War officer Lighthorse Lee and General Robert E. Lee of the Civil War. It is important to mention that another family Patriot, George Lee, has family connections to Senator Richard Henry Lee, and he will be discussed later in this book. That line is also associated with Patriot Abraham Woolery, also discussed later in this book, and with the Joshua Logan Younger line discussed above. Again, the Revolutionary War was a family affair.

We can link Grissom to Richard through wills, court orders, and probate court cases, as well as the fact that Grissom met his wife Polly Glen, whose father, Hugh Glenn Jr., was a close neighbor, and his father, Hugh Sr., was a Patriot (to be discussed later in this book). In fact, I believe that Richard and Hugh Glenn Sr. are buried in the same cemetery.

Richard served in the Third, Fourth, and, Seventh Virginia Line of the Continental Army. The multi-unit designations were not the result of reassignments but came about because the regiments were re-constituted due to losses from injuries and disease. This regiment (Third) was

---

[67] *Encyclopedia of Virginia Biography*, Volume IV. Edited under the supervision of Lyon Gardiner Tyler. Genealogical Publishing Company, Boston, Massachusetts. Page 138 recounts the lives of the Hancock Lee family from Hancock Lee Sr. for three generations.
[68] *History of New Orleans*, Volume III. John Smith Kendall, A.M. Lewis Publishing Company, Chicago and New York. Page 920 explains that Willis Lee was a civil engineer surveyor who was killed in Kentucky.

raised on 28 December 1775 at Alexandria, Virginia, for service with the Continental Army. It was merged with the Fourth Regiment prior to Ricard's enlistment, thus his official records reflect him serving in that combined regiment. I believe that during their imprisonment, the Third and Fourth Regiments were merged with the Seventh Regiment. One of its early commanders was Thomas Marshall, father of future Supreme Court Chief Justice John Marshall. A later regimental commander was Colonel William Heth, who commanded during the Valley Forge winter and later battles below. The regiment wintered at Valley Forge, Pennsylvania, for the winter of 1777–1778 and later fought in battles at Trenton, Princeton, Brandywine, Germantown, Monmouth, and the siege at Charleston, South Carolina.

Richard enlisted in October 1777 for the duration of the war and served most of the winter of 1778 at Valley Forge and the later battles mentioned above. His records reflect he was sick during part of January and February of 1778 and received a furlough following that illness. Nearly all the soldiers of this regiment were captured at the Siege of Charleston on 12 May 1780 and were discharged when released sometime prior to 15 November 1783. He received two final payments for his service in November 1783, which establishes that he was paid for his captivity. His monthly pay amounted to 6 2/3 dollars per month, and his final payment was in pounds, and that payment was for several hundred pounds. After all, he had been in prison for two years and had not been paid. This would have been a brutal captivity with high mortality rates. Prior to that he had served at Valley Forge and some of the most significant battles of the war. He is a documented survivor of the Valley Forge winter. This is an impressive Patriot story!

Richard Lee served the winter of 1777–1778 at Valley Forge, Pennsylvania.[69] This, until recently, has been studied by everyone in public schools, and we all remember it. It is the stuff of legends. This soldier survived sickness and was given leave after his health improved, and then he returned to his unit and honored his enlistment vows. What is not so well studied is the Siege of Charleston, South Carolina, from 1780–1782. Richard survived his captivity for nearly two years. Nearly all the army of Virginia Line units were held there as prisoners. He is listed in the "List of Revolutionary War Soldiers of Virginia."[70]

Richard received two land grants in Kentucky for 400 acres in 1783 and possibly one for 1,000 acres in 1785. I have also found a land patent for 350 acres in Harrison County, Kentucky, in 1789. Following the war, Richard bought and sold land in Madison County, Kentucky, and remained there until his death in 1820. His final estate consisted of 320 acres, but he had likely already dispersed most of it to his sons. His wife Elizabeth moved to Howard County, Missouri, after his death and lived with their son Richard until her death in 1838. She is buried in Howard County. Probate records reflect the settlement of his estate as well as that of his father Hancock. This was a large family and a large estate. I found records of the court documents pertaining to the civil petition filed by family members, which his son Grissom was a party to. The 1845 deed of partition for the 320 acres of his final estate names sixteen of eighteen possible children.

---

[69] Valley Forge Muster Roll. www.valleyforgemusterroll.org. Site maintained by the Valley Forge Park Alliance. Richard was listed as a soldier of the Third Virginia Regiment in a company commanded by Captain Robert Powell. The regiment was commanded by Colonel William Heth, and the division commander was Major General Marquis de Lafayette. Site accessed 1 January 2024.

[70] "List of Revolutionary War Soldiers of Virginia." Special Report of the Department of Archives and History for 1912. H.J. Eckendorf, Archivist. David Bottom, Superintendent of Public Printing, 1913. Page 183 lists Richard as a Revolutionary War soldier of Virginia.

Records exist suggesting his burial location in his plantation cemetery, identified as Paint Lick Creek Cemetery. Later research confirms his burial at the James Barnett Cemetery at Silver Creek in Madison County. It is worthy of note that Patriot Hugh Glenn Sr., discussed later in this book, owned land nearby and is also buried at Paint Lick Creek, Madison County, Kentucky. The name of this cemetery was later changed to reflect the name of a Civil War soldier.

The family of Richard and Elizabeth was large and close. There were possibly eighteen children, with the first three being born in Virginia and the remainder being born in Kentucky, except as otherwise noted below. Nearly all the children eventually settled in Missouri, one of which had Monroe County connections. I observed some of the older siblings living with their younger brothers or sisters in their final years. I resolved the names of the children from one of Richard's estate documents, and from the 1 September 1845 land partition document which I have. I must note that three of the children were not named on the 1845 deed partition, and that is so noted on the following list. The children are:

- William Thomas, 1778–1824. Married (1) Elizabeth Ann Newell and (2) Charolette Hentsmaker. Lived in Pulaski County, Kentucky, and later died in Armstrong, Howard County, Missouri. He was not mentioned in the 1845 deed partition. He is buried in the Lee Cemetery in Armstrong, Missouri, as is his mother and brother Richard. This is an unproven relationship, but he and both his wives were deceased by the time of the 1845 deed partition. I found no evidence of children, so there might have been no legal logic for him or his wives being included, due to lack of heirs.
- Charles, 1780–1842. Born in Fauquier County, Virginia, and lived in both Madison and Pulaski Counties, Kentucky. He was not mentioned in the 1845 deed partition, and this is an unproven relationship. He was deceased by the time of the deed partition but had a surviving wife and children.
- Sarah (Sally) West, 1781–1845. Married Littleton West and moved to Ray County, Missouri. She was listed as deceased in the deed partition, and her surviving husband was listed.
- Dorothy (Dolly) Titus, 1783–1869. Married Ebenezer Titus and died in Ray County, Missouri. She and her husband were listed in the deed partition.
- Ann Talitha McGuire, 1785–1872. Married Thomas William McGuire (Ned) and settled in Charleston, Delta County, Texas. She and her husband were listed in the deed partition.
- Grissom Reed, 1787–1860. My third great-grandfather and a War of 1812 soldier. Born in East Hawkins, Tennessee, and served in the War of 1812. Married Polly Ann Glen in Madison County, Kentucky, and died in Pettis County, Missouri. He was listed in the deed partition.
- Elizabeth Betsy Belsha, 1788–1845. Born in East Hawkins, Tennessee. Married Robert Belsha and lived in Madison County, Kentucky. She was deceased by the time of the deed partition, but she and her husband and children were listed in the deed partition.
- David, 1789–1875. Married Ann Gilmore and lived in Pulaski County, Kentucky, and died in Grand River, Henry County, Missouri. He was listed in the deed partition.
- Noah Green, 1790–1853. He served as a sergeant in Kentucky in the War of 1812, lived in Madison County, Kentucky, and moved to Cooper County, Missouri, by 1830. He is buried in the Lee Cemetery near Armstrong, in Howard County. He initiated the petition

that generated the 1845 deed partition. It is interesting to note that his brother Grissom named one of his sons Noah Green.

- Thomas Henry, 1795–1871. Married Gabriela Herndon and later moved to Howard County, Missouri. He was listed in the deed partition.
- Richard Washington, 1796–1882. Born in Paint Lick, Kentucky, married Nancy Harvey, and settled in Howard County, Missouri. He is buried in Howard County, as is his mother Elizabeth, who probably lived with him. He was listed in the deed partition.
- Mary Ann Polly Stephenson, 1797–1870. Born at Paint Lick, Kentucky, married James Stephenson, and settled in Nodaway, Nodaway County, Missouri. She and her husband were named in the deed partition.
- Delilah Mary Wright, 1799–1870. Married Hezekiah W. Wright and settled in Howard County, Missouri. She and her husband were listed in the deed partition.
- Nancy Ruth Todd, 1800–1840. Married Joel Todd (1801–1886) of Madison County, Kentucky, in 1822. Joel was a well-known slave abolitionist in Kentucky and assisted several former slaves in obtaining Madison County farmland prior to the Civil War. Some of the 1845 Lee partitioned land given to Joel and Nancy was probably later sold or given to slaves by them. They were both listed in the deed partition. We can speculate that because Nancy Ruth and her husband remained in Madison County, her siblings were concerned that they were preparing to distribute some or all of the land to non-family members (i.e., slaves), thus prompting the petition for land distribution to rightful heirs.
- James B., 1801–1864. He married Nedenia Cloyd in Madison County, Kentucky, and they had moved to Leesville, Henry County, Missouri, by 1840. He was a farmer and was killed by Union soldiers during the Civil War. I found no evidence he was a soldier at the age of sixty-two, but an unpublished story I discovered claimed he was beaten and hung by Union soldiers who were looking for Quantrill soldiers. He lived until the next day but did not survive the encounter. He was listed in the deed partition.
- Margaret Peggy Cloyd Dalton, 1802–1849. She was born in Paint Lick, Madison County, Kentucky, and married (1) Hugh Cloyd (1799–1833) and (2) David Dalton (1800–1840). She died in Linn, Missouri, and was listed in the deed partition.
- Irvine, 1803–1877. He was born at Paint Lick, Madison County, Kentucky, and married Elizabeth Williams in Madison County. He was a slave-owning farmer in Howard County, Missouri, by 1830 and, following the Civil War, farmed in Grand River, Henry County, Missouri. His brother David was living with him at the time of the 1870 census. He is listed in the deed partition.
- Lucinda Forrest, 1808–1861. She married Francis Preston Forrest in Howard County, Missouri, and they later settled in Bucklin, Linn County, Missouri.

As with most family histories, mysteries abound. Their son Grissom's recorded birth location in the 1850 census is Tennessee. He was born in 1787, and I believe Grissom's next younger sister, Elizabeth Betty Belsha, was also born in Tennessee nearly two years later. What was Richard and his large family of five children doing in Tennessee in the late 1780s? Grissom and Elizabeth's next younger brother, David, was born back in Madison County, Kentucky, two years later, where they had extensive land holdings. These are hard-to-ignore facts, but Grissom can soon be found in Madison County, Kentucky, where he married Polly Ann Glen, daughter of Hugh Glen Jr. and granddaughter of Hugh Glen Sr. (1735–1807), a Revolutionary War Patriot and neighbor of Richard Lee. Hugh Glenn Sr. and Richard Lee are buried in the same cemetery. Patriot Hugh Glenn Sr. will be discussed later in this book, as Emma Jo is a descendant of Hugh.

This family has been extensively researched by experienced researchers, but proof of Richard's marriage to Elizabeth Scott has not been solidly established. His will and estate documents clearly establish he was married to Elizabeth, last name unmentioned. His widowed wife Elizabeth later moved to Howard County, Missouri, and is buried there with two sons. She was the sister of General Winfield Mason Scott, which is established in his biography by Eli Chandler. Winfield Scott later ran unsuccessfully for president of the United States. I will also note that some researchers claim Richard married Elizabeth Hurst. I have records of this marriage in Northern Neck, Virginia, in 1795, but this Patriot Richard Lee and Elizabeth Scott had a family of ten of their eighteen children born by 1795. That 1795 marriage was not for a Richard Lee of the Ditchley Line, but a different Richard Lee.

Son Grissom and Polly Ann had eleven children, with their fourth daughter being Emiline (Emily) Jane, born in 1822, who married Robert Fowler in Pettis County, Missouri, on 25 September 1841. I have a copy of that marriage record of their minister. Their daughter Louvisa married John Washington Marshall Raines, my great-grandfather. Louvisa is shown on the 1860 census in Pettis County, Missouri, with the Fowler family, and I have the marriage records for her marriage to John Washington Marshall Raines.

As I mentioned above, Sarah Elizabeth Allerton, wife of Hancock Lee, was Richard's grandmother and a *Mayflower* Descendant. *Mayflower Births and Deaths* is one of the best resources documenting those passengers and some of their descendants.[71]

The *Mayflower* Connection

- Richard Lee, 1753–1820. My fourth great-grandfather
- Hancock Lee II, 1709–1762. Father of Richard
- Hancock Lee, 1656–1709. Father of Hancock II
    - Sarah Elizabeth Allerton, 1671–1731. Wife of Hancock Lee
    - Colonel Isaac Allerton II, 1628–1702. Father of Sarah Elizabeth
    - Captain Isaac Allerton, 1583–1659. Father of Colonel Isaac Allerton and a 1620 *Mayflower* passenger

Captain Isaac Allerton, my eighth great-grandfather, was the fifth signer of the Mayflower Compact, lieutenant governor of Plymouth Colony, and husband of (1) Mary Norris (unknown–1621), (2) Fear Brewster (1607–1634), and Joanna, last name unknown (unknown–1659).[72] Isaac II was the product of his father's second marriage to Fear Brewster. The book *Mayflower Increasings* lists Isaac and his son Isaac II, as well as the children of Isaac II, including Sarah

---

[71] *Mayflower Births and Deaths: From the Files of George Ernest Bowman at the Massachusetts Society of Mayflower Descendants,* **Volumes I and II**. Roser, Susan E. Genealogical Publishing Company, Inc., Baltimore, Maryland, 1992. Page 67 of Volume I lists the children and grandchildren of Captain Isaac Allerton, including granddaughter Sara Elizabeth Allerton Lee.

[72] *History and Genealogy of the Mayflower Planters and First Comers to Ye Olde Colonie,* Volume II. Leon Clark Hills. Washington D.C. August 21, 1911.

Elizabeth and her marriage to Hancock Lee.[73] The will of Captain Isaac Allerton dated 16 October 1659 names his son Isaac II.[74]

The *Mayflower* connection gets even deeper with the fact that, even though Fear Brewster was the second wife of Isaac Allerton, she was not a passenger on the first *Mayflower* voyage. She arrived on a later voyage and married Isaac in Plymouth. Fear's mother and father William (1540–1644) and Mary Wentworth (1568–1627) were on that first voyage, and William was a signer of the Mayflower Compact.[75]

Isaac Allerton II died on 25 October 1702, and his will of 1702 provided five thousand pounds of tobacco to his daughter Sarah Lee.[76] The previous sources above do not use her middle name of Elizabeth, only her first name of Sarah. Her married name of Lee was used in both sources.

The *Encyclopedia of Virginia Biography* establishes that Hancock Lee II was the son of Hancock Lee Sr.[77] I also have the marriage records of both father and son Hancock Lee.

### Captain William Scott

Born: 6 April 1747, Petersburg, Dinwiddie County, Virginia.
Died: After 1792
Burial: Diamond Springs Cemetery, Dinwiddie County, Virginia
Service: Dinwiddie County Virginia Militia
Rank: Captain
Service Dates: Not known
Wife: Ann Mason
Lineage: His daughter Elizabeth married Richard Lee, above
DAR: A101889
SAR: No

William was the son of James Scott (1720–1760) and Sarah Pegram (1724–1800), also of Dinwiddie County, Virginia. His father was born in Foreland, Aberdeen, Scotland, and moved with his parents to Virginia soon before William's birth. We have copies of Scottish church birth records that include William.

He married Ann Mason, daughter of Daniel Mason and Elizabeth Ann Winfield, in 1766. They became successful Virginia plantation owners and had seven children, the youngest of which was Winfield Scott, who became a famous general of several U.S. conflicts and served until early in

---

[73] *The Mayflower Increasings,* Second Edition. Susan E. Roser. Genealogical Publishing Company, Inc., 1995, Baltimore, Maryland. Pages 25–28 list Captain Isaac Allerton as a 1620 *Mayflower* passenger and his wife Fear Brewster. Page 28 lists son Isaac II and his wife, daughter Sarah, and her marriage to Hancock Lee.

[74] *History and Genealogy of the Mayflower Planters and First Comers to Ye Olde Colonie,* Volume II. Leon Clark Hills. Washington D.C. August 21, 1911, p. 176.

[75] *Appletons' Cyclopedia of American Biography 1600–1899,* Vol I. Edited by James Wilson and John Fisk. New York. P. Appleton and Company, 1888. Page 371 gives the life history of *Mayflower* passenger William Brewster.

[76] *A History of the Allerton Family in the United States, 1585–1885.* Walter S. Allerton. New Allerton. New York City, 1888. Page 33 gives the detail of Isaac II's 25 October will in which he left five thousand pounds of tobacco to his daughter Sarah Lee.

[77] *Encyclopedia of Virginia Biography,* Volume IV. Lyon Gardiner Tyler, LL.D. Lewis Publishing Company, New York, 1915. Reprinted by the Genealogical Publishing Company, Inc., Baltimore, Maryland, 1998. Page 139 establishes that Hancock Lee was the father of Hancock Lee II.

the Civil War, in which he was the senior army leader. He is still the longest-serving U.S. Army general. Winfield also became a presidential candidate for the Whig party, but he lost the election.[78] Ann Mason came from a prominent Virginia family and raised a large family after the early death of her husband.

The Scott family owned slaves and made a comfortable living off the land. Their plantation was called Laurel Branch and was located just a few miles from the city of Petersburg, Virginia. We have lived in Petersburg, and I can attest to the fact that it is a beautiful part of the state. DAR records show that neither he nor his wife received a pension for his service; however, I found that his wife (Ann) filed for a pension based on his name in 1831. It was approved, and she received $240 every six months until 1843. We believe she lived until that date.

The DAR awarded Patriot status to William for public service for supplying services/supplies to the army during the war. His son General Winfield Scott mentioned his service in the Continental Line in his biography; however, I could find no evidence that he served in the Continental Line. I also could find no evidence that he served in an active Virginia Line unit, but it is probable that he served in a local militia unit, specifically, the Dinwiddie County Militia. He is listed in the report "List of Revolutionary War Soldiers of Virginia."[79] I believe this militia was called to service late in the war when Virginia was anticipating invasion of the British army as it returned from the Charleston siege headed for Richmond. This service would have been late in the war, but remember, the war came to an end near Petersburg, and he likely was involved in that final battle.

Further proof of his military service was found in the form of a land warrant claimed by his wife Ann and their children in September 1824 for land in Ohio, which was awarded for his Revolutionary War service. This warrant was allegedly lost and not found until after his death. The date of his death is uncertain, as some records indicate 1789 and some 1792, but the above action on the land warrant might indicate a later death. He is buried in the Diamond Springs Cemetery in Dinwiddie County, Virginia.

My research of this family group has yielded a great deal of documentation, of which much is based on incomplete facts, making this family's history less than certain. For example, the death date of Ann in 1803 is commonly found in various references, such as DAR histories and Find a Grave files. Her headstone has the 1803 death date, but her age is not correct (too young), and the name of her husband is shown on the stone as James, not William. I believe they got it wrong, as I found records in which she claimed a land warrant in 1824 for her husband's service and also claimed a pension for his service in 1831. She collected this pension until 1843. The pension is based on the service of Captain William Scott of Virginia, and the name of Ann Scott is given on the pension. The fact that the pension was claimed in 1831 following federal legislation providing such pensions for militia members seems to support the thought that he served in the Dinwiddie County Militia, not the Continental Army, for which he would have been eligible

---

[78] *Winfield Scott: The Quest for Military Glory*. Timothy D. Johnson. University Press of Kansas, November 1998. This book describes Winfield's father, Captain William Scott, and his family.
[79] "List of Revolutionary War Soldiers of Virginia." Special Report of the Department of Archives and History for 1912, Virginia State Library. Page 271 lists William as a Virginia soldier.

for pension in 1818. Their son Winfield's statement that he had served in the Continental Line is an understandable claim made by a man running for president.

Their daughter Elizabeth married Patriot Richard Lee, discussed above. That marital relationship has not been proven, but statements made by her brother in several references and family lore seem to establish the likelihood of that marriage. Their son Grissom Lee was the grandfather of Louvisa Fowler/Raines, my great-grandmother. I believe that future research will establish Patriot status for William's wife Ann, as she may have sold farm supplies to the Virginia Army in her husband's absence. This is asserted because the DAR awarded Patriot status to William for such service.

William and Ann had the following children:

- Elizabeth, 1764–1838. She married Richard Lee, discussed above. She is my third great-grandmother.
- Martha William, 1770–1802. She married Luke Prior (1770–1851).
- Mary Mason Scott, 1772–1838. She married Theodrick Scott (1768–1861) in 1788.
- Ann Laural Walker, 1775–1872. She married Theodrick Walker (1774–1836).
- Colonel James, 1777–1841. He married Martha Pegram (1780–1855). She was likely related to James's grandmother.
- Rebecca Pegram, 1780–1850. She married Edward Henry Pegram, also likely related to Rebecca's grandmother.
- Winfield (Fuss and Feathers), 1786–1855. He married Lucy Baker. He attended William and Mary College, became a lawyer, quickly left for the army, and distinguished himself in several conflicts up to the Civil War. He was elderly at the onset of the Civil War and quickly retired. He was too large to get on a horse, and President Lincoln wanted younger officers. In his biography, he admits he did not know his family well, as he rarely visited them, and that his politics did not sell well in his home state. He was very anti-slavery.

The sources for their children's names are many, including DAR lineage records that name only Elizabeth, James, Ann Mary, and Winfield. Rebecca and Martha's information came from marriage and other records. This list may not be complete, as I believe some unnamed children did not survive until adulthood.


**Ensign Henry Carman**
Born: Before 1765, New York City, New York
Died: 1813
Burial: Unknown location, probably in Westchester County, New York
Service: New York Third Regiment, Colonel Drake's Regiment, North Westchester County Militia
Rank: Ensign
Service Dates: Unknown
Wife: Jane, maiden name unknown
Lineage: Son William B. Carman, James H.B. Carman, Margaret (Maggie) Carman/Painter (married John Thomas Painter), William Frank Painter, Oliver Painter, Emma Jo Painter/Raines

DAR: No
SAR: P128671

Henry was the son of William Carman (1739–1801) and Jane Vanderhoof of New York City, New York. William was born in Kent, England, and married Jane (last name unknown) in New York in 1759. I have those marriage records. Henry was born in New York City prior to 1765 and married Elizabeth Kom or possibly Krom. This marriage relationship is unproven.

I should note that I found a second Henry Carman, also of Westchester County, New York (1746–1816). This Henry served as a sergeant in the Revolutionary War in Benedict's Regiment, and his burial location is known and documented. I have this Henry's National Archives military records, and there were in fact two men of the same name in that county, and it is easy to confuse their life histories.

This Henry joined Drake's Third Regiment of Winchester County, New York. This regiment was one of two Drake's militia regiments of that county. Neither of these regiments saw active combat duty, and both were deactivated at the end of the war.

The Revolutionary War Pension and Bounty-Land Warrant Application Files, 1800–1900, show him on a list of applicants for invalid pension submitted to the U.S. House of Representatives by the Secretary of War on 22 May 1794 and presented in the American States papers, Class 9, page 126. The application states that on 3 November 1780, he was wounded by the accidental discharge of a pistol, with the round hitting the left side of his neck, eventually causing the loss of his left arm. The accident took place in Yorktown, Westchester County, New York, and he was authorized full pension for this injury. It requires further research with New York archives to explore Henry's service prior to his injury. I have read the description of the accident causing his injuries, and it involved a cat knocking a loaded pistol from a table. The rank ensign was not often used and was traditionally awarded to good sergeants who had served in combat and deserved a try in the commissioned ranks. I have only discovered one other ensign in Drake's Regiment. There were two Drake's regiments, commanded by brothers. Their combat exposure was slight, as they were essentially "home guard" Westchester County regiments and not committed to federal service. Westchester County is adjacent to New York City. Henry was also eligible for a land grant for his service.[80]

I found two New York court cases involving Henry. The first was a 1789 indebtedness case in which Henry was the defendant being sued by Benjamin Drake Jr. I believe the plaintiff was a son of his Revolutionary War regimental commander. Henry was the plaintiff in a 1792 case, with Elias Clapp being the defendant. I also found Yorktown, Westchester County, tax records in 1800 and 1803 in which Henry was listed as a taxpayer. Yorktown is located near the northern boundary of Westchester County.

He and Elizabeth had two known children:

- John W., 1787–1866. A farmer in Ulysses, Tompkins County, New York
- William B., 1791–1874. Emma Jo's third great-grandfather

---

[80] *New York in the Revolution as Colony and State.* Volume I. Albany, New York. J.B. Lyon Company. 18=904. Page 267.

It is fair to say that the relationship of Henry to his son William is not proven. I have proven that son William was born in New York and moved to Kentucky by 1812 and fought in the War of 1812 there. William stated in the 1860 census that he was born in New York. Although not proof, he named his first son Henry. I have collaborated with a descendant of Henry, a noted publisher, and research continues, as I am relatively certain of this relationship.

His son William B. married Elizabeth Johnston/Jaquess in 1814 in Harrison County, Kentucky, and they had eight children. I have those marriage records. William and Elizabeth were living in Marion County, Missouri, in 1823 and lived there for the remainder of their lives. He was a farmer and furniture maker and slave owner who owned one slave at the time of the 1860 census (slave schedule) in Marion County. He purchased federal land at the Palmyra Land Office and is buried in the family cemetery on that farm. Elizabeth died in 1841, and William married Sarah Calvin on 18 April 1844 in Ralls County, Missouri, and they had no children. The children of William and Elizabeth were:

- Pauline Pierce, 1817–1903. Married John Carter Pierce and lived in Macon and later in Shelby County, Missouri.
- Elizabeth America Dearing, 1817–before 1852. Married William M. Dearing, lived in Marion County, Missouri.
- Nancy W. Gibbons, 1822–1906. Married Morris Gibbons, lived in Marion County, Missouri.
- James Henry B., 1823–1908. Married Mary Ann Schulse and lived in Marion, Ralls, and Monroe Counties, Missouri. Buried in Florida, Monroe County, Missouri. He is Emma Jo's second great-grandfather.
- Harriet Heckart, 1825–1906. Married Jonathan Heckart, lived in Marion County, and died in Walla Walla, Washington.
- Mary Jane Pierce/Nelson, 1825–1899. Married (1) John C. Pierce and (2) Benjamin Nelson. Lived in Shelby County, Missouri, and is buried in Clarence, Missouri.
- Emily Ann Maston, 1827–1869. Married John B. Maston and lived in Marion County, Missouri.
- William B., 1828–1859
- Anna Eliza, Dates unknown

William's son James Henry B. was born on 4 September 1823 in Palmyra, Marion County, Missouri. He was a farmer and married Mary Schultz, and they had ten children. I have those marriage records. They moved to Florida, Missouri, and farmed in that area the remainder of their lives. Both James Henry B. and Mary are buried in Hawkins Cemetery in marked graves. This cemetery is near Florida and their son-in-law John Thomas. Painter, Emma Jo's great-grandfather, may be buried there in an unmarked grave. Thomas married Margaret Lee "Maggie" Carman, the daughter of James Henry B. and Mary, and Maggie is documented as being buried in that cemetery also in an unmarked grave. John Thomas Painter farmed and raised horses and died at the age of thirty-eight, possibly of consumption. We have no records of John being buried there, but I have helped his grandson Oliver Painter maintain that cemetery out of that belief. John T's brother George H. Painter married Maggie's sister Alma Carman, and we believe that George H. is also buried in Hawkins Cemetery in an unmarked grave. Hawkins Cemetery is east of Paris, Missouri, on County Route J a few miles west of Florida, Missouri. There are many un-marked graves in that cemetery that I found in preparation for county court testimony in 1993. I have addressed these complex relationships in depth in my book *Footprints of the Painter and Scott Families of Missouri.*

Henry's son William, mentioned above, married Betsy Johnston/Jaquess in 1814 in Kentucky. She had been previously married to Isaac Jaquess, whose father, Jonathon Jaquess, was a Revolutionary War Patriot. He is not presented as a family Patriot in this book, as Emma Jo is not his direct descendant. What I will discuss, however, is Betsy's grandfather Martin Johnston, also a Patriot; he is Jo's fifth great-grandfather. His story follows.

### Martin Johnston

Born: 1 February 1758, Culpeper County, Virginia
Died: 3 July 1820, Winchester, Clark County, Kentucky
Burial: Unknown location in Clark County, Kentucky
Service: Continental Army Third Virginia Regiment
Rank: Private
Service Dates: 3 February 1776–February 1778
Wife: Nancy Wright (1762–1843)
Lineage: Son John Johnston, his daughter Betsy Johnston/Jaquess, who married William B. Carman, their son James H.B. Carman, then his daughter Margaret (Maggie) Carman/Painter, who married John Thomas Painter, their son William Frank Painter, his son Oliver Painter, and his daughter Emma Jo Painter/Raines
DAR: A06406
SAR: P-225375

Patriot Martin Johnston was a late discovery in the final stages of documentation review of this book. It was interesting for several reasons. First, we were aware of Emma Jo's great-grandfather's connection to the Carman family. John Thomas Painter married Margaret (Maggie) Carman, and this knowledge allowed the inclusion of Patriot Henry Carman, discussed earlier in this book. The first surprise was that Maggie's mother Betsy Jaquess/Johnston was the granddaughter of Patriot Martin Johnston. The second surprise was that Patriot Martin Johnston's second grand-daughter Catherine Johnston was the mother of Narcissa Stribling, the first wife of John M. (Amos) Painter, the father of John T. Painter. These men are Emma Jo's great-grandfather and second great-grandfather. While Emma Jo is not a descendent of John M. Amos Painter's first marriage, the relationship to the Carman line establishes that she is a direct descendant of Martin Johnston. John M. Amos Painter remarried after the death of Narcissa Stribling, and Emma Jo is a product of that second marriage. To further confuse this relationship, John T. Painter's brother George married the sister of Maggie, Anna Carman. The Painter family married into the Carman line three times. While this part of the family tree is complicated, Martin Johnston is Emma Jo's fifth great-grandfather. It's that simple.

Martin is the son of William Johnston (1727–1765) and Sarah McClaren (1730–1774) of Cul-peper County, Virginia. His birth in Culpeper County is documented by his sworn statement made at his pension hearing. I have those records. His father's 1765 will also names Martin has his son. Martin enlisted in the Third Regiment of the Virginia Militia on 2 February 1776, and this was a Continental Line unit commanded by Colonel John Marshall at the time of his enlistment. I also found that he enlisted with his older brother George in the same unit that year. This unit is discussed elsewhere in this book as Patriots Lewis Murphey and Richard Lee also served in the same unit at the same time. Maybe they knew each other. All three are documented survivors of the Valley Forge winter of 1777–1778, as was Patriot Joshua Logan Younger, discussed earlier, who served in another Virginia Continental Line unit. I have muster rolls for all four men at Valley Forge.[81] This regiment was commanded by Colonel William Heth during the Valley Forge winter. Of the Patriots discussed in this book, only Richard Lee remained in the unit by the time it was captured during the Charleston, South Carolina, siege, and that story was presented earlier in this book. This is a storied unit with many battles to its credit. Martin is also listed in the "List of Revolutionary War Soldiers of Virginia."[82]

Martin's two-year enlistment ended in February 1778 as the Valley Forge winter was nearly over, and he was discharged. He was eligible for a land grant, and he was living in Clark (Clarke) County, Kentucky, shortly after 1790. He married Nancy Wright in Virginia following the war, and she lived until 1843 and made a claim for pension based on his service after his death. Martin had previously made a claim for pension 20 June 1818. He was literate and personally wrote and signed his sworn statement in which he listed witnesses who could attest to his honorable service. He also stated that President James Monroe was a lieutenant in his unit and could attest to his service. He and James Monroe had served together at the Battle of Trenton, where Monroe had been wounded. He stated he was sixty-one years old and was incapable of work and depended on others for support. His pension was approved, and his pension number is SW446 and is shown on the Kentucky Pension Rolls as being approved for $95 per year. Martin is listed in the 1835 Clark County Pension Rolls, which reflect that he was deceased. After his death, his wife Nancy applied for a pension in 1839 and gave testimony pertaining to his service. Both Martin's and Nancy's testimonies are clear, exact, and leave no doubt of the fact that he was indeed a Patriot who served in a well-known unit.

Although eligible for a land-grant, we found no evidence of him receiving one. What I did find is that in 1804, he and his wife Nancy inherited more than one hundred acres of land from her parents in Clark County, Kentucky, and they purchased additional land in that county.[83] Nancy was the daughter of Joseph Wright Jr. and Francis Isabel Hunter. Joseph is a Revolutionary War Patriot, and his story follows.

Martin and Nancy's son John Johnston was born in Culpeper County, Virginia, and moved to Kentucky with his family, where he married Francis Hawkins (1776–1850) and their daughter Betsy was born in 1791. She married Isaac Jacquess (1786–1812) of Virginia. Isaac's father Jonathon was a sailor and a Revolutionary War Patriot. Isaac died in 1812 from war injuries, and Betsy married William B. Carman in 1814 in Harrison County, Kentucky. William is the son of Ensign Henry Carman discussed above. William and Betsy moved to Marion County, Missouri,

---

[81] Valley Forge Muster Roll. www.valleyforgemusterroll.org. Site maintained by the Valley Forge Park Alliance. Martin Johnston was listed as a soldier of the Third Virginia Regiment in a company commanded by Captain John Peyton. The regiment was commanded by Colonel William Heth, and the division commander was Major General Marquis de Lafayette. Site accessed 1 January 2024.
[82] "List of Revolutionary War Soldiers of Virginia." Special Report of the Department of Archives and History for 1912. H.J. Eckendorf, Archivist. David Bottom, Superintendent of Public Printing, 1913. Page 167 lists Martin as a Virginia soldier during the Revolution.
[83] Abstract of Wills, Clark County Courthouse Book of Wills and Settlements, book 2, p 1. Will of Joseph Wright. Joseph was the father of Nancy, wife of Martin Johnston. Joseph divided his assets with his wife and eight children.

by 1823 and farmed near Palmyra for the remainder of their lives. Their children are listed in the Patriot Henry Carman story above.

I was able to prove that John was the son of Martin from a pension request submitted by Martin's wife in 1839 in which her son William presented a family bible giving the names of their children, including John. I have copies of the records of that pension hearing. I also found records of Martin's wife selling land for $1 to their sons after his death, with John being listed as one of the sons. I have marriage records of both Martin and Mary Johnston, as well as John and Francis.

Their son John Johnston, father of Betsy, was a War of 1812 soldier of Kentucky who had previously settled in Missouri prior to that war. He received a Spanish land grant on 18 June 1800 for five hundred acres on Sandy Creek in what was to become Missouri well prior to the Lewis and Clark expedition to the territory. Records show he had inhabited and cultivated this land prior to 1 October that year. His myth as an Indian fighter is probably well worth future research. John returned to Kentucky for the War of 1812 and later returned to Missouri with his family. That return to Kentucky was a short trip, as his Missouri land grant was near what is now St. Genevieve, located on the Mississippi River. He returned to the Missouri Territory after his ninety-day enlistment and spent the remainder of his life there.

Patriot Martin Johnston's lineage to the Painter family is summarized thusly:

- Son John had several daughters, but two are of special interest for this book. His daughter Betsy married William Carman. This was her second marriage. William and Betsy's son James Henry B. Carman and his wife Mary Ann Shultz had two daughters: Margaret "Maggie" and Anna. Margaret married John T. Painter, Jo's great-grandfather. Anna married John T.'s brother George. This explains two Painter marriages into this family.

- John Johnston's second daughter of interest is Catherine, who married Tandy Stribling. Their oldest daughter Narcissa married John M. Amos Painter, Jo's second great-grandfather. This was John M. Amos's first marriage, with one son and daughter born of that marriage. Emma Jo is not a descendant of that marriage. He married Eleanor Greening after Narcissa's death, and John T. Painter above is a product of that marriage. This explains the third Painter marriage into this family line.

- Therefore, the lineage to Patriot Martin Johnston is through John T. Painter and the Carman line to both Henry Carman and Martin Johnston. The John M. Amos Painter marriage to Narcissa Stribling is merely a matter of interest and family history.

Figure 4-4 illustrates these relationships, with William Painter being Emma Jo's grandfather.

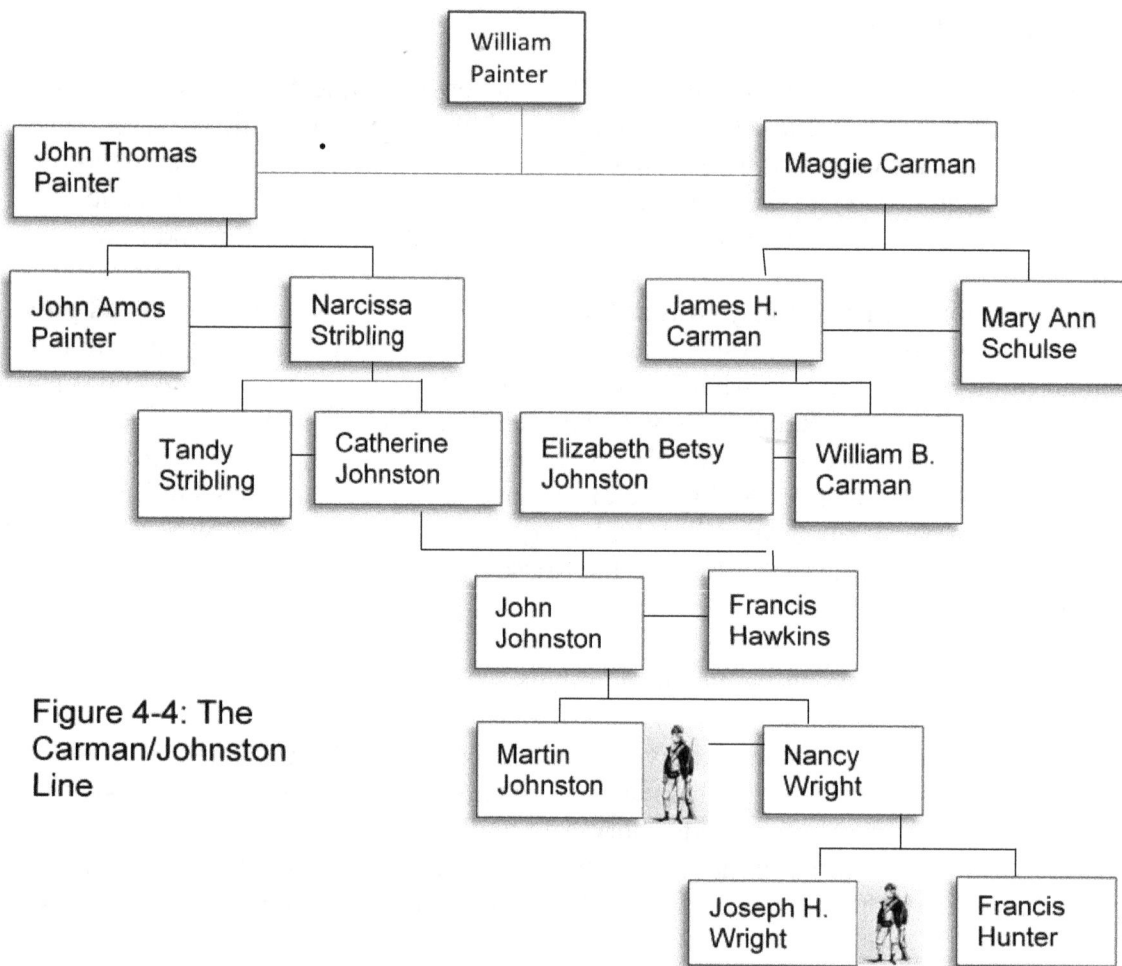

Figure 4-4: The Carman/Johnston Line

It is appropriate to point out another issue with regard to the Martin Johnston/Nancy Wright marriage. I found more than one record of their marriage, both following the war and birth of their son John. I believe John was born in 1776 and Martin and Nancy's marriage was recorded in 1779. It is not easy to explain this gap, but one can speculate that records were lost. They had relocated from Virginia to Kentucky, and marriage records were going to be needed if she were to later submit a pension claim based on his military service. Unfortunately, this marriage documented after his service would not have been recognized for her pension request until after the 1831 legislation that provided for widows married after the war. She consequently filed for a pension in 1839, and it was approved.

The known children of Martin and Nancy are:

- John, 1774–1827. Married Francis Hawkins and settled in Missouri. He is Emma Jo's fourth great-grandfather.
- William, 1780–1855. Married Elizabeth S. Lawrence and lived in New Richland, Logan County, Ohio.
- Francis Fanny Prior, 1783–1832. Married Luke Prior.

- George Washington, 1788–1888.

## Joseph H. Wright Jr.
Born: 16 June 1721, Prince William Colony of Colonial Virginia
Died: Between 16 May 1804 and 27 August 1804 in Winchester, Clark County, Kentucky
Burial: Unknown location probably in Clark County
Service: No military service
Rank: None
Service Dates: None
Wife: Francis Isabel Hunter. Married in 1742, probably in Prince William County
Lineage: His daughter Nancy married Patriot Martin Johnston, whose story was presented above
DAR: A-109316 for patriotic service
SAR: No

Joseph was the son of John Joseph Wright and Rebecca Sykes of Virginia. He was probably born in Prince William County, Virginia, where he married Francis Isabel Hunter in 1742 He lived in Culpeper County by 1760, as I found estate sale records in Culpeper County in 1760 in which Joseph purchased some items from the Henry Threlkeld estate. This information was obtained from an unpublished family history written by Jim G. Faulconer.

I found a 1783 Culpeper County tax list that included Joseph, his wife Francis, and sons William and John. In October 1780, Joseph filed a claim with the Culpeper County Court claiming reimbursement for ten bushels of rye that had been requisitioned by the Culpeper County Militia during the Revolutionary War. He later filed a claim for reimbursement in November 1781 for six hundred pounds of beef also requisitioned by the militia. These sales establish Joseph as a Patriot. The DAR recognizes his patriotic service, and members have used that service for membership claims. I found no evidence that Joseph served in the military during the Revolutionary War. However, I found a soldier with that name who served in the Richmond, Virginia, area, but he was a different person. I will note that Joseph's sons John and William served in the Culpeper County Militia on at least three different occasions, each for a total of about nine months.

Joseph and his family were living in Fayette County, Kentucky, by 1790, as he is on that 1790 tax list. He purchased land there, or it was possibly given to him as a grant. This land is rumored to have been surveyed by Daniel Boone, but that is an unproven claim in the Faulconer story mentioned above. When Kentucky was granted statehood in 1792, Clark County was formed from part of Fayette County, and Joseph and two sons and a daughter were landowners and farmers in Winchester, Clark County.

He wrote a will on 16 May 1804, and it is recorded in Will Book 2 of the Clark County probate records. The will was proven on 27 August that year, with his wife Francis, son John, and son-in-law Joshua Hazelrigg being named as executors. His death had obviously occurred between May and August. His wife and the following children were named in the will:

- Elizabeth Penhill, 1749–1813. Married James Penhill and lived in Frankford, Greenbriar County, Virginia.

- John Ellis, 1752–1816. Married Phebe Barret and served in the Revolutionary War. Settled in Clark County, Kentucky.
- Sergeant William, 1752–1836. Married Frances Hudson after serving in the Revolutionary War and moved to Clark County, Kentucky.
- Francis, 1759–1807. Married Lucinda Jones and moved to Oglethorpe, Carol County, Georgia.
- Nancy Johnston, 1762–1843. Married Martin Johnston, and they lived in Clark County, Kentucky. She is Emma Jo's fifth great-grandmother. This relationship is illustrated in the above figure.
- America Francis Hazelrigg, 1768–1861. Married Joshua Hazelrigg, and they lived in Bath County, Kentucky.

Joseph's estate may have been quite large, as there were three auctions to disperse the private property over the next two years. He was a slaveowner of at least six slaves, and he gave them to children living nearby in Kentucky via his will. He also gave 101 acres of farmland to his daughter Nancy through the will. Nancy and her husband Martin were to later buy additional land from his estate from other family members.

I discovered several claims that Joseph was descended from *Mayflower* ancestors but have not documented those claims. The DAR recognizes his patriotic service, and several members have used the Nancy Johnston line for membership. While this is not proof of relationship, it adds to the body of proof of the Johnston Patriot line.

## Sergeant Joshua Pearce Sr.

Born: 1755 (based on given age of sixty-two at 1818 pension hearing in St. Mary's County, Maryland)
Died: 1823, Sullivan County, Tennessee
Burial: Light Cemetery, Kingsport, Sullivan County, Tennessee
Service: Continental Army, First Maryland Regiment of Colonel Smallwood
Rank: Sergeant
Service Dates: 3 January 1776 until war's end in 1783
Wife: Deborah Dove (1764–1820), married on 16 April 1785
Lineage: Son Joshua Pearce Jr.'s daughter Catherine married John Quincy Adams, his son Walter Grant Adams, his son Walter Raymond Adams, his daughter Nadine Adams Raines (my mother)
DAR: No
SAR: P267267

Joshua was born in Maryland, probably in 1755 according to the age given by him at his 1818 pension hearing. I found no other records of his birth, but he was probably born in St. Mary's County, Maryland, where he joined the army and later married. He married Deborah Dove in Prince George's County, Maryland, on 16 April 1785 after he had completed his service in the Continental Army. I have those marriage records. The names of his parents are unknown. It is important to notice the spelling of his family name, as I have seen some researchers use the spelling of "Pierce." However, military, marriage, land, and census records seem to support the spelling I have used.

He joined the First Maryland Regiment commanded by Colonel Smallwood, and his company commander was initially Captain Samuel Smith. By May 1777, he was serving as a sergeant in Captain Rexbaugh's Company and later in Captain Jordan's Company of Colonel Stone's Maryland Regiment, where he served until 1783. This was the First Regiment, but the commander had changed. He reenlisted at the end of the first year of service. Records show that he served in several significant battles of the war. Some are: Battles of Long Island, Brandywine, Germantown, Monmouth, Guilford Courthouse, Camden, and Cowpens.

Later chapters in this book will discuss his regiment and Major General Mordecai Gist, who also served in that regiment as a major early in the war. There is also a chapter in this book discussing the battle at Guilford Courthouse in which the unit fought. The regiment was a Continental Line regiment and was a formidable foe for the British. This unit made a difference in the outcome of the war, as you will read in later chapters.

He was not wounded in action during the six years and many battles, but in later life he stated during his pension hearing he had been injured in accidents several times while in the army, making work difficult at his older age. The list of battles his unit participated in is impressive! He saw the war up close and was not a rear-echelon soldier. The battle at Guilford Courthouse was a pivotal point late in the war when British forces suffered enough losses to make them ineffective at the final confrontation that ended the war a year later. This was a landmark horse cavalry battle led by Lieutenant Colonel Lighthorse Lee and Colonel William Washington (cousin of General Washington). I have studied this battle as a case study in the development of cavalry tactics to be used later in the Civil War. They were outnumbered, and by all accounts they probably lost the battle, but they likely won the war, as the British fighting force never won another battle in the war. George Lee and the Rains brothers of North Carolina also fought in this battle and are discussed in later chapters. It is my contention that Lieutenant Colonel Lighthorse Lee's cavalry skills were instrumental in his grandson's later mastery of his well-known horse cavalry skills in a later war. You will see in a later chapter that Lieutenant Colonel Lee positioned the First Maryland Regiment in a critical location, as he was certain they would not retreat. They met his expectations, and they performed brilliantly, as they had at the battle of Long Island. Joshua was there.

He received a federal bounty land grant (number 11594) for his service on 7 February 1790 that amounted to one hundred acres. There are no records of him receiving a land warrant, so it is possible that he sold that bounty, which was quite common. His location after his marriage in 1785 until 1800 is uncertain. But his son Joshua Jr. was born in Sullivan County, Tennessee, around 1800. I have the 1785 Compiled Census and Census Substitute Index for Joshua in Upper Marlborough, Prince George's County, Maryland, the year of his marriage to Deborah Dove. I believe he remained in Maryland until he received the land grant.

I found records of several land transactions involving Joshua in Sullivan County in which he either sold land or bought land in partnerships with other men. He owned a considerable amount of land consisting of several hundred acres.

Joshua applied for a pension on 26 June 1818 while living in Sullivan County, Tennessee, at the age of sixty-three. He stated he had lived in Sullivan County for fifteen years and in Tennessee for more than twenty years. That seems to place he and Deborah in Tennessee around 1798. That pension was approved, and he received $8 per month until his death in 1823. The pension number was S39004. He stated in a later 1820 pension hearing that his wife had died a few months earlier, and records do show that Deborah had died in 1820. He stated that his children were grown and were on their own at that time.

I found only three children of Joshua and Deborah, and in his 1818 pension hearing, he stated that he had three grown children. William (1788–1848) also lived in Sullivan County, Tennessee, and married Elizabeth Smith. His second son, James McClellan (M.), was born in Tennessee and owned land in Sullivan County. Joshua Jr. was born in Tennessee and later moved to Liberty, Adams County, Illinois, in 1832.[84]

Adams County, Illinois, was a designated land grant county in which Justice Perrigo also settled after the War of 1812. I have records of Joshua Jr. buying and selling land in Sullivan County until 1829–1831 before he moved to Illinois. He married Sarah Golden in Sullivan County in 1820. Joshua Jr.'s daughter Catherine, who was born in Sullivan County, married John Quincy Adams, my great-great-grandfather.

The Adams County History states that Joshua Jr. owned a 320-acre farm and was involved in a partnership with A.D.D. Butts in a mercantile business. Joshua also operated a mill powered by horses. This county history also states that he fought in the Black Hawk War after arriving in the county.[85] Joshua Jr. was murdered in 1833 in Adams County, and I have a record of the grand jury ruling showing a warrant for his murderer. This is the same county in which Justice Perrigo, the son of Patriot David Perrigo, lived, which is near present-day Quincy, Illinois. The Adams and Perrigo families became acquainted with each other at that time, and several marriages soon followed. The Adams/Perrigo relationships continue until this day.

I cannot prove the connection between Joshua Pearce and his son Joshua Jr., but it is a likely relationship for several reasons.

- I found land transactions in Sullivan County involving these men as well as son William.
- Joshua Jr. married Sarah Golden also in Sullivan County.
- I found land transactions involving her father and William, brother of Joshua Jr.
- Joshua Sr. stated in his pension hearing that he had three children. He did not name those children, but I have land transactions involving Joshua Jr., William, and James M.
- Tax records for Sullivan County show only sons Joshua Jr., William, and James M. Other researchers have speculated Joshua Sr. might have been excused from paying taxes due to age. I found land transactions involving Joshua Jr. after the death of his father in Sullivan County, thus eliminating the possibility that Joshua Sr. was the seller or buyer. The last

---

[84] *Portrait and Biographical Record of Adams County, Illinois, Containing Biographical Sketches of Prominent and Representative Citizens,* Chapman Brothers, 1892. Page 498 states that Joshua and his wife and family moved to Adams County in 1832 and that he fought in the Black Hawk War after arriving.
[85] Ibid., p. 498.

transaction was in January 1831 and was witnessed by William Pearce, his likely brother. The other witness was Benjamin Golden, who was a brother to his wife Sarah. Further proof of this relationship is hampered by the fact that many Sullivan County records were destroyed during the Civil War.

- Finally, the same given name is a clue.

The lineage from Joshua Pearce Jr. to the Adams family line is given in the Adams Patriot stories earlier in the book.

## Nehemiah Patch

Born: 7 January 1741, Ipswich, Essex County, Massachusetts
Died: 24 September 1830, Ipswich, Massachusetts
Burial: Ipswich, Massachusetts
Service: Minutemen of Ipswich and the Continental Army
Rank: Private
Service Dates: 19 April 1775–1777
Wife: Hepzibah Wells (1740–1830)
Lineage: Daughter Mary married John Adams, my third great-grandfather, who was a son of Patriot Samuel Adams discussed above.
DAR: No
SAR: P-266415

Nehemiah was born in Ipswich, Massachusetts, to John Patch Jr. (1722–1799) and Abigail Somers (1722–1812). His father was governor of Ipswich and a farmer in the Ipswich area. They had twelve children, of which Nehemiah was the oldest. One of his childhood homes still stands in Ipswich. His father, John Patch Jr., was also a Patriot, and his story follows. His birth is recorded in the Massachusetts, U.S., Compiled Birth, Marriage, and Death Records 1700–1850 for Ipswich, Essex County, Massachusetts, which also lists the name of his father. Nehemiah is also listed in his father's 1799 will in Essex County, Massachusetts.

Nehemiah married Hepzibah Wells in 1763,[86] and they had four children, of which Mary, their youngest, married John Adams, son of Samuel Adams, a Patriot described earlier in this book, thus making Nehemiah my fourth great-grandfather. Mary's birth is recorded in the Massachusetts, U.S., Compiled Birth, Marriage, and Death Records 1700–1850 of Ipswich. They spent the entirety of their lives in the Ipswich area, and records of their births, marriages, and deaths are recorded by the excellent city records. I have the marriage records of Mary's marriage to John Adams. Nehemiah inherited his father's farm after his father's death in 1799. This was a large farm, and he and his family lived comfortably. He lived until he was ninety-one years old.

He served in Captain Moses Jewitt's Company of Colonel John Baker's (Third Essex County) Regiment of light horse of the Ipswich minutemen and served during the Battles of Lexington and Concord on 19 April 1775 for three days. He later served as a private in the Continental

---

[86] *Colonial Families of the USA 1607–1775*, Ancestry.com Operations Inc. Lehi, UT, 2016. Pages 515 and 516 give the marriage date of Nehemiah and Hepzibah Wells and provide the name of her father, Captain Nathaniel Wells.

Army in Robert Perkin's Company of Major Charles Smith's Third Regiment of light horse volunteers. During this enlistment, he fought in the Battle of Ticonderoga and at the surrender of Burgoyne on 16 October 1777.[87] There are no records of land grants or pensions based on this service.

Nehemiah is buried in the Ipswich, Massachusetts, cemetery in the old south section of the cemetery, and there is no known marker for his grave.

Nehemiah's wife Hepzibah was the daughter of Nathaniel Wells III, also of Ipswich. Nathaniel also served in the Revolution, and his story follows later. Their children were:

- Hepzibah Morgan, 1764–1854
- Anna Doctor, 1766–1804
- John, 1770–1858
- Mary Adams, 1782–1836. Married John Adams, son of Patriot Samuel Adams III. My third great-grandmother.

**John Patch Jr.**
Born: 1721, with 3 March 1727 baptism date
Died: 18 December 1799
Burial: Old South City Cemetery of Ipswich, Massachusetts
Service: Patriotic service on the Committee of Correspondence and Safety of Ipswich, Massachusetts
Rank: None
Service Dates: None
Wife: Abigail Somers (1722–1812), married on 8 July 1840 in Ipswich
Lineage: Son Nehemiah Patch discussed above, his daughter Mary Patch/Adams, wife of John Adams, son of Patriot Samuel Adams III, discussed above, my fourth great-grandfather
DAR: AO88514
SAR: P-266406

John Jr. is the son of John Patch (1699–1775) and Abigail Bowls (1700–1721) of Ipswich, Essex County, Massachusetts. His baptism was recorded by the town of Ipswich and lists his father as John, with his baptism date being 3 March 1727. It is interesting that his younger brother James was also baptized on the same day.[88] The failure to register his birth might be explained by the fact that his mother died the year of his birth in October. His father soon married Mercy Potter, and John's baptism was delayed until the second son, James, was baptized.

He was recognized for patriotic service by the DAR for serving on the Committee of Correspondence and Safety for the city of Ipswich, County of Essex, Massachusetts. This is further

---

[87] "Revolutionary War Archives," Massachusetts Office of Secretary of State of the Commonwealth, vol. 12, p. 163, and vol. 22, pp. 57 and 58.
[88] *Vital Records of Ipswich, Massachusetts, to the End of the Year 1849,* Volume I: Births. Essex Institute, Salem, Massachusetts, 1910. Newcomb and Gaus, Printers, Salem, Massachusetts, p. 280. This contains the birth records for most of the Patch family of Ipswich from 1634 until 1849, including John.

documented by the research of Hamline Elijah Robinson.[89] He was also the deputy governor of Ipswich, Massachusetts, during the Revolution. His son Nehemiah, discussed above, served in the Revolution as a minuteman and later in the Continental Army.

John was probably a lawyer and a member of the Massachusetts General Court in 1780, 1782, 1784, and 1787. He owned and outfitted several privateers under letters of marque and reprisal with a Colonel Pierce. The privateers he outfitted and sponsored were recognized by the British as pirates, and had the colonists lost the war, he would have surely been hanged. Even the fact that he served on the Committee of Correspondence and Safety would have assured reprisal by the British. His privateer activities gained him some wealth. He also farmed and owned over four hundred acres of land that he inherited from his father in his 1775 probate case. I have a copy of that will. The privateer activities are documented in two SAR applications and in the William Cutter book that gives the stories of several family members.[90] Cutter does not always enjoy my full support as for accuracy, as I spent a full year reviewing his work in another of his books during my research for my book on the Perrigos. You will see in the later Perrigo chapter of this book that, while the "Cutter Account" is sometimes correct, it is wrong on some important claims. Here is what I am confident about concerning John Patch Jr., as I have multiple sources for these facts:

- He was a son of John Patch and lived most of his life in Ipswich at the times stated.
- He owned a four-hundred-acre farm as well as a home in Ipswich.
- He served on the Ipswich Committee of Correspondence and Safety.
- The names of his children are correct.
- His support of a privateering operation is true.
- He was the owner of at least two wigs (his probate case inventory).

I am unsure of his profession as a lawyer. I did, however, find at least six probate cases in which he was appointed to inventory or act in an official capacity while those cases were settled. I did not confirm his serving in the Massachusetts House of Representatives. If he served in the years indicated, then he would have certainly been involved in writing the Massachusetts Constitution, which was quickly used as a basis for the U.S. Constitution just two years later by future President John Adams of Boston, Massachusetts.

John's home in Ipswich remains standing and is recognized as the Burnham-Patch House on 1 Turkey Shore Road. It is believed to have been built around 1730 by Thomas Burnham, using the foundation and materials from a 1670s home on that site. John purchased that home in 1742. The Ipswich 1771 tax records also reflect his ownership of a home at 232 Argilla Road that was built

---

[89] "Colonial and Revolutionary Ancestry: Some Account of the New England Descent of Hamline Elijah Robinson." This brochure was written and distributed in limited numbers by Hamline Robinson, vice president of the Missouri Historical Society. Page 24 establishes that John Patch was elected to the Ipswich Committee of Correspondence and Safety on 18 December 1775 and that he also served as deputy governor of Ipswich.

[90] *New England Families Genealogical and Memorial: A Record of the Achievements of Her People in the Making of Commonwealths and the Founding of a Nation*, vol. 2. William Richard Cutter. Lewis Printing Company, New York, 1914, p. 715.

in 1760. These tax records also show his son Nehemiah possibly owning the Burnham-Patch home by then.[91]

His son Nehemiah and Nehemiah's daughter Mary are well documented by Ipswich city birth records, as is Mary's marriage to John Adams. John was the son of Patriot Samuel Adams, discussed above in this book. John's son was John Quincy Adams, also born in Ipswich, later moving to Adams County, Illinois, and later to Shelby County, Missouri. His son Walter Grant was my great-grandfather and is buried in Shelbyville, Shelby County, Missouri.

I found it interesting that the various Ipswich records I reviewed during the preparation of this story contained mention of several other of my Ipswich family members, namely John Adams, my third great-grandfather, and Mathew Whipple, the grandfather of Jemima Whipple, the wife of Samuel Adams III, as well as William Adams. William was the second great-grandfather of Samuel Adams III and settled in Ipswich soon after its founding in 1634. I noted more than one Patch-Adams marriage in that era.

John and Mary had the following children, all named in his November 1799 will except Sarah, who died in infancy:

- Nehemiah, 1741–1830. My fourth great-grandfather discussed above.
- Abigail Cogswell, 1744–1829
- Jemima Brown, 1746–1822
- Joanna Baker, 1748–1816
- Martha Appleton, 1750–1810
- Mercy Clinton, 1750–1810
- Mary Lakeman, 1753–1831. (Also mentioned in the news article.)
- Elizabeth Choate, 1753–1813
- Sarah, 1755–1755
- Lydia Patch, 1759–1844. Married a Patch.
- Hephzibah Smith, 1761–1848
- Martha or Mary Appleton, 1763–1861

The Yarmouth Genealogies No. 98 of 25 March 1902 gave family information that he left seventy-eight grandchildren and twenty-four great-grandchildren for a total of 114 descendants (including his children) at the time of his death at the age of seventy-eight. His wife Abigail died in 1812 at the age of eighty-nine. This story was based on an earlier *Yarmouth Herald* newspaper article.

---

[91]*Ipswich in the Massachusetts Bay Colony*. Thomas Franklin Waters, president of the Ipswich Historical Society, Ipswich, Massachusetts, 1905, Salem Press, Salem, Massachusetts. Page 478 documents the purchase of a home on the corner of Turkey Shore Rd. and Poplar St. by John Patch in 1752.

**Nathaniel Wells III**
Born: 24 April 1699
Died: 27 May 1790
Burial: Highland Cemetery of Ipswich, Massachusetts
Service: Ipswich Militia and the Continental Army of Massachusetts
Rank: Ensign
Service Dates: 19 April 1775, July 1775, and July 1777 to February 1780.
Wife: (1) Mary Parshall Hall (1700–1722) and (2) Sarah Kinsman (5 July 1705–July 1772)
Lineage: His daughter Hepzibah, daughter of his second wife Sarah, married Patriot Nehemiah Patch above. Their daughter Mary married John Adams, the son of Samuel Adams above.
DAR: No
SAR: No

The Wells family was an old Ipswich family with records dating to the earliest days of the city. Some of the early family lived in the Maine territory, which was disputed with the Massachusetts colony and located near Ipswich. I found records of Indian attacks on an uncle's home in 1703 in Ipswich in which the entire family was killed when the father was not at home.[92] Nathaniel III is my fifth great-grandfather.

He was the son of Captain Nathaniel Wells Jr. (1669–1717) and Mary Crandall (1671–1722) of Ipswich, Massachusetts.[93] The Ipswich town birth records also record his birth date and the names of his father and mother.[94]

Except for his military service, Nathaniel spent his entire life in and around Ipswich, Massachusetts. His father Nathaniel fought as a captain in King George's Army in the French and Indian War (this was a Massachusetts campaign). The given name Nathaniel was carried for at least four generations, with this Nathaniel being the third. He is buried in the Highland Cemetery in Ipswich with a stone-marked grave. Find a Grave reflects that he is buried in the old Ipswich cemetery, but that is incorrect. The picture of his stone is next to a relatively modern house, and there are no modern homes near the Ipswich city cemetery. City records reflect the correct Highland location.

Nathaniel served for nearly the entire Revolutionary War in several units. He reenlisted at least twice with different units in the Continental Army and served throughout Massachusetts. Following are his enlistments based on military records that I have found:

First: Served as an ensign in Thomas Bonham's Company of Ipswich minutemen. He served starting on 19 April 1775 at the Battle of Lexington, and he served for three days.

---

[92] North American Histories 1500–2000. Database online. Provo, Utah. Ancestry.com Operations, Inc. Wells Family History, page 14, gives the account of the death of the wife and children of Thomas Wells, a sibling of the father of Nathaniel III on 10 August 1703.
[93] *Colonial Families of the USA, 1607–1775*, Volume III. Mackenzie, George Norbury and Nelson Osgood Rhodes, editors, 1912. Reprinted by Genealogical Publishing Co., Inc., Baltimore, Maryland, 1966–1995. Page 578 gives the birth date and father and mother of Nathaniel Wells and his siblings.
[94] Massachusetts, U.S., Town and Vital Records, 1620–1988. Database online. Provo, Utah. Ancestry.com Operations, Inc. 2011. Ipswich births. Page 389 lists the birth date and names of Nathaniel's mother and father as well as several other family members.

Second: Enlisted in July 1775 in Captain William Judson Ballard's Company of Colonel James Frye's Regiment until October 1775.

Third: Served in the Continental Army in Captain William Prescott's Company of Colonel Bishop's Regiment in York County from January 1777 to 28 February 1780 in defense of eastern Massachusetts.

His service is documented in *Massachusetts Soldiers and Sailors of the Revolutionary War*, Volume 16, page 605. The National Archives has limited records of his service, but *Colonial Families of the USA* documents his extended service. Nathaniel was in his seventies during the war, and that is an advanced age for combat, but his second wife died in 1772, and his children were grown. I found no evidence of an application for pension, as his death preceded the establishment of the pension act of 1810. I did, however, find land warrant eligibility with S-1826. I cannot determine if that pension and warrant eligibility pertained to him or to his son Nathaniel IV.

Given Nathaniel's age at the beginning of the war, I first examined the life of his son Nathaniel IV, thinking it was probably he who had served, and he did serve in the Massachusetts Militia and is recognized by the DAR (A122575). Nathaniel's death records list him as "gentleman." This was not a poor family.

The DAR has not awarded any memberships based on his service. The DAR records show his service and list a few names of his family members. I have found at least two SAR applications in his name, but they were not approved because the listed family lines of the applicants were not correct.

I believe no children were born by his first marriage to Mary Hall, whom he married on 11 April 1717. She died in 1722. He then married Sarah Parshall Hall on 7 July 1723. All his twelve children were born after this marriage. They were:

- Sarah Lord, 1724–1797. Married Nathaniel Lord, a Revolutionary War Patriot. Listed in her father's will.
- Elizabeth Smith, 1725–1815. Married Adam Smith, a Revolutionary War Patriot. Listed in her father's will.
- Mary Wheeler, 1728–1810. Married Moses Wheeler. Ipswich birth records record her father and mother.
- Susanna Smith, 1730–1779. Married Ephraim Smith. Baptism records record her father and mother. Not mentioned in her father's will, but she was deceased before his death in 1790.
- Lucy Lord, 1732–1765. Married Jeremiah Lord, who also died in 1765. Her baptism records reflect her father and mother. Not listed in her father's will but was deceased by the time of his death in 1790.
- Nathaniel IV, 1734–1810. Patriot of the Revolutionary War in Ipswich. (DAR: A122575.) Birth recorded in Ipswich birth records. He is listed in his father's will.
- Lydia Wallace, 1735–after 1790. Married Quaker Samuel Wallace. She is listed in her father's will, and her birth is listed in *Colonial Families of the USA*.

- Abigail Kinsman, 1738–1772. Married John Kinsman. Her birth is recorded in *Colonial Families of the USA*. She was not listed in her father's will, as she was deceased by the time of his death in 1790.
- Hepzibah Patch, 1740–1830. Wife of Nehemiah Patch and my fourth great-grandmother. Her birth is recorded in *Colonial Families of the USA*. She was not listed in her father's will. Her marriage to Nehemiah is recorded in Ipswich.
- Simeon, 1742–1822. Not listed in his father's will, but his birth is recorded in *Colonial Families of the USA*.
- Hannah Friend, 1744–1829. Married John Friend. Her birth is reported in *Colonial Families of the USA*.
- John, 1748–1790. Listed in his father's will and *Colonial Families of the USA*.

I used multiple sources to document the birth of his children noted above. Their later lives are well documented in Ipswich following their births.

The Adams family linkage to the Nathaniel Wells line was not difficult to establish. The Ipswich city records reflect the marriage of Nathaniel and Sarah as well as the birth of Hepzibah and her marriage to Nehemiah Patch and the birth and marriage of their daughter Mary to John Adams. The Adams family is well documented up to present generations.

**Ellis Jones**
Born: 1747, probably Baltimore, Maryland
Died: 1838, Brooke County, Virginia, now West Virginia
Burial: Family Cemetery near Bethany, West Virginia
Service: Baltimore Maryland Militia, Soldiers Delight Hundred
Rank: Private
Service Dates: Not known
Wife: (1) Phrania Elizabeth Reice and (2) Ann Crawford
Lineage: Son Lewis Reice Jones, daughter Eliza Pamelia/Plummer, daughter Sarah Sallie Plummer/Younger, daughter Blanche Younger/Raines (my grandmother)
DAR: No
SAR: No

The Ellis Jones story will begin to bring the focus onto my proposal made early in the book that the Revolutionary War was a family affair. This is the intersection of the Reinecker and Gist family lines already discussed. The son of Ellis, Louis Reice, married Elizabeth Pamilia Gist, the granddaughter of Patriot Joseph Gist of Maryland. Later you will see Plummer and Woolery family Patriot stories and then see how Joshua Logan Younger, discussed earlier in the book, fits into the bigger story of this fascinating family.

Ellis Jones's birthplace has not been proven, but Baltimore County is a reasonable guess, as he spent more than seventy years of his life in and around Baltimore. He lived there at the times of the 1790, 1800, and 1810 censuses. He also served in the Revolutionary War in Baltimore, and all his children were born there. His occupation was reported as a Baltimore coachmaker from

1804 to 1818.[95] His location for the 1790 census of Patapsco Lower 100 seems to fly in the face of a Baltimore business location, but this can be explained by a move from Patapsco just a few miles away, to Baltimore by 1800.

His father's name is likely Charles Robinson Jones (1727–1792); he is found in the Baltimore County area, now Anne Arundel County, in the 1790 census. Anne Arundel County was formed from part of Baltimore County after the war. I have few sources that establish this relationship. The first source is a family story written by great-grandson J.H. Jones on 27 April 1892.[96] This information was important in establishing the birth year for Ellis, the name of his first wife, and the family move to Virginia. The second source is an SAR Application dated 6 December 1849 and submitted by George Robinson Jones, a grandson of Ellis. This application gives the father of Ellis as Charles Robinson Jones, whose wife was Catherine Cling. The application states that Ellis lived in Brooke County, Virginia. In the application, George claimed Patriot status for his grandfather Charles Robinson, who served in the Revolutionary War in a Pennsylvania regiment. The application was not approved because Charles did not serve in Pennsylvania, but in Maryland. The remainder of the application seems to be very accurate. Charles Robinson was a Patriot, but more on that later.

The final source for the Jones family consists of an extensive family history written by an unnamed descendant in a recently discovered unpublished story. This history claims the arrival of the Jones family in Virginia in the early 1600s. The family line is traced through Charles Robinson Jones and his son Ellis to the Pettis County, Missouri, line, which is my family line. Little documentation is provided with this eloquent story, but the names, dates, and locations of Ellis and his descendants seem to match my research. This is certainly not proof, but it is useful information. I do not cite this reference, as the author is unnamed and few sources were given for Charles Robinson and Ellis Jones.

I am claiming the Revolutionary War service firstly due to the statement made by his great-grandson mentioned above in 1892; however, this is not sufficient evidence to claim DAR or SAR membership. Secondly, I have a published history of Baltimore County militias, and there are several Joneses listed in these regiments, but no given name provided—just the initial of their given names. I believe Ellis was one of the "E. Jones" listed in that history of Baltimore County militias.[97]

I do not believe that Ellis served in the Continental Army—as did his proposed father—or a Maryland Line unit, as my search of those records did not produce his name. Because of the Maryland conscription laws requiring all able-bodied men to serve in the militia, that is the likely source of his service.

---

[95] The UK and US Directories, 1680–1830, of Ancestry.com Operations, Inc., 2003, of Provo, Utah, seem to establish that Ellis was a coachmaker at 54 Albemarle St., West Side, in 1804 and again in 1817.

[96] "Family History of Ellis Jones Family," J.H. Jones, 27 April 1892. This biography gives the birth location, the names of one of his wives, and the names of his children. It also gives the location of his Brooke County homestead in what is now West Virginia. It also establishes his Revolutionary War service.

[97] *The Maryland Militia in the Revolutionary War.* S. Eugene Clements and F. Edward Wright, Heritage Books Inc., 2008.

Ellis may have served in the same Maryland Militia as Joseph Gist, included above as a family Patriot. Remember, Ellis's son Lewis Reice married Elizabeth Gist, the granddaughter of Joseph Gist, so these families knew each other, and they moved to Brooke County, Virginia, at about the same time following the Revolution.

There were possibly twenty Maryland Militia units locally organized and supervised by the various Committees of Safety. Most saw little or no action, as there were no major battles in that colony. My research has shown that Ellis served in the Soldiers Delight Hundred Company. That is an interesting designation for a military unit and requires some explanation. It is likely that this unit was a company-sized unit of the Soldiers Delight Regiment of the Baltimore Militia commanded by Colonel Thomas Gist. The Gist family story is presented in a later chapter in this book.

The Soldiers Delight was a tract of land several thousand acres in size located in western Baltimore County. Note that Baltimore County consisted of most of occupied Maryland prior to the Revolution. It was later divided into several smaller counties. The Soldiers Delight area, now an environmental area, was heavily wooded, but some of it was rich farmland in the western portion of the county. It was farmed by working, non-slaveholding farmers. There were only two roads leading in or out of this region. Those living there often did not leave this area except to vote once a year. They kept to themselves. The heavily wooded part of the region was filled with open pits that had been dug in search of iron ore, which could be found there with little digging. It was a dangerous place to roam at night. There were several militia companies organized in this section of the county, and both Ellis Jones and Joseph Gist were members of these. Ellis was assigned to the Soldiers Delight Hundred. The term "hundred" was an old English political subdivision smaller than a "shire." Many of the early settlers had received English land grants in the "hundred" division.[98] Following the war, Baltimore County was partitioned into Kent, Cecil, Hartford, Carroll, Frederick, Howard, and Anne Arundel Counties.

Ellis's grandson J.H. Jones wrote his family history on 27 April 1892 and stated that his grandfather was a Revolutionary War soldier. His family history appears to be accurate in every other account, so until proven otherwise, we should consider him a Patriot. Census records of 1790, 1800, and 1810 place him in the Baltimore area. The 1820 and 1830 census records place him in Brooke County, West Virginia. J.H. Jones was the son of Lewis Reice Jones, my third great-grandfather. I have studied the published history of the Soldiers Delight units and, as local militias, their records are far from complete. It is understandable that written records of enlistment did not survive.

After 1814, Ellis and his family moved to Brooke County, West Virginia, and settled on a large tract of land on Buffalo Creek, now the site of Bethany College. He is buried in what was the family cemetery about ¼ mile from Bethany College. His first wife died in the 1810 in Baltimore, and he married Ann Crawford on 9 Feb 1815 in Brooke County, and she is also buried on the farm there. Ellis and his first wife Phrania Eliza Reice had eleven children. They were:

---

[98] *Maryland Historical Magazine* published under the authority of The Maryland Historical Society, vol I, Baltimore, 1906. Page 141 contains a presentation about the Soldiers Delight Hundred given in 1881.

- Elizabeth Counselman, 1778–1842. Not named in her father's 9 July 1838 will. Married John Counselman (1788–1867). Died in Brooke County, West Virginia.
- David, 1780–1820. Not named in his father's will. Married Sarah Anderson. Moved to Wellsburg, Brooke County, West Virginia, by 1820.
- Mary Worthington, 1785–1856. Named in her father's will. Married Nicholas Worthington (1779–1841). Died in Wellsburg, Brooke County, West Virginia.
- Rebecca Miller, 1788–1860. Not named in her father's will. Married Charles Miller (1788–1842) in Wellsburg, West Virginia, and died there.
- Phrania Chesbrough, 1789–1828. Not named in her father's will. Married Isaac Marks Chesbrough in Baltimore, Maryland, and remained there for the remainder of her life.
- Caleb, 1790–1852. Not named in his father's will but lived next door to him in the 1810 census and later in the 1820 and 1830 censuses. Married Hannah Stockton (1787–1860). May have died either in Illinois or Missouri.
- Catherine Seawright, 1791–1862. Named in her father's will. Married Alexander Seawright (1788–1846). Died in Bristol, Morgan County, Ohio.
- Ellis Jr., 1795–1828
- Lewis Reice, 1798–1877. My third great-grandfather. Named in his father's will. Married (1) Elizabeth Pamilia Gist (1798–1824) and (2) Nancy Ann Crawford. Died in Heath's Creek, Pettis County, Missouri.
- Jane Purcell, 1801–1865. Named in her father's will. Married William Purcell (1805–1850) in Brooke County, West Virginia. Died in Bristol, Morgan County, Ohio.
- Ann H. Rice, 1803–1891. Named in her father's will. Married Thomas Rice (1800–1850) and died in Lexington, Dawson County, Nebraska.

His son Lewis Reice Jones married Elizabeth Pamelia Gist, the daughter of Cornelius Howard Gist, the son of Joseph Gist, discussed above as a family Patriot. She is listed in her father's will, and I have those marriage records. Their daughter Elizabeth (Eliza) Pamelia married Franklin Plummer, and they were the parents of Sarah "Sallie" Plummer/Younger who was the mother of my grandmother Blanche Younger/Raines. I have those West Virginia marriage records. This Younger line back to Cornelius Gist has been recognized by the DAR for many membership applications.

Lewis's first wife, Elizabeth Pamilia, died in 1824 after about four years of marriage. She was the mother of Eliza Pamilia Plummer. Lewis then married Nancy Ann Crawford in 1826. They remained in Brooke County until after 1850 and then moved to Pettis County, Missouri.

Their daughter Eliza Pamilia was born in Brooke County, West Virginia, on 28 May 1821. She married Franklin Plummer (1819–1889) in Brooke County on 12 April 1849. Franklin was the son of George Gilbert Plummer (1780–1865) and Leah Wells (1794–1845). Leah was granddaughter of Captain Alexander Wells, a Revolutionary War Patriot whose story follows this story. Alexander is my fifth great-grandfather.

Franklin and Eliza were living in Cooper County, Missouri, by 1850, and by 1854 they were farming near Blackwater, Saline County, Missouri. Their daughter Sarah "Sallie" was born in 1854 and married Coleman Washington Younger on 27 September 1871 in Saline County. Their daughter Blanche Betrand Raines (1887–1957) was my grandmother. My membership in the

SAR is based on proven lineage to Patriot Joseph Gist through the Younger, Plummer, Jones, and Gist lines.

The proposed father of Ellis, Charles Robinson Jones, also served in the Revolution in the famed Maryland Third Regiment.[99] It falls to further research to prove the kinship of Charles Robinson to Ellis; thus, Charles Robinson is not included in this book as a Patriot. Charles's father, Captain Robert Jones III, has an extensive documented history as a slave trader. He died in Africa while on a trading expedition prior to the war. That is an interesting story, but much remains to be proven in this instance; however, I have proven the kinship of Charles Robinson to his father, Captain Robert Jones.

### Captain Alexander Wells

Born: 12 March 1727, Baltimore County, Maryland
Died: 9 November 1813
Burial: Wells Burying Ground in Cross Creek Township, Washington County, Pennsylvania
Service: Second Soldiers Delight Company and Baltimore County Militia
Rank: Captain
Service Dates: 1776
Wife: Leah Owings, married 12 July 1753
Lineage: Son Richard's daughter Leah married George Gilbert Plummer, father of Franklin Plummer. His daughter Sarah Sallie Plummer/Younger's daughter was Blanche Younger/Raines, my grandmother.
DAR: A122281
SAR: P-316131

Alexander was the fifth of six children of Captain James Wells (1692–1771) and Ann Thornborough (1690–1771) of Baltimore, Maryland. Their births are recorded in the St. Paul's Episcopal Church of Baltimore.[100] Additional records also reflect the births of both his parents and Alexander.[101] The referenced "Little Wells" story is a thoroughly researched and well-written unpublished story I found useful in the preparation of this story. I have further added information concerning his military experience and business dealings. Alexander is my fifth great-grandfather in the Younger family line.

He married Leah Owings on 12 July 1753 at the Garrison Forest Episcopal Church in Baltimore. Leah was the daughter of Captain Henry Owings (1692–1763) and Helen Sinchcomb (1702–1763). The Owings' plantation, "Long Acre," was in Baltimore County. Leah had six siblings. I have a copy of those marriage records.

Alexander and Leah's plantation in Baltimore County was known as the "Wells' Inheritance," located in the suburbs of present-day Baltimore. They owned other tracts of land in Baltimore

---

[99] *The Maryland Militia in the Revolutionary War.* S. Eugene Clements and F. Edward Wright, Heritage Books Inc., 2008. A. Roberts, Comptroller, the Press of Brandow Printing Company, Albany, New York. Documents Charles Robinson's service in a Maryland Militia unit.
[100] Maryland, U.S., Births and Christenings, 1662–1911. FHS Film number 1396.
[101] "The Little Wells Family in North America—Alexander Wells (1727–1813)," Harold Henry and Nadine Hull Arnold, 1969. Edited and reorganized by Harold Hull Arnold in 1998. This is a twenty-page unpublished account of Alexander Wells and his family including his military service and land holdings in Pennsylvania.

County amounting to several hundred acres.[102] Neither I nor other researchers have determined if the Wellses lived on the Wells' Inheritance plantation or one of the other parcels of land owned by them. I found no indication that the Wellses used or owned slaves for their plantation operations, but there is evidence of use of indentured workers. Below in figure 4-5 is an ad published by Alexander to aid in recovering an indentured worker that seemingly violated his agreement with the family.[103] [104] If found, the worker would probably be fined by the court system and indentured time added to his agreement before he could be declared a free person. This was not slavery, as the family had likely paid for the servant's trip from England to the colonies in return for a defined period of service with pay.

---

### TEN POUNDS REWARD

Ran away from the Subscriber, living near Soldier's Delight, in Baltimore County, on the 9th of June last a Servant Man named David Wickenden, an Englishman, about 5 Feet 6 Inches high, about 30 Years old, thin Visage, dark Complexion, dark brown Hair, has a speck in the Sight of his Eye of a palish blue, floops a little in his Walk, is fond of Liquor, much given to chewing Tobacco, and is a notorious Rogue. He is well known in Baltimore and Ann-Arundel Counties, having served Mr. Henry Dorsey on Elk Ridge 7 Years. He is fond of Plowing or driving a Team. Whoever takes up the said Servant, and brings him to the Subscriber shall have the above Reward, paid by

Alexander Wells

---

Figure 4-5 Reward for an indentured servant offered by Alexander Wells

His military service started with his service prior to the Revolution as a lieutenant in the minutemen and continued later with the Second Company of the Soldiers Delight Regiment. Patriot Richard Gist, also discussed in this book, was an officer in that regiment. After the war began, he enlisted as a captain.[105] He also signed an Oath of Fidelity to Baltimore and renounced his loyalty to England and King George.[106]  found no records of his seeing military action, as he was forty-five years old at that time. This was probably a common act in Baltimore, where public figures joined a local militia to show public support for the Revolution. I found no records of any

---

[102] Copied from card indexes of patents and surveys, etc. in Maryland State Land Office, Annapolis, Maryland, in 1963 and 1964. Twelve patent transactions were found dating from 1750 to 1772 for parcels ranging from 1¼ acres to more than 600 acres.

[103] "The Little Wells Family in North America—Alexander Wells (1727–1813)," Harold Henry and Nadine Hull Arnold, 1969. Edited and reorganized by Harold Hull Arnold in 1998.

[104] "Maryland Gazette (of) Annapolis, Maryland, Micro Film Reel 5, Issue No. 974. Thursday January 6, 1764. University of Texas Library.

[105] Alexander Wells Family Listing and Service in the Militia, located in The Maryland Historical Society, Baltimore, Maryland. This listing gives the militia duty of Alexander in the Soldiers Delight Militia Regiment beginning on 13 May 1776. It also lists his wife and his children, including Richard.

[106] Journal and Correspondence of the Council of Maryland, 1778–1789.

Baltimore militia fighting, as few battles were fought there. It is true that Maryland fought and fought hard in the Revolution, but just somewhere else in very important action discussed elsewhere in this book. Alexander's oldest son, Henry, fought in the Revolution and is recognized by the DAR and SAR, as is Alexander.

Alexander began acquiring land in Pennsylvania as early as 1772, but the actual move by him and his family from Baltimore was delayed until about 1782. They sold their plantation, Wells' Inheritance, on 27 April 1780 to Johnathan Hudson for 30,000 pounds. A second piece of property, the "Wells' Delight," located in Frederick County, was sold to Samuel Owings. He remained in Baltimore until that sale. On 9 January 1782, he gave Thomas Owings a power of attorney to sell his remaining property. He was living in Washington County, Pennsylvania, by that date.

Alexander purchased land in Cross Creek Township in Washington County starting in 1772.[107] Those purchases included:

1. 1,500 acres in partnership with Nathan Cromwell
2. 500 acres in partnership with Nathan Cromwell
3. The Cliffs, 400 acres
4. Mayfield, 389 acres
5. Rocky Ridge, 407 acres
6. The Grove, 199 acres
7. Skillton, 423 acres, later sold to his youngest son, Richard, grandfather of George Gilbert Plummer, who was the father of Franklin Plummer

I found records showing that Alexander established several grist mills in the township. The flour was boated down Cross Creek to the Ohio River and on to New Orleans. He also established Ft. Wells on his land called "Mayfield" for the defense of the mills. The DAR recognizes him for establishing and maintaining that fort. He also operated a distillery in Washington County. This and other distilleries in Washington County were at the center of the Whiskey Rebellion of 1794. This is discussed elsewhere in this book. The federal "whiskey tax" and subsequent rebellion may have motivated Alexander and his wife to soon move to Brooke County, Virginia, now West Virginia. Brooke County was relatively close to Washington County, Pennsylvania. I discussed Brooke County earlier in the book during the Gist and Ellis Jones stories. I imagine that these families were known to each other because of their connections from the Revolutionary War in the Baltimore area.

Alexander began selling his Washington County property on 1 January 1795 when he sold "Skilton" to his son Richard and his wife Helen. He later sold "Mayfield" and "The Cliffs" to Richard and his wife in 1798 for 2,500 pounds. This included both the mills and the fort. This transaction can easily be confused with another Richard Wells who owned property nearby: Richard "Graybeard" Wells.

---

[107] *History of Washington County, Pennsylvania*, Boyd Crumrine, 1882: "Cross Creek Township," "Early Settlements."

Among the first permanent settlers in the area was Richard "Graybeard" Wells, who emigrated from Baltimore County in 1772. He was born in Baltimore County, Maryland, on 25 October 1742. Graybeard acquired land in the area and built a fort.

Richard Graybeard Wells was the son of Alexander's older brother James (1716–1797). The Graybeard fort, according to Earl B. Forrest, *History of Washington County Pennsylvania*, vol. 1, 1926, p. 54, was in what is now West Virginia, six miles northeast of the Alexander Wells Fort in Washington County. According to this source, troops were stationed at both forts during the Indian Wars. While West Virginia generally lies south of Pennsylvania, local border variations appear to exist which would make a northeast course possible.

Alexander died in Brooke County, Virginia, on 9 December 1813, and his wife Leah a little over a year after that. They are both buried in the Wells family cemetery in Washington County. In his will, he left property to some of his children and grandchildren. By the time of his death, he had sold or given much of his estate to his children, including Richard. We see in his will that he left a small sum of money to Helen, twin sister of Richard.

Despite the many sources used in producing this story, I found mainly indirect proof of the relationship between Richard and his father, Alexander. I could not find the church records for him or several of his children. We can speculate on that circumstance, but it is just that—speculation. Alexander began the task of establishing the family's presence in Pennsylvania around 1772. He certainly traveled between Baltimore and Washington County many times between 1772 and the final relocation to Pennsylvania in 1782, ten years later. Several children were born in that span. Their association with the church may have lagged. Here is the documentation I have:

- Baltimore County historical records reflect the names of his children, including Richard, as well as his military service.
- He sold most of his valued Pennsylvania real estate to Richard and his sister Helen in 1795.
- Richard and Helen's marriage is recorded in the Episcopal Church records of Baltimore. Both lived there at the time of their marriage. This is the same church that contains birth records of his father and mother.
- The DAR recognizes Richard as the son of Alexander. While not proof of relationship, many memberships have been approved based on this assertion over may years. It also recognizes Richard's relationship to the Wells Fort in Washington County.
- Even though I found no mention of son Richard in his will, I found little of other adult sons in that will either, as he had already provided for them with land sales and gifts. His only mention of his oldest son, Henry, was for identifying his grandson Nathaniel Wells, who was a son of Henry. He did not mention sons Bezalell, Michal, or James in this will. The fact that Richard was not mentioned seems consistent—he had provided for him already.

It is fact that there were at least three other Richard Wells of this family line living in Washington County. They were sons of brothers or grandsons, and I have eliminated them from this search. I have seen records that show Richard's twin sister, Helen, married a first cousin named Richard Wells.

Alexander and Leah had the following children:

- Henry, 1754–1814
- Alexander Jr., 1756–1846
- Anne Nancy Griffith, 1758–1840
- Michal Owings, 1759–1831
- Nathaniel, 1761–1789
- Bazaleel, 1763–1830
- James, 1765–1847
- Richard, 1775–1830. Father of Leah, who was mother to Franklin Plummer. He is my fourth great-grandfather.
- Helen Wells, 1775–1826. Married another Richard—first cousin Richard Wells.

Multiple sources were used to document the names and vital information of his children:

- The Alexander Wells Family Listing and Service in the Militia noted above for his military service also lists some of his children.
- Alexander's will of 3 November 1821 in Brooke County, Virginia. Located in the probate records of Brooke County, West Virginia.
- "Story of Early Brooke County Settlers" made available by the Brooke County Historical Society contains a biographical sketch of five early influential settlers of Brooke County, including Alexander Wells and his family.
- Some of the children of Alexander and Leah Owings Wells are listed in the records of St. Thomas Parish (Garrison Forest Episcopal Church) in Baltimore County.

Son Richard married Helen Ellen in Washington County, Pennsylvania, on 22 March 1788, and they remained there operating the mills and distilleries he purchased from his father. Richard and Helen had the following children:

- Leah Plummer, 1794–1845. Mother of Franklin Plummer. My third great-grandmother.
- Ruth, 1795–Unknown death date
- Bazaleel, 1796–1846
- Joshua, 1800–1836

We know that Leah is the daughter of Richard, as her grandfather's probate papers list her as daughter of Richard and show her last name as Plummer in 1813. Her father's will of 1822 and later codicils show she was given the land and mills on that land. Leah died in 1845 and is buried in the Wells Burying Ground, as is her husband, George Gilbert. I have not found the marriage records of George and Leah.

George Gilbert Plummer and Leah Wells had the following children:

- Franklin, 1819–1889. My second great-grandfather.
- Ruth D. Buxton, 1820–1866

- Christina, 1821–Unknown death date
- Jerone, 1823–1898
- Sarah Ensley, 1831– Unknown death date
- Gilbert Lafayette, 1834–1862
- Rebecca, Dates unknown

Son Franklin married Eliza Pamelia Jones in Brooke County, West Virginia, in 1849. Eliza was the daughter of Lewis Reice Jones, son of Patriot Ellis Jones, discussed earlier in this book. Lewis Reice Jones married Eliza Pamelia Gist, granddaughter of Patriot Joseph Gist, also discussed elsewhere in this book. Franklin and Eliza's third daughter, Sarah "Sally," married Coleman Washington Younger, and they are my great-grandparents. These Plummer relationships are documented with marriage and census records as well as more than one hundred DAR and SAR memberships claiming these Wells, Jones, Gist, and Younger Patriots.

I found non-documented records showing that Leah Wells may have used the given name "Sarah," even though all legal records we have found show Leah. If that was true, is it possible that my great-grandmother Sarah Younger was named after her?


**Lawrence Abraham Woolery**
Born: 9 April 1739
Died: 9 April 1839
Burial: Mount Nebo Cemetery, Cooper County, Missouri
Service: Continental Army, Colonel Sherburne's Infantry of Foot Regiment
Rank: Private
Service Dates: 15 April 1777–15 April 1780
Wife: Margaret Horn
Lineage: Son Lawrence George's daughter Jane Woolery married Charles Lee Younger Jr. His son Coleman Washington Younger was my great-grandfather.
DAR: No
SAR: P-324566


Lawrence is my fourth great-grandfather and was born to recent German immigrants Henrich (Henry) Ullerich (1703–1802) and his wife Anne Elizabeth Stichman (1710–1810). He was either born on the boat or soon after they landed in Philadelphia in 1739.[108] The name was pronounced "Ullery," hence the change to Woolery. It sounded the same and no doubt led to confusion about correct spellings in his records. Records show that his father settled in North Hampton County, Pennsylvania, but I am not sure where Lawrence Abraham lived until the Revolutionary War began thirty-seven years later. Some family researchers have said he moved to Kentucky prior to the Revolution and that he married Margrieta Peggy Horn (1749–1837) there, but that is unlikely. Even Daniel Boone found that to be a rough neck of the woods prior to the Revolution. He did marry Margrieta Peggy Horn, but that almost certainly took place in New York or eastern

---

[108] *Names of Foreigners Who Took the Oath of Allegiance to the Province and State of Pennsylvania, 1727–1775.* Pennsylvania Archives Volume XVII, Second Series, Harrisburg, 1890. Reprinted for the Genealogical Publishing Company, Baltimore, 1967 and 1976. Page 190 shows the father of Lawrence, Henrich Ullerich, as a passenger on the ship *Friendship* that arrived in the Port of Philadelphia on 3 September 1737.

Pennsylvania following the war. They were possibly married in 1778, but I found no documentation supporting that claim. Their first son, John, was born in 1779.

He enlisted in Colonel Sherburne's regiment, a Continental Army force, on 15 April 1777 for three years and served in Captain John Smith's Company of that regiment. As the war waged on, the number of men assigned to that regiment dwindled to the point that it was declared a battalion, still commanded by a colonel. The regiment served in New England and fought several battles there. There are no recorded battles in Pennsylvania. I originally thought that Lawrence had belonged to a Pennsylvania militia regiment, but a search of 134 Pennsylvania regiments revealed he had not joined in his home state, although it is likely the regiment recruited there. I found no records of him requesting a pension or land grant based on his service. I have copies of his National Archives records consisting of a muster roll call at about the time of his discharge.

Soon after the war, Lawrence Abraham settled in Madison County, Kentucky, with Margaret (Margrieta) Horn. She was born in Holland and, as with Abraham, her name was changed from Van Horn to Horn, with her first name also undergoing a change from Margrieta. Abraham and Margaret had at least eleven children, and I believe all were born in Madison County prior to their immigration to Cooper County, Missouri. That move probably occurred prior to 1830, as he and his family are shown in Missouri in that census. He bought two tracts of Missouri land from the federal government: one on 30 September and one on 14 November 1835, one of which was in partnership with his son George. The land descriptions are section 26 range 18W Township 47N and section 4, range 18W, Township 46 N, both in Cooper County. He had either homesteaded that land from the time of his arrival prior to 1830 or had bought it on a deferred payment plan which would have allowed him five years to make a final payment. The Missouri deferred payment plan set the land price at $2 per acre, with 10 percent due at the time of purchase and the remainder due in five years. Cash payment price would have been $1 per acre.

Kentucky records show that three of his sons—James, Jacob, and Abraham—joined Captain John D. Thomas's Company of Infantry of the Kentucky Militia from 8 March to 3 September 1813. I at first believed that father Abraham had enlisted with two sons until I discovered a son Abraham; however, I cannot discount the possibility that Abraham Sr. served in that war also.

A newspaper account of his death credits him with being an early settler of Cooper County. His son Henry established a family cemetery near what is now the Nebo Cemetery and church. This church is one of the older churches west of the Mississippi River. His grave is marked and is recognized by the SAR. I believe his grave is marked with a non-engraved stone. We have a photo of that unmarked stone.

Lawrence Abraham and Margaret had twelve children I am comfortable in listing. There may be at least two additional children, but I have been unable to document those relationships. I list a possible son Michael out of belief that he may in fact be a son, but this is unproven.

- John James, 1779–1823. Married Susannah Eads and moved to Lawrence County, Indiana. Kentucky War of 1812 veteran.
- Michael, 1781–1823. Married Jane Todd and moved to Lawrence County, Indiana. I cannot document him as a son of Abraham, but it is likely. Kentucky War of 1812 veteran.

- Peter, 1783–1840. He married Maragret Peggy Cross and remained in Madison County, Kentucky.
- Francis, 1784–1856. He married Ruth Francis Henderson and moved to Palmyra, Marion County, Missouri.
- Henry W., 1786–1842. He married Nancy Corum, and they moved to Cooper County, Missouri.
- Jacob, 1786–1866. Married Susannah Hannah Todd and moved to Lawrence County, Indiana. Kentucky War of 1812 veteran.
- George B., 1788–1844. My third great-grandfather. He married Ann Matilda, daughter of Patriot George Lee, discussed below. Their daughter Jane married Charles Lee Younger, father of Coleman Washington Younger, my great-grandfather. They settled in Cooper County, Missouri.
- Margaret Jones, 1792–1864. She married Lewis "Jessie" Jones, and they settled in Cooper County, Missouri.
- Abraham, 1794–1864. Married Emily Jane Branum, and they settled in Cooper County, Missouri. Kentucky War of 1812 veteran.
- Isaac, 1796–1851. Married Frankie Watson and remained in Madison County, Kentucky.
- Stephen Andrew, 1799–1871. We have a photo of Stephen. He married Hannah Briscoe, and they settled in Cooper County, Missouri.
- James, 1801–1840. Married Margaret Watson and remained in Madison County, Kentucky. Kentucky War of 1812 veteran.

This line represents the intersection of the Woolery, George Lee, Joshua Logan Younger, Ellis, Plumber, and several other Patriot lines discussed throughout this book. George Lee's story follows.

**George Lee**
Born: 6 October 1742, Buckingham County, Virginia
Died: 1803, Madison County, Kentucky
Burial: Unknown
Service: Montgomery County Militia of Virginia
Rank: Private
Service Dates: 1780–1782
Wife: Martha George (1755–1810), married 25 December 1777
Lineage: Daughter Ann Matilda married George B. Woolery, and their daughter Jane married Charles Lee Younger, whose son Milton Toney Younger was the father of my great-grandfather Coleman Washington Younger. Lawrence George Woolery was the son of Patriot Lawrence Abraham Woolery, discussed above.
DAR: No
SAR: No

George Lee was the son of planter Richard Henry Lee Jr. (1707–1795) and Mary Gresham (1709–1767) and was born in Buckingham County, Virginia. That county generally lies south of the James River in central Virginia and was founded in 1761, with its boundaries changing several times during the colonial period. I believe that Richard Henry lived most of his life in this county until his move to Ballston, Virginia. George's second wife was Elizabeth Miller, and after her death, he moved to Jackson County, Tennessee, to live with family members.

It is important to devote extra attention to this generation of the Virginia Lee family, as George's father is easily confused with Senator Richard Henry Lee of the Continental Congress. They are not the same men, but of the same family line of the Virginia Lees. This Richard Henry was a planter and, as far as I could determine, never a politician or army officer. Several court documents I discovered used the term "Esquire" following his last name. He was not a lawyer either, as this term was then not a formal term but merely used out of respect. The father of this Richard Henry was Richard Henry Sr., and his father was William Lee. We believe William was born in England and that most of the Virginia Lee family descended from him.[109]

I found a letter written by Miller Lee, son of Richard Henry Jr., in 1850 in which he names his father, grandfather, and great-grandfather. We also found a letter written by George Washington Lee, great-grandson of Richard Henry Jr., in 1869 in which he confirms the names of his immediate family.[110] Both these documents also name George Lee as the son of William Henry Lee Jr. I also found other family letters later published in historical journals confirming these family relationships.

William Henry Lee Jr. and Mary Gresham had ten children, with eight additional children being born after his marriage to Elizabeth Miller. I could not document the birth location of their son George, but I found numerous documents attesting that George spent nearly all his early pre-military life in Buckingham County, so an assumption was made about this birth location.

We know little of George's life in Virginia except that he married Martha George on 25 December 1777 prior to his military service, and their first child was born in 1789.[111] His military records are few, except for a muster card or two, but that was enough to learn much more about his service. As a matter of note, there were only maybe two George Lees serving during the Revolutionary War, with the other George serving in Delaware in the Continental Army in Lee's Rangers. Both Georges probably had a lot to talk about following their service in these very active units. He served under an officer I personally refer to as the "George Armstrong Custer of the Revolutionary War." That was not his name, but he was probably every bit as colorful. Colonel William Campbell, later General Campbell, lived a hard, fast, but short life, and George Lee was close to these exploits, which I will recount below. In fairness, the other George Lee served under Lieutenant Colonel Lightfoot Lee in "Lee's Rangers." More on them in the chapter on the Guilford Courthouse Battle.

By 1780, when George joined the army, Colonel William Campbell commanded the Montgomery County Militia. The regiment was assigned a mission by the governor to protect the lead

---

[109] *Ancestors and Descendants of Gresham Lee of Buckingham County, Virginia.* Richard Edward Lee. Gateway Press, Baltimore, Maryland, 1991. This gives an accounting of the wives and children of William Henry Lee, land owned by him, and the location of that land.

[110] *The Virginia Genealogist*, edited by John Frederick Dorman, Washington, D.C., October–December 1996, vol. 40, no. 4. Pages 257–258 contain the letter of George W. Lee written to his son Abner Grisham Lee, who was living in the Montana Territory on 9 October 1867.

[111] *Virginia Marriage Records*, extracted from *The Virginia Magazine of History and Biography*, the *William and Mary College Quarterly*, and *Tyler's Quarterly*. Baltimore, Maryland. Bentley, Elizabeth Petty, indexer. Genealogy Publishing Co., Inc., 1984. Page 610 gives the marriage date for George Lee and Martha George on 25 December 1777.

mines in Washington County, which is located generally in the southwest end of the state adjoining North Carolina. Lead was an important commodity not only to the colonists but also to the British. The side controlling this commodity might control the outcome of the war. The Comanche Indian tribe was also not happy with either side's presence in their territory. Colonel Campbell was a well-known Virginian who married Elizabeth, the sister of the then governor of the colony, Patrick Henry. The Lees no doubt knew the Campbells, so George certainly would have felt comfortable serving with a name familiar to the family. William Campbell was a young man on his way up.[112]

Both Loyalists and Indians had contributed to a very dangerous and unstable situation in Washington County, and the mission given to Colonel Campbell was to settle the unrest. He quickly became known as a very brutal commander and was known to have shot or hung several Loyalists for their activities in that county without a trial. Justice was swift. He was well respected by his men and quickly gained a reputation as a very effective leader who paid little respect to the legal aspect of his mission. The Virginia General Assembly became aware of this dilemma and quickly granted him legal immunity from criminal and civil prosecution. Remember, his wife was sister to the governor. Also remember, the Virginia Continental Line was being held as prisoners of war in Charleston, and the outcome of the war might well rest on the colonies' ability to defend themselves from the obvious future campaign by Cornwallis and the Loyalists, who were causing a lot of unrest in that region. Colonel Campbell and his troops seemed to be just what was needed. They soon met that expectation.

On 15 June 1780, the governor named Colonel Campbell commander of an expedition against the Cherokees in eastern Tennessee. George Lee would have been a part of that expedition, but it did not occur. The regiment was diverted to again protect the lead mines of Montgomery County, and they were again successful, and the campaign ended in August 1780.[113] The next month the regiment was sent to Kings Mountain in North Carolina. The battle occurred on 7 October 1780 ten miles south of Kings Mountain, North Carolina, in South Carolina. Colonel Campbell was appointed the leader of the attack up the mountain by his fellow commanders, in which he quickly headed up the hill with his troops and won the battle, killing the senior British officer.[114] This was a very important victory, as it was the first success since the British had captured Charleston. Campbell was recognized by the Virginia General Assembly for his actions, and he and his soldiers were recognized as heroes. This victory allowed General Nathanael Greene to organize his troops to counter the Cornwallis movement through North Carolina to Virginia. A later chapter of this book will discuss the Kings Mountain battle, in which two Gist brothers were killed.

In early 1781, Colonel Campbell's Regiment joined with General Greene's Army to face the British as they moved into North Carolina, and within nine days of his joining Greene's force, they found themselves in the Battle of Guilford Courthouse. Campbell served under the command of Lighthorse Lee on the left of Greene's line. Campbell's forces took the brunt of the Cornwallis attack and suffered severe losses.[115] General Greene praised Campbell for standing

---

[112] *History of Southwest Virginia, 1746–1786, Washington County, 1777–1870*, Lewis Summers, 1903, pp. 584–587.
[113] Ibid.
[114] *The Road to Guilford Courthouse: The American Revolution in the Carolinas.* Buchanan, John. John Wiley and Sons, 1997, New York. Pages 215–221 give an account of Colonel William Campbell's contributions to the battle.
[115] Ibid. Pages 215–221 give an account of Colonel William Campbell's contributions to the Battle of Guilford Court House.

his ground and keeping American losses to a minimum. Colonel Campbell later claimed his unit had been sacrificed by Lighthorse Lee. This was a tactical loss but strategic victory for the Americans. I will devote a chapter to this significant battle later in the book due to the number of family Patriots who were present for this battle.

Following the Guilford battle, the Virginia General Assembly appointed Campbell as a brigadier general. His unit was to join General Marquis de Lafayette in eastern Virginia. Campbell, however, soon met with bad luck, as in August 1781 he died of a heart attack at the age of thirty-six.[116] He had certainly lived fast and died young.

George Lee joined the army to protect some Virginia lead mines under the command of a popular, colorful commander and found himself involved in two of the most brutal yet important battles of the Revolutionary War! He helped make history and then quietly moved on to go to Kentucky and raise a family. I believe he may have received a land grant but did not find those records.

There are some questions about George's marriage. I have Virginia marriage records showing he married Martha George on 25 December 1777.[117] Other researchers show he married Nancy Pinkston (1773–1850) in North Carolina in 1793. If he married Nancy Pinkston, then she would have been about twelve years old when we find George in Kentucky. Given that multiple researchers have associated Nancy with George, I will merely mention this claim, but I will maintain the George Lee and Martha George relationship until more information is produced.

By 1785 we find George in Madison County, Kentucky, where the circuit court bound Leonard Neal to George in the amount of 30 pounds.[118] The Madison County tax records for 1792, 1795, 1799, 1800, and 1801 also reflect his living there. Kentucky did not become a state until 1792, explaining the 1792 tax record, which would have been the first for the state. Madison was previously a Virginia county, and the pre-1792 court records were officially Virginia court records. Their children were:

- Ann Matilda, 1789–1844. Ann married George B. Woolery (1786–1844), whose father was a Patriot discussed above in this book. Ann Matilda is my third great-grandmother.
- Stephen, 1792–1854. Married (1) Rachel Kidwell (1798–1818) and (2) Elizabeth Flood-McDonald (1802–1834) and (3) Leanna Roley (1821–1915). Lived in Illinois and later Texas. His family bible gives his father's name.
- Nancy Walters, 1795–1869. Married Abraham Walters (1784–1863) and lived in Illinois.
- Enoch Walters, 1798–1871. Married Catherine Kidwell (1806–1891) and lived in Clark County, Illinois.
- Rachel Kidwell, 1801–1894. Married James E. Kidwell (1798–1867) lived in Clark County, Illinois, and later in Parker, Texas.

---

[116] *History of Southwest Virginia, 1746–1786, Washington County, 1777–1870*, Lewis Summers, 1903, pp. 584–587.
[117] Virginia Marriages 1750–1850. Database online. Provo, Utah. Ancestry.com. Page 610 has the marriage of George Lee and Martha George in December 1777.
[118] Madison County, Kentucky, Circuit Court Case Number 2777, dated 25 October 1785 and modified in November 1789. Leonard Neal bound to George Lee in the amount of 30 pounds.

- George Jr., 1804–1857. Married Louvicy Louisa Kidwell and lived in Clark County, Illinois. Later moved to Texas and died with a wagon train en route to California. He is buried along the Rio Grande River in Texas.

Their six children were all born and married in Lincoln County. I found no records of their births there and did not expect to find them, given that few births were recorded there until post-1800. Marriages were, however, recorded, and they were important in placing these children in Madison County at an appropriate time. Daughter Ann Matilda married George B. Woolery in Madison County in 1810, and they remained there until their relocation to Cooper County, Missouri, prior to 1824. Their daughter Jane was born in Cooper County in 1824.

George B. Woolery and Ann Matilda Lee had at least two children, and their second child, Jane, married Charles Lee Younger, the great-grandson of Patriot Joshua Younger, another Patriot discussed earlier in this book. Their marriage was in Cooper County in 1845. This Charles Lee Younger was the father of my great-grandfather Coleman Washington Younger. We have a large portrait of Charles and Jane hanging in our library. Charles was a Confederate soldier in Missouri and later a farmer.

**Jesse Oglesby**
Born: 15 March 1763, Goochland County, Virginia
Died: 1 October 1852, Madison County, Kentucky
Burial: Paint Lick Cemetery in Garand County, Kentucky
Service: First Virginia Militia Regiment assigned to the Continental Line as the Second Virginia Regiment
Rank: Private
Service Dates: 9 June 1777–August 1781
Wife: Celia Witt (1765–1855)
Lineage: Daughter Maria married Ellis Roney, and his daughter Elizabeth Roney married Fielding Murphy, whose son Joseph Roney Murphy was the father of Bessie Pauline Murphy/Scott, Jo's grandmother. He is Emma Jo's fourth great-grandfather.
DAR: A085821
SAR: No

Jesse was born on 15 March 1763 to Jacob Oglesby and Ann Bailey in Goochland County, Virginia.[119] This information is also documented by the Oglesby family bible.[120] The Oglesby family was a well-established Colonial Virginia family with land holdings throughout Goochland County, which was later divided into several current counties, including Amherst and Fluvanna Counties. The Oglesbys' land was in what is now Amherst and Fluvanna Counties near Richmond.

---

[119] *North American Family Histories 1500–2000.* Lineage Book for the Daughters of the American Revolution. Volume 85. Page 15 gives the birth year for Jesse Oglesby, the name of his parents, and his birth county. It also gives his military unit and commander.
[120] The Oglesby Family Bible. Bible owned by Dr. Harry Field Parker, Warrensburg, Missouri. Copied by Fannie L. Avery Oglesby. Contains the names of the parents of Jesse and his birth date of 15 November 1763.

Some records show that Jesse was born in Goochland County and some Fluvanna County. Fluvanna County was not formed into its present configuration until 1774, so it is likely that Jesse was born in the part of Goochland County that later became Fluvanna County. I found records that establish his birth date as 1759, and his tombstone shows a 1761 birth date, but his family bible and the 1850 census reflect the 1763 birth date that I have used.

National Archives military records show that Jesse joined the Virginia Militia First Regiment commanded by Colonel Dabney on 9 June 1777 early in the war as a private. This was a militia regiment that was later reorganized into the Second Virginia Line Regiment and later assigned to the Continental Line. This unit served in and around Richmond for most of the war and was later assigned under the command of General Lafayette during the conflict with General Cornwallis in the final battles of the Revolutionary War. In fact, Cornwallis passed through Goochland County on his way to his defeat at Petersburg. Jesse served under the company command of Captain James Burnett and helped protect his home county during that part of the campaign. The DAR recognizes his service in that command, and I have his National Archives records, including his pension request. He is also recorded in the "List of Revolutionary War Soldiers of Virginia."[121]

An interesting twist to his military service arose when I studied his request for a pension, which he submitted in October 1832 more than fifty years after his service. In this sworn statement, he stated that he joined this regiment to serve for a friend, Richard Perkins, in 1781. The agreement was that if he were to be drafted during this term of enlistment, Richard was to serve for him. He stated that he served that ninety-day enlistment and later joined the regiment again on his own account rather than be drafted into another regiment. He gave considerable detail on the movement and operations of his regiment and validated that he served until the end of the war. He did not account for the time between the recorded enlistment date of 9 June 1777 and 1781. I believe that this account was taken by another person during his application process, as he could not write, and that the failure to account for the actual enlistment date was a simple error since he could not read the completed statement prior to placing his "X" upon it. This confusion does not detract from the fact that he served his enlistment in and around Goochland County and that he served until the end of the war. The actual unit records of Colonel Dabney's Regiment seem to agree with Jesse's account of battles and locations. His company commander, Captain James Burnett, also verified his service in that unit. His pension number is W1987. His wife Celia made a second pension request after his death in 1853, and it was approved. His name and service unit are contained on the Kentucky Pension Roll of 1835, and this establishes his initial pension payment date as 1833. This is a telling date. Jesse would have been eligible for pension in 1818 if his service had been in the Continental Line, even though historical records indicate otherwise. I believe that his unit probably was assigned to the Continental Line, then very soon reassigned back to state control as a militia regiment. That was not unusual. This thought is further supported by the combat record of the unit—they never left Goochland County for more than a few days. In fact, the Virginia Continental Line units were taken as prisoners at the Siege of Charleston, and only state line and militia units were left to protect the state.

---

[121] "List of Revolutionary War Soldiers of Virginia." Special Report of the Department of Archives and History for 1912. H.J. Eckendorf, Archivist. David Bottom, Superintendent of Public Printing, 1913. Page 225 lists Jesse Oglesby as a Virginia soldier.

In his pension request, Jesse stated he lived in Amherst County when he enlisted and lived there for fifteen years before moving to Madison County, Kentucky. He married Cecilia Witt on 15 September 1794 and moved to Madison County, Kentucky, following his marriage and prior to the birth of his daughter Maria. The spelling of his wife's given name is in question, as marriage records show it as "Celia" as opposed to "Cecilia."

I found no records of a land grant for his service, but much of Madison County, Kentucky, was settled primarily by land grant recipients, so it is likely that he received such a grant. He was a farmer in both Virginia and Kentucky. The 1820 Kentucky census shows that he owned one slave. This was a surprise in that neither his father nor brothers owned slaves. Upon researching Celia's father's records, I found that her father, David Witt Jr., owned slaves and that he left one slave to Celia. His will was written in 1818, and he died later that year, which might account for the slave on Jesse's census records in 1820.[122]

Their daughter Maria married Ellis Roney on 12 February 1823 in Shelby County, Kentucky. Ellis was the son of Patriot Hercules Roney II, discussed later in this book, and is Emma Jo's third great-grandfather. Their first daughter, Elizabeth, born in 1823, married Fielding Murphy in 1852 in Oldham County, and their son Joseph Roney Murphy was the father of Emma Jo's grandmother Bessie Pauline Murphy Scott. I should note that Fielding Murphy's father, John Lewis Murphy, married Betsy Ashby, daughter of Patriot Fielding Ashby discussed earlier in this book. The Ashby family and their contributions are discussed in a later chapter in this book. The Murphy family line accounts for six Patriots, all discussed in this book—Murphy (2), Ashby (3), and Roney—further evidence that the Revolutionary War was a family affair.

Jesse and Celia had the following nine children:

- Sarah, 1794–1855
- Jacob, 1798–1860
- David, 1799–1850
- Maria Roney, 1800–1853. Emma Jo's third great-grandmother
- Jane Foley, 1807–1850
- Malinda Alderson/Callison, 1810–1860
- Nancy Witt, 1812–1891
- John, 1814–1895
- Jesse, 1815–1822

Jesse left a will in September 1850 in which he mentions all his children. His marriage to Celia (Cecilia) Witt is recorded in Virginia, and she is documented in his request for a pension. The Scott family bible documents Maria's marriage to Ellis Roney.[123] I am uncertain of Maria's death date. Ellis died in 1850, and I found an Iowa special census report and death records for 1853 in her name. The lineage of the Ellis Roney line is covered in the Patriot Hercules Roney story later in this book.

---

[122] Virginia's Wills and Probate Records, Nelson County. Will Book Vol. B, 1818–1822, p. 353.
[123] The Scott Family Bible. This bible, which we no longer have access to, belonged to Gorda and Bessie Scott. The information we have was provided by Lou Callis of Paris, Missouri, from her personal records obtained from that bible.

Jesse is buried in Paint Lick Cemetery in Garrard County, Kentucky, and his grave has a headstone. There are Patriots from the Raines line buried in that cemetery, all discussed above.

Jacob Oglesby Jr., the father of Jesse Oglesby, is recognized for patriotic service, and his story follows:

**Jacob Oglesby Jr.**
Born: 1736, Goochland County, Virginia
Died: January 1813, Albemarle County, Virginia
Burial: Unknown location
Service: Patriotic service
Rank: None
Service Dates: None
Wife: (1) Ann Bailey (1740–1780) and (2) Mildred Martin (1741–1827)
Lineage: Son Patriot Jesse Oglesby, featured above
DAR: A085819
SAR: No

Jacob Jr. was born in 1736 to Jacob Oglesby Sr. (1709–1780) and Constance Perkins (1709–1769) in Goochland County, Virginia. There is some debate concerning the family name of his wife Constance. The family name of Perkins can be questioned, as the marriage records I found merely show her given name as Constance. Some researchers maintain that her family name was Christian. What seems to be certain is that they were married in 1726 in Goochland County. The relationships of the Oglesby family—Richard, son Jacob Sr., Jacob Jr., and Jesse—are proven by the Oglesby family bible located in Missouri, as well as marriage, probate, and census records noted above.

Grandfather, father, and son were all farmers and plantation owners in Goochland and Albemarle Counties of Virginia. As a matter of note, Albemarle County was formed from parts of Goochland and other counties in 1776. The father of Jacob Sr. was Richard, a large landowner who had married a lady who herself was a large landowner. Their crops consisted mainly of tobacco and hemp. Jacob Jr. served as a tobacco inspector for his county for several years, according to the 1810 state census and other records. Albemarle County operated a tobacco warehouse, and they employed a corps of inspectors whose job was to weigh and record purchases of hemp. This was a public-appointed position that he held for several years. This warehouse had previously belonged to a family who had moved to Kentucky, and the county continued its operation in support of local tobacco production.[124]

---

[124] Albemarle County, Virginia, 464, 1297, p. 58. After 1789, Milton, Virginia, was the seat of a public tobacco warehouse called Henderson's, which was equipped with a corps of tobacco inspectors for many years. Jacob Oglesby was listed as one of the inspectors.

I also found evidence of him serving as a constable, which again involved weighing and certifying the purchase of tobacco and hemp.[125] He also served as a juror at least once in Albemarle County.[126]

I could not document the size of Jacob Jr.'s plantation, but his land holdings may not have been as large as those of his father or grandfather. Virginia land office records show he received several grants for Albemarle County land during the period of 1790–1799. These grants were in partnership with William Clark:

- 152¾ acres—Land Office Grants No. 23, p. 342, Reel 89, in 1790-1781
- 800 acres—Land Office Grants No. 30, p. 524, Reel 96, in 1794
- 400 acres—Land Office Grants No.30, p. 524, Reel 96, in 1794

A Virginia Colony 1780 reconstructed census shows Jacob owned four slaves that year. The 1790 federal census shows two slaves, and the 1800 census two slaves, but given his age, perhaps his slaves had been sold or passed on to his sons. I will speculate that prior to 1780, it was not practical to own slaves in Albemarle County due to the fact that it was a dangerous county because of Indian unrest. His sons who remained in Virginia owned slaves, and those sons who moved to Kentucky did not take slaves with them. It is a well-established fact that Thomas Jefferson held slaves in this county, but I believe it was well after the 1760s. As discussed earlier in the book, son Jesse owned a slave in Kentucky, but his wife Celia inherited that slave from her grandfather of Virginia.

Jacob Jr. married Ann Bailey in Goochland County on 14 February 1760, a fact supported by the above family bible and Virginia marriage records. Ann died in 1780 at the age of forty after six children were born. They were:

- Thomas, 1761–1840. Died in Christian County, Kentucky
- Jesse, 1763–1852. Emma Jo's fourth great-grandfather. Died in Madison County, Kentucky.
- Jacob III, 1764–1817. Died in Virginia
- Pleasant, 1766–1847. Died in Cooper County, Missouri
- John, 1775–1802. Died in Virginia
- Martha "Patsy" Dinsmore, 1778–1868. Died in Indiana
- Mary Christian Estes, 1780–1838. Died in Lincoln County, Missouri
- Elizabeth Whitney Fagg, 1782–1851. Died in Pike County, Missouri

The mother of the final two children was Mildred Martin, whom he married in 1780. I cannot discount the possibility that not all their children are included in this list, as the referenced family bible is badly damaged and has missing parts.

---

[125] Albemarle County, Virginia, Court Papers, 1290, 1744–1783, p. 37. 1768 Folder: Jacob Oglesby, Constable of Albemarle, certifies he has weighed 3004 lbs hemp, the property of John Scott of this county, 10 Aug 1768.
[126] Albemarle, Virginia, 1293, p. 47. Jacob was listed among the names of jurors that sat in Charlottesville for inquests of property owned by Loyalists in 1779.

I found no records of Jacob Jr.'s military service, but it is probable that he served in the local militia in 1758 during the French and Indian War. Most free men were expected to participate in the Albemarle Militia for the purpose of protection from the Indian population. The French and Indian War in 1756 had left the area in a state of unrest. I have searched the various lists of militia members in that county and was unable to find his name, but these lists are incomplete. During my research of the Ashby family of Virginia I found that Albemarle County was frontier during the French and Indian War. Thomas Ashby commanded Ft. Ashby nearby; his job was to provide security to the area. He did a fair job at that task, but he needed quite a bit of supervision from his commander, Colonel George Washington. That story will be revealed in the later Ashby chapter.

Jacob Jr. is credited for patriotic service during the Revolutionary War for several acts:

- He served on a jury for the purpose of inquiry into property owned by Loyalists. Loyalists ranked directly below Indians in popularity. Their land was subject to seizure by the courts.[127]
- Following the war in 1782, he made a claim and was reimbursed for a gun that was impressed by the militia, also for grain and meals and bacon for the militia. His claim was approved.[128] [129]
- He signed the Albemarle County Declaration of Independence in 1779. I noticed a fellow Albemarle County resident signing this document. His name was Thomas Jefferson—a colonel in the county militia at the time and, of course, a future president.[130]

The date of his death is uncertain. Some researchers have given January 1813 as the date, but I found little evidence to support that date. I, however, found partial probate papers containing the date of his estate inventory being filed: 1 May 1815.[131] His burial location is unknown.

**David Witt Sr.**
Born: 11 April 1720, Goochland County, Virginia
Died: 27 June 1808, Patrick County, Virginia
Burial: Witt family cemetery in Henry County, Virginia
Service: Patriotic service recognized by the DAR and SAR
Rank: None
Service Dates: None
Wife: Sarah "Sally" Harbour (1732–1814)

---

[127] Ibid.
[128] Virginia Revolutionary War Claims, p. 12, Albemarle County. Jacob Oglesby for a gun impressed for militia, 20 pounds, 20 shillings, for 6 diets (meals), 6 shillings, 8 diets for prisoners, 8 shillings, 1 bushel of corn, 8 shillings. He was reimbursed for these goods and services in 1782. The DAR has recognized this act as a patriotic act.
[129] Virginia Revolutionary War Claims, p. 20. He was reimbursed 50 pounds of port, 32 pounds of bacon, and 1 bushel of corn taken by CPL, 1 pound and 3 shillings.
[130] Virginia Declaration of Independence, dated 21 April 1779. Located at the Virginia Historical Society in Richmond, Virginia.
[131] Probate 1 May 1815, Albemarle County, Virginia. Albemarle County Court Records, pp. 58–59, book unknown. Inventory of Jacob Oglesby submitted to Albemarle County on 1 May 1825. John Fagg purchased a folding table and other things from the estate. Inventory performed by Charles Handstep and others. Note: John Fagg was probably the husband of his daughter Elizabeth.

Lineage: David is Emma Jo's sixth great-grandfather. Son was David Jr., and his daughter Celia married Patriot Jesse Oglesby, featured above.
DAR: A127231
SAR: P-323091

I will start the Witt family story in which my previous research has left some questions about the father of David. In my book *Footprints of the Painter and Scott Families of Missouri,*[132] I made the statement that they were French Huguenots from France. I used three sources supporting this claim:

1. *Huguenot Magazine,* Number 3, page 32.
2. An SAR application for membership by John M. Witt filed on 13 December 1923 and approved in June 1924. He stated he was the second great-grandson of David, and that the family was of Huguenot descent. He also claimed that a brother of David's father, Benjamin, was a member of the Virginia House of Burgess.
3. *My Virginia Kin: Comprising the Hamlett, Witt, Giles, Wills, Eubank-Fortune, Mullenix, Lynchard, Talbot, and Kight Families, with a Short Treatise on the Loving Family.* Blanche Hamlett Baldridge. Strawberry Point, Iowa: Press-Journal Pub. Co., 1958. Page 48 claims that the early Virginia Witt family was of Huguenot descent.

Other researchers have now challenged that long-held assertion for several reasons. The first being that it appears that David's father and grandfather were members of the Church of England. I have those records. Secondly, I believe the birth of his grandfather Robert was in England. Lastly, I believe that it seems unusual or unlikely for a Huguenot descendant (David) to be a slave owner. Both David and David Jr. were documented slave owners.

I remain undecided on this issue; however, my leaning is that they are of British descent, which rules out the Pilgrim claims. I recently obtained a published work on the Virginia John Witt family.[133] David was the son of John Witt and Elizabeth Mildred Daux of Charlottesville, Virginia, and his father had extensive land holdings in Albemarle and Goochland counties in Virginia. Most of these holdings were in present-day Nelson County. David Sr. moved to southern Virginia in Henry County prior to the Revolutionary War.

Both John and his son David Sr. owned and traded land, and some records seem to involve other Witt and Harbour family members. In fact, David was probably a cousin of his wife Sally.

At first, I did not fully understand his presence in southern Virginia by the time of the Revolution, but I have since found other Witts also living in Henry County and believe them to be brothers (William) and nephews. His brother Benjamin served in the Virginia House of Burgess, and it is speculation that David Sr. received a Virginia land grant there.[134] His son David Jr. remained in Nelson County and made considerable additions to those land holdings. They grew tobacco, a major cash crop. This family was a slave-holding family, with slaves being passed from

---

[132] *Footprints of the Painter and Scott Families of Missouri,* Virgil E. and Emma Jo Raines, Compass Flower Press, Columbia, Missouri.

[133] *Descendants of John Witt, the Virginia Immigrant,* Robert W. Witt, Heritage Books Inc., Westminster, Maryland, 1998, p. 1. This family history makes no mention of a Huguenot connection and speculates that the family came from Hertfordshire, England.

[134] *Descendants of John Witt, the Virginia Immigrant,* Robert W. Witt, Heritage Books Inc., Westminster, Maryland, 1998.

generation to generation. In fact, I noticed David providing for the support of a young disabled male slave named Isaac in his will. This young slave was described as "simple" and was being provided for, as he was probably unable to work.

David did not serve in the military during the Revolutionary War, but he did sign a loyalty oath in Henry County, Virginia, in November 1777.[135] He also sold supplies to the Virginia Militia during the war. Both the DAR and SAR recognize these activities and have recognized his patriotic service. Interestingly, his son David Jr. was approved as a DAR Patriot for several memberships based on these acts. During my research, I realized that son David Jr. probably never lived in Henry County but remained in Nelson County his entire life. It was his father David Sr. who lived in Henry County. Additionally, it became apparent that David Jr. was not old enough in 1776 or 1777 to sign a legal oath—he would have been maybe seventeen years old. The DAR has now blocked the David Witt Jr. line for future memberships, probably for that reason. David Sr. is the Patriot based on his patriotic service.

I used multiple sources for constructing the names of their children, as his will did not name them. The Witt book does name them.[136] David and Sally had the following children:

- Nannah Dotson, 1747–1850
- David Jr., 1750–1818. Emma Jo's fourth great-grandfather
- Martha Mildred Moore, 1754–1826
- John, 1755–1826
- William, 1758–1840
- Sylvanus, 1761–1855
- Joel, 1763–1812
- Elizabeth Dillon, 1765–Unknown death date
- Sarah Smith, 1772–1850

David Witt Jr.'s daughter Celia married Patriot Jesse Oglesby, discussed above. Celia is named in Jesse Jr.'s 1818 will and was left a slave called Nully. I believe Nully is the slave mentioned in a Kentucky census as being held by Jesse and Celia. Celia and Jesse were subjects of a probate lawsuit brought by Celia's sister Melinda "Linney" against the executors of their father's will. I have that will and the court challenge.

I also found a deposition by David and Sally in a civil court case that seemed to challenge his will in which David left one half of his land and property, including slaves, to Benjamin Moore, the husband of their daughter Martha Mildred. One can assume that the estates of David and his son David Jr. were extensive and court challenges might be expected, especially given the fact that the wills were written several years before their deaths.

---

[135] Ibid., p. 49.

[136] Ibid., p. 49.

### Lewis Murphy (Murphey)
Born: 1740, Virginia
Died: 1803, Kentucky
Burial: Unknown Jefferson County, Kentucky, location
Service: Continental Army, Virginia Line, Third Regiment
Rank: Private
Service Dates: 1777–February 1779
Wife: Anne Johnston (possibly second wife)
Lineage: Son John Lewis Murphy, son Fielding Murphy, Joe Murphy, daughter Bessie Murphy Scott (Jo's grandmother)
DAR: No
SAR: No

Lewis Murphy was born in Virginia (county not known). He enlisted in the Continental Army's Virginia Third Regiment in early 1777 for a period of two years.[137] Colonel Thomas Marshall commanded the regiment, and his company commander was Captain John Peyton. Colonel Marshall was the father of John Marshall, who would later be the chief justice of the supreme court. The regiment was formed in Alexandria, Virginia, so it is likely that Lewis was living nearby when he enlisted. His unit was a very active Virginia regiment that wintered at Valley Forge during the winter of 1778–1779.[138] He is a documented survivor of the Valley Forge winter with General Washington.[139] He is also recorded in the "List of Revolutionary War Soldiers of Virginia," page 222. His regiment was later captured at Charleston in 1780, but Lewis had been discharged by then. As I discussed earlier, Colonel Marshall was an early commander of the regiment, but Colonel William Heth was the commander for most of the Revolutionary War.

It is worthy of note that Richard Lee, discussed earlier, also served in the same unit. Lewis enlisted in October 1777 for two years after Richard's enlistment, so he was not in the unit at the time of their capture at Charleston. They almost certainly knew each other. Patriot Martin Johnston, discussed earlier, also served in the same unit at the same time.

His military records reflect his presence at Yorktown in July 1777, and his regiment fought battles at Trenton, Princeton, Brandywine, Germantown, and Monmouth during his enlistment. There are no federal records of his receiving a pension, but his death in 1803, not long after his probable second marriage, would have been before the availability of pensions in 1810. He did not live long enough to apply for a pension, and he was not married to Anne during the war, so she would not have been eligible.

Little is known of his activities following the war until he marries Anne Johnston in Jefferson County, Kentucky, on 20 July 1800. He had one son, John Murphy, who married Betsy Ashby, whose father was Fielding Ashby, a Patriot with a story told above. It is likely Lewis received a

---

[137] "List of Revolutionary War Soldiers of Virginia." Special Report of the Department of Archives and History for 1912. H.J. Eckendorf, Archivist. David Bottom, Superintendent of Public Printing, 1913. Page 222 lists Lewis as a Virginia Soldier in the Revolution.
[138] *Historical Register of Virginians in the Revolution: Soldiers, Sailors, Marines.* Edited by John H. Gwathmey, Richmond, Virginia, 1938. Volume 13, page 574 lists Lewis Murphy in the Third Virginia Regiment.
[139] Valley Forge Muster Roll. valleyforgemusterroll.org. Site maintained by the Valley Forge Park Alliance. Lewis Murphy was listed as a soldier of the Third Virginia Regiment in a company commanded by Captain John Peyton. The regiment was commanded by Colonel William Heth, and the division commander was Major General Marquis de Lafayette. Site accessed 1 January 2024.

land bounty in Kentucky, as he would have been eligible. Jefferson County, Kentucky, contains the city of Louisville, one of the older cities in the state. He is shown on the Jefferson County tax records in 1800, so he likely lived there until his death in 1803. His burial location is not known. There is some confusion about the spelling of his name. Virginia records of his birth show it spelled without the "e," and later records contain that letter. This family connection took considerable research to confirm. It simply required full research of all the numerous Murphy and Murphey families living in Kentucky after the Revolution. Some had remarkable military records, but they did not ever live in Jefferson County, Kentucky, or have a son named John. We suspect that the letter "e" was added when he joined the army. The records of his marriage to Anne Johnson show the spelling without the "e."

**John Murphy Sr.**
Born: Circa 1764, Virginia
Died: After 1840, Jefferson County, Kentucky
Burial: Possibly in the Murphy Cemetery in Oldham County, Kentucky
Service: Virginia Line, Clark's Illinois Brigade
Rank: Private
Service Dates: 1779–1781
Wife: Margaret Martin, married 1790
Lineage: Son John Lewis Murphy Jr., his son Fielding Murphy, his son Joseph Roney Murphy, and his daughter Bessie Pauline Scott (Emma Jo's grandmother)
DAR: No
SAR: P-254331

John was the son of Lewis Murphy, discussed above, and an unknown mother of Virginia.

His father Lewis married Anne Johnson in Jefferson County in 1800, so she was not the mother of John. Lewis died in 1803, three years after his arrival in Kentucky. As John Sr. was born around 1767, we continue to search for his mother. The circa 1767 birth date is based on his age claim at his 1835 pension hearing. I added the suffix of Sr. to his name for clarity purposes. No records were found using that suffix.

John was a Patriot of the Revolutionary War. Family historian Lou Bridgeford Callis made that statement in her 1987 research of the family, so that was a good start to our research of him, as she was very familiar with that family history from the Scott and Murphy family bibles.[140] He was one of several persons with that name who served, but I quickly found John Murphy listed as a Revolutionary War pensioner of Jefferson County, Kentucky. That listing gave his age at the time he filed the claim (in 1835) as seventy-six. This listing also stated he was a Virginia Line soldier. That narrowed down my search to only a few Patriots.

---

[140] Scott Family of Missouri Bible. Beginning with Davis Scott through Cerra Scott documenting the Scott, Murphy, and Roney families of Missouri. In possession of the Scott family.

No person has used John Murphy as a Patriot for membership in the DAR. That does not imply he is not a Patriot; it merely means no person has filed a membership application using that name. I did find that the SAR recognizes his service, but that is likely based on his pension application.

I eventually found his claim for pension filed in 1835 in Jefferson County. This request was approved, and the pension number is S-13998. During his interview, his memory seemed fine, and he was able to make clear statements concerning his service. He was a member of the Illinois Brigade and a member of the dragoons battalion. The Illinois Brigade was a Virginia Line unit commanded by General John Rogers Clark. Clark was an older brother of William Clark of Lewis and Clark fame.[141] I have researched that unit for years and suffice to say that they were tough, well-led men with a difficult mission in the Illinois Territory. John was proud to be a member of that unit. He was a private and served for two combat-filled years, and he was eligible for a land grant for his service. The land warrant number is 1015, dated 23 June 1783. But I found no records for a Kentucky grant, so it is likely he quickly sold that warrant and got his start in Jefferson County, but that is speculation. Jefferson County was not a military land grant county.

John was a farmer with at least sixteen slaves in Jefferson/Oldham County. He is shown in the Kentucky 1800 tax list, as is his father, and again on the Kentucky 1810, 1820, 1830, and 1840 censuses. I found no census records after 1840. The Kentucky pension list states he died in 1840 in Jefferson County; however, Find a Grave records show a death of 24 August 1848, with burial in the Quertermous-Martin Cemetery in Jefferson County. Ownership of that number of slaves in Jefferson County seems to indicate he owned a large farm for that region.

We have Murphy family bible notes showing that his son John Lewis Jr. is the father of Fielding Murphy. The Kentucky census reports of the early 1800s seem to support that relationship. The Murphy connection to Jefferson/Oldham and Shelby Counties in Kentucky is well documented with tax, census, marriage, and military records, and I have been unable to find other Murphys in those counties using tax and census records, as well as military pension listings and probate records.

John Sr. married Margaret Martin in Jefferson County on 19 March 1790, and I have the marriage record. One son, John Lewis Jr., and a daughter, Mary, have been found. John Lewis Jr. married Elizabeth "Betsy" Ashby in Shelby County on 12 February 1816. Betsy was the daughter of Patriot Fielding Ashby, discussed elsewhere in this book. John and Betsy had four children:

- Lewis, 1818–1869
- Rebecca Hess, 1820–1903
- Matilda Elizabeth Ashby, 1821–1903
- Fielding, 1824–1900. Emma Jo's second great-grandfather

---

[141] *Dear Brother: Letters of William Clark to Johnathan Clark*, James J. Holmberg, Yale University Press, New Haven and London. A compilation of letters written by William Clark discussing his brother's life and financial problems.

All four children settled in Monroe County, Missouri, and are buried in the Pleasant Hill Cemetery there with well-marked graves.

According to family legend, John Jr. left Shelby County headed for Monroe County, Missouri, with a large sum of money in his possession for the purpose of buying land there. He made it to the Mississippi River and was never heard from again. We are unsure of the date, except of it being before 1840. We find his wife Betsy in Shelby County, Kentucky, living with her sister as a neighbor to her father Fielding Ashby for the 1840 census. She died there in 1855 and is buried in the Ashby family cemetery. Fielding Murphy, probably named after Fielding Ashby, is Emma Jo's great-grandfather. We have a photo of him at his Missouri home below in figure 4-6.

Figure 4-6 Fielding Murphy family with Fielding seated in front. Taken between 1792 and 1800 in Monroe County, Missouri. The photo is in possession of the Scott and Raines families.

## Ensign Henrich "Henry" Myers

Born: 1755, Fayette County, Virginia, now Westmoreland County, Pennsylvania
Died: 1824, Mount Sterling, Montgomery County, Kentucky
Burial: Myers Cemetery in Jeffersonville, Montgomery County, Kentucky
Service: Monongahela Regiment of the Virginia Militia
Rank: Ensign
Service Dates: 1781–1782
Wife: Hannah Miller (1756–1836)

Lineage: Daughter Barbary married George Allen, their daughter Melinda married Joseph Morris Crooks, and their daughter Fannie Braden was the wife of DeMarquis Scott (Emma Jo's great-grandfather)
DAR: A083809
SAR: No

Henrich "Henry" is Emma Jo's fourth great-grandfather, and his parents were Johan Ulrich Myers (1727–1777) and Hannah Frick (1725–1799), who immigrated from Wurttemberg, Germany, to Philadelphia, Pennsylvania, in 1752 prior to the birth of Henry in 1756. They took the Oath of Allegiance to the Pennsylvania Colony after their arrival on 8 November 1752.[142] The Myers family soon moved to German Township, Fayette County, Pennsylvania, and began farming. Fayette County was disputed by both Virginia and Pennsylvania until the dispute was later settled by the Continental Congress. The township was referred to as German Township for the simple reason that there were many German settlers in the area.[143] Henry served in the Revolutionary War in a local regiment and is listed in the 1786 septennial census for Fayette County. He remained in that area until they moved to Montgomery County, Kentucky, around 1800. He is listed in the Montgomery County tax list in August 1800. There were at least three siblings of Henry that moved to Kentucky with their spouses at about the same time that year. His father Ulrich died earlier in 1777, and his Pennsylvania land was divided between his wife Hannah and the four children and spouses. The children of Ulrich and Hannah were William, Henry, Mary, and Hannah. Henry purchased land in Montgomery County after arrival there in 1800.

Fayette County, Pennsylvania, was a border county with West Virginia and Maryland. During the Revolutionary War, Virginia claimed much of the land west of the mountains, including what is now parts of West Virginia, Pennsylvania, and Ohio. This area was disputed until the federal government settled the dispute in favor of Pennsylvania and Westmoreland County. Fayette County was formed from Westmoreland County in 1783, so the county did not actually exist during the war; however, I found several references to the county dating prior to 1783. Fayette County was the center of the Whiskey Rebellion in 1793 that was quelled by then President George Washington. You will see more of that incident below and later in the book.

Henry joined the Monongahela Regiment of the Virginia Militia as an ensign in 1781 for a campaign to quell Indian disturbances brought on by the British. Colonel Thomas Gaddis, his regimental commander, had a long history in this region, first during the French and Indian War and later during the Revolution. In 1776, he was appointed as captain of the Monongahela Militia and was quickly promoted to lieutenant colonel and then colonel. Gaddis was aware that a substantial number of settlers in the region had taken an Oath of Allegiance to the United Kingdom and that some were planning to attack the arsenal at Redstone, Pennsylvania. He stationed additional troops at that arsenal and was successful in its defense.

---

[142] *Names of Foreigners Who Took the Oath of Allegiance to the Province and State of Pennsylvania, 1727–1775*. Pennsylvania Archives, Volume XVII, Second Series, Harrisburg, Pennsylvania. Reprinted for Clearfield Company, Inc. by Genealogical Publishing Company, Inc., Baltimore, Maryland, 1996. Page 374 lists Urlich Myers as taking the Oath of Allegiance on 8 November 1752 after arriving on the ship *Snow Louisa* from Rotterdam after a stop in England. Ulrich was the father of Henry.
[143] *History of Fayette County, Pennsylvania: with Biographical Sketches of Many of Its Pioneers and Prominent Men*, edited by Franklin Ellis, pp. 591–592.

In hope of putting an end to Indian attacks on American settlers, Gaddis and his regiment took part in the ill-fated Sandusky Expedition along the Sandusky River in 1782. They began recruiting troops in 1781, when Henry enlisted. I have a copy of some of his National Archives military records that support this enlistment, as well as the registry of Virginians in the Revolutionary War.[144] As with some other Pennsylvanians serving in the Revolution, this regiment was a Virginia Militia unit operating in a portion of the colony being claimed by Virginia.

Word of this expedition reached the Indians and British well prior to their arrival, and the regiment was forced to retreat. This was a vicious and bloody battle lasting several days as they retreated. About seventy men and officers were captured and killed.[145] Henry Myers was certainly part of this expedition, as his enlistment papers explain this as the purpose of this enlistment. Henry did not claim a pension for his service, as he died in 1824 before pensions were available to militia soldiers. Think about the complexity of such a claim, had it been made. A Kentucky resident previously living in Pennsylvania fighting in a Virginia Militia regiment in the Ohio territory. His military records exist, and such a claim would likely have been approved, as Colonel Gaddis lived in the region for many years following the war and would certainly have remembered an officer of his regiment.

Colonel Gaddis is also known for his activities during the Whiskey Rebellion. He was the leader of the "Whiskey Boys," a group that was enraged that Congress had imposed a tax in 1791 to pay its debts for the Revolutionary War. In 1794, the Gaddis home was the site of a "liberty pole" raising, which was a public protest that was illegal, and he was accused of a misdemeanor by the governor. He was the famous Revolutionary War officer that attracted the nation's attention about the tax and its implications. He was pardoned by the president, and the tax was repealed in 1800. George Washington led the young U.S. Army to Pennsylvania to quell the riots and defend the new Constitution. Colonel Gaddis was quick to recognize that President Washington was not to be trifled with and quickly subsided in his activities. You will see another story involving that liberty pole later in this book.

Henry and his family moved to Montgomery County, Kentucky, in 1800, as we find him on the tax rolls there in August of that year. Sons Henry Jr., Daniel, and Lewis also bought land in Montgomery County and lived on adjacent land. I could not find evidence of a Kentucky land grant for Henry, but it is likely that is what brought him there, as many of the early settlers in Montgomery County had received land grants for their Revolutionary War service. Patriots discussed earlier in this book received such grants in Floyd County, but changes in county boundaries resulted in Floyd County being formed from part of Montgomery County.

Henry died in Mount Sterling Township of Montgomery County, Kentucky, in 1824 and is buried in the Myers Cemetery there. I was not able to determine the exact location of the cemetery and could not find records of a government headstone; however, I have a photo of the headstone for him and his wife Hannah.

---

[144] *Historical Register of Virginians in the Revolution: Soldiers, Sailors, Marines.* Edited by John H. Gwathmey, Richmond, Virginia, 1938, p. 576.

[145] *An Historical Account of the Expedition against Sandusky under Colonel William Crawford in 1782,* Consul Willshire Butterfield, Clark and Company, 1873. Gives a good account of the Monongahela Regiment.

I believe that Henry and Hannah had thirteen children. I questioned the fact that Hannah, born around 1756, was still having children as late as 1800 at over forty years of age, particularly Aaron, born in 1796, and Ruth in 1850, but they are all children of Henry and Hannah, as they are all named in his will and associated 1826 probate documents.[146]

- Elizabeth Rachel Jenkins, 1774–1837
- Hannah Kirk, 1777–1853
- Daniel, 1778–1826
- George, 1780–Unknown death date
- Johnathan, 1782–1859
- Lewis, 1782–1823
- Barbary, 1784–1855. Married George Allen, and they are Emma Jo's third great-grandparents.
- Henry Jr., 1785–1828
- Solomon, 1788–1870
- Francis "Frank," 1789–1888
- Rebecca Overturf, 1790–1833
- Aaron, 1796–1870
- Ruth, 1800–1850

We know that Barbary was the daughter of Henry Myers from his will and the 1850 census from Montgomery County, Kentucky, as well as a deed book that recorded his land transfers after his death, which also gave the name of Barbary's husband, George Allen.[147]

I do not have the marriage records of George and Barbary. They were likely married in Montgomery County, but that is speculation. I must mention that other researchers have assumed she married another man as she is shown as living with the family of Austin Johnson in Bath County in the 1850 census. Austin Johnson was her son-in-law, not her husband. Her husband died in 1839 in Hancock County, Illinois, and was buried there, and that seems to cast doubt on his marriage to Barbary, who was still in Kentucky. In fact, he was probably visiting their son William in Hancock County at the time of his death. William unfortunately died at the age of thirty-one only a month after George, and I have a bill of sale with George paying a $7 down payment for two coffins. The balance of $13 for this bill was later charged to George's estate in Kentucky. We can speculate that George was visiting his ill son when he also became ill. They are both buried in the Cozad Cemetery in Hancock County.

There has been confusion as to Barbary's husband. Other researchers have attributed her marriage to Samuel Allen of Henry County, Virginia, who later moved to Floyd County, Kentucky. The Virginia Samuel Allen married Sarah Prather and later moved to Floyd County adjoining Montgomery County in Kentucky. I was one of those researchers who recorded the Samuel Allen/Barbary Myers relationship for a few years until I came to realize that these two men had different wives who outlived them. The Henry Myers probate records clearly establish that George

---

[146] The Deed Book 13 of Montgomery County, Kentucky, dated 25 March 1826. Pages 1–5 show the children of Henry, including Barbary and her husband George Allen.
[147] Ibid.

married Barbary, who was living in Kentucky while Samuel Allen was still living in Henry County, Virginia, married to a lady with the last name of Prather. Samuel remained in Virginia until he served in the Virginia Militia for the War of 1812. George served as a lieutenant in the Kentucky Seventh Militia Regiment during that war.

George's proposed father, John Allen (1744–1804), was a Patriot who served in the New Hampshire Militia during the Revolutionary War and later moved to Montgomery County, Kentucky. I believe George was born in Montgomery County, but his relationship to his father is unproven. Consequently, I am unable to tell the Patriot John Allen story in this book.

We later see George and Melinda living in Bath County, Kentucky, for the 1830 census, where he had received a 214-acre land grant for his service. Did they move from Montgomery County? Probably not, as Bath County was formed from a part of Montgomery County in 1811. I am uncertain if they moved or if the county reorganization changed their reported residence.

Barbary and George's daughter Melinda (1818–1880) was born in Bath County, and we see a female of the correct age group listed in George's household in the 1830 census in Bath County. Melinda married Joseph Morris Crooks (1814–1866) in Morgan County, Illinois, on 7 June 1837, and I have those records. Joseph and Melinda lived in Bath County until we find them in Monroe County, Missouri, in 1860 for that census. Joseph died in Monroe County in 1866.

Their daughter Fannie Braden Crooks (1855–1911) is shown in the 1860 census at the age of five living with her mother Melinda as head of the household in Monroe County. Her father is shown in that census on neighboring property. Fannie Braden married DeMarcus Scott, Emma Jo's great-grandfather of Monroe County, Missouri.

Joseph Morris Crooks has been the subject of an extensive research project for another book of mine, and I believe his father was killed in the War of 1812 and that both his grandfather and great-grandfather were Revolutionary War Patriots. I have been unable to prove the father-son relationship with Joseph and his father, James Crooks IV, therefore they are not included in this book with their Patriot stories.

I have the marriage records for Fannie Braden and DeMarcus Scott and both their death records. They are buried beside each other in the Pleasant Hill Cemetery in Monroe County, Missouri. Her grave has a stone, and his does not.

### The Roberts Family

The following three Patriot biographies tell the story of the Roberts family and their relationship to my family line. They were Sergeant Joseph Roberts, his father Benjamin Roberts, and Joseph's father-in-law, Thomas Triplett. I will begin with the story of Joseph and trace his lineage forward to my grandmother Blanche Perrigo/Adams, followed by his father Benjamin's story and then the story of Thomas Triplett (my fifth great-grandfather), whose daughter married Sergeant Joseph Roberts.

**Sergeant Joseph Roberts**
Born: 17 August 1740, Culpeper County, Virginia
Died: August 1823, Shelby County, Kentucky
Burial: Unknown location
Service: The Illinois Brigade under General George Rogers Clark
Rank: Sergeant
Service Dates: 1777–1782
Wife: Francis Triplett (1768–1849)
Lineage: Son Joseph Thomas Roberts Jr., his son John Samuel Roberts, his daughter Stella Catherine Roberts married Andrew Jackson Perrigo, their daughter Blanche Francis Perrigo/Adams (my grandmother)
DAR: A096964
SAR: P-280040

Joseph is the grandfather of John Samuel Roberts, my second great-grandfather. John Samuel fought for the Union side in the Civil War and settled in Shelby County, Missouri, later in his life. His wife was Lucinda Catherine Pruitt, who he married in Indiana prior to the Civil war. Our family has known of John Samuel for years, and I have visited his grave several times in Shelby County, Missouri, but the identity of his father has been elusive. John Samuel moved to Marion County, Indiana, with his mother and siblings apparently after his father's death in 1860. The 1860 census in Indiana indicated his birth state as Kentucky. That seemed to be an easy trail to explore, but there were just too many Roberts surnames, most in Shelby County, so it took some detective work. I eventually stumbled onto his brother Dudley's death certificate, and it revealed his father's name. I had found Dudley on an Indiana 1860 census with his mother and brother John Samuel, so I had the right guy.

John Samuel's father was Joseph Thomas Roberts Jr. (1809–1860) of Shelby County, Kentucky, who had been a farmer and slaveholder in that county. It was not difficult to trace his heritage to Culpeper County, Virginia, with three Patriots to be discussed. The father of Joseph Thomas Jr. was Sergeant Thomas Roberts, with his father being Benjamin Roberts Sr. The father of Sergeant Thomas's wife, Thomas Triplett was also discovered and is presented below.

We know that Joseph Thomas Jr. was the son of Sergeant Thomas Roberts for several reasons. Firstly, Sergeant Roberts was located in Shelby County, Kentucky, by 1800, as he was shown on the state tax list in August of that year. Secondly, the wills and probate records of both Sergeant Joseph and his wife Ann Triplett account for Joseph Thomas Jr. in Shelby County. Lastly, I believe their Kentucky land holdings adjoined.

Joseph enlisted in the Illinois Brigade of the Northwest Territory shortly after its formation for the duration of the war.[148] Illinois was not yet a state, or even a recognized territory. It was, however, of strategic importance to the colonies, especially Virginia. It was a source of Indian unrest brought on by the French and then English presence there. Hence the need for a Virginia Line

---

[148] "A Roster of Revolutionary Ancestors of the Indiana Daughters of the American Revolution," vol. I. Commentaries of the United States of America bicentennial, 4 July 1976. Evansworth, Indiana. Page 542 lists both Benjamin and Joseph Roberts, their families, and their service during the Revolution.

unit, controlled by the governor. This was not a Continental Line unit. *Revolutionary Soldiers in Kentucky* also contains unit rosters that list both Joseph and his brother Benjamin Jr.[149]

Joseph was promoted to sergeant on 10 August 1779 and was a member of Captain Robert Todd's Company of that brigade. I have Joseph's National Archives military records. His military service is recognized by both the DAR and SAR. His older brother Benjamin Jr. was a captain in that brigade. His wife was granted a pension for his service on 10 December 1840. His pension number was 5945.[150] I also found Shelby County court records attesting that Joseph and Benjamin had a brother named William. He served as an ensign in this regiment but soon died intestate without heirs, leaving his Kentucky land to his brothers. I have, however, been unable to find further genealogy records for William.

The Illinois campaign, also known as Clark's Northwestern campaign (1778–1779), was a series of events in which a small force of Virginia Line soldiers led by Clark seized control of several British posts in the Illinois Territory. Some researchers refer to this unit as a regiment, but it was more than that, reflected by the fact that it was commanded by a general rather than a colonel. He had several lieutenant colonels under his command and at least eight company-sized units. We should note that this brigade was not a Continental Line unit under the command of General Washington, but a Virginia Line unit under the command of Governor Patrick Henry. While Washington was certainly aware of this campaign, I doubt if he played any role in its operations. This is a classic example of a military operation crossing the boundaries from tactical local protection to regional operational policy to strategic importance and great long-range magnitude.

The need for this campaign is debated now and has been since the war. Many Virginia researchers hold that the war was won in Virginia and few other campaigns in other locations really made a difference. One fact casts doubt on that notion: the British ceded the northwest territories to the colonies in the 1783 treaty because Clark had kicked their behinds and they lost control of that region. Without that provision, that territory would likely have remained owned and controlled by the British following the war. It is mere speculation whether the War of 1812 would have resolved that dispute. Also, the disruptions caused by the campaign in that region forced the British to focus more attention in that area instead of in the eastern colonies, especially Virginia. Most importantly, I believe this campaign focused colonial attention on migration across the mountains into the Northwest Territory many years earlier than might have normally happened. The Ashby chapter, "Nothing There but Indians and Ashbys," later in this book discusses that contention. I believe this campaign hastened the westward expansion of settlers by years.

The story of the capture of Vincennes, of the then Illinois territory, in February 1779 best describes the type of actions and conditions that confronted this small, isolated unit. The unit involved in this campaign consisted of maybe 170 volunteers from Virginia, several Kentucky hunters, and some Kentucky volunteers. They had to be careful to leave enough Kentucky volunteers at home to protect their families from Indian attack as they moved into Illinois. This was

---

[149] *Revolutionary Soldiers in Kentucky*, compiled by Anderson Chenault Quisenberry from various sources. Reprinted by Southern Book Company, Baltimore, Maryland, 1959. Republished by Genealogical Publishing Company, Baltimore, Maryland, 1998. Page 20 shows Joseph Roberts as a private. He was later promoted to sergeant. Page 18 shows his brother Benjamin Jr. as a sergeant. He was later promoted to captain.
[150] *Revolutionary Soldiers in Kentucky*, compiled by Anderson Chenault Quisenberry from various sources. Reprinted from *Yearbook*, Kentucky Society of the Sons of the American Revolution. Louisville, 1896. Pages 17 lists Benjamin, the brother of Joseph, and page 39 lists Joseph as a member of the regiment.

surely a small force for the task at hand, which was to capture Vincennes from British Colonel Hamilton, who was hated by the Americans for paying the Indians to deliver American scalps. Clark and his men traveled across southern Illinois in freezing weather and high water. They waded in water nearly the entire distance due to flooding and built boats to cross rivers such as the Wabash. Sometimes they waded in cold water chest-deep. They took Vincennes by surprise on 25 February, and Hamilton was taken as a prisoner to Williamsburg. This territory was after this point referred to as the Northwest Territory. Modern historians often point out that Clark never conquered that territory, and that at best, he helped the French and Indian inhabitants of the territory remove themselves from the control of the British.

The operation was not well funded, and most of those who invested their money in the military operations were never to be repaid, including George Rogers Clark, who spent most of his remaining life repaying those debts.[151] Congress refused to honor his claims. This fact is discussed elsewhere in this book. General Clark was the brother of William Clark, who gained fame on the Lewis and Clark expedition in 1804–1806. Perhaps the justification for Congress not reimbursing Clark was that this was a state line unit, not a Continental Line organization. It was a Virginia debt. I used the following sources to gather information about this campaign:

- George Rogers Clark Memoir. Published under various titles including *Colonel George Rogers Clark's Sketch of his Campaign in the Illinois in 1778-1779*, New York: Arno, 1971.

- *George Rogers Clark Papers,* 2 Volumes, James Alton, ed. Originally published 1912–1926. Reprinted New York: AMS Press, 1972.

- *Dear Brother: Letters of William Clark to Johnathan Clark*, James J. Holmberg, Yale University Press, New Haven and London. A compilation of letters written by William Clark discussing his brother's life and financial problems.

After the Revolution, Joseph returned to Culpeper County and purchased 471 acres from his brother John of Mountain Run and received a 411-acre land grant there.[152] He moved to Shelby County, Kentucky, well prior to 1800. In fact, records for Louisville, Kentucky, show Benjamin Roberts Jr., Joseph Roberts, and William Toole drawing for town lots on 24 April 1779. The drawing was primarily a speculation, with winners selling their lots to others. Jonathan and Squire Boone also participated in that drawing. In May 1780, many of the same individuals petitioned the Legislature of Virginia to establish Louisville as a town in the county of Kentucky to get state protection from the Indians.[153] It is likely that he was still in the military when he participated in that drawing, and that proceeds from selling those lots helped finance his farm in Culpeper County, but that is speculation. Kentucky was a county of the Virginia colony during the war.

---

[151] *Dear Brother: Letters of William Clark to Johnathan Clark*, James J. Holmberg, Yale University Press, New Haven and London. A compilation of letters written by William Clark discussing his brother's life and financial problems. Contains a good firsthand account of the war compiled by William Clark, the brother of John Rogers Clark, well after the end of the Revolution.
[152] *Virginia Northern Neck Land Grants*, Volume III, Book U: 1775–1800, Gertrude E. Gray, Genealogy Publishing Company, 1993, Baltimore, Maryland. Page 122 shows Joseph Roberts received a 411-acre land grant on 21 July 1892 in Culpeper County following the war.
[153] *The Centenary of Louisville*, Reuben T. Durrett, 1893, John P. Morton and Company, Louisville, Kentucky. Pages 149–144 and pages 149–151 give the account of the drawing for land and subsequent petition to the Colony of Virginia for protection.

Joseph received three land grants in Shelby County, Kentucky, for his service. They were:

- 2 November 1796: 1,000 acres on the Jepthea Water Course
- 20 August 1798: 300 acres on the Jesse Water Course
- 20 August 1798: 800 acres on the Jesse Water Course

I am not certain when Joseph and his family moved to Shelby County, but the 1800 census and Shelby County tax records record his family and slaves living there. The slave count (probably inherited slaves) was fourteen in the 1800 census and fifteen in the 1810 census. He died in 1823, and his wife drew a pension based on his service from her eligibility in 1835 until her death in 1848. Their names are on the Kentucky Widows Pension Report of 1835.

Joseph and Francis Triplett had nine children:

- George, 1786–1879
- William, 1787–1846
- Thomas, 1789–Unknown death date
- Henry, 1791–1823
- Elizabeth, 1792–1868
- Hannah Clifton, 1795–1860
- Mary Magdalena (Polly) Gibson, 1796–1871
- Mildred O'Bannon, 1798–1856
- Joseph Thomas Jr., 1800–1860. He was the father of John Samuel, my second great-grandfather.

His son Joseph Thomas Jr. was born on 28 December 1800 in Shelby County, Kentucky. He was designated as the executor of his father's 20 October 1823 will. His brothers William and Henry signed that probate inventory order. Willis Roberts also signed that order, but I am not sure of his relationship to the family.

Joseph Thomas Jr. married Mary Davis (1802–1860) on 20 December 1825 in Shelby County. I have those records. They possibly had six children:

- S. Roberts, 1835–Unknown death date. Female and unproven descendant.
- Richard, 1839–Unknown death date. Unproven descendant.
- Dudley, 1841–1901. Moved with his mother, brother John Samuel, and sister Mary E. to Marion County, Indiana. They are on the 1860 census there. His 1901 death certificate reflects his father's name as Joseph Roberts and that he was born in Kentucky.
- E. Roberts, 1844–Unknown death date. Female and unproven descendant.
- John Samuel, 1845–1884. My second great-grandfather.
- Mary E., 1847–1940. Moved to Marion County, Indiana, with her mother and two brothers by 1860. She married (name unknown) and died in Kentucky as a widow.

His son John Samuel is shown on the Shelby County, Kentucky, 1850 census in the household of J. Roberts and M. Roberts with five siblings, as shown above. I have confirmed that Dudley, John Samuel, and Mary E. later moved to Marion County, Indiana, with their mother Mary by 1860 (1860 census). John Samuel and brother Dudley later served in the Civil War in K Company, Fifty-Second Indiana Infantry Regiment, for the Union. Dudley later received a pension for injuries received during the war.

John Samuel married Lucinda Catherine Pruitt of Marion County on 14 September 1867 in Marion County, Indiana, and I have those records. Their daughter Stella Catherine was born in Marion County on 26 May 1879. John Samuel and his family had moved to near Bethel, Shelby County, Missouri, by 7 June 1884, where he died of typhoid. He and Lucinda are buried in the Shiloh Cemetery north of Bethel. His grave is marked with a military stone, and no stone for her can be found, but there is an unmarked grave site beside his.

Their daughter Stella Catherine (1879–1948) married Andrew Jackson Perrigo (1896–1967) on 25 November 1896 in Knox City, Knox County, Missouri. I have those records. They had nine children, of which their oldest, Blanche Francis (1897–1996), was my grandmother. I have her death records listing her father. Their oldest daughter was Ruby Nadine, my mother.

I will note that the Perrigo line has been the subject of a book of mine that traces that line back to England and documents Revolutionary War Patriots in New England.[154] A later chapter in this book will cover the story of a few of the Perrigo Patriots from which I am descended.


**Benjamin Roberts Sr.**
Born: 1705
Died: 14 February 1782
Burial: Unknown location
Service: None, but a member of the Culpeper County, Virginia, Committee of Safety and therefore recognized by the DAR and SAR for patriotic service
Rank: None
Service Dates: None
Wife: Anne Delaney
Lineage: Son Patriot Sergeant Joseph Roberts, Son Joseph Thomas Roberts Jr., son John Samuel Roberts, daughter Stella Catherine Roberts Perrigo, daughter Blanche Francis Perrigo Adams (my grandmother)
DAR: A096896
SAR: P279890

Benjamin Roberts Sr. was the father of Patriots Captain Benjamin Roberts Jr. and Sergeant Joseph Roberts and is my fifth great-grandfather of the Adams/Perrigo line.[155] This is an old Virginia line, and the given names Benjamin and Joseph are quite common. It was important to get it right, as even the DAR has faced challenges in keeping it straight. There were possibly three

---

[154] *The Problem of the Perrigo Patriots of Pownal*, Virgil Raines, Compass Flower Press, Columbia, Missouri, 2024
[155] *North American Family Histories 1500–2000*. Lineage Book for the Daughters of the American Revolution. Volume 101. Page 256 establishes that Benjamin married Anne Dulaney and that his son was Captain Benjamin Roberts.

Virginia Benjamin Roberts of that era, and all except this one fought for the colony in the military. We confirmed that this Benjamin was a very active member of the Church of England in Virginia and was married to Anne Delaney by that church. None of the others were married by that church.

He was born in Spotsylvania County to John Roberts (1658–1724) and Elizabeth Trammell (1682–1730).[156] He later moved to Culpeper County and spent the remainder of his life there. He was an active community leader in St. Mark's parish of the county[157] and served as vestryman and church warden of their chapter of the Church of England. Prior to the war, the members had become quite dissatisfied with the English clergy that had been provided, and he became a lay minister by reading church services once the clergy was removed. He sponsored a protest to the governor over the Stamp Act tax, and he was also one of twelve justices of the peace for Culpeper County. Most important, he is recognized by the DAR for Patriot status for his service on the Culpeper Committee of Safety.[158]

I believe that it is likely that Benjamin served as a captain in the Culpeper militia during the French and Indian War under the command of Colonel Thomas Slaughter, as did Patriot Francis Triplett. Some researchers attribute that rank to him, but I could not prove his service or rank. The story referenced below concerning his resigning his rank in 1765 seems to support this claim.

The original church building constructed in 1763 no longer stands and was replaced in 1773. It is now the Little Fork Church and is the oldest remaining colonial church building in the United States.[159] Thomas would have attended services in both buildings. As a matter of interest, the one entry and exit door required members to pass the pulpit before entering or leaving. That might tend to discourage late arrivals and early departures. Maybe Benjamin had something to do with that arrangement. I have a modern photo of that church. I also have an unpublished story saying that Benjamin served as a vestryman and warden of the church. It also maintains that he signed a petition to the governor in 1765 protesting the Stamp Act. He also resigned his commission as a captain in that protest.[160] This resignation seems to support the possibility of military service during the French and Indian War.

I found five children of Benjamin and Ann Delaney who were named in his will of 14 February 1782:

- Mary DeLaney, 1725–1799
- Anne Fields, 1727–1782
- Jemima Kirtley, 1730–1818
- Benjamin Jr., 1738–1781. A Revolutionary War Patriot

---

[156] Spotsylvania County Records 1721–1800, Book A: 1722–1749 Wills. Page 1 shows that his father John left Benjamin land adjoining Roger Abbot's in 1724.

[157] Culpeper County tax list for 1783 shows he was a citizen of St. Mark's Parish.

[158] *Lineage Book: National Society of the Daughters of the American Revolution*, Vol C. Press of Judd and Detweiler Inc., 1928, Washington, D.C. Page 76 establishes that Benjamin Roberts was a justice of the peace and a member of the Committee of Public Safety for Culpeper County, Virginia.

[159] *Virginia's Colonial Churches: An Architectural Guide*. Rawlings, James S., Garrett and Massie, 1963, Richmond, Virginia, pp. 139–140.

[160] Unpublished story by Wendy Guion.

- Joseph, 1740–1823. My fourth great-grandfather. He was named as executor in his father's will.

His father's will lists sons, grandsons, and their wives. Benjamin left nearly a thousand acres of Virginia farmland to sons Benjamin Jr. and Joseph. He also left nearly a dozen slaves to each son and several to his daughter Jemima. We see son Joseph as a slaveholder later in Shelby County, Kentucky.

Both the DAR and SAR support the names of his children, with multiple memberships based on that assumption, but both organizations state that is not proof of lineage. I will assume those prospective members did not have access to his will, which I have discovered. Joseph's business dealing with sons Benjamin Jr. and John of Culpeper County seems to support this relationship, and military service with Benjamin Jr. strengthens this claim. Study of both county and church records in Culpeper County seems to support there was not another Roberts line in that county during the Revolution. Both Benjamin and Joseph moved to Shelby County, Kentucky, at about the same time, and I found business dealings between them in that county. Joseph also married Anne Triplett, daughter of Thomas Triplett of Culpeper County. They were members of the same church. The Triplett story follows.

### Thomas Triplett

Born: 25 November 1727, King George County, Virginia
Died: April 1778, Cumberland County, Virginia
Burial: Cumberland County, location unknown
Service: Service on the Culpeper County Committee of Safety. The DAR has recognized his public service and awarded him Patriot status.
Rank: None
Service Dates: None
Wife: Hannah Claiborne (1729–1781)
Lineage: Daughter Francis married Patriot Sergeant Joseph Roberts, whose story and lineage are shown above.
DAR: A1166629. See discussion below.
SAR: No

Thomas Triplett was son of William Triplett II and Elizabeth Hedgeman of Culpeper County, Virginia. The Triplett family was a large and influential family of Colonial Virginia with more than fourteen family members credited with Revolutionary War service. The given name of Thomas appears often in Virginia Revolutionary War history, and research of this family can be fraught with confusion and errors. One Thomas Triplett was a member of the Committee of Safety for Fauquier County, Virginia, and was a close friend of George Washington. This Thomas was later invited by Martha Washington to George's funeral service years later. He served under Washington during the French and Indian War and was recommended by Washington to the county Committee of Safety. Another Thomas Triplett served as a captain during the Revolution, and he settled in Shelby County, Kentucky, as did some of the Virginia Roberts family discussed earlier in this book. We found as least two Triplett females from Virginia receiving credit for patriotic service. The Triplett family was obviously deeply committed to the Revolution, but I needed to sort them out.

I isolated this Thomas Triplett from other Virginia namesakes and centered research on Culpeper County. This Thomas served as a vestryman at the same Saint Marks' parish church as did his father, William.[161] Benjamin Roberts Sr., father of Thomas Roberts, also served in that capacity in that church. Thomas Triplett's daughter Francis married Sergeant Joseph Roberts.

Thomas was not a young man at the time of the Revolution, so he did not serve in the military then, but he served as an ensign during the French and Indian War under Colonel Thomas Slaughter of the Culpeper Militia.[162] Two of his sons served in the Revolution—George, and Peter Hedgeman Triplett.

Research of this family was challenging due to the number of Triplett family members serving in the war under similar given names. As discussed above, there were at least three Thomases of this generation in Virginia serving in one official capacity or another. The DAR has granted Patriot status to this Thomas Triplett based on the service of another Thomas Triplett. They have recognized the error in approval of this application and frozen the family line until his service is proven. I was nearing a roadblock in research until discovery of the *William and Mary Quarterly* volume on genealogies of Virginia families noted above, where I found discussion of this Thomas and his family. This journal proved that Francis was his daughter and that he lived and owned land in Culpeper County.

Thomas's father, William Triplett II, might have been a colorful man, as he was a large land-owner, was involved in several lawsuits, and was recognized as a "Gentleman" in those court cases. He left land to his children in Culpeper County.[163] I believe that William II also served in the French and Indian War.

Thomas and Hannah had five children:

- George, 1752–1833. Served in the Revolution as a captain.
- Peter Hedgeman, 1755–1851. Served in the Revolution. Note that Peter's middle name is his mother's maiden name.
- Amelia, 1756–Unknown death date
- Thomas, 1763–1833. Became a lawyer and later helped Patriots file claims for pension in Kentucky.
- Francis, 1756–1848. Married Patriot Sergeant Joseph Roberts, my fourth great-grandfather.[164]

---

[161] "Children of William Triplett/Elizabeth Hedgeman," *William and Mary Quarterly*, Volume V, Thompson-Yates. Page 207 lists sons of William and Elizabeth as John, Thomas, Nathaniel (dead by 1753), James, and William.

[162] Ibid. Page 213 lists Francis as the daughter of Thomas Triplett. It also establishes that Thomas served as an ensign in Colonel Slaughter's Regiment in the French and Indian War in 1756.

[163] Culpeper County Deed Book A, p. 258. This deed, dated 19 July 1753, records a deed from William Triplett, Gentleman, to sons John, Thomas, and Nathaniel (dead by then). William had removed from Culpeper County to Prince William County. It referenced William's will dated 10 May 1748.

[164] Culpeper County Deed Book A, p. 258. This deed, dated 19 July 1753, records a deed from William Triplett, Gentleman, to sons John, Thomas, and Nathaniel (dead by then). William had removed from Culpeper County to Prince William County. It referenced William's will dated 10 May 1748.

In addition to the Deed Book reference above that establishes Francis as the daughter of Thomas, she is listed in her father's 1777 will.[165] I speculate that Francis's name was derived from her grandfather's middle name of Francis.

Thomas died in Cumberland County, Virginia, and is buried in an unknown location.

**Hugh Glenn Sr.**
Born: 1735, Lancaster County, Pennsylvania
Died: 7 December 1807, Paint Lick Creek, Madison County, Kentucky
Burial: Paint Lick Creek area in Madison County, Kentucky
Service: Continental Army, Eighth Pennsylvania Regiment
Rank: Private
Service Dates: 19 June 1779–1 January 1783
Wife: Elizabeth Martin
Lineage: Son Martin Glenn, his daughter Mary Ann Polly, wife of Grissom Lee, their daughter Emiline Jane, wife of Robert Fowler, their daughter Louvisa Fowler/Raines (my great-grandmother)
DAR: No
SAR: P-166990

Hugh was the son of Thomas Glenn (1700–1755) and Christina Wilson (1700–1765) of Lancaster County, Pennsylvania. Thomas was born in Londonderry, Ulster, Ireland, and married Christina in Philadelphia, Pennsylvania, on 12 January 1719 in the First Presbyterian Church. I found family claims of his royal connections in Ireland but did not research the line beyond his birth. Hugh is my fifth great-grandfather in my Grissom Lee, Robert Fowler, and Raines family line.

His father lived in Philadelphia and moved across the river to Chester County after his marriage to Christina Wilson in 1719. I have those marriage records. The family later moved further west to what was to become Lancaster County, later moving to Cumberland County. It appears Hugh and his siblings also moved at about the same time, and I believe Hugh's parents died in Cumberland County. I have lived in Cumberland County and can attest that the farmland is of top quality. It was probably worth the move from Chester County.

His pre-Revolution records in Pennsylvania at first appear to belong to more than one person with that name. I found tax records and an Oath of Allegiance from Chester County, land warrants from Lancaster County, and a 1790 census from Cumberland County. Were there multiple persons of that name, or did he merely move several times? While he may have moved one or more times, the correct answer is likely that the Pennsylvania county lines changed. Lancaster County was part of Chester County until 10 May 1729, when it was established as a separate county. Then, on 27 January 1750, Cumberland County was formed from parts of Lancaster County.[166] Official records are often slow to reflect these political boundary changes, hence the confusion. Chester County was originally established as part of the William Penn Charter of

---

[165] Culpeper County Will Book Volume A-B, 1749–1783, lists Francis as a daughter of Thomas Triplett.
[166] Counties of Pennsylvania. Pennsylvania State Archives. Archived from the original (index of 67 Pennsylvania county histories) on 6 March 2009. Retrieved on 4 October 2005.

1681 and consisted mainly of former German settlers who received grants to settle there. Hugh was of Scotch descent, and his wife Elizabeth Martin was probably of Swiss descent. Hugh was probably quite successful in that setting.

He received a 150-acre land warrant on 18 November 1772 in Lancaster County, Pennsylvania.[167] I also found a 250-acre land warrant (WS 3202) dated 26 March 1767. I was unable to determine if he made a claim for a land grant based on these warrants or if he sold the warrants. He is found listed in a state census of 1770 in Chester County owning fifty acres, two horses, and other livestock. Maybe he sold the warrants to get a farming start.

Hugh Glenn joined the Eighth Pennsylvania Regiment of the Continental Army on 19 June 1779 for the duration of the war. He would have been in his mid-forties with eight children and a wife, Elizabeth, at home. He was a landowner and farmer, so this was probably not a whimsical decision. It is also fact that Pennsylvania had a conscription law, and he would have been required to at least join a militia. As discussed above, Pennsylvania was tasked by the Continental Congress to raise 8 regiments. They were quite successful in this undertaking, raising more than 130 regiments. Most of these recruited regiments served as local home guard units providing security to towns and counties. Philadelphia was the nation's capital and presented special challenges for its security. Eight of these regiments were transferred to continental control, of which this regiment was one. Money was essentially non-existent for the common man at this time in our nation's history, so an enlistment bonus would have been an important motivator. Most of the Pennsylvania residents were first- or second-generation Americans with strong ties to European tradition, in which conscription was a fact of life. This is opposed to the Massachusetts or Virginia Colonies, where soldiers might be fourth- or fifth-generation citizens who enjoyed a strong independent streak. There was strong social pressure for young Pennsylvania men to defend their freedom. Hugh Glenn was not a young man, but the 113 2/3-dollar enlistment bonus might have been a factor in his decision. His five male sons were old enough to maintain the farm, but for whatever reason, Hugh Glenn went to war.

The Pennsylvania Eighth Continental Regiment, commanded by Colonel Daniel Broadhead IV for most of the war, provides a stark contrast in how the Revolutionary War was fought by Contnental units with regard to assigned missions. The regiment was transferred to federal control in November 1776, even though it had been in existence for several months and had fought some battles under the control of the colony. The unit was originally known as MacKay's Battalion. Soon after transfer to federal control it was reorganized as a regiment and moved to New Jersey; they fought several battles there with a noted lack of success. It was effective in losing battles early in the war, as was the entire Continental Army. In fact, their first commander (Lieutenant Colonel MacKay) and his second-in-command died of disease in New Jersey. After Colonel Broadhead assumed command in 1777, the unit soon returned to Pennsylvania, where it wintered at Valley Forge (although I do not believe Hugh was at Valley Forge). At the beginning of that winter, the unit had nearly 270 soldiers, with only 68 soldiers surviving the winter. Most were lost due to expired enlistments or illness. After the Valley Forge winter, the unit built its strength to eight companies of over one hundred men each. The unit participated in the 1778 battles of Bound Brook, Brandywine, Paola, and Germantown, and they suffered significant losses

---

[167] Pennsylvania Land Warrants, 1733–1952, Pennsylvania State Archives, Lancaster County, Harrisburg, Pennsylvania.

at Paola. Later that year, the regiment was assigned to the Western Department, a frontier mission with a ninth company added.

This new mission contrasted with earlier typical combat operations wherein large unit formations, frontal assaults, flank security, and classical tactics ruled the day. Frontier operations consisted of manning remote outposts and performing road construction. Basic survival skills were important, not to mention dealing wisely with the many powerful Indian tribes that inhabited western and northern Pennsylvania. General Washington respected Colonel Broadhead and quickly assigned him as the western frontier area commander. He was a skilled commander, but compared to his counterpart to the south, General George Rogers Clark, he was an amateur, and his shortcomings played a significant role in the future of this unit and its soldiers.

General George Rogers Clark of the Illinois Brigade (this was a Virginia Line Brigade) had the benefit of recruiting mountain men from Virginia and North Carolina who only knew life in the wilds and were adept at knowing which Indians to trust and which to avoid. They made their own clothing, and game was plentiful. Logistics was not a weakness of this unit. They flourished as soldiers and made a difference in the Illinois, Indiana, and Ohio territories in which they fought. The Indian tribes and British army went out of their way to avoid General Clark. General Clark's younger brother William grew up around his brother, admired him, and served in the army following the Revolution in the western frontier, where he became a noted explorer and woodsman. It was these skills that later attracted Meriwether Lewis to recruit him for the Lewis and Clark expedition in 1802.

Colonel Broadhead's focus was that of equipping his unit, and that is a critical skill a regimental commander must develop. The continental forces did not normally look to their home colony for support, but to the Continental Congress, and replacement uniforms and weapons were supplied when the commander requested these supplies. Pay was monthly and depended on monthly muster roll calls that were required. My review of Colonel Broadhead's requests revealed that he was insistent that his soldiers be clothed and not naked. Pennsylvania is a cold state, and my personal experience there revealed ten months of winter with two months of poor skiing and large mosquitos. His soldiers suffered due to lack of bedding and clothing. Their mission involved road building and construction of forts and outposts, which would take a toll on modern clothing, not to mention period military uniforms that were ill-suited for hard labor. His requests often went unfulfilled. In fact, he gained a reputation as a complainer with his fellow commanders. I believe that General Washington was quite familiar with the true nature of their mission, as he spent his early working years leading survey crews in a similar environment. General Washington eventually provided some relief to their clothing needs as the war progressed, but their pay and ability to operate in this hostile territory did not improve with new clothing.

I researched the 1779 Sullivan Expedition, in which the unit was involved in moving up the Allegheny River in Pennsylvania into upstate New York. This was a four-hundred-mile journey involving six hundred men, and they were to meet up with other federal forces belonging to General Sullivan at Cuylerville, New York. They never accomplished this mission, as they could not find Cuylervillle. They did not have a guide that knew the route, and they were essentially lost for three months. They were somewhat successful in avoiding the Indians but did accidentally stumble into an Indian camp, in which a few shots were fired. I should mention that Cuylerville,

New York, still exists with a population of 297 citizens, and I doubt if I could find it without an automobile and GPS. It is a few miles south of Rochester, New York. I believe that Hugh Glenn Jr. participated in this expedition shortly after his enlistment, as the unit had recently recruited in the county where he lived.

During research of National Archives records, I found few pay records for Hugh Glenn and the men of his regiment for 1778–1780. At that point, it was obvious they had not been paid. That problem manifested itself in January 1881 when several regiments mutinied. Jacob Painter's sixth regiment, discussed above, was one of those regiments. This problem came to General Washington's attention very quickly. Nearly all his Virginia regiments were guests of the British army in a Charleston, South Carolina, prison camp, and now there was unrest in his northern army. The general's normal response would probably have been a public hanging, but their grievances were real, and harsh punishment was not called for. The Eighth Regiment was located over one hundred miles from the mutiny, but they were guilty by association. Remember, Colonel Brodhead had a reputation as a complainer, and this reputation was well known. General Washington wisely paid those soldiers and then proceeded to disband the participating units and discharge every soldier with three or more years of service, except noncommissioned officers. Most of the discharged soldiers reenlisted in the new units and fought until the end of the war. I believe that Hugh Glenn continued until 1883, perhaps in the Second Pennsylvania Regiment. This would have been Jacob Painter's regiment also. Remember that the second regiment was a Chester County unit.

I found final payment records for Hugh Glenn dated 1 January 1783. This was for his service from 1 January 1781 to 1 January 1783. It was for $80, which included 6 percent interest for that amount due to the late payment. The final payment voucher (78123) was dated 30 October 1784. I found certificates filed by fellow soldiers upon his daughter's claim for pension in which they testified he served from 1778 until 1784, or five years. These sworn statements were filed in 1813 after his death, and their memories may not have been correct. I believe he served from June 1779 until January 1783, or 3½ years, but it is quite possible that he enlisted in MacKay's Battalion prior to 1779 and that the 1779 enlistment was a reenlistment into the newly formed regiment. He may well have served after January 1783, but I found no payments for that period.

It is also worth mentioning that pay for the western frontier soldiers was a common problem. George Rogers Clark had similar problems, and his solution was to pay his soldiers out of his own pocket, assuming the Continental Congress would reimburse him after the war. He borrowed much of that money and spent the remainder of his life repaying his debt, as the Continental Congress refused to reimburse him.

Hugh's commander, Colonel Daniel Broadhead IV, was so respected by General Washington that he called on the colonel to be a regimental commander during the Whiskey Rebellion of 1790. President Washington personally commanded the troops he sent to quell the rebellion. I have a prized painting on one of my walls of General Washington with Colonel Broadhead IV marching through Carlisle, Pennsylvania, as they proceeded to western Pennsylvania near Pittsburgh. Maybe Colonel Broadhead had taken geography lessons by that time and was more familiar with the state!

Hugh Glenn remained in Pennsylvania until after 1790. Federal census and state tax records support that contention. It appears that his youngest son, Hugh Jr., moved to Madison County prior to the family move, as there is a Hugh Glenn on the 1795 county tax records for that year. Hugh Jr. would have been about twenty-one years old at that time.

By 1800 he and his family were living in Madison County, Kentucky, where he is shown on tax records, and he lived at Paint Lick Creek until his death in 1807. His granddaughter Mary Ann Polly Glenn, daughter of his son Martin Glenn, met her husband Grissom R. Lee there, married in 1820, and moved to Pettis County, Missouri, in 1828. Grissom Lee's father, Richard Lee, was a neighbor and a Patriot discussed earlier in this book and was also buried at Paint Lick Creek. I had difficulty in locating that cemetery until I discovered it was later merged with the James Barnett Cemetery. I am not certain if Hugh is buried in the Barnett cemetery, but this is likely, as his neighbor Patriot Richard Lee is buried there.

I found records that Hugh Sr., in his later years, turned his Kentucky farming operations over to his youngest son, Hugh Jr. When Hugh Sr. passed away, his wife Elizabeth was still alive and inherited his estate. Probate records reflect a dower estate, meaning he had no will, thus leaving his farm to his wife. Hugh Jr. soon convinced his mother to transfer her land and other property to him. His siblings discovered that fact upon the death of Elizabeth one year later in 1808, and their only recourse was civil litigation.[168] It is likely that Hugh Jr. was required to sell the land, after which he moved to Howard County, and Randolph County, Missouri, which was formed from parts of Howard County. Hugh Jr. was a slave owner of one slave, reflected on the 1810 census. I have read family accounts that stated that Hugh Sr. furnished the slaves for his son's farming operation, but I found no records supporting that claim.

After the death of Hugh Sr., his daughter Margaret, who had married and remained in Pennsylvania, filed for his pension in 1813. She claimed she was his sole surviving heir and that she was eligible for his pension authorized by Congress in 1811. Several local men who had served with Hugh attested to the fact that he had served and that she was his lawful daughter. That request was approved, and the pension file number is BLW 634-100. I have that file, and her claims as to his military service are consistent with his official records. It is interesting that Hugh's neighbor Richard Lee's children also fought over his estate, also at Paint Lick Creek. I do not believe Margaret shared the pension with her brothers and sisters who lived in Kentucky. It is interesting to note that Margaret was a party to the civil case brought against her brother Hugh Jr., so the family had remained in contact over the years. Hugh and Elizabeth had eight children, according to the court case involving his son Hugh Jr. and his siblings in 1808. They were:

- Ann Elizabeth Courtney, 1761–1856
- Margaret McCluskey, 1755–1815. Remained in Pennsylvania and filed for pension based on her father's service.
- Jean Flak, 1755–1855
- William, 1757–1830. William settled in Boone County, Missouri.

---

[168] Madison Co., Kentucky, Wills, Probate Records: Vol. A - A1, 1787–1813. Kentucky State Archives Roll # 7012790, Madison Co., Wills, 1787–1829, 16mm film.

- Joseph, 1759–1812. Joseph was dead before 1812 in St. Louis, Missouri, and was not listed in the civil probate case of his siblings.
- Martin, 1765–1833. My fourth great-grandfather.
- Susannah McCormack, 1767–1856
- Hugh Jr., 1774–1834. Later settled in Crawford, Randolph County, Missouri

Following the civil case involving his father's estate, Hugh Jr. was living in Missouri prior to 1817, where he received a license as an Indian trader. The source for this is a reconstructed census of the territory. I found evidence that another Hugh Glenn also made trips to New Mexico and became a large wheat farmer in California, but this person was of a later generation. He hailed from Carlisle, Pennsylvania, in Cumberland County. I am uncertain of his relationship to this family, but he was likely some kind of kin.

I have a copy of his military records, as Colonel Broadhead kept good records. After all, it was a Continental Line unit. At least one membership to the SAR has been approved based on Hugh's service. I also found another application for membership awarded to a descendant of the husband of daughter Margaret. She is shown on that application. Margaret also requested and received a pension based on his service.

Hugh's son Martin married Anna More (1765–1834) in Madison County, Kentucky, and remained there the remainder of his life. They had eight children, of which their daughter Mary Ann Polly (1793–1860) was the oldest. I have the 24 September 1810 marriage records of Polly to Grissom Reed Lee, my second great-grandfather, as well as the court records involving Grissom Lee and his siblings in his father's estate case, in which Polly is named. Grissom Lee's connection to my family is given in the Richard Lee story told earlier in this book. Grissom and Polly settled in Pettis County, Missouri.


**Hercules Roney III**
Born: 1750, Donegal, Ireland
Died: July 1812, West Finley, Washington County, Pennsylvania
Burial: Unknown
Service: Third Battalion of the Washington County Militia
Rank: Private
Service Dates: 1781–1782
Wife: Margaret Buchanan (1741–1822)
Lineage: Son Ellis, his daughter Elizabeth married Fielding Murphy, their son Joseph R. Murphy was the father of Bessie P. (Scott), Emma Jo's grandmother
DAR: A097629
SAR: No

Hercules was born in Donegal, Ireland, to Hercules Roney Jr. and Elizabeth Mary Barnes. I use the "III" suffix with his name to distinguish him from the other namesakes in his line, but I found no evidence of that being used during his lifetime. He probably arrived in Bucks County, Pennsylvania, around 1775, just prior to the Revolutionary War, with his father, mother, and brothers.

His grandfather served as a surgeon in the Irish Army, so military service was probably familiar to him. I have seen genealogies claiming he was born in Pennsylvania, but the DAR and a published Washington County history say he was born in Ireland.[169] Regardless, both Hercules and his brother James were living in the frontier county of Washington, Pennsylvania, in West Finley Township, by the time of Revolutionary War. His father and other siblings remained in Bucks County. *Roney Family History and Genealogy* lists the children of Hercules Jr. and places Hercules in Virginia and Kentucky later in his life with at least one brother.[170]

We have family stories that both Hercules and brother James served on a Virginia survey crew and ended up owning land in Pennsylvania. Remember that part of Pennsylvania was claimed by the Virginia colony. We found records that Hercules owned at least four hundred acres of farmland.[171] This may have been a land grant for his survey work. Washington County is near the southwest corner of Pennsylvania within just a few miles of the West Virginia line. The referenced warrant attests that he had occupied and improved the land since 1774. The colony of Virginia included what is now West Virginia, so it is easy to understand the colony's claim to this land, even though the colony of Pennsylvania was an original colony and did eventually win the claim with the new Continental Congress. This was a similar situation to that of Fayette County, Pennsylvania, where Patriot Henry Myers, discussed earlier, lived. They were probably happy with their new-found religious freedom and the concept of land ownership, but there were those who contested the very idea of them being there in the first place: the various Indian tribes that spent their summers there on hunting trips. The Roneys were aware of that fact and were forced to deal with the realities of living in Indian territory. The British were not necessarily their only enemies at this point in history.

Both Hercules and brother James enlisted in the Third Battalion of the Washington County Militia in late 1781. Pennsylvania's conscription laws were clear and heavily enforced. All able-bodied men were required to enlist or arrange a substitute. The Third Battalion was commanded by Lieutenant Colonel David Williams, and both brothers were in a company commanded by Captain George Sharp.

Reading the rosters of these eight or nine companies for each of at least eight battalions of the Washington Militia is like reading the names in a telephone book. Nearly every adult male was listed. Recruiting was no problem. I found a letter from Lieutenant Colonel Henry "Lighthorse" Lee to General Washington wherein he stated that the Scotch-Irish citizens of Pennsylvania joined the military in droves and were not only willing to fight, but anxious to do so.

The rosters of this militia spoke volumes about their activities, or lack thereof. The rosters were adequate for accounting for soldiers who enlisted and were discharged, but not adequate for wartime accounting and control. For the most part, they did not do a lot of fighting as a large unit but were involved in small, detached operations involving only a few soldiers at a time on a short-term basis. This was typical of local militias. I did find one exception: a special unit of

---

[169] *The History of Bucks County, Pennsylvania: From the Discovery of the Delaware to the Present Time*, William W. H. Davis, The Lewis Publishing Company, New York and Chicago. Page 458 shows that Hercules was the son of a surgeon in the Army of Queen Anne and lists his sons.
[170] *Roney Family History and Genealogy, 1690–1972*, Doris Roney Bowers, Stevens Publishing Company, 1978, Astoria, Illinois. Page 25 lists the children of Hercules and places Hercules III and his brother Joseph in Virginia and Kentucky later in their lives.
[171] Pennsylvania Land Warrants, 16 September 1785.

volunteers was formed as the Ninety-Ninth Rangers, and they were involved in the expedition against the Moravian Indians commanded by Lieutenant Colonel David Williams of the Third Battalion. Brother James Roney participated in this operation, but I could not find evidence of Hercules's involvement. Several men were killed in this expedition. Some of the officers and all non-commissioned were elected by the soldiers. I found one account of James Roney as a lieutenant, but the unit rosters reflect his and brother Hercules's rank as private. Maybe James was elected as an officer for the expedition? The Revolutionary War enlistees were called for a final muster or rendezvous on 18 May 1782. Their pay was computed, but most were not paid until 1784. The Third Battalion Militia was not disbanded and continued for several years manned by volunteers.

It is speculation, but there is a possibility that Hercules did not participate in the Williams Expedition but remained behind to protect his family. He had a wife and three children, and James also had a family in need of protection. This was not a safe neighborhood—I found accounts crediting Hercules with building a stone farm building that was sometimes used by the local community as a part-time fortress for protection from attacking Indians. Hercules was recognized by the DAR for his military service. He was also recognized for patriotic service—the stated reason was deprivation. There was no shortage of enemies. Peace did not arrive at their doorsteps when the Revolutionary War ended, but the threat of Indian attack increased as the local militias were disbanded.

Hercules lived and farmed in Washington County until his death in 1812. He left a will leaving his land and possessions to his wife and sons James, William, and John. I noticed that son Ellis was not mentioned in his will written in 1805, but I quickly realized that Ellis was born after the will was written that year and the will was never updated. I could find no later documents accounting for any inheritance due to son Ellis, thus making proof of lineage questionable, and I decided to not include him in this book. But I got lucky! Notes from the Murphy family bible taken by Emma Jo's cousin, the late Richard Scott, attest to the fact that Ellis Roney was the son of Hercules Roney III. These notes also gave the name of the wife of Ellis—Maria Oglesby. The daughter of Ellis and Maria Roney, Elizabeth, married Fielding Murphy, the second great-grandfather of Emma Jo. The Oglesby and Murphy families were disused earlier in this book.

I believe Hercules and Margaret had ten children:

- James, 1778–1842
- William, 1781–1831
- John, 1783–1831
- Mary Reed, 1790–Unknown death date
- Elizabeth Cooper, 1794–1850
- Joseph, 1796–1841
- James, 1799–1869
- Hercules IV, 1804–Unknown death date
- Ellis, 1805–1853. His daughter Elizabeth married Fielding Murphy, Emma Jo's second great-grandfather.
- Daniel, 1810–1847

I later found added evidence of lineage solidifying the Roney-Murphy relationships. Ellis Roney and siblings James, John, and William moved to Shelby County, Kentucky after their father's death. They owned land and continued to do business with each other for the remainder of their lives. I found Ellis on Kentucky tax records and census reports until 1850. The 1850 census shows Ellis with nine slaves and no daughter named Elizabeth, but Elizabeth is shown on that census living with Joseph Roney, age sixty-four. This discovery provided another break in the lineage to the Murphys. This detective work was complicated by the fact that the 1850 census featuring Ellis was for Oldham County, Kentucky, not Shelby County. Were there two Ellis Roneys? I quickly realized Oldham County was formed from the large Shelby County in 1821. No one had moved. This mystery of Ellis and possible daughter Elizabeth was eventually solved the old-fashioned way: a broad search of both Shelby and Oldham County probate, court, marriage, and land records. I found:

- Daughter Elizabeth and husband Fielding Murphy are named in probate records after the death of Ellis.
- Marriage records of Fielding Murphy and Elizabeth Roney on 11 September 1851.
- Ellis was married twice. His second marriage was to Melinda Hall.
- Ellis received eleven slaves in settlement of a debt from Nancy Roney, wife of Joseph Roney, in 1842. This seemed to explain why a Pennsylvania Irish man would own slaves.
- Evidence of land sales from Ellis Roney to Benjamin Roberts Jr., the son of Patriot Benjamin Roberts. Both Benjamin Roberts Jr. and brother Joseph Roberts settled in Shelby County, Kentucky, after the Revolutionary War. The Roberts are ancestors of the Raines/Adams line discussed earlier in this book.

It is also interesting to discuss the Kentucky family connections of several of the Patriot families we have discussed. Fielding Murphy, Emma Jo's second great-grandfather, who married Elizabeth, daughter of Hercules and Margaret Roney, was the son of John Lewis Murphy and Betsy Ashby, also of Shelby/Oldham County, Kentucky. John Lewis was the son of Patriot Lewis Murphy, discussed earlier in this book, and Fielding's mother Betsy Ashby was the daughter of Patriot Fielding Ashby, also discussed earlier in this book. The Roney, Murphy, Ashby, and Roberts families all lived in Shelby/Oldham County before moving on to Missouri. I also found records of land transactions between Patriot David Ashby and the Roberts family. The Raines-Painter family ancestors knew and did business with each other in Kentucky!

I would like to emphasize that the Missouri Murphy family bible was extremely helpful with documentation of this family line, as was the research done by Emma Jo's cousin, the late Richard Scott. I was ready to abandon the Roney Patriot story of the book until I discovered Richard's work of 1987 that had been given to Emma Jo. That revelation motivated me to further my research of these Shelby County connections.

I am uncertain of the burial location of Hercules in Pennsylvania; I found a photo of his tombstone with the correct dates and will eventually find his burial location.

## The Duncan Family

Following are the stories of the Duncan family Patriots—John Duncan, his son Sergeant John Duncan Jr., and his son Joseph Duncan. John Jr. had three Patriot sons and a daughter, Elizabeth Embree (married Thomas Burris Embree). Elizabeth lived to be 101 years old and settled in Missouri before it became a state. Three of her children settled in the Territory of Oregon and recorded notable accomplishments there, and her daughter Nancy Ann Scott was Emma Jo's second great-grandmother. The Embree family also married into the Missouri Fowler family, from which I am descended. These stores recount the American westward expansion as we see the Duncan and Embree families migrate from Virginia to Kentucky and westward to Missouri and on to Oregon in less than fifty years.

### John Duncan Sr.

Born: 15 July 1715, Prince William County, Virginia
Died: 4 April 1795, Fauquier County, Virginia
Burial: Fauquier County, Virginia
Service: Patriotic service
Rank: None
Service Dates: None
Wife: Willkey McClanahan (1731–1793)
Lineage: Son John Jr., his son Joseph Sr., Daughter Elizabeth "Betsy" Embree, daughter Nancy Ann Scott, wife of Davis Scott (Emma Jo's second great-grandfather)
DAR: A034930
SAR: P-340500

John was the son of Marshall Duncan and Mary Ann Durron of Prince William County. John was a plantation owner who once offered land for the Fauquier County Courthouse, but Governor Dinwiddie declined and instead took an offer from Richard Henry Lee.[172] Thomas Marshall was noted in the above reference as the county surveyor; he was appointed to this role by the college leadership of William and Mary College. Marshall, a neighbor and a lawyer, wrote the will of John Duncan on 4 April 1788, in which he named his wife and children, including son John Jr.[173] When the will was probated after his death in 1795, mention was made that son John Jr. was deceased—he had died soon after the will was written in 1788. Thomas Marshall witnessed the will. This is the same Thomas Marshall who served as a regimental commander early in the Revolutionary War and was the father of Supreme Court Chief Justice John Marshall. Several Patriots discussed in this book served under Colonel Thomas Marshall. I believe that Thomas Marshall had been a militia regimental commander prior to the Revolutionary War, and shortly after that regiment was committed to the Continental Army, he relinquished command to a younger man. Thomas then became the surveyor for Fauquier County and continued a law practice.

---

[172] *Abstracts of Fauquier County, Virginia: Wills, Inventories, and Accounts, 1759–1800*, Gott, John K., Baltimore, Maryland: Clearfield, 1999. This account said that the county court's opinion was that the John Duncan plantation was the proper and convenient location for the next court of the county and that the governor be advised of the decision. The governor apparently did not concur and directed that the next court be held at the house of William Jones on land owned by William Henry Lee.
[173] Fauquier County Will Books 1–2, 1759–1796. Page 424 lists the wife and sons of John Duncan.

John did not serve in the military during the Revolutionary War but is credited with patriotic service by both the DAR and SAR—he sold supplies to the military, as did some Ashby Patriots of Fauquier County discussed elsewhere in this book.[174]

John and Willkey McClanahan had the following seven children who are documented by name in his April 1788 will. I do not have John and Willkey's marriage records, but she is named in his will. I also discovered the records of his 1795 probate case naming his wife Willkey but claiming dower rights for her. That would indicate he had no will, but I am uncertain of the dower claim. Maybe the will was filed without the family's knowledge of the will. Their children were:

- John Durron Duncan Jr., 1730–1788. (Middle name is his grandmother's maiden name.) He is Emma Jo's fifth great-grandfather and a Revolutionary War Patriot to be discussed next.
- Willis, 1742–1796
- Moses, 1767–1845. Named as will administrator.
- Elias, 1768–1845
- Enoch, 1769–1832
- Millie Henderson, 1773–1789
- Linda, Birth and death date unknown.

We know that John Jr. was his son because he was listed in his father's will and because of Fauquier County land transactions listed in SAR applications. They owned adjoining land, and the father sold land to his son in 1766.

I do not know where John is buried except that he is buried in Fauquier County.

It is important to note that research of this family line from Virginia is challenging, as several persons with the name John Duncan lived in the Virginia colony at about the same time. Another John lived in Culpeper County, served in the French and Indian War, and also sold supplies to the colony during the Revolution. While Culpeper County is near Fauquier County, they could not be the same men. I relied solely on original documents that were considered in the context of time, location, and common sense. I believe I have it right. This is an important family line that made history after the Revolutionary War. I expected to discover that John or his son were slave owners, but I did not find that to be the case, as no mention was made of slaves in his will. His son John Jr. served in the military during the Revolution, and John Jr.'s son is also a Patriot recognized for patriotic service. Their stories follow:

---

[174] *Virginia Revolutionary Publick Claims*, Janice Abercrombie and Richard Slatten, Iberian Publishing Company, Athens, Georgia. Volume I, page 346 lists John Duncan as providing supplies in Fauquier County, Virginia.

**Sergeant John Durron Duncan Jr.**
Born: 15 July 1727, Prince William County, Virginia
Died: 6 November 1788, Fauquier County, Virginia
Burial: Unknown location in Fauquier County, Virginia
Service: Fourth, Eighth, and Twelfth Virginia Regiments, Continental Line
Rank: Sergeant
Service Dates: Prior to May 1776 until at least December 1778
Wife: Dianah Bradford (1726–1788)
Lineage: Son Joseph Duncan Sr., daughter Elizabeth Betsy Embree, daughter Nancy Ann Scott, wife of Davis Scott (Jo's second great-grandfather)
DAR: A04932
SAR: P-151099

John was the son of John Duncan Sr. and Wilkey McClanahan of Prince Henry County, Virginia, later of Fauquier County, Virginia. He was probably born in Prince William County, as Fauquier was formed from Prince William after his birth. He married Dinah Bradford in 1747, and I have those marriage records from Fauquier County. They both died in 1788 in the same county, he at the age of fifty-eight and she at the age of sixty-two.

Again, the name of his father is confirmed in his father's will and the fact that they owned adjacent land in Fauquier County, with father selling land to son. Although not proof of relationship, both the DAR and SAR have accepted this relationship on many applications for membership. The DAR records also reflect Dianah as his wife.

John is listed as a member of the Fauquier County Militia on 25 September 1761.[175] This is pre-Revolutionary War service, but the referenced orders state that the service was for the French and Indian War. The Ashby and Gist chapters later in this book give an insight into the conflict at that time.

As I discuss elsewhere in this story, there were several other John Duncans of Virginia of this era. At least three of them served in a Virginia regiment during the Revolution. Two of them lived long enough to claim pensions after the 1832 Pension Act: one in Virginia and one in Tennessee. One of these Johns is John Jr's. son. John Jr. did not live until 1832, as he died in 1788, well prior to any pensions being available.

This John Duncan enlisted in the Virginia Fourth Regiment of the Continental Line. The Fourth Regiment was merged with the Virginia Eighth Regiment following the winter at Valley Forge. I have the National Archives records of his service in the combined Fourth/Eighth Regiment. Patriot Joshua Logan Younger also served in this regiment, serving under Colonel James Woods. Patriot Richard Lee also served in this unit at the same time.

This regiment is a storied regiment, serving in some of the most important and brutal battles of the Revolutionary War. The Fourth Regiment wintered at Valley Forge during the winter of

---

[175] *Virginia Military Records: From the Virginia Magazine of History and Biography, the William and Mary College Quarterly, and Tyler's Quarterly,* The Genealogical Publishing Company, Inc., Baltimore, 1983. Page 161 lists John Duncan Jr. as a member of the Fauquier County Militia on 25 September 1761.

1777–1778. By the end of the winter, unit strengths had fallen so drastically that the Fourth and Eighth Virginia Regiments were merged. This combined regiment participated in the Charleston, South Carolina, siege in May 1780 after a five-hundred-mile march, and the soldiers were taken captive and served the remainder of the war as prisoners. Few records attest to his imprisonment, as the units ceased to exist after capture. What I am reasonably sure of is that his initial enlistment was for three years and that he is recorded as present with the unit in May 1776. He was a sergeant in the unit in March 1777. If this was a three-year enlistment, he would likely have been present in the unit until May 1779; however, I have found no unit rosters containing his name after December 1778. The National Archives file of his service contains more than fifty pages, and it appears this file is not complete, as I found no final payment records. Perhaps he reenlisted after making sergeant, or perhaps he was discharged after serving three years and before the unit's capture in 1780. His son William served in the same unit. The May 1776 records also seem to establish that John wintered at Valley Forge with his unit, as did Patriots Joshua Younger and Richard Lee.

I could find no evidence of pension requests, and expected none, as both he and his wife died well before the pension act was passed in 1819. His son William received a hundred-acre land grant based on the service of his father in 1887.

We can only speculate on the seemingly early deaths of both John and his wife Dinah in the same year. It would be easy to believe his life was shortened due to injuries received in the war and possibly while a prisoner. Remember Joshua Younger suffered several injuries and was discharged after a serious injury.

John and Dinah had the following children:

- John III, 1749–1833. Served in the Revolutionary War and settled in Floyd County, Virginia.
- William, 1750–1830. Served in the same regiment as his father and died in Culpeper County, Virginia.
- Joseph Sr., 1752–1826. Revolutionary War Patriot for patriotic service. Emma Jo's fourth great-grandfather. Discussed below.
- Rose Murphey, 1756–1830
- Chloe Kirk, 1762–1821
- Leanna, 1764–1830
- Alamander, 1766–1856. Served in the War of 1812.

As John died with no will, I documented his children with DAR records. Although not proof of relationships, I feel confident that I found the members of this very important family.

**Joseph Duncan Sr.**
Born: 1 January 1752, Fauquier County, Virginia
Died: 25 March 1826, Clark County, Kentucky
Burial: Unknown location in Clark County, Kentucky
Service: Patriotic service
Rank: None
Service Dates: None
Wife: Nancy Ann Stevens (1757–1832)
Lineage: Daughter Elizabeth "Betsy" married Thomas Burris Embree, their daughter Nancy Ann married Davis Scott, their son Demarcus Scott was Emma Jo's great-grandfather.
DAR: A03492
SAR: No

He is the son of Sergeant John Durron Duncan Jr. and Dinah Bradford of Fauquier County, Virginia. His father and grandfather John Duncan Sr. and Jr. were Revolutionary War Patriots discussed above. His brothers William and John served in the Virginia Line. I could not confirm any military service on the part of Joseph, but he is recognized by the DAR for providing substantial support to the Revolution in Virginia. He claimed reimbursement from Fauquier County following the war. I discovered another Joseph Duncan, also born in Fauquier County, who also moved to Kentucky and who served in a Virginia regiment, but after careful study, I concluded it was his son.

We know that Joseph was the son of Sergeant Duncan from lineage records provided to the DAR for membership applications. He is also documented in a Kentucky historical review.[176] I do not consider a historical society publication as proof of relationship, but when taken in consideration with other records, such as the DAR records, it is an acceptable assumption.

He married Nancy Ann Stevens in Orange County, Virginia, on 22 May 1757. I have those marriage records. This marriage is also documented in the above reference.[177]

Joseph Sr. is Emma Jo's fourth great-grandfather, as his daughter Elizabeth "Betsy" is the mother of Nancy Ann Scott, the wife of Davis Scott, Emma Jo's second great-grandfather.

Following the war, he and his family moved to Clark County, Kentucky, by 1787. He later served in the Kentucky Seventeenth Regiment during the War of 1812.[178] Joseph and Nancy had fourteen children, one of which died in childhood:

- Sarah Montague Collins, 1757–1822. Married and remained in Clark County, Kentucky.
- James, 1775–1842. Settled in Lincoln County, Missouri.

---

[176] *Genealogies of Kentucky Families: From the Register of the Kentucky Historical Society*, A–M (Allen–Moss). Genealogical Publishing Company, Inc., 1981. Page 283 lists the several Duncan families of Virginia, including Joseph of Fauquier County, Virginia, son of John, who married Nancy Stevens and moved to Orange County, Virginia, and then to Clark County, Kentucky.
[177] Ibid.
[178] *Kentucky in the War of 1812,* Anderson Chenault Quisenberry, Kentucky Historical Society, Frankfort, Kentucky, 1915. Page 175 lists Joseph Duncan as a soldier in the Kentucky Seventeenth Regiment.

- Elizabeth "Betsy" Embree, 1776–1877. Emma Jo's third great-grandmother. Settled in Monroe County, Missouri. See her story below.
- Peggy Daniel, 1777–1818. Married and settled in South Carolina.
- Nancy Watkins, 1779–before 1845. Married and remained in Clark County, Kentucky.
- Charles, 1781–1818. Remained in Clark County, Kentucky.
- Mary Stevens Daniel, 1784–1872. Remained in Kentucky.
- John, 1785–1795. Died as a youth.
- Anthony Thomas, 1787–1848. Settled in Troy, Lincoln County, Missouri.
- Carey, 1787–1848
- Lewis, 1789–1873. Settled in Galveston, Texas.
- Dianah Lampton, 1795–1851. Settled in Monroe County, Missouri.
- Joseph Jr., 1796–1870. Remained in Clark County, Kentucky.
- Lucinda M. Smith, 1799–1896. Remained in Kentucky.

Joseph and Nancy's daughter Elizabeth "Betsy" married Thomas Burris Embree (1774–1845) in Winchester, Clark County, Kentucky, on 24 August 1796, and they bought land there in 1808. This land consisted of two one-hundred-acre parcels, one of which he purchased from his father John. I have those marriage records and land descriptions.

Thomas and Betsy left Clark County for Missouri by wagon train in 1820, along with their eleven sons, three daughters, and three slaves.[179] They were among the early settlers in Howard County, Missouri, that year and purchased 159 acres of land there in 1825 (NE ¼ of Section 6, Twp 049W, R16W) about two miles northwest of present-day Boonville. They later moved to Randolph County, Missouri, by 1836. That land of 160 acres (SE ¼ of Section 1, R-13W, Twp 53N) was in Randolph County but later Monroe County because of those county lines being redrawn.

To be historically correct, those county lines changed several times before and following Missouri statehood. Pike County absorbed parts of Howard County, and the Randolph and Monroe County lines were changed following the establishing of Monroe County in 1831.

That family group (Burris/Embree) is credited with being among the first pioneer families to settle in what was soon to be Monroe County, Missouri, near the present-day village of Middle Grove.[180] Their neighbors were the Ezra Fox family, the first settlers to arrive. The Embrees are buried in Burris-Embree Cemetery near the current Monroe and Randolph County line north of Middle Grove, near the Junction of Monroe County Roads YY and 1099. That is located a mile or so northwest of the Ezra Fox family cemetery, which is credited with being the oldest cemetery in Monroe County. Elizabeth lived to the age of 101 years old after having fourteen children and surviving hazardous living conditions in early Howard and Monroe County, Missouri.

---

[179] *Old Families of Randolph County, Missouri: A People's History,* edited by H.W. Marshall, published by the Randolph County Historical Society, Moberly, Missouri, 1976.

[180] *Old Families of Randolph County, Missouri: A People's History,* edited by H.W. Marshall, published by the Randolph County Historical Society, Moberly, Missouri, 1976. This gives the account of Thomas Burris Embree in Clark County, Kentucky, including his land ownership there and the move to Howard County, then Monroe County, Missouri.

Thomas Burris and Elizabeth had at least fourteen children that survived to adulthood:

- Isham Prewitt, 1795–1872. Settled in Fayette, Howard County, Missouri. He was a slave-holder.
- Martillas, 1796–1850. Moved to Pettis County, Missouri, and died of cholera on the Oregon Trail in Nebraska en route to Oregon. He may have been a minister. His wife had remained in Pettis County.
- Demarcus D., 1797–1845. Moved to Howard County, Missouri, and died near Madison, Monroe County, Missouri. I believe Emma Jo's great-grandfather DeMarcus Scott was named after him.
- Lucinda Ford, 1799–1874. Married Nathaniel Ford and settled in Dallas, Polk County, Oregon by 1850. See their story below.
- Luvina Elkin, 1802–1900. Married John Elkin and settled in Howard County, Missouri.
- Joseph W., 1804–1865. Married Eliza Harter. He moved to Dallas, Polk County, Oregon by 1860. An Oregon constructed census shows him living in Dallas, Polk County, by 1860, but he had purchased land in Randolph County, Missouri, so his relocation occurred between 1856 and 1860. His wife Eliza was deceased by 1845, and I do not believe any of his children relocated to Oregon. I found a probate case that seems to establish he died intestate in eastern Oregon around 1865 and that there were no known family members at that location.
- Carey, 1806–1900. Married Lucinda Fowler in Pettis County, Missouri, and they moved to Dallas, Polk County, Oregon, by 1844. See their story below.
- Mary Jane Cox, 1807–1864. Married Francis M. Cox and settled in Monroe County, Missouri.
- Thomas I., 1808–1845. Married Eliza Harter, and they settled in Pettis County, Missouri.
- Nancy Ann Scott, 1811–1886. She married Davis Scott, and they settled in Monroe County, Missouri, by 1831. She is Emma Jo's second great-grandmother. See their story below.
- Rosa Moss Brockman, 1813–1893. She married Jacob E. Brockman and settled near Keytesville, Chariton County, Missouri.
- Milton Jackson "Apple Jack," 1815–1902. Married (1) Lucinda Lampton and (2) Nancy Jane Stevens and lived near Middle Grove, Monroe County, Missouri.
- Sarah Mariah Ayres, 1816–1845. Married Walter Ayres and lived in Saline County, Missouri.
- Lewis Perry, 1818–1865. Married Sallie Sarah Ann Ford and lived near Keytesville, Chariton County, Missouri.

Daughter Lucinda married Nathaniel Ford in Howard County, Missouri. Nathaniel was a slave-holder when they moved to Polk County, Oregon, in the 1840s. I believe there were two slaves. He became a political leader in Oregon—a territorial governor and a political representative for the territory. He had promised to free his two slaves brought from Missouri upon their arrival in Oregon, but he failed to keep that promise. Later one of the slaves brought a lawsuit for his freedom, and both slaves were freed in that decision.[181] [182] When formed, Polk County was much

---

[181] *Bancroft's Works*, Volume XXIX, Oregon Biographical Sketches, Bancroft, Hubert Howe, retrieved on February 26, 2008.
[182] Pioneer History: Polk County 1846–1855. Churches of Christ & Christian Churches in the Pacific Northwest.

larger than the present county, and it bordered the California territory and occupied most of southwestern Oregon. Nathaniel and Lucinda lived on Rickreall Creek near what was to become the city of Dallas, the current county seat of the county. I have a photo of their old home still standing, but in poor repair.

Son Carey married Lucinda Fowler (1807–1881) in Pettis County, Missouri. Some documents reflect the spelling of his first name without the "e." I note that Lucinda was the daughter of John Fowler (1765–1826) of Pettis County. John was the father of Robert Fowler, who was the father of Louvisa Fowler Raines, my great-grandmother, thus making Lucinda distant kin (by marriage) to both Emma Jo and I. Carey and his family departed for Oregon on 18 April 1844 with two teams of oxen and some livestock and less than $20. Their trip and subsequent life in Oregon is recorded in a well-written unpublished story, "The Fowler-Embree Oregon Trail in 1844," by a family member—Francis Dempsey. They were under pressure to cross the mountains before winter and were short on money. The trip along the Columbia River required Lucinda and their children to walk along the riverbank while her husband took the high ground inland and above the river with the livestock. That would have been a very difficult and risky journey for the entire family. The river route was the route used by Lewis and Clark about forty years earlier. After arrival, they borrowed money from a trading company to survive the first winter. Three years after arriving in the Oregon Territory, Carey ventured to California during the gold rush there. He was apparently successful and returned to the Oregon Territory, where he purchased large land holdings and remained in the Willamette Valley area for the remainder of his life. His probate estate consisted of several thousand acres.

Thomas and Elizabeth's daughter Nancy Ann married Davis Scott of Howard County in 1828, and they soon moved to Monroe County east of Paris, Missouri, probably in 1831. Davis Scott had arrived in Howard County from Kentucky while the War of 1812 hostilities still lingered around 1818.

They too are credited with being early Monroe County settlers. Davis and Nancy Ann are the second great-grandparents of Emma Jo. We have their 1828 Howard County marriage and property records. This was the second marriage for Davis. Davis and Nancy Ann sold their Howard County property by 1830 and purchased Monroe County land at the Palmyra land office. I believe they were completely moved by 1831, the year the city of Paris was incorporated. Among their children was DeMarcus Scott, Emma Jo's great-grandfather. DeMarcus ventured to New Mexico as a gold prospector and returned to Missouri during the mid-1860s. Davis Scott was a successful farmer, part owner of the Paris Bank, and probably a lawyer, and two of his sons became doctors. The son of DeMarcus was Cera Gorda Scott, Emma Jo's grandfather. I believe that the father of Davis was probably a Patriot, but more on that later.

### William Webb III

Born: 11 May 1754, Washington County, Maryland
Died: 12 February 1807, Washington County, Maryland
Burial: Webb Family Cemetery in Leitersburg, Washington County, Maryland
Service: Seventh Maryland Regiment, Continental Line
Rank: Private
Service Dates: March 1777–January 1783
Wife: Eleanor Charlton
Lineage: Daughter Mary Poly married Alexander Cooper Baker, their daughter married Henry Boren, and their daughter Louise B. married Albert G. Dilts, whose daughter Stella was Emma Jo' grandmother in the Painter line.
DAR: No
SAR: No

William was the son of William Webb Jr. and Isabella Charlton of Washington County, Maryland. He married Eleanor Charlton (1748–1818) in 1773. William's lineage seems to be established by his grandfather's will of 26 August 1759, in which he provides for his son William Jr. and grandson William III.[183] His grandfather William Sr. (1700–1783) immigrated from England and settled in Chester County, Pennsylvania. His father William Jr. relocated from Pennsylvania to Washington County, Maryland, when he married Isabella in 1742.

Other than his time in the service, he spent his entire life in and around Washington County, Maryland.

He served in the Maryland Seventh Regiment commanded by Colonel John Grunby, in a company commanded by Captain Johnathan Morris. The unit was organized in March 1777 in Baltimore and Frederick Counties. It was assigned to the First Maryland Brigade and to the Continental Line and was commanded by Colonel Smallwood. This brigade was soon commanded by General Mordecai Gist, a family member discussed extensively later in this book. Patriot Joshua Pearce, discussed earlier in this book, also served in the First Maryland Brigade.

The Seventh Regiment entered Valley Forge on May 1778 with 235 men. The had previously fought in engagements in the Philadelphia campaign and in New Jersey. Of the 235 assigned men that entered Valley Forge, only 131 were fit for duty by winter's end. The unit needed a rest. History credits this regiment with successfully blocking the British army from following George Washington after his being ejected from Long Island. Had they caught up with the colonial army, the war might well have ended early. I believe that unit rosters for this unit during the Valley Forge period no longer exist, so I could not verify that William was there. His company commander is listed as present, so I will infer that William was also present.

Following Valley Forge, the unit was assigned to the southern department in May 1880. It had already fought in the battles of Brandywine, Germantown, Monmouth, Camden, and Guilford Courthouse. See the later chapter devoted to the Guilford Courthouse battle.

---

[183] Pennsylvania Wills and Probate Records, 1683–1933, Ancestry.com, Provo, Utah, 2015.

The regiment was disbanded on 1 January 1783 at Annapolis.[184] The personnel rosters of this unit have not completely survived. I did, however, find the final payment records for William as the unit was being disbanded. He was paid 86 pounds and 11 shillings. This is a substantial sum of money and represents his pay for the war. This was a tough battle-hardened unit that Generals Washington and Greene depended on to never retreat. They lived up to that reputation.

I did not find a pension request for William, and did not expect to find one, as he died before Congress passed the pension act in 1819. His wife would have been eligible, but she also died prior to 1819.

I also found a fidelity oath taken by William in early 1777 prior to joining the army. This act alone would qualify him for DAR recognition as a Patriot. It is possible that his father signed that oath, as he was alive and living in Washington County. If the signature belonged to his father, we might be able to claim his Patriot status, but the question remains as to who signed that document, father or son.

He is shown on both the 1790 and 1800 censuses for Washington County, Maryland. His father was deceased by 1790, so it was this William Webb being recorded.

William and Eleanor had five children:

- Elias, 1776–1814
- Sarah, 1783–Unknown death date
- Mary Poly Baker, 1786–1859. Married Alexander Baker. She is Emma Jo's third great-grandmother.
- Johnathan, 1788–1865
- Susanna Cooper, 1792–1882

I found birth records for Mary Poly documenting her father, and she was born following the war. She married Alexander Cooper Baker—son of Maurice Baker of Hartford County, Maryland—on 1 March 1808 in Washington County, and I have those records. Maurice is a Patriot, and his story follows below. By 1840, they and all their children had moved to Marion County, Missouri. They operated a large farm there near Hannibal until Alexander died in 1860. Both Alexander and Mary Poly are buried in the Bellefontaine Cemetery in St. Louis, Missouri.

They had twelve children, of which daughter Ann Elizabeth married Henry Boren of Marion County. The children are:

- John, 1810–1890. Died in Carroll, Ohio.
- Morris, 1813–Unknown death date. Died in Marion County, Missouri.
- Mary Stover, 1815–1851. Died in Marion County, Missouri.
- Anne Elizabeth Boren/Pendleton, 1817–Unknown death date. Emma Jo's second great-grandmother.

---

[184] *The Continental Army*, Robert K. Wright Jr., Center of Military History, United States Army, Washington D.C., 1981. Page 121 lists the Vally Forge units. Page 277 lists the participating Maryland units.

- Rachel Heckert, 1818–1850. Died in Shelby County, Missouri.
- Thomas Alexander, 1819–1854. Died in Marion County, Missouri.
- Catherine Anne Cash/Davis, 1821–1890. Died in Pike County, Missouri.
- Louisa Mary, 1823–Unknown death date.
- Pointon, 1826–Unknown death date.
- Benjamin Franklin, 1829–1880. Died in Lake, California.
- Hiram Nicholis, 1832–1891. Died in Colusa, California.
- Mary, 1834–Unknown death date.

I documented daughter Anne Elizabeth with census and marriage records. The 1850 census for Missouri shows her birth state as Maryland. I have her marriage records for her marriage to Henry Boren in Washington County, Maryland. Her husband Henry became a wagon maker in Hannibal, Missouri, who died in the mid-1860s. Ann later remarried. Their daughter Louise B. married Albert G. Dilts Jr., whose daughter Stella was Jo's grandmother. These relationships are documented with census reports, marriage records, and cemetery records. The Dilts family has been extensively documented in my book *Footprints of the Painter and Scott Families of Missouri.*

## Maurice Baker

Born: 8 July 1748, Baltimore County, Maryland
Died: 1830, Washington County, Maryland
Burial: Unknown location in Washington County, Maryland
Service: Patriotic service
Rank: None
Service Dates: None
Wife: Mary Elizabeth Allender
Lineage: Son Alexander Cooper, his daughter Anne Elizabeth married Henry Boren, his daughter Louise married Albert G. Dilts (Emma Jo's great-grandfather)
DAR: No
SAR: No

Maurice was born in Baltimore County, Maryland, and was the son of Alexander Baker and Zipporah Hilliard. I have the Saint Paul Episcopal Church of Baltimore records recording his birth and his parents' names. It is an interesting note that his mother was a Quaker and Maurice attended meetings with her. Maurice is Emma Jo's fifth great-grandfather in the Painter/Dilts lines.

This line of Bakers can be traced to very early Virginia settlers and then to early Maryland. I will also note that the given name of Maurice in this family line appears multiple times in colonial times in Maryland and Virginia. This Maurice is but one of several in early American history.

I have seen a claim that Maurice served in the Maryland Militia during the Revolution, but the Maryland Militia records are incomplete, and future research is continuing with available records. I have the published records of most of the Maryland Militia rosters, and there are several Bakers shown, but their first names are sometimes not given or they are listed with a first name initial. I have been unable to find National Archives military records for him, but most Maryland Militia records were never recorded by the National Archives. Maryland State Line and

Maryland Continental Line records were certainly maintained, as those units played an important role in the Revolution, as reflected in other stories in this book. As there were no Revolutionary War battles of note in Maryland, those militia units have received little attention from historians.

What I do know, however, is that he took a sworn fidelity oath in 1778 in Washington County. That single act placed him and his family at risk of retribution by Tories or British and would be recognized by either the DAR or SAR for Patriot status. I have those records.

He married Mary Allender on 15 December 1777 in Washington County in what may have been his second marriage. I have a copy of those records. The 1790 census of Washington County shows twelve individuals besides his wife. He had four sons under sixteen and one male over sixteen besides Maurice himself at age forty-two.

Mary Allender and her sister, Sarah, each inherited a slave, Joe and Fann respectively, from their uncle John Day in 1784, and a slave shows on each of their 1790 censuses.

Maurice and Mary Elizabeth had seven children documented by the Tuscarawas County, Ohio, history. At least one of their children migrated to Tuscarawas County, and the records of those family lines are recorded there.[185]

- Maurice Jr., 1778–1860. Settled in Carroll County, Ohio.
- Nicholas, 1780–1839. Settled in Tuscarawas County, Ohio.
- Alexander Cooper, 1782–1860. Emma Jo's fourth great-grandfather. Settled in Marion County, Missouri.
- Mary Webb, 1786–1862. Remained in Washington County, Maryland.
- John, 1788–1854. Remained in Baltimore, Maryland.
- Richard, 1790–1859. Settled in New Castle, Indiana.
- Catherine Barrington, 1794–1866. May have lived in Pennsylvania, but later returned to Baltimore, Maryland.

Maurice's death date is uncertain. We see him in the 1820 census, but he cannot be found on the 1830 census for Washington County. I use the 1830 death date, as Find a Grave gives that date, but no documentation or location of his grave is given. It is a guess.

His son Alexander Cooper married Mary Poly Webb, and their daughter Anne Elizabeth married Henry Boren. Henry Boren's daughter Louise B. married Albert G. Dilts Jr., who is Emma Jo's great-grandfather. Alexander Cooper Baker settled in Missouri between the 1830 and 1840 censuses and is buried there. The Bakers were large plantation owners in Marion County. This county includes parts of the city of Hannibal, and the town of Palmyra is also in that county. It had a large slave population prior to the Civil War. I was not surprised to find records of slave-holdings on the plantation, but his sons and nephews served as coopers and wagon makers on that farm.

---

[185] *The History of Tuscarawas County, Ohio*, Warner, Beers & Company, 1884.

I have the marriage records for Alexander Cooper Baker and Mary Poly Webb in Washington County, Maryland. Mary is the daughter of Patriot William Webb II, who is discussed above in this book. I have the birth records of their daughter Anne Elizabeth, who married Henry Boren, also in Washington County. Henry was born in Pennsylvania, but I have not discovered his birth family. Their daughter Louise B. (1848–1917) married Albert G. Dilts Jr., and they are Emma Jo's great-grandparents. I have those marriage records, and they are buried in the Paris, Missouri, Walnut Grove Cemetery with well-marked graves.

Maurice was descended from Jamestown, Virginia, settlers. I have ample documentation from church records, and from Anne Arundel County property, marriage, and probate records, to establish this interesting family history in Baltimore and southern Maryland. This family line was living in America 125 years prior to the Revolution, and the family lineage is solid based on the records noted. His early family is listed below:

| | |
|---|---|
| Father of Maurice: | Alexander Baker, 1705–1750 |
| Mother of Maurice: | Zipporah Hilliard, 1713–1782 |
| Father of Alexander: | Maurice Baker III, 1675–1762[186] |
| Wife of Alexander: | Sarah Nicholson Baker, 1671–1762 |
| Father of Maurice III | Maurice Baker Jr., 1635–1700[187] |
| Wife of Maurice III | Lady Elizabeth "Lisa" Hill Griniff, 1635–1703 |
| Father of Maurice Jr. | Maurice Baker Sr., 1622–1660[188] |
| Wife of Maurice Sr. | Joan Greenfield, 1620–1660 |

Maurice Baker Sr. was born in Moulton Parish, Northamptonshire, England, and married Joan Greenfield prior to coming to the Virginia colony of Kent Isle. He died in 1660 on Kent Isle.

Maurice settled on Kent Isle, the largest island in the Chesapeake Bay. It has been a part of Queen Anne's County, Maryland, since the colonial era. It was first established as Kent Fort in 1631, making it the oldest settlement in Maryland and the third-oldest English settlement in the Americas following Jamestown and Plymouth, Massachusetts.[189]

William Claiborne, a resident of Jamestown, founded a settlement on the island in August 1631. The island served as a trading station for trade with Indians. The colonies of Virginia and Maryland disputed the ownership of the island until the Revolutionary War, when it became part of the colony of Maryland.[190]

I believe that Maurice Baker Sr. and Joan Greenfield arrived on the island in 1651, and I have a ship manifest. He is also listed in *Early Virginia Immigrants, 1623–1666,* also reflecting that

---

[186] *Baltimore County Families, 1659–1759,* Robert W. Barnes, reprinted for the Clearfield Company, Inc., Baltimore, Maryland, 1966. Page 19 states that Maurice Baker moved to Maryland from Virginia by 1675 and acquired land in Anne Arundel County. It also states that his wife's name was Elizabeth and he had a son named Maurice.
[187] Ibid.
[188] *Early Virginia Immigrants, 1623–1666,* George Cabell Greer, Genealogical Publishing Company, Inc., 1982. Page 18 shows Maurice Baker arriving in 1651 sponsored by Thomas Thornbrough, Northampton Company.
[189] "History of Kent Island," Kent Island Heritage Society. Retrieved 13 August 2008.
[190] Ibid.

date of arrival.[191] By 1651, when they arrived, the Jamestown settlement was being abandoned, and the settlers moved to the new colony capital of Williamsburg. The king had revoked the Jamestown corporate charter and established Williamsburg as the capital. The Bakers may have arrived in Williamsburg before moving on to Kent Isle, but that is speculation. Future research will involve search of colonial records for their stay in that settlement and their move to Kent Isle.

I found it interesting that his possible older brother John Baker, at the age of fifteen, arrived in 1623 in Charles City County, Virginia, as an indentured servant and later became a landowner in that county adjacent to the Jamestown settlement.[192] This is an unproven relationship. I believe that John and Maurice Sr. were both from Northamptonshire.

This Baker line is one of the older family lines of the Raines/Painter line following Lydia Hayward, wife of James Perrigo. Lydia is a 1620 *Mayflower* Descendant, and William Adams settled in Essex, Massachusetts, in 1628. See the Patriot Samuel Adams story above and the James Perrigo story later in the book.

## Ishmael Rains

Born: 1741, Caroline County, Virginia
Died: 17 December 1790, Randolph County, North Carolina
Burial: Unknown location in Randolph County, North Carolina
Service: Patriotic service
Rank: None
Service Dates: None
Wife: Sarah Caveness (1742–1840)
Lineage: Son Ambrose Rains, son Charles Rains, son John Washington Marshal Raines, William P. Raines, V. Elwood Raines Sr. (my father)
DAR: A212817
SAR: No

Ishmael was a farmer in Chatham/Randolph County, North Carolina, during the war. I believe his land was on or near the county lines, and that Randolph County was formed from parts of Chatham soon after his arrival in the colony. He and his brothers and mother had been there as early as 1772 after moving from Caroline County, Virginia. This was truly the "Wild West" at that time. North Carolina residents faced a variety of risks during the Revolution in addition to British soldiers and Tory residents. Indians were a constant risk, and many settlers were killed by them as they attempted to settle their land. In fact, Ishmael's possible brother John Jr. was recruited as a ranger company commander by his home county after he had served in the Revolution as a soldier. His job was to protect the county from Indians, and he seemingly did an excellent job. More on that later.

---

[191] *Early Virginia Immigrants, 1623–1666*, George Cabell Greer, Genealogical Publishing Company, 1982, Baltimore, Maryland. Page 18 shows his arrival date as 1651 and that he was sponsored by Thomas Thornbrough of the Northampton Company.
[192] *Early Virginia Families along the James River: Their Deep Roots and Tangled Branches*, Charles City County–Prince George County. Volume II. Compiled by Louise Heath Foley, Clearfield Publishing Company, Baltimore, Maryland, p. 18.

During the war, Ishmael sold supplies and provided services to the North Carolina or Continental Army. This service is documented in *North Carolina Revolutionary Army Accounts*, Vol XII, Part XI, p. 1445, and Part XIV, pp. 1938–1943. This act may appear to be just a business transaction, but it may have been far from that. Military officers issued vouchers for supplies and services while there was no promise of immediate payment, or if payment was not possible. North Carolina and the federal government did not establish a process for making claims for payment until the war ended. In fact, there was no currency with which the army could make payment. Those who supplied the army faced retribution from local Tories, and this was often violent retribution. The Tory/Revolutionist relationships festered throughout the war, especially in the southern colonies. Following the war several Tory instigators were hung. Ishmael was probably adept at maintaining a fine-edged relationship with the local Tories. One of his brothers was captured by the Tories and held as a prisoner during the war, so they knew the risks.

The Rains brothers' contributions to the Revolution are notable and worthy of further discussion and will be covered in some detail later in chapter five of this book.

The following two Patriot stories, David and James Perrigo Sr., my fifth and sixth great-grandfather respectively, are taken from the book I have written named *The Problem of the Perrigo Patriots of Pownal*. While the stories remain largely unchanged from that book, the documentation and references have been updated with the latest available information.

I will also add that chapter nine contains the stories of other Perrigo Patriots who are the brothers of both David and James and the sons of those brothers, for a total of fifteen Patriot stories.

### David Perrigo

Born: Circa 1738, unknown location in Massachusetts, maybe Bridgewater
Died: After 1804
Burial: Unknown location, but probably in Essex County, New York
Service: French and Indian War in Connecticut. Revolutionary War in the Continental Army in the Twenty-Sixth Regiment of Massachusetts. Later designated the Second Massachusetts Regiment. His father also served in that regiment.
Rank: Private
Service Dates: 1757, 1758, and 1780.
Wife: Susanna Varrel, married on 21 February 1765, Gloucester, Essex County, Massachusetts
Lineage: Son Justus J. Sr., his son Justus Jr., his son Martin VanBuren, his son Andrew Jackson, and his daughter Blanche Francis Adams (my grandmother). He is almost certainly my fifth great-grandfather.
DAR: No
SAR: No

The Perrigo family, from which I am descended, has been extensively researched by other family members for many years. Despite those early efforts, it seems no one was successful in establishing the early Perrigo history in New England. Particularly who my fourth great-grandfather, father of Justus Perrigo Sr., might be. So, I set out to settle that mystery, and my research led to my ultimately publishing a book—*The Problem of the Perrigo Patriots of Pownal*—in 2024. I will discuss this effort later in the Perrigo chapter of this book. I will sum up my efforts by stating that I was not completely successful in my attempt, but the following story of David Perrigo stands as the most thorough investigation I have seen, and I believe the preponderance of evidence points to a logical conclusion as to who the father and grandfather of Justus Perrigo Sr. might be.

David is the unproven son of James Perrigo Sr. and Lydia Hayward of Stoughton, Massachusetts, and later Pownal, Vermont. I have not found church or city birth records recording that birth. I will discuss their family relocation from Stoughton in Norfolk County to Bridgewater, Plymouth County, around the year of his birth when I discuss his father James's story next. They were quickly warned out of Bridgewater, and his birth may have simply not been recorded. I have extensively searched city records of Massachusetts during that period and am convinced his birth was not recorded in any city. I will offer a possible reason for that mystery later with his father's story.

David married Susanna Varrel (1738–Unknown death date) in Gloucester, Essex County, Massachusetts, and I have those records. The distance from Plymouth to Gloucester is about sixty miles, and he was about twenty-seven years old. The marriage was in February 1765, and it seems he wasted no time in getting to Pownal, Vermont, as we see him there with his father later that year, based on a census report from 1771. That report placed them in Pownal as early as 1765. Perhaps he arrived earlier, and he returned to marry, but that is speculation. Interestingly, that 1771 Vermont census report reflects him as being from Connecticut. Maybe he remained in Connecticut following to the French and Indian War and remained there until his marriage.[193]

His presence in Pownal is documented with several documents, petitions, and appointment notices. I have a copy of a petition taken from *State Papers of Vermont*, Volume V, on 3 January 1779, showing that David signed a petition requesting land from the colony. I saw no evidence that it was approved.

He served in the French and Indian War for at least fifteen days in 1757, in the Connecticut Fourth Regiment Militia under the command of Colonel Wooster in the First Company. His brother Robert also served in the same unit in 1759. His cousin John Kemp Perrigo was killed while serving in the same unit in 1757. David would have been nineteen or twenty years old while serving. The source I consulted establishes this fact, but it does not relate where they enlisted or served.[194] His cousin John Kemp Perrigo died in a hospital in Albany, New York, because of his injuries from an accidental shooting, so the unit may have been operating near Albany in 1757. His brother Robert also spent some time in that hospital the same year, and he is also listed as a soldier in that unit. I have researched French and Indian War records for several years and have observed that enlistments were for specific campaigns, not for a specific period as with the Revolutionary War and later conflicts. I believe that few men served in this war for only fifteen days. The records I found claimed fifteen days for David, but what I have is not an original record, but an extraction of an official record taken by a researcher a hundred years after the fact. That may only be part of the story. Remember I discussed earlier that brothers James Jr. and John also served in the French and Indian War, but in a Massachusetts regiment, at about the same time, and they also served in New York. Brother Robert went to Rhode Island after the

---

[193] *Vermont 1771 Census*, Jay Mack Holbrook, Holbrook Research Institute, Oxford, Massachusetts, 1982.
[194] *Rolls of Connecticut Men in the French and Indian War*, Volumes I and II, Connecticut Historical Society, Hartford, Connecticut, 1903.

war, and James Jr. remained in Massachusetts. John and David may have worked in New York or Connecticut and later relocated to Pownal with their father by 1765.

On 19 March 1787, David was appointed as surveyor and viewer of fences for Bennington County.[195] The surveyor description is clear, but the viewer of fences should be explained. The Pownal area in Bennington County was being developed from the arrival of the first settlers twenty years earlier. David was among that early group, based on him being listed in the 1771 census that placed him there by 1765. Descriptions of the land earlier in the book revealed that it was decent farming land, as opposed to most Vermont land west of the mountains. Fencing was made mainly from stones cleared from the fields rather than from wood rails. Once a fence was in place, it was difficult to adjust its location. Real property descriptions used landmarks such as rivers and large trees. Rivers changed over time, and trees died. A fence, once in place, would become a log-term property boundary; therefore, locations of those fences was important. David would need to know the basics of survey techniques and also need to be familiar with the community. This was an important job. It also indicates he was literate and a respected member of the community.

The 1779 petition mentioned above was probably not approved, so this might explain his next act. He joined the Continental Army in Williamstown, Massachusetts, on 29 June 1780. He served 5½ months and was discharged on 6 December that year. It is an interesting part of the story that his father, James Sr., joined the same unit in April 1777, was AWOL by May that year, and later returned for duty in January 1778 at Valley Forge. This is an interesting story that leads a person to imagine many questions that are not easy to answer. David's service is recorded in *Massachusetts Soldiers and Sailors of the Revolutionary War*, Volume 12, page 187, as is his father's service. Neither of these men lived to claim a pension. James Sr. may not have been eligible, because of his absence. The Massachusetts enlistments are easy to explain, as Williamstown, Massachusetts, is about four miles from Pownal, Vermont.

When this story is viewed in a larger perspective, there were eighteen Perrigo men, descendants of James Sr., living in and around Pownal at the time of the Revolutionary War. Ten of them were serving in the army at about the same time, from 1776 to 1780. The remaining eight men were too young to serve. Would this fact explain the actions of James Sr.? Did he return to care for the remaining families? When the regiment was converted into a Continental Line unit, an act that ensured the unit was leaving the colony, perhaps James Sr. opted to stay with the family.

I did not find any evidence of a land grant for his service in the Revolutionary War. I am not sure the colony of Massachusetts awarded any land grants, as the colony had no land to award, as did the New York and Virginia colonies who awarded land in in New York and Kentucky respectively.

We know of three children of David and Susanna:

- Frederick Howard, 1765–1850. Patriot of the Revolutionary War.

---

[195] *Vermont Historical Gazetteer*, Volume I, Burlington, Vermont. Page 493 references the appointment of David as surveyor and viewer of fences on 19 March 1787.

- Justus J. Sr., 1768–1832. War of 1812 veteran and my fourth great-grandfather.
- Charles, 1770–1856

I have researched Wales Perrigo, who I believe may be a son of David and Susana, but I have insufficient documentation to pursue this relationship further. Wales was born in 1774, making him a younger brother of Frederick, Justus, and Charles. I have further evidence of his children, but the lack of birth and other records from Pownal prevents me from listing him as a son of David. Wales lived in Dutchess County, New York, and had several children, one of which was Wales Jr., a noted soldier of the Black Hawk War.

I am not sure of the death date of his wife Sussana Varrel. I believe she may have died prior to the 1800 census, as it appears David may have lived with his son Frederick Howard at the time of that census. He was the only elderly male in that household with Frederick.

I believe that David moved to New York before the 1790 census. His oldest son Frederick moved before this census, and David may have lived with or near him. I see David in the Willsborough, Essex County, tax rolls there in 1803 and 1804. I believe that he lived with his son Frederick Howard in the same location for the 1800 census, as there is one adult over forty-five along with Frederick's wife and family. His son Justus Sr. also lived near there and appeared on the same tax rolls. I have established his death date as after 1804 in Willsborough, New York, based on the tax list for that year.

**James Perrigo**
Born: 1702, Raynham, Bristol County, Massachusetts
Died: 2 February 1786, Pownal, Bennington County, Vermont (unproven date and location)
Burial: Unknown location, probably in Vermont
Service: Sixth Company of Colonel John Bailey's Continental Army, Twenty-Sixth Regiment of Massachusetts. Later designated as the Second Massachusetts Regiment of the Continental Army.
Rank: Private
Service Dates: 10 April 1777 until January 1778, with a break of AWOL
Wife: Lydia Hayward, married March 1727 or 1728 in Bridgewater, Plymouth County, Massachusetts
Lineage: His son David was the father of Justus J., and his son Justus Jr. was the father of Martin Vanburen, his son was Andrew Jackson, and his daughter was Blanche Francis Perrigo Adams (my grandmother). James would be my sixth great-grandfather.
DAR: No
SAR: No

James is a third-generation Perrigo and the son of Robert Perrigo Jr. and Mary (last name unknown). He was born in Raynham, Bristol County, Massachusetts. We know he is the son of Robert Jr. as he is mentioned with his brother Ezekiel in a court summons pertaining to his grandfather's estate in 1719.[196] This document also gives his town of residence at that time. The

---

[196] 1719 court summons to Henry Peterson regarding the probate of the will of Robert Perrigo. New London County court records, held in the Connecticut State Library in Hartford.

Cutter Account[197] also supports this relationship, as do the Bishop "Perrigo Papers."[198] I could find no official records establishing his birth; however, I was able to locate a source that attributes the births of his sons and daughter to him and his wife Lydia.[199] James is a great-grandfather to most of the current Missouri line of Perrigos.

He married Lydia Hayward (1708–1791) on 4 March 1727 or 1728 in Bridgewater, Massachusetts. This marriage is documented in both the Town of Stoughton records and Bridgewater records. He probably filed this marriage both in his town of residence and Lydia's town of residence. This listing was an "intention to marry" entry from 1727, with the marriage in 1728. The book *Mayflower Families through Five Generations* also supports this marriage.[200]

Lydia was the daughter of Joseph Hayward Jr. and Sarah Crossman of Bridgewater. Lydia is listed as their daughter in *The Brett Genealogy*.[201] I also have a copy of her Bridgewater birth records for 1708 listing her parents.

The Haywards were long-time citizens of Bridgewater and were landowners there. Her mother, Sarah, was the daughter of Joseph Crossman and Sarah Alden of Taunton, Massachusetts, and later Bridgewater. I have her birth records. Sarah is a *Mayflower* Descendant, and so is her daughter Lydia. Her second great-grandfather John Alden was a crewmember on the 1620 *Mayflower*, which would not automatically make him a *Mayflower* Descendant, but he chose to remain in the colonies and thusly is recognized as a passenger. I suspect his choice was logical, as he soon married Priscilla Sarah Mullins, who was a passenger on the ship with her family. Her father William and mother both died on the ship the winter after its arrival in Massachusetts. John was the seventh signer of the Mayflower Compact and was the last male survivor of those who came on the *Mayflower*.

I remember being taught in grade school that John's friend Myles Standish was interested in proposing to Priscilla, so he asked his friend John to inform Priscilla of his intentions. Her response, according to William Webster, was, "John, you should speak for yourself." This response apparently led to the following genealogy:

- Parents of Lydia:
    - Joseph Hayward Jr., 1673–1746
    - Sarah Crossman, 1686–1746
- Parents of Sarah Crossman:
    - Joseph Crossman, 1659–1696
    - Sarah Alden, 1685–1713
- Parents of Sarah Alden:

---

[197] *Genealogical and Family History of Northern New York,* Volume I, William Richard Cutter, p. 1169. Note: I refer to this as the "Cutter Account" in this book.

[198] The Perrigo Papers, compiled by Prof. Robert E. Bishop of Bradenton, Florida, Volume I and II, from 1980 to 1982.

[199] *The Record of Births, Marriages and Deaths and Intentions of Marriage in the Town of Stoughton and the Town of Canton from 1727–1845,* Canton, Massachusetts, printed by William Bense, 1896.

[200] *Mayflower Families through Five Generations,* vol. 16 pt. 3. Society of *Mayflower* Descendants, 2004, Plymouth, Massachusetts. Page 47 establishes the marriage of Lydia Hayword and James Perrigo.

[201] *The Brett Genealogy,* Parts I, II and III, compiled by L.B. Goodenow. Murray and Emory Company, Cambridge, Massachusetts, 1915, p. 73.

- o Joseph Blunden Alden, 1626–1697
- o Mary Simmons, 1638–1697
- Parents of Joseph Blunden Alden:
  - o John Alden, 1599–1687. *Mayflower* passenger. He would be my tenth great-grandfather.
  - o Priscilla Mullins, 1602–1685. *Mayflower* passenger.

These are the references I used to establish the John Alden and Hayward relationships:

- *Mayflower Births and Deaths: From the Files of George Ernest Bowman at the Massachusetts Society of Mayflower Descendants,* Volumes I and II, Susan E. Roser, Genealogical Publishing Company, Inc., Baltimore, Maryland, 1992.
- *Memorial of the Descendants of the Hon. John Alden*, Ebenezer Alden, Randolph, Massachusetts, 1687, pp. 1 and 2.
- "Signers of the Mayflower Compact," published by the *Mail and Express*, New York, 12, 19 and 26 November and 24 December 1898.
- *North American Family Histories 1500–2000*, Provo, Utah, 2016, p. 564.
- *Mayflower Families through Five Generations*, vol. 16, pt. 3 (John Alden). General Society of *Mayflower* Descendants, 2004, Plymouth, Massachusetts, pp. 47 and 48.

I will not list the proof of relationships for the Hayward, Crossman, and Alden families, but I have the birth, marriage, and probate records for the four generations of this well-researched family connecting Lydia to the Aldens.

The John Alden home of about 1630 and still stands in Duxbury, Plymouth County, Massachusetts and is a national historical landmark. It is a ¾ Colonial-style home with two stories and has probably not changed much since he lived in it.

It is always interesting to consider the question: How did James and Lydia meet? Her family had deep Pilgrim roots, and the Perrigo family was likely not known for religious fervor, and I suspect they were not particularly wealthy, perhaps poor. James lived several miles away on the south side of Boston in Stoughton and Lydia in Plymouth County southeast of Boston. I present two thoughts for consideration in this question. First, James was born in Raynham, not far at all from Bridgewater. These towns are in different counties, but only about seven miles separates them. Second, the Haywards owned property in Taunton, south of Raynham, and would have likely passed through the town of Raynham on the way from Bridgewater to Taunton on the old "King's Highway."

I know of four sons and a daughter of James and Lydia:

- Robert, 1729–1808. Lived in Rhode Island and New York and was a Revolutionary War Patriot.
- James Jr., 1731–1808. Lived in Massachusetts and was a Revolutionary War Patriot.
- John, 1733–1811. Revolutionary War Patriot. Died in Chittenden, Vermont.

- Mary, 1737–1761. Died at the age of twenty-four in Killingly, Windham County, Connecticut.
- David, 1738–1808. Father of Justus Jr., my fourth great-grandfather. Died in Chelsea, Vermont. He too was a Revolutionary War Patriot discussed above.

All their children's births are recorded in the Staunton city records of birth and death except for David, discussed above.

It is important at this point in the James Perrigo story to establish a residency timeline of James and Lydia, as I have some questions concerning where the family lived at an important point of their lives, the period of 1739–1765. It is important to note that all these locations are not more than twenty-five miles apart, except for Pownal, Vermont.

### James Perrigo Timeline

| Date | Event | Location | Source |
|------|-------|----------|--------|
| 1702 | Birth | Raynham/Bristol | City records |
| 1719 | Summons | Stoughton/Norfolk | Court documents |
| 1728 | Marriage | Bridgewater/Plymouth | City records |
| 1729 | Birth of son Robert | Stoughton/Norfolk | City records |
| 1731 | Birth of son James Jr. | Stoughton/Norfolk | City records |
| 1733 | Birth of son John | Stoughton/Norfolk | City records |
| 1737 | Birth of daughter Mary | Stoughton/Norfolk | City records |
| 1738 | Birth of son David | Unknown | None |
| 1739 | Warning Out | Bridgewater/Plymouth | City records |
| 1754 | Warning Out (Robert) | Bridgewater/Plymouth | City records |
| 1760 | Probate Witness | Bridgewater/Plymouth | Court records |
| 1765 | Colony Census | Pownal/Bennington | State records |
| 1777 | Military | Pownal/Bennington | National Archives |

Here are some notes for the timeline:

- It is worth mentioning that the county of his birth, Bristol County, is adjacent to Plymouth County and that Raynham is only about seven miles from Bridgewater in Plymouth County, the home of Lydia.
- The 1719 summons for his grandfather's estate establishes he lived in Stoughton in 1719.
- He married Lydia in Bridgewater, Plymouth County, Massachusetts, 1728.
- His son David was possibly born in Bridgewater, Plymouth County, Massachusetts, in 1738.
- James was a witness to son Robert and Sarah Shorey's legacy case involving her inheritance from her father Miles Shorey in 1760. Robert and Sarah lived in Bristol County, so perhaps James lived nearby. He was born in Raynham, Bristol County. Perhaps they were safe from "warning out" in Raynham. More on that issue below.
- James and Lydia and sons John and David were living in Pownal, Vermont, by 1765.[202]

---

[202] *Vermont 1771 Census*, Jay Mack Holbrook, Holbrook Research Institute, Oxford, Massachusetts, 1982. This census records the residents of Pownal for the year of 1765, which included James Sr., John, and David Perrigo

I have documents proving his birth location in Raynham, Bristol County, in 1702 and then his residence in Stoughton from as early as 1719 until 1737. Son David may have been born in Bridgewater in late 1738. In March 1739, the entire family was warned out of Bridgewater, the hometown of Lydia. I have been unable to document James and Lydia's location from 1739 (in Bridgewater) until 1765, when they appear in Pownal, Vermont, except that James seems to be in Bristol County in 1760 to witness his daughter-in-law's legacy case. It also interesting to note that son Robert and his wife were married in Plymouth, Massachusetts, in 1753 and they too were warned out in 1754. Robert soon moved to Rhode Island.

Records show James and his family were warned out of Bridgewater in March 1739 by the constable. Warning out was a mechanism for denying residency based on a previous English practice in which a town would advise a poor transient person or family that the town was financially unable to provide them assistance. It was English law that towns provide support to persons in need. Therefore, the town leadership "selectmen" would determine if the town could financially support additional poor arrivals. If not, they would order the constable to warn the new arrivals of the situation. See the figure below for a copy of the warning document.

The book *Warning Out in New England* gives some detail on the need for this practice and the supporting legislation in several New England colonies and towns. On 5 January 1739, an act was passed in Massachusetts establishing that citizens were not eligible for financial support even if they had paid taxes in that town.[203] I think this legislation probably motivated the Bridgewater selectmen to warn out families and individuals they had failed to warn out in the past. Perhaps the James Perrigo family was not destitute, but just poor, and the town needed to ensure they did not become a burden. The fact remains, when you were warned out of town, you had to leave, and James Perrigo and family did just that. Figure 4-7 below depicts the record of the warning out.

---

[203] *Warning Out in New England, 1656–1817*, Josiah Henry Benton, Boston W.B. Clarke Company, 1911, p. 52. This book discusses the New England practice of "warning out" and was used in the research of the James and Robert Perrigo stories.

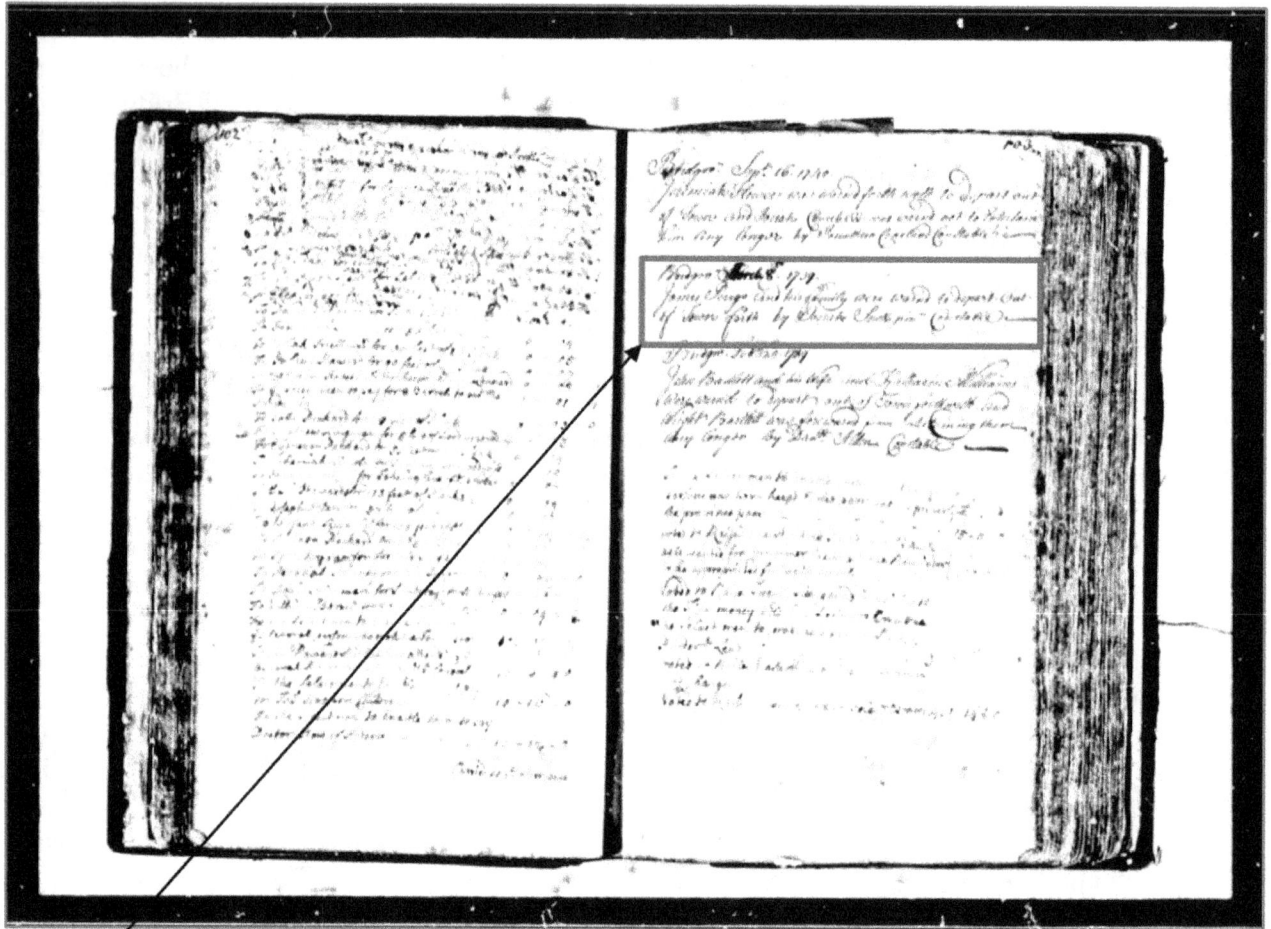

March 8, 1739. James Perrigo and his family were warned to depart out of town forth(wright) by Dansk Chapman Constable.

Figure 4-7. James Perrigo warning out notice. Massachusetts U.S. Town and Vital Records, Bridgewater, Plymouth County, Massachusetts, 1620–1988.

Stoughton was settled in 1713 and incorporated in 1726, two years before their marriage. It was named after William Stoughton, who was the chief justice of the Massachusetts Colonial Courts and was a strong supporter of the Salem witch trials. David Thomas Vosel wrote *An Early History of Stoughton and Historic Canton*. Canton was part of Stoughton until 1797, when it was split into a new town. He stated that in 1727 Stoughton had a population of 182, with 121 houses and 763 cattle and horses. The economy was based on six or seven sawmills, two gristmills, and four ironworks. The Neponset River provided excellent waterpower for those industries. By 1769, the population was given as 2,100 citizens. Given the importance of early industry in Stoughton, we must consider that James worked in one of those mills. I doubted if he was a

Taunton in 1732 and that he had sold several parcels of land.[204] While I believe he lived in Stoughton in 1732, Taunton is less than twenty miles from Stoughton, and Taunton is near his birthplace.

It appears that James and his family experienced a financial setback in Stoughton in 1737 and/or 1738. They left their home of several years and moved to Lydia's hometown and were quickly ordered to move on. This fact seems to explain why a man over sixty years old would move to the frontier in Vermont. They were probably more welcome there. Land grants were possible, and sons John and David had experienced the French and Indian War, lived in New York briefly, and moved on to Pownal. What did he have to lose? The church information was taken from the Vosel book mentioned above. It also mentioned there was not a school in Stoughton until around 1739.

A mystery related to the financial setback discussed above is that I and other researchers have been unable to document the birth of their youngest son, David. He seems to have been born at about the time of the warning out of Bridgewater. One must consider that registering the birth of a newborn required a trip to the city hall. If James was at all concerned about being vulnerable to warning out, then maybe he chose to skip this formality. That is a real possibility we are forced to consider. Remember, his first three children were not recorded by a church, but at the Stoughton City Hall. David was likely not born in Stoughton, or his birth would have almost certainly been recorded in that town. The only church in town until 1739 was the English Anglican Church, with Baptist and Catholic churches being established that year. None of the other family births were recorded in a church.

I cannot overlook this lack of documentation, because we have little other proof of relationship with his father and mother. His father did not leave a will. My research of the records of nearly every town in southern Massachusetts has not been fruitful. I am convinced that his birth was never recorded, given the extensive research performed by myself and others.

These are the facts that seem to establish a father/son relationship, but this is not proof:

- David and brother Robert were hired to serve in the French and Indian War at the same time in the same unit. The documentation for this service used the term "hired" as opposed to "enlisted."
- David and his proposed father were counted in the Pownal, Vermont, 1771 census, which established their residency in that town in 1765. I believe they were the first Perrigos to settle there, and brother John arrived one or two years later.
- David and his proposed father signed a petition in Pownal at the same time.
- David and his proposed father joined the same Massachusetts Revolutionary War unit; however, they did not serve at the same time. They enlisted in Massachusetts, but that town was four miles from Pownal.

---

[204] *Mayflower Families through Five Generations*, vol. 16, pt. 3. Society of *Mayflower* Descendants, 2004, Plymouth, Massachusetts. Pages 47–48 establish that James was a brickmaker and that he had sold two parcels of land in Taunton.

My research of Revolutionary War Patriots over the years has revealed several respected historians claiming that nothing of consequence took place outside of Virginia during the Revolutionary War and immediately prior. While one should not discount the activities of Thomas Jefferson nor disregard William Henry Lee's ability to persuade the Virginia House of Burgess to enact an early version of the Declaration of Independence, Massachusetts contributed to the beginnings of the Revolution also. The Boston Tea Party was encouraged by Samuel Adams and did much to stir New Englanders to action. A lesser-known event also encouraged by Samuel Adams took place in Stoughton, the previous home of James and Lydia and their family. To be correct, James and Lydia were citizens of Pownal, Vermont, by the time of these activities, but their son James Jr. and his family certainly remained there after their departure. In fact, even though he lived in Wrentham, James Jr. joined a military unit in Stoughton early in the war.

The Suffolk Resolves were compiled at Doty's Tavern on 16 August 1774, and some historians hold that these resolves were the basis for the Declaration of Independence, written the following year. This meeting included such notables as Rev. Samuel Dunbar and Paul Revere, and the location was chosen by Samuel Adams and Dr. Joseph Warren. Dr. Warren might not be a well-known name, but one can argue that the Revolution might not have been possible without his leadership. He was unfortunately soon killed in the Battle of Bunker Hill.

Why would a tavern be chosen as a meeting location? Meetings other than church services were prohibited, so Samuel Adams encouraged that this meeting be held a little farther from the coast than Boston. Doty's Tavern was a well-established meeting place with a reputation as a clean, well-run establishment, often patronized by influential citizens. This location might not attract the unwanted attention of the British. The tavern was located on what was known as the Taunton King's Highway, which linked Taunton with Boston.

The meeting resulted in written resolves that were voted on and passed and eventually approved by the Continental Congress in Philadelphia at Carpenter's Hall on 17 September 1774. This story can be found in the article "Doty Tavern" by Daniel T.V. Huntoon.[205] The history of Stoughton was taken from Wikipedia and its listed references.

I do not propose that James was involved in this important meeting, although I am certain he and Lydia were citizens of Pownal, Vermont, by then. But I am convinced he was aware of it and the resolves after the fact. One only needs to follow this story with the activities of three generations of the James Perrigo family to gain an appreciation for their desire for liberty and belonging to a community. They helped make history, and this meeting may have stirred their motivations to fight for their freedom. It is noteworthy that James Jr. had connections to Stoughton when this important meeting occurred and that he wasted no time in enlisting in the Continental Army when war began. He was already a member of the minutemen.

We are uncertain of his arrival in Pownal, Vermont, but we see at least one petition signed by him there in 1776. I have also discussed the Vermont 1771 census, which establishes his presence in Pownal as early as 1765 along with his son David.[206] That census is listed with the

---

[205] "Doty Tavern," Daniel T.V. Huntoon, *Potter's American Monthly*, July 1876, vol. 7 no. 5, pp. 24–26. Used for the James Perrigo story.

[206] *Vermont 1771 Census*, Jay Mack Holbrook, Holbrook Research Institute, Oxford, Massachusetts, 1982. This census records the residents of Pownal for the year of 1765, which included James Sr., John, and David Perrigo.

references below. He signed as a witness in his son Robert and his wife Sarah Shorey's legacy case in which she inherited from her father's estate. This was in 1760 in Bristol County, Massachusetts. These facts seem to date his movement from Massachusetts to Vermont between 1760 and 1765. It appears his sons John and David also moved to Vermont, while son Robert moved to Rhode Island and son James Jr. remained in Massachusetts.

He was a Patriot in the Revolutionary War in a Massachusetts regiment. This fact requires some explanation, as he was Vermont resident. *Massachusetts Soldiers and Sailors of the Revolutionary War* reports him as being from Pownal, Vermont. As a matter of note, I have seen his service records reporting him as being from Pownal, New York. That is explained by the fact that the New York colony claimed Vermont as a territory until the matter was settled by the First Continental Congress in 1791. It is important to note that Massachusetts also claimed the Vermont territory. I maintain that this confusion resulted in the colonies of Massachusetts and New York failing to require towns and cities to establish systems for keeping vital records. Remember, there also were no record-keeping churches in early Pownal.

We are left to ponder his livelihood in Pownal, as he signed a petition for land in that small town in 1887. He no doubt acquired land as a very early settler and may well have earned a living as a farmer. I have questioned the likelihood of Pownal being a farming region, but early descriptions of the land in and around Pownal describe the soil as being suitable for farming, as opposed to land outside of Bennington County being rough and rocky.[207]

James joined the Sixth Company of what I believe was the Twenty-Sixth Massachusetts Regiment of the Continental Army on 10 April 1777 at Williamstown, Massachusetts. I have a copy of his National Archives records. This was just a few miles across the Vermont/Massachusetts state line. We have seen documents stating it was only four miles from Pownal to Williamstown. James had a short military career, as he was reported absent without leave on 2 May of that year. We find him later in January 1778 in Captain Warner's Company of the same regiment at Valley Forge. He was present for a muster that month, and it is unclear how much longer he served. The Massachusetts records do not mention the designation of the unit, but research has shown that Colonel Bailey commanded that unit, and it was probably in northern Massachusetts in April that year. This unit did see some important action, but its assignment to the Continental Army was changed to a state line unit and back again twice in 1777. It was, however, truly a Continental Line unit while at Valley Forge. While serving as a Continental Line unit, it was designated the Second Massachusetts Regiment of the Continental Army. It was commonly referred to as "Bailey's Regiment."

We should not be too quick to be harsh with the manner of his service, because he was not a young man—he was over seventy years old. His record is not to be confused with his son James Jr., who was in Massachusetts at that time, as we have his records of the Revolutionary War in another unit. Their military records clearly establish that they were different men. He was a landowner, and his absence from the military from May to January might be explained by his farming responsibilities. We have the right man here; he merely did what he could. Still a Patriot even

---

[207] *A Gazetteer of Vermont: Containing Descriptions of all the Counties, Towns, and Districts in the State, and of Its Principal Mountains, Rivers, Waterfalls, Harbors, Islands, and Curious Places*, John Hayward, Boston: Tappan, Whittenmore, and Mason, 1849.

if his records reflect that he deserted. We should furthermore consider that James enlisted in a state militia that was soon reassigned as a Continental Line unit. This change would certainly result in the unit leaving Massachusetts, which is probably more than he had bargained for. It is also important to note that James rejoined his regiment at Valley Forge in December after being AWOL since April. His records do not reflect how long he remained at Valley Forge. His service is recorded in *Massachusetts Soldiers and Sailors of the Revolutionary War*.[208]

His death date and location are uncertain. His wife Lydia died in 1791 in Stephentown, Rensselaer County, New York. She was probably living with their son David. I believe James died in Pownal, but that has not been documented.

---

[208] *Massachusetts Soldiers and Sailors of the Revolutionary War*, Volumes 1–17, Boston, Massachusetts, Secretary of the Commonwealth, Wright and Potter Printing, 1896–1908.

**I am not a Virginian, but an American**
*-Patrick Henry*


### Chapter Five: The Rains Brothers—Six, Seven, or Eight, Ain't They Great?

I have been familiar with my Rains genealogy for many years. Ishmael, my fourth great-grandfather, was documented by my mother and brother many years ago in their research. Later, during some of my research projects, I found several men who were probably his brothers, but not much additional work was done by myself in that pursuit. As I began the Patriot program, I discovered a DAR application claiming that a potential father of Ishmael, Henry Raines Jr., was a Patriot. That application was disapproved based on DAR research that seemed to support the fact that Ishmael was a Tory. I have not been able to confirm that assertion, and in fact, in 2018 he was designated a Patriot by the DAR based on his patriotic service to the army. That fact drew me back into research mode. I had already discovered eight possible brothers, several of whom had served in the Revolution.

It is probably important to discuss the spelling of the Rains surname, as I have always spelled it differently. Where did the "e" come from? The story provided by my father was that his second great-grandmother was a landowner in Pettis County, Missouri, after her and her son's arrival from Randolph County, North Carolina. Her land records were seemingly recorded with the modified version containing an "e," and she was advised that it was easier and cheaper to change her name than to change land records. My research for the book about a Civil War ancestor—William Rains—seems to point to another reason, but I will merely state that "Rains" was the way they did it then.

Collaboration with my brother Gary has yielded a 1908 letter written by Mary Rains McNary, granddaughter of George Rains Sr., discussed below. She stated that when her grandfather and his brother Lawrence moved from North Carolina to Ohio, there were three brothers remaining in North Carolina. Since brothers Ishmael and Robert were dead by the time the brothers moved, that would seem to account for at least seven Rains brothers. I have attempted to account for Ishmael's brothers and their service to the nation, and that evidence abounds for those who served in Virginia. There are six brothers I have confirmed, with other candidates that may never be proven without DNA evidence. Four of the six known brothers are Patriots, and one may be qualified as a Patriot with further research, as Randolph County Militia records are in very poor condition. There may be at least one more missing brother, or maybe not. The Rains brothers were brothers of my fourth great-grandfather, and they were:

1. **Robert**
Born: 1740, Caroline County, Virginia
Died: 1794, Randolph County, North Carolina
Service: Fourth Regiment of Foot of the Virginia Militia
Wife: Hannah Elizabeth Barker (1751–1854)
DAR: No
SAR: No

Robert was a witness to his brother Ishmael's will of 17 December 1790 in Randolph County, North Carolina, so this makes him one of the seven possible brothers. I have a copy of this will. This birth date is proven by Virginia soldier records. He likely moved to Randolph County after the Revolutionary War, as he did serve in a Virginia regiment. His nephew Ambrose, who is my third great-grandfather, was a witness to the will. I believe his wife's name was Elizabeth, but no marriage records have been found. Robert died in Randolph County, with burial location being uncertain.

He joined the Virginia Fourth Regiment of Foot commanded by Colonel John Newill and Captain Kirkpatrick for the duration of the war. I have a copy of his National Archives records. This regiment was later consolidated with the Virginia Third Regiment, and his service has not been used for any applications for either the DAR or SAR. He probably enlisted in May 1779, but his discharge date has not been determined. His records reflect that he mustered every month after May until December that year. His regiment was a Virginia Line unit, not a militia or Continental Line unit. Colonial Virginia records show that he was eligible for a land grant for his service, but a patent was never issued. This eligibility would seem to indicate that he served until the end of the war, which would have been a typical Virginia enlistment. His wife would not have been eligible for a pension, as he died before the pension laws were passed starting in 1811 and he was not married while in the service.

The 1790 census places him in Randolph County, North Carolina, and he was a witness for his brother Ishmael's will in 1790. He died in 1794 leaving four children—John, James, and Mary—who are mentioned in his will. As he fought in the Virginia Army, he probably did not move to Randolph County until after the war. His children's names were:

- Robert Rains Jr., 1770–1850. Settled in Alabama
- John Rains, 1773–1858. Settled in Tennessee
- James Rains, 1776–1866. Settled in North Carolina
- Mary Rains, 1782–Unknown death date

## 2. Ishmael

Born: 1741, Caroline County, Virginia
Died: 17 December 1790, Randolph County, North Carolina
Wife: Sarah Caviness (1742–1840)
DAR A212817
SAR: No

Ishmael, my fourth great-grandfather discussed in the previous chapter, was probably born near Fredericksburg in Caroline County, Virginia, and moved to Randolph County, North Carolina, as early as 1772. He farmed there for the remainder of his life and owned land. He appears in the Cumberland Association census as early as 1772. This was true frontier country at that time, and hostilities by Indians were not uncommon. He farmed during his adult life in Randolph County and later in bordering Chatham County and died on 17 December 1790. I doubt if he moved, as Randolph County was formed from parts of Chatham and Guilford Counties in 1779. He and his wife Sarah Caviness (1742–1840) had three sons who are named in his 17 December 1790 will:

- George Rains, 1769–1845. Settled in Ohio.
- Ambrose Rains, 1772–1831. Lived in Randolph County, North Carolina. My third great-grandfather.
- John Rains, 1780–1835. Settled in Kentucky.

Even though Ishmael did not serve in the military during the Revolutionary War, he has been awarded Patriot status by the DAR based on patriotic service.[209] He rendered services and sold goods to the militia during the war and claimed reimbursement following the war. I found a receipt issued by the North Carolina Hillsborough District on 11 September 1783 that certified that Ishmael had been paid (amount illegible) pounds and 8 shillings apiece for an unknown product. I will speculate livestock, but the certificate was nearly unreadable. It is likely that his second claim was for services rendered. His support of the revolutionary forces probably placed him and his family at risk of retribution from Tories. You will see below that his proposed brother was taken prisoner by the Tories. This was a civil war in this part of the country, and Indians and Tories were abundant and violent. The Cumberland Association records attest to the violence existing there before and following the Revolution.

The Cumberland Association was formed by the colony of North Carolina around 1772 to establish efficient government of the early settlers along the Cumberland River in what was to become parts of North Carolina and Tennessee. The association was formed upon the signing of the Cumberland Compact with the granting authority being the colony of North Carolina. Their records describe frequent conflicts with Indian tribes in that region that were severe enough to cause farmers to remove their families from the area. The association then offered land grants to those men that remained to protect the land, crops, and livestock. While it might appear that the association was based in Tennessee, its records show that the Rains family was farming in North Carolina well prior to the Revolution. Tennessee was not a state at that time, so North Carolina residents probably recognized that as North Carolina territory. John Rains discussed below, or possibly his father, was an early explorer for the association and is mentioned several times in their records.[210] It is likely that the association made it possible for brother George to settle in Tennessee in the early 1800s and for brother Lawrence Wesley to live there for a few years as he migrated to Ohio.

### 3. George Sr.
Born: 1750, Caroline County, Virginia
Died: 1840, Warren County, Tennessee
Wife: Rosanna Graham (1752–1805)
DAR: No
SAR: No

---

[209] *North Carolina Revolutionary War Accounts*, Book A, Part VII, Part XI, p. 145 and Part XIV, p. 1938. Weynette Parks Haun. Reflects that Ishmael was paid on two accounts for services rendered to the North Carolina Militia, thus making him eligible for patriotic service recognition.
[210] *1770–1790 Census of the Cumberland Settlements: Davidson, Sumner, and Tennessee Counties*, compiled by Richard Carlton Fulcher. Genealogical Publishing Company, Baltimore, Maryland. Pages 99 and 100 list the families of Captain John Rains Sr. and John Rains Jr. in Davidson County.

George is one of the seven brothers inferred by his granddaughter Mary Lucinda McNary's letter of 1907. He is shown in a special Randolph County census of 1782, the first federal census of 1790, and Randolph County tax records of 1799. He is on the early tax list for Tennessee in 1812.

He and his wife had seven children. The names are of interest, as I have seen some of these names reported as brothers of Ishmael and most of them lived in Randolph County at one time or the other.

- Joab Rains, 1770–1856. Settled in Indiana
- Asahel Thomas Rains, 1772–1861. Settled in Tennessee
- George Rains Jr., 1773–1875. Settled in Ohio
- Hannah Rains Woodward, 1774–1860. Settled in Texas
- James Rains, 1775–1860. Settled in Tennessee
- John Rains, 1777–1856. Settled in Indiana
- Robert Rains, 1784–1877. Settled in North Carolina

George Sr. moved to Jacksboro, Tennessee, around 1800 and built a home on Caney Branch near Jacksboro in Warren County. He spent the remainder of his life in that area and left his home to Asahel, his second son, who lived out his life there. There are no records of his service in the military, but research is continuing. His family's move to Tennessee seems in conflict with the statements made by his granddaughter that he moved to Ohio. Further research has confirmed that George Sr. probably did not move to Ohio, but that his son George Jr. did move there. George Jr. was the father of Mary Lucinda McNary. George Jr.'s children later moved to several states, including Ohio, Iowa, and Texas.

4. **Lawrence Wesley**
Born: 24 December 1752, Caroline County, Virginia
Died: 20 November 1823
Service: Randolph County Militia of the Hillsborough District Brigade of the Continental Line
Wife: Ann McManus (1759–1821)
DAR: A214285
SAR: No

Lawrence was an executor for the will of his brother Ishmael; thus, he is one of the Rains brothers in Randolph County, North Carolina. He was probably born in Caroline County, Virginia, but this has not been proven. He can be found in Randolph County until after 1800, where he received a Randolph County land grant in 1784 for 160 acres (Randolph 258-93). This was likely for his Revolutionary War service. He is shown on the Randolph County censuses of 1790 and 1800. The military records from Randolph County, North Carolina, are in very poor condition, handwritten and incomplete. He was awarded a pension (number R-8623) and served under Colonel Barbour (Balfour), so he was certainly a Patriot. Colonel Balfour commanded the Randolph County Militia, which was assigned to the Continental Line and the Hillsborough District Brigade. This regiment was established on 2 February 1779 when the county was formed from the southern third of Guilford County. If Lawrence joined the regiment shortly after its being formed, then he likely remained in the unit until the end of the war. This fact is important when considering which brothers fought in the Battle of Guilford Courthouse in 1781, which was just a few miles from his home. While this brigade and its subordinate regiments did not make the headlines for critical battles, as did some Virginia regiments of the Continental Line, they fought and made a difference in the outcome of the war. I will cover their likely roles in the Battle of Guilford Courthouse in a later chapter.

Lawrence was reimbursed for goods and services by the North Carolina military, as were his brothers Ishmael and Anthony and two other family members to be discussed later. This would make them eligible for DAR and SAR recognition as Patriots for patriotic service in addition to military service.

The 1820 Ohio Ross County census shows him in the Eagle/Hockey township. Other records show that he established a grist/sawmill in Eagle Township on Eagle Run Creek as early as 1813. His will of 21 May 1817 includes eleven children. His wife Ann died in 1821, and he died on 20 November 1823. His children are:

- Isaac Rains, 1781–1836. Settled in Indiana
- Ruth Rains Dixon, 1785–1875. Settled in Ohio
- Catherine Rains Moffatt, 1787–1850. Settled in Ohio
- Lawrence Rains Jr., 1790–1863. Settled in Mills County, Iowa
- John Rains, 1792–1874. Settled in Ohio
- Elizabeth Rains Cox, 1797–1851. Settled in Ohio
- Ann Elizabeth Rains Comer, 1797–1875. Settled in Ohio
- Rebecca Rains Dixon, 1800–1872. Settled in North Carolina
- Benjamin J. Rains, 1806–1869. Settled in Ohio
- Hannah Rains Cox, 1809–1871. Settled in Ohio
- Nathan Rains, 1809–1848. Settled in Mills Iowa

## 5. Anthony

Born: 13 October 1757, Caroline County, Virginia
Died: 25 March 1837, Randolph County, North Carolina
Service: Chatham County Militia of the Hillsborough District Brigade of the Continental Line
Wife: Nancy Graham (1760–1841)
DAR: A093504
SAR: P3300086

Anthony is one of the brothers of Ishmael. He was born in Caroline County, Virginia, and was alive when he applied for his military pension (number SW1481) in 1834. In his application, he stated he came to Randolph County in 1772 with his mother and family. He spent the remainder of his life in Randolph County. This statement about the move is important in that it establishes the date as well as the fact that his father did not accompany the family.

He served in the Chatham County Militia under Colonel Luttrell. Both the DAR and SAR have approved memberships based on this service.

His wife Nancy, in her claim for pension, stated he had enlisted in the Randolph County Militia under Colonel Lyteral (Luttrell) and served for about eight months. She filed for the pension after his death in the state of Tennessee. The request was approved, and she received a pension of $26.66 per year. My research of North Carolina regiments has led to the fact that Anthony was in the Chatham County Regiment under the command of Colonel Luttrell, not the Randolph County Militia as stated by his wife. This mistake is easy to understand due to the reorganization of counties in 1779 as discussed above. These dates seem to establish his being involved in the Guilford Courthouse battle.

He received a two-hundred-acre land grant from the state (288-593) on 18 August 1789.

He and his wife Nancy had twelve children, but not all survived to adulthood. The names of their children are familiar Rains names and seem to lead to the confusion about some of Ishmael's brothers, as some of them were old enough to appear on the first and second federal censuses, which did not reflect ages.

- Elizabeth Rains Craven, 1775–1849. Settled in Missouri
- John, 1785–Unknown death date. Settled in Tennessee
- Isaac Rains, 1787–1862. Settled in Tennessee
- Hannah Raines Steed, 1788–1853. Settled in North Carolina
- Elizabeth Rains Poe, 1790–1840. Settled in Indiana
- Rebecca Rains Hay, 1792–1850. Settled in Tennessee
- Jane Rains Bray, 1794–1890. Settled in Tennessee
- Mary Rains Phillips, 1796–1877. Settled in Tennessee
- Balaam Rains, 1801–1888. Settled in Tennessee
- William Rains, 1807–1900.

I have long considered the following John Rains as a brother of Ishmael; however, it is possible, even likely, that he may be a cousin or a more distant relative. Maybe it is coincidence that he also lived in Randolph County and had a familiar given name. Whether he is a missing brother or not, he is an extremely interesting man who left his mark on history. If he was a brother, he would have been the "wild youngest brother."

## 6. John

Born: 2 August 1759, Fredericksburg, Virginia
Died: 28 January 1835, Bledsoe County, Tennessee
Service: Randolph County Militia of the Hillsborough District Brigade of the Continental Line
Wife: Letitia "Lety"
DAR: A093540

His wife Letishia, in her claim for pension on 3 June 1839, stated that John was born near Fredericksburg, Virginia, and moved with his father and mother to Randolph County, North Carolina, around 1772. It is likely that Ishmael's father was dead before he moved to North Carolina, but the year of movement is consistent with the date of Ishmael's movement to that county. That statement calls into question the possibility that Ishmael and John were brothers. The spelling of Letitia's given name has several variations in records I found. I will use the spelling used with her Widow's Pension Application File of 1843. Her family connections are probably quite interesting, but unproven. Her proposed father Bryant B Ward "Indian Trader" and mother Nancy Ward Fivekiller deserves further investigation.

He entered the Randolph County Militia on 1 December 1779 under Captain Robertson and Colonel Coylar (Collier) and was discharged on 1 March 1880. While being interviewed for his pension (number SW982), he said he was drafted. He stated he had participated in a skirmish against the British and Tories near Ceraw (Cheraw) Hills in South Carolina. After his discharge he was captured by the Tories in June 1880 and held for about two months and escaped capture near Wilmington, North Carolina. Wilmington is a coastal town in the extreme southern tip of the state near adjoining South Carolina. The DAR recognizes him as a POW. He stated that he then went to live with his father for three or four months. I am unsure whether his father still lived in Randolph County, North Carolina, or if he had relocated to Sevier County, Tennessee, where I believe his father probably died.

In April 1781, he was appointed as a captain of a ranger company that would patrol the counties of Randolph, Chatham, Cumberland, and Moore, where he served in that capacity for six months. This is probably the reason that the DAR granted him Patriot status, but he was also recognized for patriotic service since it is documented that he was also reimbursed for goods and services sold to the military.[211] During his Revolutionary service the statement that he served under the command of Colonel Collier establishes that he served in the Randolph County Militia, not the Chatham Militia, as did brother Anthony. I think it is likely that he fought in the Guilford Courthouse battle.

Following his military service, he moved to Sevier County, Tennessee. He married an Indian lady named Letitia, of the Virginia Powhatan tribe, on 8 March 1787, possibly in Caroline County, Virginia, so his efforts at settling the Indian problem must have been successful. He stated in the pension hearing that he lived in Sevier County, Tennessee, for twenty-one or twenty-two years and moved to Overton County, Tennessee, for three years. He then moved to Bledsoe County, Tennessee, where he lived for the remainder of his life. He is buried in the Collier Cemetery in Pikeville, Bledsoe County.

His and his wife's pension statements seem to complicate my long-held belief that he was a brother to Ishmael, Lawrence, George, and Anthony. Then who was his father, who seemingly brought John to Randolph County? The census reports show several Johns of that area, so one of them was probably his father. It seems his father was alive after his escape from Tory captivity in 1781 before he signed on with the ranger company. I am unsure where he lived from late 1881 until he married Letitia in Caroline County, Virginia, in 1787. It seems he moved to Sevier County, Tennessee after the marriage. He did own land in that county, as did several other Rainses. I discovered land transactions in that county when a railroad purchased land for construction in 1824. Several Rainses were involved in those transactions.

Several years ago, I read of a fellow "long hunter" associate of Daniel Boone. His name was John Rains of Virginia. When this John was preparing to move to Kentucky, Daniel Boone

---

[211] *North Carolina Revolutionary War Accounts,* Book A, Part VII, Part XI, p. 145 and Part XIV, p. 1938. Weynette Parks Haun. Reflects that John was paid for providing services, thus making him eligible for patriotic service recognition.

recommended that he consider Randolph County, North Carolina, instead. Boone then took Rains to Randolph County, and Rains then went back to Virginia and returned to North Carolina with his family.[212] This John may well have been the father of this John Rains. I believe the elder John eventually moved to Sevier County and was followed by his son Captain John after the war. This might explain Letitia's statement that John had moved to Randolph County with his father. I have had possession of this well-written and well-documented article for several years. While it is interesting history, it is my opinion that the author has confused the long hunter John Rains with another John Rains of Sevier County, possibly the father of Captain John Rains. The long hunter Rains, I believe, settled near Nashville, Tennessee. I am unable to resolve this mystery and will leave this question to subsequent generations. I will venture speculation that John's father, John Sr., was a brother of Ishmael's father. I will develop this proposal in the next chapter.

John and Letitia had seven children named in his will, all born in Sevier County, Tennessee:

- James Rains, 1788–Unknown death date. Settled in Tennessee
- Robert Rains, 1790–1890. Settled in Arkansas
- Letitia Rains Britt, 1790–Unknown death date. Settled in Tennessee
- Samuel Rains, 1794–1849. Settled in Arkansas
- John Rains Jr., 1796–Unknown death date
- Charles Rains, 1798–1840. Settled in Tennessee
- Josiah Rains, 1800–1880. Settled in Tennessee

---

[212] "Long Hunters," Emory L. Hampton, *Historical Sketches of Southwest Virginia*, Southwest Virginia Historical Society, 1970.

**"The God who gave us life gave us freedom at the same time"**
*-Thomas Jefferson in 1774*

## Chapter Six: Six, Seven, or Eight, Your Daddy's Great, but Who Was He?

My search for Rains Patriots led me to consider the preceding generation of Ishmael and his brothers: Was there a Patriot lurking in that far distant edge of our tree? If some of the brothers departed Virginia just prior to the Revolution, and if brother Robert remained behind to fight in the Virginia Fourth Regiment, then what about the remainder of the Rains line? Speculation about the identity of the father of Ishmael was just that—speculation. The given names of Henry, John, Ambrose, and William seem to be a starting point, as those names continued to be used by this Rains line for generations. Caroline County was also a good starting point due to statements made by one or more brothers discussed above, as well as that of Letitia, wife of possible brother John.

The Rains Virginia lines were diverse until I narrowed searches to Caroline County. Records of Henry Rains, while not plentiful, do exist, and they—as well as several other researchers—told me enough to know that this line was probably worth further research to make connections with the North Carolina brothers.

I seriously considered not including this chapter in the book for two reasons. First, the information gathered does not meet the professional standards adhered to with the preceding Patriots, and second, I doubted I would find more Patriots. While I was relatively sure I had the parents and grandparents of Ishmael and his brothers, there is insufficient information to publish these best guesses as facts. Much is not known or not proven. It may never be proven for several reasons. I will publish what I know not so much from my desire to inform, but from my desire to challenge future generations to continue the search along this line. It simply must be extracted from the volumes of records that exist in Virginia courthouses not destroyed during the Civil War, and from the University of Virginia Library. It will be useful to skip a generation to begin the story of the Virginia Rains line.

First, something about Caroline County, Virginia, and how it became a Virginia county. That county exists today in what is known as the "Tidewater" area of eastern Virginia. It generally follows the Rappahannock River, with Spotsylvania County to the north side and Caroline County bordering on the south. Henry Rains owned land in both counties, with some of it bordering that river. These two counties were formed from the British Essex, King and Queen, and King William Counties, which were long corridors running from southeast to northwest along the Rappahannock River. Caroline County was formed in 1728, and the county seat is Bowling Green. Interstate 95 traverses through both Caroline and Spotsylvania Counties at Fredericksburg. This was then, and is today, prime real estate because of its riverside location. Much of the land once owned by Henry has been added to the current US Army Garrison Fort Walker, formerly Fort A.P. Hill. There is a present-day unincorporated area named Raines Corner near that base. Early in my military career, I was quite familiar with that base and the Fredericksburg area. I have traveled the Interstate 95 corridor from Richmond to Washington D.C. often and pondered the fact that my possible great-grandfather owned land near the bridge crossing the Rappahannock. Prime real estate indeed.

The proposed grandfather of Ishmael and brothers is:

**Henry Rains Sr.**
Born: Circa 1685, Wiltshire, England
Died: Between December 1766 and February 1767
Burial: Unknown, but probably in Caroline County
Wife: Esther Chapman of Virginia

Henry was a first-generation American and was a freeman, meaning he was not indentured to anyone and paid his way to America. He was allowed to own slaves and hold indentured servants, and he probably brought some indentured servants with him, or they followed him. The book *Cavaliers and Pioneers: Abstracts of Virginia Land Patents and Grants*, Nell M. Nugent. Volume III, 1695-1792. page 184 documents his status.

He owned several tracts of land in that area and received a couple of grants or patents from the king. The fact that he paid his own way to the colony would have made him and his wife eligible for a fifty-acre grant for each of them. He received grants in Drysdale Parish in 1716 and several later grants in the 1720s. These grants are recorded in the above reference and in *Virginia Colonial Abstracts*, volume 28, King and Queen County, Beverly Fleet. page10. Some of these references spell his name as Reins and Raynes, but we have the right man. He received a couple of grants and purchased some land, and in all he may have owned 1,200 acres of farmland. He was not a large landowner, but he was not a subsistence farmer either. Records show that Henry considered himself a planter.

Henry was appointed as a constable for Drysdale Parish of Caroline County for several years. This made him a law enforcement officer for that parish, which was a lifetime appointment, and I found that he served at least three terms. This was essentially the "Wild West" at that time, and being a law-enforcement officer was not a safe appointment. Most constables either quit or were killed. *Colonial Caroline: A History of Caroline County, Virginia*, by T.E. Campbell, The Dietz Press Inc., Richmond, Virginia, page 361.

Juries formed an effective means of enforcement of British common law, without political influence. I found records of Henry serving on at least three juries from 1732–1745. While this may seem like a normal function of any citizen, that was not actually the situation. Wealthy citizens would consider this act beneath their dignity and would not serve. Henry was a landowner and a freeman, and he likely had no problem with doing so. Above Caroline County History, page 351.

There are records of Henry presenting indentured servants to court after they escaped and were recaptured. An indentured servant would owe their landowner up to five years of service for payment of their transportation to the colonies. After satisfactorily completing this service, the servant was declared a freeman and could vote, own land, and marry. These deserters were re-captured, presented to the court, and fined, and their service period was lengthened to cover the cost of their recapture. Caroline County History, page 321. Remember, Henry was a constable, and maybe that allowed him to recapture them himself.

Henry's will was dated 27 December 1766 and was probated on 12 February 1767. He died be-tween those dates, probably in late January or early February. A surviving copy of his will was found by Ed Neal in June 2000. It was a hand-written copy used in a Spotsylvania County court case—Hill vs. Purvis—and a copy remains there today. He identified himself as Henry Rains of Drysdale Parish, county of Caroline, and as a planter. He used an "X" to sign the will, but he may not have been physically able to write. His will was witnessed by a William Rains, who may have been a brother. We believe that Henry's father was named William Rains (of Wilt-shire, England), but he did not come to America. The names of his children are contained in that will:

- John Rains, 1716–Unknown death date
- Ignatius Rains, 1722–1799
- Henry Rains Jr., 1725–1772. He is my proposed fifth great-grandfather
- Mary Rains Duval, 1726–Unknown death date
- Olivia Rains Pearce, 1728–Unknown death date
- Cordeliah Rains Perry, 1739–Unknown death date
- Ambrose Rains, Dates unknown

His will does not mention disposition of slaves, so he probably owned none. His land holdings were probably not substantial enough to produce tobacco using slave labor. I did, however, find census records stating that son Ambrose owned two slaves in Johnson County, North Carolina, by 1800. I found no records of Rains slaves in Randolph County, North Carolina.

No land was left to Henry Jr., but the will indicated that he had already been given land. Henry gave the remainder of his land to John, Ambrose, and Ignatius. I am not certain of the birth dates of these children, and Henry Jr. may well have been the oldest, since he had already received some land from his father. While I use a birth date for Henry Jr. of 1725, this date is probably too late given the birth of his oldest son, Robert, in 1740. Robert's birth date is proven. I found rec-ords of Henry Jr. involving some later land transactions there, as well as serving as a witness in a court case. I believe that Henry Jr. married Mary Rosanna Hammer, and she survived him and moved to Randolph County, North Carolina. She lived until at least 1793. Mary's father may have moved to Randolph County from Virginia, so this may help to explain her presence there with her children by 1772. The route taken by Mary to North Carolina is probably different than one might take today, as I believe they would have proceeded west to the Ashby Gap (see the Ashby chapter later in the book). This route would have taken them down the Shenandoah Val-ley to North Carolina. That is the route used by those entering the Cumberland Country. Today we merely proceed southwest on a more direct route. That was a dangerous migration route in 1772. I could speculate that Henry Jr. began that trip and never finished it.

I followed the lives of brothers John, Ignatius, and Ambrose, and they soon left Virginia for Kentucky and North Carolina. John moved to Kentucky and perhaps later Tennessee, and Ambrose to Johnson County, North Carolina. I found no records of these brothers serving in the Revolutionary War.

A mystery unfolded when I found records of a Henry Rains of Caroline County who joined the Caroline County Militia Third Regiment. He served aboard the Virginia navy's ship the *Mosquito*, which was taken by the British ship *Aranda* on 4 June 1777. This ship was manned by Caroline County men, and they were taken prisoners by the British. This Henry Rains remained prisoner for some time, became ill, and was eventually released and cared for by William Arnold, who received 10 pounds for nursing him to health during a bout of smallpox. Caroline County History, page 378. If this Henry Rains was the son of Henry Rains Sr. above, his story does not account for a wife and family in North Carolina by 1772 and the story of his death prior to that. Additionally, I am not sure this Henry was nursed to health from smallpox; he may have died from that disease. I simply do not know how this Henry Rains fits into the family group presented. Maybe he was the father of Ishmael, maybe not. Perhaps his family departed for North Carolina following his death in 1772.

Here is what we know about Henry Rains Jr.:

1.  He existed. His father's will establishes that, as does a statement made by son Anthony in his pension application. He was a witness in one or more Caroline County court records and was recorded as Henry Rains Jr.
2.  He never lived in Randolph County, North Carolina, a belief established by statements made by Anthony.
3.  The name of his wife was Mary Rosana Hammer. Her full name is not proven, and the marriage date is not known.
4.  He owned land in Caroline County, as property records show Henry Rains Jr. transferring land.
5.  He had at least five sons, as I have established that Anthony was a son, and he was a brother to Ishmael. Therefore, there were at least five brothers. Capt. John Rains of Randolph County may be a son, or maybe he is a son of John, the brother of Henry Jr.

His death was in 1772; again, Anthony made that statement. His location at time of death is unknown. Maybe he died or was killed during the trip from Caroline County to North Carolina, or perhaps he died from disease from military captivity. I have been unable to explain why his wife Mary would leave Caroline County with five sons and travel to a frontier territory, with many hazards along the way down the Shenandoah Valley. Read the Ashby chapter below to understand the many risks one might encounter in this area at that time. I recognize that son Ishmael was married during this migration, and his brothers were also adults, so she was not totally on her own. Then again, maybe Henry Jr. began that risky trip.

Henry Jr.'s wife Mary Rosanna Hammer is of further interest and has captured our attention for several reasons. She was a Quaker and was probably born in Pennsylvania. Her father, John Hammer, is a well-documented Quaker who also settled in Randolph County, North Carolina, after living in Virginia. Mary outlived her husband by several years after migrating to Randolph

County in 1772. She is shown on at least one Randolph County special census (1779), and more importantly, she sold goods and services to the North Carolina military during the war on at least three occasions and was reimbursed in 1783 for those actions. She appeared there on the first U.S. census of 1790. Mary would be the first Rains female eligible for Patriot status from the DAR and SAR. I have discovered a Randolph County land grant in 1793 for Mary Rains, and I can find no other Mary Rains of Randolph County who would have been an adult that year. Lastly, her Quaker upbringing would have surely prevented her from marrying into a slaveholding family in Virginia. While this statement is speculation, I believe that the fact that no slaves were listed on the will of Henry Sr. and the fact that the family did not move slaves to North Carolina supports that contention. I have further reasons supporting the contention that the Rainses were not slaveholders, but that is open for future debate and research. I did not include Mary Rosanna Hammer/Rains as a Patriot in this book, because I cannot prove she was the mother of the Rains brothers. Research will continue along that line.

The discovery of a final Rains Patriot was a late surprise in my research. While my third great-grandfather Ambrose Rains was only a few years old at the time of the Revolution, he did something that seems to place him in the Patriot category. You be the judge.

### Ambrose Rains
Born: Circa 1772, Randolph County, North Carolina
Died: 25 May 1831, Chatham County, North Carolina
Wife: Rachael Rushton
DAR: No
SAR: No

Ambrose is my third great-grandfather, son of Ishmael, and he is listed in his father's 17 December 1790 will. (Randolph County, North Carolina, Record of Wills and Inventories & Settlements of Estates, Book 1: 1779–1793, page 99.) His birth date is not certain but is based on the belief that he was born after his parents' arrival in North Carolina that year. Add to that the age categories on his and his father's census and other records, and that date is certainly a close guess.

He farmed in both Randolph and Chatham Counties and owned land in both counties at various times, and the recording of his deeds can be found in both counties' records. His land was usually located somewhere near Brush Creek. The earliest record of a land transaction is 7 July 1794, in Randolph County (Deed Book 6, page 69), where he received land grant number 195 from the state, lying on the Black Branch of Deep River. He again received land from the state on 29 May 1797, in Randolph County on the waters of Broad Mouth Creek. When Ambrose purchased 131 acres of his land on Big Brush Creek in 1809, a survey was made in 1810, and his sons John and Henry (then about thirteen years old) are named on the survey record. In those days, to save money on the survey, it was common to have teenaged sons used as chain carriers in the survey process. It is believed that the land Ambrose owned when he died is in the vicinity of Brush Creek Church. Ambrose died without a will. At the Court of Pleas and Quarter Sessions, 9 August 1831, the administration of his estate was granted to Abraham Lane. He entered a bond of $900 for security, and it was then ordered that he be given leave to sell the perishable estate. Court records also record the estate sale on 10 August 1831, listing all goods, who bought them, and the amount. The sale total was $190.75, with the highest-priced item being a gray stud horse with bridle for $90.59. Charles was present and purchased a "rifle gun and shot bag." A Lettis Rains bought a bureau, and it is possible that this is the Letitia Rains that we find later in Missouri.

After the death of Ambrose, his wife Rachel filed for her dower rights, which allowed her 1/3 of the land, and a committee was appointed. This process may have taken at least a year, or at least until after the crop harvest that year. That date is important when placing Rachel in Missouri either in 1832 or 1833 with her son Charles and daughters Hulda and Letitia. Son Henry had moved to Howard County, then Pettis County, Missouri, several years earlier.

He was only four years old by the start of the Revolution and ten by the end of the war. He did not fight but did claim reimbursement in 1783 for a rifle "donated" to the army, and he was paid nearly $10 for that loss. I make no claims of patriotism or of service to our nation except that he somehow lost a rifle to the army and was old enough to make a claim for that weapon at the age of about ten after the war. I am certain that an interesting story accompanies that loss, but that is likely lost to history and left to our imaginations. That claim was filed with the North Carolina Revolutionary War Accounts.[213]

As he died without a will, the names of his children were constructed from other records. There are ten known children: John F., Henry Ambrose, William, Jane, Hilda, Mary, Letitia, Catherine, Charles, and Hulda. These names continue the tradition of much-used Rains given names. Notably the name of Letitia may add evidence that John discussed above was possibly Ishmael's brother, as his wife was also named Letitia. Son Charles Henry is my second great-grandfather. His son William served in the Union Army during the Civil War, and I have written a book on the life of William Rains: *Horse Sense—William Rains and the Missouri Seventh Volunteer Cavalry.*

The Rains family lives are centered in Randolph County. Randolph County exists today, but county lines in North Carolina have changed several times since the Revolution. Randolph County was established in 1790, so in what county did the Rainses reside prior to that date? Chatham County is an original county of the colony, and it is shown as Ishmael's location at the time of his death. Military records for the Revolution establish that there was a Randolph County Militia, even though the county was not organized until after the war. Randolph County was formed from the southern part of Guilford County. Confusing, but it's clear that the Rainses lived and served in both Chatham and Randolph Counties prior to and following the Revolution, probably with only few moves.

---

[213] *North Carolina Revolutionary War Accounts,* Book A, Part VII, Part XI, p. 145 and Part XIV, p. 1938. Weynette Parks Haun. Reflects that Ishmael was paid on two accounts for services rendered to the North Carolina militia thus making his eligible for patriotic service recognition.

> **"Remember that it is the actions, and not the commission, that make the officer, and that there is more expected from him than the title."**
>
> *—George Washington's address to the officers of the Virginia Regiment,*
> *Thursday, 8 January 1756*

## Chapter Seven: Nothing There but Indians and Ashbys

The Ashby family, the French and Indian War, Colonial Virginia history, George Washington, and the Revolution are inextricable names and terms. This family settled in the gateway to the Shenandoah Valley region of Virginia, leaving their mark on that state. They were amongst the early settlers in that region, and they established a relationship with George Washington as a young man that continued for nearly forty years. They are the stuff of legend, and their story is worth recounting. Much has been written about them, and I will recount a few of the notable stories. One early Virginia explorer, when considering his planned explorations west of the Alleghenies, asked another explorer what he might find there, and the reply was, "Nothing there but Indians and Ashbys."

As I discussed earlier in chapter four, the purpose of this chapter is to tell the stories of the brothers and cousins of Thomas Edward Jr., Robert, David, and Fielding Ashby.

It is important to recognize as I tell these stories that I tell them from the perspective of colonists of that era. These were brutal and turbulent times. I have British friends that are quick to point out that the likes of the Ashbys were considered traitors of the time. They were not considered heroes. Another point of view is represented by current researchers that depict those Americans fighting Native Americans as less than patriotic, even portraying them as haters not worthy of positive historical treatment. I suppose even the French explorers would not have held them in high regard. I have Vietnamese friends that do not consider our operations in their homeland as heroic or even legitimate, but we nonetheless can discuss history from each other's viewpoint and learn from those discussions. I hope that we can do the same here. This is history, like it or not, and we can learn from it. Just keep in mind that history often depends on the perspective of those living it and recording it.

This family was heavily involved in the idea of the colonists' migration from the Virginia Colony westward into the Shenandoah Valley, including the initial Lord Fairfax land surveys, the French and Indian War, later Indian conflicts, the Revolutionary War, and later the Civil War. I must also mention that there were four generations of Ashby slave owners. I found slaves being passed to later generations in probate proceedings. Much of this family's success was built on the backs of slaves. I wish I could recount these slaves' important stories.

There were four generations, starting with the second American generation—father, son, grandson, and great-grandson—who served in the Revolution. The first American generation, Thomas Edward Sr., would no doubt have served had he lived long enough, but his six sons did fight in the French and Indian War and the Revolutionary War. I discovered more than twenty-three Ashby descendants of Captain Edward Ashby Sr., who fought in the Revolutionary War. In fairness, the fifth-generation Ashby family had one Patriot—Fielding Ashby, son of David, with his story told in chapter four above, as he is a direct ancestor of Emma Jo, my wife.

A geography note: Frederick County is now Clarke County, Virginia. Fauquier and Frederick Counties met at the crest of the Blue Ridge Mountains.

The French and Indian War is generally perceived as one war in current times. Various dates are given for the length of the conflict, generally from 1754–1763. Colonial records portray this conflict as several wars, or more properly campaigns, the most well-known being Braddock's campaign. Braddock was a British general who commanded at least two Virginia colonial regiments led by Colonels George Washington and William Byrd III, and soldiers were generally recruited for a specific campaign, not the duration of the war. Virginia soldiers received little pay but were awarded bounties of land in Virginia or the Kentucky territory. Of course, there were several other prominent colonial military leaders in other colonies during the French and Indian War, but their influence and operations were for the most part not in the colony of Virginia.

The sources for this chapter are documented with footnotes within the story, but it is worth emphasizing that the published documents I reviewed, although helpful, were often incomplete or just plain wrong. Even original documents can be misleading. For example, last wills and testaments are considered original documents, but one must recognize that they are often not complete. Some beneficiaries were not shown for any number or reasons, so I searched numerous other records, such as court and other family probate records, to confirm my belief that sons were omitted from Thomas Ashby's and his sons' wills. They were there, and I found them! I have also consulted with current Ashby family members, and we do not always agree on some dates, names, and places, and I suspect similar disagreements existed in those times. Family history is complex and not an exact science, but I will try to do justice to these great stories.

The first known American member of the Virginia line of Ashbys is Thomas Edward Ashby Sr. His story follows and then the stories of his six sons and their families, covering five generations of the family.

### Captain Thomas Edward Ashby Sr.

Born: 1682, Leicestershire, England
Died: 4 August 1752 in the Shenandoah Valley, Clarke County, Virginia
Burial: Centenary Reformed UCC Cemetery, Frederick County, Virginia
Wife: Rosanna (Rose) Berry

He is the seventh great-grandfather of Emma Jo Painter/Raines. The lineage is:

> Captain Robert Ashby, Emma Jo's sixth great-grandfather
> David Ashby, fifth great-grandfather
> Fielding Ashby, fourth great-grandfather (her DAR Patriot)
> Daughter Elizabeth Betsy (married Fielding Murphy), third great-grandmother
> John Murphy, second great-grandfather

Joseph Roney/Murphy, great-grandfather
Bessie Pauline Murphy/Scott, grandmother
Lita Blanche Scott/Painter, mother
Emma Jo Painter/Raines

The Ashby line from Patriot Feilding Ashby to Emma Jo Raines has been used for DAR applications and is very well documented. I believe I have adequately documented the earlier three generations from Captain Robert to Fielding Ashby in the following stories.

Thomas was born in Leicestershire, England, in 1682, immigrated to Frederick County, Virginia, between 1690 and 1700, and later moved to Fauquier County.[214] He married Rosanna Berry by 1700 in Virginia.

Thomas and Rosanna had at least ten children. All six of their sons fought in the Revolution, as well as the French and Indian War and earlier conflicts, not to mention the husbands of their daughters and grandchildren. The names of their known children are:

- Captain John Ashby, 1707–1789. Patriot
- Captain Robert, 1710–1792. Patriot and Emma Jo's direct family ancestor
- Captain Thomas Jr., 1714–1783. Patriot
- Captain Benjamin, 1722–1804. Patriot
- Elizabeth Hardin 1723–1758
- Rose Timmons 1724–1760
- Henry Ashby, 1725–1798. Patriot
- Captain Stephen, 1710–1797. Patriot
- Sarah Byrum 1727–1752
- Ann 1733–1752

These children are confirmed descendants, as they were included in his will.[215] Some published records claim at least twelve children, and I found possible candidates but could not document them. While the death dates of their sons have been documented mostly by wills and court documents, I have been unable to document their birth dates with certainty. The exciting stories of the Patriot sons follow, as well as those of the Patriot grandsons.

Thomas settled in the Shenandoah Valley by 1742 after receiving a small land grant.[216] He was among the early white settlers on the ridge of the Blue Ridge Mountains. He discovered an Appalachian Mountain gap used to this day named "Ashby's Gap." He soon owned at least 1,269 acres, and land adjacent to his land had been surveyed in his sons' names. He also owned a ferry across the Shenandoah River a few miles west of the gap near Winchester, Virginia. This gap often followed Indian trails and later became a very important road used during the Revolution and

---

[214] *Encyclopedia of Virginia Biography*, Volume V. Lyon Gardiner Tyler. Lewis Historical Publishing Company, New York. Page 1124 gives the account that Thomas Ashby initially settled in Fauquier County, Virginia, between 1690 and 1700, later moving to the Shenandoah Valley.
[215] *The Buckners of Virginia and the Allied Families of Strother and Ashby*, published privately for William Dickinson Buckner by the Genealogical Association, 1907. Pages 242 and 243 contain a copy of the Thomas Ashby will and list his children and the various land holdings.
[216] *Shenandoah Valley Pioneers and Their Descendants: A History of Frederick County, Virginia*, T.K. Cartmell, 1909. Page 16 shows that Thomas Ashby received a two-hundred-acre grant on the north side of the Shenandoah River from the Fairfax Estate on 1 February 1742.

Civil War and later westward expansion. As a matter of interest, land he earlier owned in Frederick County is now part of the Marine Corps Base Quantico, not far from present-day Washington D.C.

The Ashby Gap is recognized by a roadside historical marker today. This marker commemorates that his son John Ashby is known to be the first person to move the first "hogshead" of Virginia tobacco to eastern Virginia markets. Emma Jo and I recently visited that region and in particular Paris, Virginia, which is at the entry of the Ashby Gap. We obtained a room in the Ashby Inn, located in Paris, from which the gap can be viewed.

In 1742 and 1743 he served in the Fauquier County Militia as a captain, helping protect local settlers from Indians.[217] He received more than one land grant for that service, which might account for his large land holdings. The Shenandoah Valley was rich in natural resources such as game. It was highly valued by the Indians and, even though they may not have resided there all year, it provided a bountiful travel route from their summer to winter homes. The French fur traders were close business partners with the Indian tribes, and the appearance of English settlers threatened that valuable relationship. They were not thrilled to see the Ashby bunch, especially given the fact that they were surveying the land for future settlement. In about ten years, the colonists' presence in the valley would lead to the French and Indian War, in which the Ashbys and George Washington would find themselves tightly embroiled. This was a politically sensitive region. The British did not want colonists to settle in the Shenandoah region due to concern about conflict with the French, so they prohibited it. The treaty with Britain following the Revolution did not include that region, and I have studied scholarly claims that this shortcoming resulted in the War of 1812. There were certainly other reasons, but this was among them.

Thomas kept an inn on the Shenandoah River in 1748. That year he and his sons and grandsons assisted as chainmen, rod bearers, and recorders on several land surveys in the area supervised by a young George Washington. Washington's records show he stayed in the Ashby Inn during that period. The pay the Ashbys received for their work probably consisted mostly of land grants. The Washington and Ashby relationship continued from this early survey project through two wars and the Washington presidency.

Consequently, Thomas had substantial land holdings in Virginia, and in April 1752, prior to his death in August, he willed his real estate and personal holdings to his heirs. He held slaves, and some of his sons lived on land they were to inherit. One son, Thomas Jr., received only 1 pound cash and "no more," but he had probably already been given land by his father.

Thomas Ashby Sr. did not live to see the Revolutionary War, but he no doubt influenced his sons, grandsons, and later descendants to not shirk their duty to their new nation. This is a story worth telling, and I will recognize the six known Patriot sons, as well as their sons and grandsons, as appropriate. I have discovered more than twenty-three Revolutionary War Patriots who were descendants of Thomas and Rosanna, and their stories follow the stories of the six sons.

---

[217] *Virginia's Colonial Soldiers,* Lloyd DeWitt Bockstruck, Genealogical Publishing Company, Inc., Baltimore, Maryland, 1988. Page 28 shows that Thomas Ashby served as captain of foot on 23 March 1742–1743.

## 1. Captain John Ashby (Captain Jack)
Born: 1707, Delaplane, Fauquier County, Virginia
Died: 1789
Burial: Winchester, Virginia
Wife: (1) Jane Combs and (2) Catherine Huffman
DAR: A003417
SAR: P-11044928

John is a sixth great-uncle in the Raines/Painter line. Sometimes referred to as "Jack," he was born in Delaplane, Virginia, only about six miles east of Paris, Virginia; both are located on what is now Virginia Highway 50. He grew up near the Ashby Gap at Paris, and some researchers claim the gap was named after him, not his father. One story, "Life of Turner Ashby" by Thomas Almond Ashby, goes:

> He first comes into notice when, as a mere youth, he gave his name to Ashby's Gap in the Blue Ridge Mountains, through which the early settlers crossed over from the Piedmont section into the Shenandoah Valley. He has the credit of being the first white man to have piloted a wagon through this gap, and an accident that happened to him on this trip, because of his failure to lock the wheel of his wagon, is said to have given his name to the gap.

> The story goes that it was the custom in those days in going down a steep incline to cut down a tree and attach it to the wagon to hold it in check, for the wagon chain was not then in general use. John Ashby failed to take this precaution, and when the wagon in its descent ran over the horses and spilled the load on the ground, making a bad mix-up, he was asked why he had not locked the wheels. His reply was: "Damn a pair of horses that can't outrun a wagon."[218]

While I, and others, have attributed the naming of the gap to his father, figure 7-1 below depicts a roadside marker located at the gap along Virginia Highway 50 attributing the name to John.

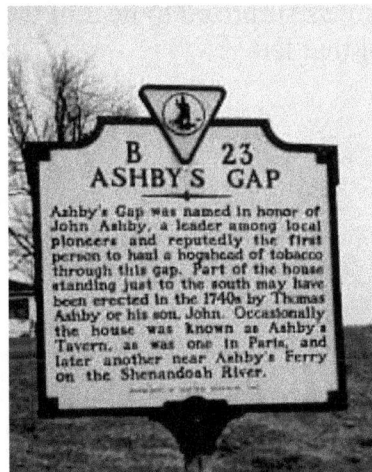

Figure 7-1 Historical marker near Ashby Gap, Virginia. Raines photo.

During the French and Indian War, Thomas served in the Second Virginia Rangers as a captain and commanded a company of rangers. His service dates were 1752–1756. During the war, he commanded Fort Ashby on the junction of Patterson Creek and the Potomac River and worked for Colonel George Washington, who commanded the Second Colonial Militia Regiment. Fort Ashby was in Hampshire County, now West Virginia, immediately west of Frederick County. His brother Robert, discussed below, also served under Washington. As a matter of record, Colonel Washington did not appoint John Ashby. Governor Dinwiddie appointed him as a ranger company commander to go to the Shenandoah River and help defend Washington, who had suffered a defeat or two by the Indians, and several settlers had been killed by the Indians. Colonel Washington knew Ashby well and had visited him and stayed in his home several times while surveying the Shenandoah region prior to the war. In fact, John and his father and brothers had served on his surveying crew. Ft. Ashby remained a well-known and often-used landmark for several years and served as an assembly point for federal forces during the Whiskey Rebellion, in which President Washington as commander in chief led federal forces to quell that uprising. One can imagine that the president knew that area well, having surveyed and fought two wars in and around that area.

His command of Ft. Ashby was brought to the attention of Colonel Washington several times during the war, and for several problems, most of which centered on lack of discipline. In December 1755, at least ten soldiers summarily left the fort to go home. George Washington, upon hearing of this, sent a captain and twenty soldiers to the fort to investigate. They discovered that there were in fact missing soldiers, but also, the remaining soldiers were mutinous and preparing to leave. The investigating officers convinced those soldiers to remain or be tried and hanged. They left an officer to assist Ashby in regaining control. After about three weeks, that officer left the operation back in Ashby's hands.

Ashby continued to be plagued by problems caused by unruly soldiers, which resulted in Washington writing a letter to him indicating he was surprised to hear of the many irregularities he was allowing. This is a transcribed copy of that letter:

Letters, Orders and Instructions, December 1755 28th
To Captain John ASHBY of the second Company of Rangers

I am very much surprized to hear the great irregularities which were allowed of in your Camp. The Rum, although sold by Joseph COOMBS, I am credibly informed, is your property. There are continual complaints to me of the misbehaviour of your Wife; who I am told sows sedition among the men, and is chief of every mutiny. If she is not immediately sent from the Camp,- or I hear any more complaints of such irregular Behaviour upon my arrival there; I shall take care to drive her out myself, and suspend you.

It is impossible to get clothing here for your men. I think none so proper for Rangers as match-coats; therefore would advise you to procure them. Those who have not receive clothing, for the future will receive their full pay without stoppages; and those already made, will be repaid them.

Those who have been clothed must either return them or allow stoppages. I would have you consult your men and fall upon some method to supply them immediately. I have heard very great complaints about the mens pay; and that it has been misapplied: to prevent any for the future

> I Order, that you have your accompts with the men properly stated against I come up. And always after you make payments hereafter, to take two receipts from each man: one of which you are to have entered in a Book kept for that purpose, for your own use; the other must be taken upon a sheet of paper, and transmitted to me monthly.

> I have sent you one of the mutiny Bills which you are (as far as it relates to the men) to have frequently read to them. Further; acquaint them, that if any Soldier deserts, altho' he return <u>himself</u>, he shall be hanged.

> Given Ye. at Winchester: December 28. 1755.

> G.W.[219]

Another well-documented story about Captain Ashby involved him delivering a message to Governor Dinwiddie of Virginia after General Braddock's defeat by the French and Indians. The letter was delivered by Ashby and the governor's response returned to Washington before they were aware he had even left his camp. Ashby soon disappeared for several weeks, and it was rumored the Indians had killed him, but he reappeared in good health. Maybe he feared reprisal from Colonel Washington more than the Indians. It is worthy of note that Washington's performance during this war was not spotless, but he did a good cover-up.

Although George Washington and John Ashby were at odds on several occasions during the French and Indian War, they remained on friendly terms. He first met Ashby in 1748 when he spent the night at Ashby's home while doing survey work for Lord Fairfax. He later spent eight days at Ashby's home in 1769, and Ashby later visited George Washington at Mt. Vernon after he became president.

In 1774, John traveled to Kentucky to survey additional land he had received as bounty for his service during the French and Indian War. He had received three thousand acres of land in the very center of the territory of Kentucky.[220] This was adjacent to another two-thousand-acre tract owned by Colonel Thomas Marshall, father of future Supreme Court Justice John Marshall. Thomas Marshall was later to command a Revolutionary regiment in which several Patriots discussed in this book served. After John surveyed this land—remember, he was a qualified surveyor—he returned to Virginia via a very complex and dangerous route, as the Revolutionary War had begun. He departed with two other men down the Ohio River to the Mississippi River to New Orleans. They then ventured east by land to Pensacola, Florida, and on to Charleston and Virginia. One man died during the journey.

During the Revolutionary War, he served as a captain in the Virginia Third Regiment. He received a land grant for that service. The records for that service are not clear, but he was either wounded or became ill soon after joining, as he served three years at half-pay, then was discharged. Following the war, he applied for a pension, which was denied because of his half-pay situation.

---

[219] George Washington Papers, Series 2, Letterbooks. (Original transcription from *The Writings of George Washington from the Original Manuscript Sources, 1745–1799*, John C. Fitzpatrick, Editor., vol. 01; re-transcribed by C. Hammet, 25 Mar 1999.)

[220] *Annals of Southwest Virginia 1769–1800*, Lewis Preston Summers, Abingdon, Virginia, 1929. Page 652 reports that John Ashby received a thousand-acre land grant on the head branches of the Bear Grass Creek branch of the Ohio River and on 23 June a grant of two thousand acres on the north-side Kentucky branches of the Ohio River.

At some point following the French and Indian War, John used the title of colonel. I found no records supporting that title, but who was to question him? Not even Colonel and later General and President Washington cared to do that. We found numerous other stories depicting the life of Colonel Ashby, all true we are sure, but we believe we have set the tone for a very colorful and independent American family story.

John owned land in the Shenandoah Valley near Winchester, Virginia, and grew tobacco and had slaves. One story I found involved his relationship with a slave:

> One day Capt. John Ashby sent a hogshead of tobacco by a trusted slave named Ephraim to Dumfries for sale. The inspector reduced the grade below what Ephriam believed to be true, and in order to prevent it getting into the hands of cheats, land sharks and grafters, he rolled it into the Quantico Creek, there to rot, and went back home.

> Capt. John Ashby asked how he got through with the tobacco, and Ephraim straightforwardly replied, "Poorly."

> "What did you do with it?" asked his master.

> "Them rascals down in Dumfries," said Ephraim, "wanted to reduce yo' tobacco to nothin' an' sooner 'an let you be cheated, why I jes' rolled it into the creek."

> The uncompromising old ranger sprang to his feet and instead of a reprimand, exclaimed, "You did right, sir; you did as your master would have done had he been there! But, Eph, the fish of Quantico Creek will not forgive you for the next six months for making them drink bitter water." Capt. John and Ephraim passed the incident off with several drinks of honest whisky.

> Capt. John Ashby died about 1797 and left a name and reputation long treasured by his countrymen, who admired the sterling character of this diamond in the rough.

> *Notes found in Florence Chiles Maltsberger and Isabel Gaddis family papers.*

John was the great-grandfather of Confederate General Turner Ashby Jr. and Captain Richard Ashby of the Civil War. Turner was killed during the war while serving for Stonewall Jackson and was promoted to general after his death.

The DAR has awarded Patriot status to John, not for his military service but for patriotic service by providing material aid.[221]

John had eight children with his first wife, Jane Combs:

- Elizabeth Peters, 1742–1837. Married Patriot Colonel John Peters, and they settled in Woodford County, Kentucky.
- Lewis, 1746–1806. Patriot. Remained in Virginia.
- Lieutenant Nathaniel, 1748–1811. Patriot. Settled in Kentucky.
- Jane "Jennie" Darnall, 1750–1822. Husband Colonel Joseph Darnall was a Patriot, and they settled in Woodford County, Kentucky.
- Mary, 1750–1751

---

[221] *Virginia Revolutionary Publick Claims*, Janice Abercrombie and Richard Slatten, Iberian Printing Company, Athens, Georgia, 1992, pp. 346, 352, and 354.

- Edward, 1754–1809. Probably settled in Frederick County, Virginia, but he almost certainly lived and did business in Kentucky.
- Captain John Jr., 1756–1774. War of 1812 Virginia soldier who settled in Kentucky.
- Nancy Ann Smith, 1762–1793

John married Catherine Huffman in 1783, and he and Catherine had one daughter:

- Charlotte Statterwhite/Parker 1785–1851

I used multiple sources for the names of his children. I found a transcribed copy of his October 1788 will (the original may have been destroyed in a Fredericksburg courthouse fire), which is in the possession of a modern family member. This copy was provided by Gary David Ashby, a descendant of Patriot David Ashby. I am indebted to Gary David Ashby for this document.

There are some disagreements as to both the birth and death dates of John. Some sources give a 1797 death date and some 1789. His will was dated October 1788, and it appears his estate was divided accordingly prior to 1797, so the 1789 death date may be correct. Both DAR and SAR records reflect the 1797 date. It seems all his children were alive and mentioned in his will and received Virginia or Kentucky land as well as several slaves. Some of these slaves assisted on the move to Kentucky.

After the death of John, several of his children moved to Woodford County, Kentucky, and settled the land he had obtained from his French and Indian War service. Daughter Elizabeth and her husband Colonel Peters, and sons Nathaniel, Edward, and John Jr., were probably in that group.[222] Several years had elapsed since John surveyed and recorded the deeds to this large tract before the arrival of his descendants. Some of this land contained squatters that had to be evicted before permanent homes could be built.

John's oldest son, Lewis (1746–1806), was a Patriot who served in the Fauquier County Militia under the command of Captain Benjamin Harrison. I believe that this Benjamin was the grandfather of future President Benjamin Harrison. He married Leannah Ann Buckner Darnell (1754–1809), and they had ten children. His grandson William, a son of Buckner's, was essentially killed by the last bullet of the last battle of the Civil War. He was killed on 9 April 1865 at the Appomattox Court House.[223] Lewis remained in Virginia and is buried in Frederick County.

His son Lieutenant Nathaniel (1748–1811) served in the Revolutionary War as a lieutenant in the Virginia Third Continental Line Regiment until 1777. DAR records show that he served as a lieutenant, as do his National Archives records in my possession. *The Buckners of Virginia* states that he continued his service following the war on the frontier as a captain.[224] He married (1)

---

[222] *History of Woodford County, Kentucky*, William Edward Railey, Roberts Printing Company, 1928. Pages 360–362 give the history of John Ashby's children after their arrival in Woodford County, Kentucky, after 1800.
[223] *The Buckners of Virginia and the Allied Families of Strother and Ashby*, published privately for William Dickinson Buckner by the Genealogical Association, 1907, p. 244.
[224] Ibid., p. 245.

Marquerite "Peggy" Mauzey (1748–1802) and (2) Ann (last name unknown). Ann was mentioned in his 1811 will, as well as his twelve children. He received a land grant for his service and settled near Lexington in Fayette County, Kentucky, where he lived the remainder of his life. The Buckner book referenced above states he was a very successful farmer and that his children were also quite successful, including his son Dr. Mauzey Quincy (1787–1873), who became a well-known doctor.

## 2. Captain Robert R. Ashby

Born: 1710, Delaplane, Fauquier County, Virginia
Died: 27 Feb 1792, Delaplane, Fauquier County, Virginia
Burial: Ashby Cemetery in Delaplane, Virginia
Wife: (1) Dorothy Baylis (1713–1774) and (2) Catherine Combs (1742–1791)
DAR: A003422
SAR: P-104933

Robert is the second son of Thomas Edward Ashby Sr. and Rosanna Berry, the father of David Ashby, and the grandfather of Fielding Ashby, making him the sixth great-grandfather of Emma Jo. As I have already recounted his story in chapter four above, I will not repeat the details of his life. He had ten known children. They were:

- William, 1735–1772. Married Mary Tibbs. Served in the French and Indian War and as a captain in the Fauquier County Militia in 1771.
- David, 1737–1803. Patriot and Jo's fifth great-grandfather.
- Robert Jr., 1738–1780. Married Ann Walters.
- Captain John, 1740–1815. Patriot. Married Catherine Huffman.
- Winnifred Peters/Piper, 1741–1790. Married James Peters.
- Captain Nimrod, 1742–1764. Married Francis Wright and was killed in the French and Indian War.
- Mary (Molly), 1743–Unknown death date.
- Captain Benjamin, 1744–1823. Patriot. Married Jane Ash.
- Ann Farrow/Smith, 1745–1807. Married William Smith.
- Captain Thomas Enoch, 1747–1790. Patriot.

The marriages of his children are documented in the Fauquier County Records.[225] Of his seven sons, four served in the Revolutionary War, and two did not serve, failing to survive until that war. One was killed in the French and Indian War in 1763 (Nimrod), and William was serving in the Fauquier County Militia at the time of his death prior to the war. Robert Jr. did not serve but died in 1780 before the end of the war.

Son David's story was presented in chapter four and will not be repeated here.

---

[225] *The Buckners of Virginia and the Allied families of Strother and Ashby*, published privately for William Dickinson Buckner by the Genealogical Association, 1907, p. 276.

Son Captain John Ashby (DAR: A217936 and SAR: 340080) served in the Third Regiment of the Continental Army and was seriously injured in New York. Those injuries required that he be evacuated back to Virginia, and he served the remainder of the war as a recruiter. John also served in the Fauquier County Militia in 1770 prior to the Revolution. He died near Delaplane, Virginia.

Son Benjamin Ashby served in Morgan's Rifle Regiment or the Third Virginia Continental Line Regiment during the Revolutionary War and later received a land grant and claimed a pension. He also took the Oath of Allegiance in 1778 and paid the Virginia Supply Tax in 1783.

Thomas Enoch (DAR: A003409), Robert's youngest son, served as a private in the Fauquier County Militia under the command of Captain Benjamin Harrison, who was to later become president of the United States. He also paid the Virginia Supply Tax in 1783. He died in Fauquier County, Virginia.

### 3. Captain Thomas Edward Ashby Jr.
Born: 19 February 1714, Frederick County, Virginia
Died: 23 May 1783, Harpers Ferry, Jefferson County, West Virginia
Burial: Harpers Ferry, West Virginia
Wife: Mary Elizabeth (Betty) McCullough (1716–1760)
DAR: A003426
SAR: No

Thomas is the son of Thomas Edward Ashby Sr. and Rosanna Berry of Frederick County, Virginia. He is the sixth great-granduncle of Emma Jo and a brother of John, Benjamin, Henry, Robert, and Stephen Ashby, also discussed in this chapter.

Thomas Edward Jr. served under Captain Daniel Morgan in the Virginia State Second Regiment during the Revolution. He enlisted on 1 November 1775 and mustered out on 23 May 1783. He received one hundred acres for a land grant (warrant #959) on 20 June 1783. He and his wife Mary Elizabeth McCullough had at least six children, of which at least three sons also served in the Revolutionary War. He and his wife settled at Harpers Ferry, West Virginia, and are buried there. I have shown a DAR Patriot number for Thomas, but the DAR has frozen this listing until several vital facts concerning his residence and death date are proven. I have a copy of his National Archives records, but these records do not reflect his residence when he enlisted. His records show he enlisted in the Virginia Second Regiment, and the book *Historical Virginians in the Revolution* shows he was a member of the state militia.[226] I'll note that this reference indicates a state unit, but other records reflect militia, which is a county unit. I believe the Second Regiment was a State Line unit in which other family members served.

I have documented six children of Thomas and Mary Elizabeth, and there may be two older sons, but I was unable to fully document their connection with this family.

---

[226] *Historical Register of Virginians in the Revolution: Soldiers, Sailors, Marines, 1775–1783*, John H. Gwathmey, Genealogical Publishing Company, Inc., 1973, 1975, Arlington, Virginia, p. 23.

- Jesse, 1738–28 November 1823. Served in Lord Dunmore's War in 1771. Married (1) Nancy Williams and (2) Tamar Ruby. Settled in Kentucky.
- Henry, 1745–29 June 1833. Patriot recognized for patriotic service. Married Ann Shumate and settled in Kentucky. Served in the Kentucky Militia during the War of 1812.
- George, 1745–1817. Patriot in the Eighth Virginia Regiment of the Continental Line.
- Stephen, 1747–1831. Patriot in the Washington County, Pennsylvania, Militia. See his story below.
- Mary Rude, 1749–1820
- Peter, 1751–1833. Patriot in the Virginia Line.

Jesse was the oldest son of Captain Thomas Ashby and Mary Elizabeth McCullough. He married (1) Nancy Williams (1738–1776) and (2) Tamar Ruby (1756–1841). Although the DAR has awarded membership based on his Revolutionary War service (A000340), his only military service was in 1771 and 1773, when he served, as did his father, in Lord Dunmore's War in Captain David Morgan's Company. He received two land grants in what is now West Virginia for what I assume was two enlistments. Those enlistments were for specific campaigns usually of short duration. Even though the DAR has approved memberships based on his service and awarded a bronze plaque on his gravestone, this line is frozen for future membership until actual Revolutionary War service can be established. I believe he did not serve in that war, as his first wife, Nancy, died in 1776, leaving him with several children. He died in 1823 in Ohio County, Kentucky. Adding confusion to his military service, he is listed in the *Historical Register of Virginians in the Revolution.* John H. Gwathmey. Genealogical Publishing Company. 1996. on page 23, but no dates or unit are given. I have been unable to locate his Revolutionary War military records.

Henry, the second son of Captain Thomas Ashby and Mary Elizabeth McCullough, married (1) Judith Ann Shumate (1770–1851) and (2) Alice Alsey (1745–1818). He did not serve in the military during the Revolution but has been awarded Patriot status by the DAR for public service (A132729). He provided pasturage in Virginia during the war. He moved to Kentucky after receiving a land grant and later served in the War of 1812 under the command of Captain William R. McGreevy in Colonel Henry Renik's Kentucky Regiment.

His son George served in the Continental Line's Eighth Virginia Regiment, and this regiment was captured at the Charleston siege in 1780. I have his final pay record of 1783 denoting a large final payment for his captivity. This is a similar entry we see for other Charleston siege prisoners, so he spent two years in captivity. George's service is recognized by the DAR (A003441).

Son Stephen moved to Cecil Township, Washington County, Pennsylvania, prior to the Revolutionary War and later enlisted in Captain Robert Miller's Company of the Fourth Battalion of the Washington County Militia. His service in this unit is recognized by the DAR (A003424). See more of his story below.

Thomas Edward's youngest son, Peter (1751–1833), also served as a private for two enlistments during the Revolutionary War. During the first enlistment, he served under the command of

Captain James Parson in the Virginia Militia for ninety days in 1778. He again enlisted in 1780 under the command of Captain Thomas Neal for a period of ninety days. He applied for a pension at the age of eighty-one in Hopkins County, Kentucky. He married Winnifred Timmons (1764–1839) in 1776, and they had five children.

The following is a sad story involving son Stephen and his family as they migrated to Kentucky following the war. It is an Indian captivity story, and as with most similar events, the records consist mainly of interviews conducted years later by sometimes unknown authors. I have examined interviews of former captives in similar stories that were conducted by different authors resulting in vastly different accounts of the related events. I obtained several accounts of the Stephen Ashby family captivity, and as expected, time plays tricks on our memories, but the basic facts are common in all versions of the stories I reviewed. Firstly, the family was captured, and lives were lost. Secondly, there were one or more escapes, and I was unable to determine if all the escapees were reunited. Lastly, Stephen, his wife, and some of their children were reunited after seven years. I also do not have the Indians' side of this story, but I am certain they had a long list of grievances and had certainly suffered greatly from American westward expansion.

I relied on these sources for the preparation of the following story:

- The *Indiana Magazine of History*, Volume 9, 1813, page 109. Based on an interview by Judge William Polke, a friend of Stephen Ashby and his family.
- *The Ashby Book* by Lee Fleming Reese, published by Reese, San Diego, California, 1976. This is an excellent two-volume book of Ashby family history.
- An article in the *Fort Wayne Times* in 1842. This three-page article is partially based on the Polke version described above, but it offers some added details about the family's experiences after capture and upon being reunited.[227]

In 1788 Stephen and his family were making their way to settle land he had been awarded for his Revolutionary War service in Shelby County, Kentucky. There were already a couple of Ashby families settled in that area, including an uncle, Stephen Ashby (1710–1797), also a Patriot who had retired and moved to Kentucky with a land grant. His story is below. They were traveling on a raft on the Ohio River near present-day Louisville, Kentucky, through wilderness and unfriendly territory. The party consisted of Stephen, his wife Susannah Miles, and possibly eight children and an unnamed aunt. As they pulled the raft to shore near the Louisville rapids to begin their overland portion of the journey, they were attacked by a war party of Indians of the Potawatomy tribe. Stephen allegedly had one weapon in poor working order, and they were quickly overwhelmed. His oldest son, Miles, became involved in hand-to-hand fighting and was quickly killed by several arrows. One story of the family said Miles had been opposed to accompanying the family, as he was considering marriage in Virginia. A warrior quickly cut out his heart, and the war party took the remainder of the family prisoner. They quickly set out with their captives with the apparent intent to get far from the river. The tribe was probably based in the northern Illinois Territory and were far from their home base.

---

[227] The Indina Magazine of History. Volume 9. 1913. Page 109. This story was taken from a series of sketches written by Judge William Polke and later published in the Fort Wayne Times in 1842.

At the end of the day and not far from the river, they camped, and the Indians ate the son's heart. The next day, it quickly became apparent that the Indians were preparing for extended travel to northern Illinois. The Indians seemed unconcerned about any escape attempts, due to the remoteness of that area. They took Stephen to help look for materials to make pack saddles to load some of their belongings on the horses. Stephen realized he could easily make an escape, but he decided to return to camp and inform his oldest son Obediah "Beady" of the plan and take him with him. One version of the story told that his wife informed him before he escaped that the Indians were planning on burning him the next morning. They soon slipped away from the camp, located two of the Indians' horses, and proceeded to the Ohio River. They made it to the river, but the horses would have nothing to do with swimming, so they abandoned them and swam the river to relative safety. Stephen nearly drowned in the swift waters but was rescued by Beady. The Indians soon realized they were missing with two horses and gave chase. They quickly found the horses near the river and wet, so they probably assumed the two had drowned, and no further search was attempted. They returned to camp and told the remaining family they had killed Stephen and his son.

Even after swimming the Ohio River to safety, they were still weeks away from any known settlements or military forts. After about two weeks, they found the safety of a military fort at Louisville and received assistance. Stephen and his son remained at the fort assisting the military in their search for his family. Stephen sold his land to finance the search for his family, which was held captive for nearly seven years until a treaty between the army and several tribes in the Ohio territory was made. This was the 1795 Treaty of Greenville, and there were provisions in this treaty for the safe return of any captured Americans, but it still took months for the captives to be located and moved to freedom. When Stephen was informed that his family was being returned, he set out to meet them. He soon met the party, which contained just his wife with a number of warriors. Stephen quickly recognized the brave that had killed his son, and after greeting his wife, he told her he would kill the brave. His wife wisely told him to stay calm—their children were following this party by a day or two, so this was not a good plan. He complied with her request.

During their captivity, one infant daughter soon died en route to their summer camp, and within a year or so at least two sons escaped; one made it to safety and was reunited with his family.

His wife later related stories of their seven-year captivity. She and her children were treated well but were servants. She soon began asserting some authority over the women of the tribe, as their status was equal to the prisoners. By the end of their captivity, she seemed to be in charge of the tribal women, to the delight of the braves.

He was reunited with the remainder of his family in a few days, and they continued to Caldwell County, Kentucky. Stephen later became a Baptist minister in 1809 and spent the remainder of his life in Kentucky. I gathered the names of their children from several sources, including a "Survivors List" from the Papers of the War Department, 1784–1800 (from the Anthony Wayne Collection from Kent State University) and the DAR list of surviving children whose descendants later filed for membership based on his service.

- Stephen Jr., 1768–Unknown death date. Not on survivors list of 1795.
- Susannah Miles, Dates unknown. Listed on the survivors list of 1795.
- Miles, Dates unknown. Killed during the attack.
- Absalom, 1770–1841. On the 1795 survivors list. He became a Kentucky state representative in 1822.
- Obediah "Beady," 1772–1825. Escaped with his father and remained in Shelby County, Kentucky.
- Robert, 1773–1830. On the 1795 survivors list. He remained in Shelby County, Kentucky.
- Thomas, 1775–1850. On the 1795 survivors list; however, he had escaped about one year before the family was reunited in 1795. He settled in Spencer County, Kentucky.
- John Miller, 1774–1839. On the 1795 survivors list. Possibly settled in Texas.
- David, 1776–1850. On the 1795 survivors list. He settled in Platte County, Missouri.
- Stinson, 1772–1822. On the 1795 survivors list. He later replaced his father as constable in Shelby County, Kentucky.
- Polly, Dates unknown. On the 1795 survivors list.
- Enoch, 1777–Unknown death date. On the 1795 survivors list.
- Infant. Died in captivity.

It appears son Stephen Jr. either died in captivity or escaped and was never reunited with his family.

## 4. Captain Benjamin Ashby

Born: 1722, Fauquier County, Virginia
Died: 1 September 1804, Hampshire County, Virginia
Burial: Unknow location in Hampshire County
Wife: Hannah Seaver (1730–1814), married prior to 1752
DAR: No
SAR: P-104917

Benjamin was the son of Thomas Ashby and Rosanna Berry and was born in Fauquier County. He was named in his father's will and inherited land and slaves.

I believe it likely that Benjamin served in the French and Indian War, as did his brothers; however, I found no records supporting that claim. He did, however, serve in Lord Dunmore's War in 1774 in Captain John Harniss's Ranger Company.[228] This was a short Indian conflict led by Lord Dunmore into the Ohio territory to quell recent Indian disturbances following the French and Indian War. I believe that Benjamin received a small land grant in Hampshire County as pay for that expedition.

He later joined the Seventh Virginia Continental Line Regiment as a lieutenant and later captain for the Revolutionary War under Colonel Daniel Morgan in 1777. He served more than three

---

[228] *Virginia's Colonial Soldiers,* Lloyd DeWitt Bockstruck, Genealogical Publishing Company, Inc., Baltimore, Maryland, 1988. On pages 137 and 138 Benjamin is listed as a soldier in John Harniss's Ranger Company having received a land grant.

years and was awarded a bounty land grant (warrant #2147) for 2,600 acres in Hampshire County, Virginia, now West Virginia. He and his wife are buried there.

They had at least three children. I found evidence of a second son named John, who may have also fought in the Revolution, but he is an unproven son. These three children were listed in his 29 September 1779 will in Hampshire County, Virginia:

- Lottie Ross, 1753–1788
- Elizabeth Acton, 1755–1784
- Jerimiah, 1761–1842

This large land grant can be explained by the fact that his regiment was captured in Charleston and Benjamin was likely still in the regiment at that time as a prisoner. These prisoners were usually given large land grants for that service. He is shown in the *Historical Register of Virginians in the Revolution* as serving in the Continental Line.

I believe Benjamin had a marriage prior to the 1752 marriage to Hannah, but this is not proven. His wife Hannah was mentioned in his will.

## 5. Henry Ashby

Born: 1716, Frederick County, Virginia
Died: 1798, Mercer County, Kentucky
Burial: Unknown location
Wife: Eleanor "Nelly" Bounds (1716–1814)
DAR: A132729
SAR: A132729

Henry is the son of Thomas Henry Ashby and Rosanna Berry and was born in Frederick County, Virginia. He later moved to Fauquier County with his family as a child. He remained in Fauquier County as a farmer until he received a land grant in Mercer County, Kentucky, around 1780. He is noted as serving on George Washington's survey crew around 1748 and receiving a land grant in Virginia from Lord Fairfax for that service.

He served in the French and Indian War with the Frederick County Militia and later received a land grant in Mercer County, Kentucky, as a lieutenant; I believe this may have been for this service. His brother Stephen also later received a land grant in Mercer County.

Henry has been awarded Patriot status by the DAR for patriotic service during the Revolutionary War for providing pasturage for the military.[229]

He married Eleanor "Nelly" Bounds in 1748. She was born in 1716 and outlived him by sixteen years. They had nine children who are listed in his 5 February 1797 Mercer County will. (Kentucky Mercer County Will Book 2, page 80.) They were:

---

[229] *Virginia Revolutionary "Publick Claimes". Volume II.* Janice L. Abercrombie and Richard Slatten. Iberia Publishing Company. Athens, Georgia. Page 81.

- Captain Stephen, 1749–1798. Patriot of the Virginia Continental Line. He was a POW after the Charleston siege and was deceased by the time of his father's will.
- George, 1752–1811. Patriot. He served in the Eighth Virginia State Regiment.
- Argyle, 1752–1823
- Elizabeth Campbell, 1754–1846
- Robert, 1755–1835
- Sarah, 1756–1797
- Mary Jones, 1762–1798
- Nancy Harding, 1767–1846
- Robert, 1776–1844

His son Stephen, born in Stafford County, Virginia, joined the Eighth/Twelfth Virginia Continental Line Regiment as a captain in 1776. The designation of this regiment has been explained elsewhere in the book. This historical regiment was the result of unit consolidations early in the war by George Washington. Later in the war while the soldiers of that unit were serving as prisoners following the Charleston siege, the Third Regiment was merged with the Eighth and Twelfth Regiments. Stephen served in that unit for the entire war. I must mention that Stephen Ashby (1710–1797), son of Thomas Edward Ashby Sr., also served in the same unit early in the war. His story follows below. This Stephen is a documented survivor of the Valley Forge winter as well as most of the battles the unit engaged in during the war. He received a substantial land grant of four thousand acres for his service (warrant #3591). He also received a considerable pay settlement at the time of his discharge in 1783 for back-pay earned in captivity. He settled in Mercer County, Kentucky, and his will of May 1797 names his wife Mary and his seven children.

Son George, born in Stafford County, Virginia, joined the Virginia Eighth State Regiment in May 1777 and served until May 1778. This state regiment fought in several battles and was certainly a different regiment than the Eighth Continental Regiment that his brother Stephen served with. The DAR recognizes his service in the war (A003411). The regiment served initially in the southern theater in Charleston, South Carolina, as a Virginia regiment. By the time of George's enlistment it was assigned to the main army under the command of George Washington, but it never served as a Continental Line unit and remained within the state of Virginia under the command of Colonel James Wood. It fought in the battle of Germantown in October 1777, and George would have certainly been in the unit at that time. This regiment was later merged with the Virginia Fourth Regiment and marched to Charleston, South Carolina. They were later taken prisoner by the British and remained as POWs until the end of the war, but I found no evidence that George was assigned to either unit after May 1778. Following the war, George received a land grant in Ohio County, Kentucky, and resided there for the remainder of his life. Ohio County was originally bordered on the north by the Ohio River and is now bordered on the north by Hancock County, where several other Ashby family members settled.

**6. Captain Stephen A. Ashby**
Born: 1710, Prince William County, Virginia
Died: 12 May 1797, Hopkins or Mercer County, Kentucky

Burial: Ashby family farm cemetery in Mercer County, Kentucky
Wife: Elizabeth Robertson (1732–1797), married in 1753
DAR: A0034525
SAR: P-104936

He was a son of Thomas Edward Ashby Sr. and Rosanna Rose Berry and is Emma Jo's sixth great-granduncle. He served under Colonel George Washington during the French and Indian War, as I found a company roster to that effect. Other researchers and I have struggled not to confuse this Stephen Ashby with his nephew Stephen (1747–1831), son of Thomas discussed above, who was captured by Indians. Both these men served in the Virginia Continental Line at nearly the same time and served their nation in extraordinary ways. They are an important part of the Ashby story.

He married Elizabeth Robertson (1732-1797) in Virginia in 1753, and she also died in 1797, probably before Stephen as she is not mentioned in his will. She is recorded as his wife in the DAR records, but Stephen's line requires future applicants to prove their descendancy from her. I did not find his marriage records, so it is likely the DAR also has not seen that documentation.

Stephen served in the French and Indian War as a captain in the Fauquier County Militia in 1758.[230] As did his brother Benjamin, he also served in Lord Dunmore's War in 1774 as a captain of rangers.[231] He would have received a land grant for his service in both conflicts.

Stephen then joined the Woodford Regiment of the Eighth Virginia Continental Line on 9 September 1776 as an ensign. I will add that his nephew Stephen also served in that regiment, as did several other Patriots featured in this book. This Stephen was later promoted to lieutenant and then to captain despite his age. If I have his correct birth year, he was nearly sixty-six years of age at the time of enlistment.

He did not serve as a company commander but as regimental quartermaster, and his records support that statement. He served the winter of 1777–1778 at Valley Forge, and I have read stories that he was retired because of his age in 1778 and given a large land grant for his service. The unit consolidation occurred in the spring of 1778 at White Plains, New York, when General Washington consolidated fifteen Virginia regiments into eleven after the brutal winter at Valley Forge. His 14 September 1778 muster card reflects that he was "supernumerary" by choice, meaning he was on the active rolls but would not be counted in the total force of the eleven regiments after they had been reorganized. He received a 1,000-acre land grant in Kentucky for his service (warrant #3591) in December 1784. I have seen Kentucky records attributing 2,500 acres of land grants to him also in 1784. I will speculate that he also was given a land grant for his service in the French and Indian War in Hopkins County, as was his brother Henry, discussed above. He was retired from the Continental Army, but I am unsure of the date. His nephew Stephen was retired in 1783 after serving as a prisoner of war.

---

[230] *Colonial Soldiers of the South, 1732–1774*, Clark, Murtie J., Baltimore, Maryland: Genealogical Publishing Co., 1999. Page 513 reflects his service in the French and Indian War.
[231] *Virginia's Colonial Soldiers,* Lloyd DeWitt Bockstruck, Genealogical Publishing Company, Inc., Baltimore, Maryland, 1988. Page 138 lists Stephen as a captain of rangers.

It is likely that the Kentucky land grant(s) resulted from his French and Indian War service, because his surviving children and grandchildren applied for a land grant based on his service in the Revolutionary War on 15 May 1847 nearly fifty years after his death. This request (BL 2420-300) was filed by an attorney, William Gordon, Esq., to the commissioner of pensions. His children and grandchildren were named in this request. His voluntary retirement rather than an "earned" retirement appeared to be at issue, and the attorney made a case with previous practices to strengthen their consideration in the request. All his children except for daughter Letiita (Lety) were named in this request. I note that none of the eight children were surviving at the time of the filing of this request. Stephen's earlier land grants were almost certainly French and Indian War grants, as Revolutionary War grants were considerably smaller, especially for the rank of captain.

Following the war, he moved to Hopkins County, Kentucky, and remained there until 1797, as his will of 19 May that year was written in Mercer County, where he may have lived until his death later that year. Hopkins, Christian, and Mercer Counties were not formed until after his death. Given his large land holdings, it is likely he owned land in all three counties. His will was found in Mercer County Court Records Will Book 2, page 36. His probate inventory listed seven slaves by name.

The town Ashbury in Hopkins County was named after him in 1829. I found it interesting that Kentucky records indicate the town was named after General Stephen Ashby, probably a descendant of this Stephen. I believe he likely had relocated to Kentucky before his nephew Stephen was captured in 1787 in central Kentucky while en route to Shelby County. In 1946 a DAR chapter was formed in this Stephen's name at Madisonville, Kentucky, in Hopkins County. The children named in his will were:

- Enos, 1755–1808. Patriot in the Virginia Line.
- Letitia "Lety" Neal, 1757–1846
- Ensign Daniel, 1759–1834. Patriot serving in Virginia regiments.
- Absolom, 1765–1841
- Anne Prather, 1765–1822
- Rose Timmons, 1767–1812
- John, 1776–1841
- Stephen Jr., 1776–1841

Son Enos is documented in his father's 1797 will in Hopkins County, Kentucky. I have been unable to document the Revolutionary War service, but he received a military land grant of two hundred acres in Hopkins County, Kentucky, and settled there near his father. This grant almost certainly signifies military service.

His son Daniel is also mentioned in his father's 1787 will and settled in Hopkins County, Kentucky. Daniel served in the Revolution late in the war by enlisting in Colonel Glen's Virginia Regiment in 1780. He then marched with the regiment to South Carolina and back to Hillsborough, North Carolina, where he detached to aid in gathering the prisoners taken at the Battle of Cowpens. He then marched back to Albemarle Barracks, Virginia. From there he was discharged and returned home after serving six months. In 1781, he was appointed an ensign in the

Hampshire County Militia and served in Captain William's Company in Colonel Van Meter's Regiment going out against the Tories at various times until November 1781. He then marched to Winchester, Virginia, where he guarded the prisoners taken at Yorktown, serving three months. The DAR has recognized his service (A203307). He filed for and received a pension in 1832 (S14927).

I also note that son Daniel became one of the first Kentucky state senators from Hopkins County. This information was obtained from a presentation by Mrs. Poly, a family descendant who was instrumental in formation of the Hopkins County DAR chapter named after his father.

**"The right wing, where I stood, was exposed to and received all the enemy's fire...I heard the bullets whistle, and believe me, there is something charming in the sound."**

*—George Washington's letter to his brother John A. Washington, Friday, 31 May 1754*

## Chapter Eight: A Story of Leadership, Exploration, and Tragedy—The Gists of Baltimore

In chapter four I presented the lives of two Gist Patriots, my fifth and sixth great-grandfathers Joseph and William, but that did not sufficiently tell the story of this very interesting family. They are somewhat overlooked by history, and this is my effort to begin telling their story. This was not a particularly wealthy or successful family, as they had their failures and personal tragedies, but when viewed 250 to 300 years after the fact, their contribution to our independence is awe-inspiring. Their contributions relate to military leadership and exploration of frontiers west of the Alleghenies. This family produced twenty-one Revolutionary War Patriots from three of the first five American generations. I have collected stories of these five American generations and have included them in this chapter. Here are some of their noteworthy contributions:

- There were four generations of French and Indian War veterans and Revolutionary War Patriots.
- One great-grandfather was one of the first citizens of Baltimore, Maryland.
- One family member surveyed the city of Baltimore, Maryland.
- Eight family members served in the French and Indian War.
- Twenty-one family members served in the Revolutionary War.
- A family member saved the life of George Washington two times in one day. This member served as a guide for Washington and contributed to his success and survival in the French and Indian War.
- One family member became a general in the Revolutionary War and arguably saved the Revolution in an early battle.
- Two family members were killed in the Revolutionary War and another later in a Mexican expedition.
- Members of five generations served in leadership positions in the city of Baltimore, and in Virginia, North Carolina, and Tennessee.

Members of this line of Gists of Baltimore quickly spread south and westward from Baltimore prior to the Revolution and lived in Virginia, South Carolina, North Carolina, Pennsylvania, and what was to become Tennessee and Kentucky. They served in military, exploratory, and political leadership roles in each of those colonies or territories. They left their mark on history.

My approach to telling this story is to focus on individuals and their stories starting with the first Gist in America and outlining each member's contribution to American independence. While school history may remain silent about this family, there are many original historical documents revealing interesting facts. This effort will strive to consolidate these facts into a story worth remembering and telling.

The purpose of discussing the two generations prior to the Revolutionary War is that, for this family, the French and Indian War shaped their involvement in the Revolution to the extent that both stories must be told to fully explain their contribution to history. Furthermore, family given names tend to be repeated over several generations in this family line, so I hope to help reduce the confusion generated from repeats of given names like Christopher, Richard, Nathaniel, and Joshua. The story will be told by generation (starting with the first American generation) and by family group within that generation.

I cannot separate the Gist family story from controversial facts, nor do I think that necessary. History is history, and the better we understand the issues of those times, the better we are able to understand modern social problems. First, I believe most of the first five generations of the American Gist family were slaveholders. You will see slaves passed down from one generation to the next in last wills and testaments. I think at least one family line may not have owned slaves, but further research is needed to confirm that statement. Second, the relationships with Native Americans are documented in several Patriot stories below. It seems one family member was quite realistic in his dealings with tribal leaders and was treated with mutual respect. You will see a likely Gist descendant with a Native American mother, as well as a Gist descendant in command of Native American Patriots. You will also see Gist descendants in direct confrontation with Native American tribes. I make no excuses and have endeavored to present the stories as accurately as possible, letting you be the judge.

## The First Generation of American Gists

### Christopher Richard Gist

Born: 8 August 1650, Wiltshire, England
Died: 9 March 1690, Back Bay, Anne Arundel County, Maryland
Wife: Edith Cromwell, daughter of Oliver Cromwell, the lord protector of England

He was the son of Sir Christopher Gist (1616–1658) and Lady Ann Washington (1621–1662) of Malmesbury, Wiltshire, England.

Christopher arrived from England in the Baltimore area around 1679 and was a planter and justice of Baltimore County and a member of the grand jury of that county.[232] He married Edith Cromwell around 1682.[233] Christopher and Edith Cromwell had four children.[234] Edith came from an influential and important English family.[235] Christopher and Edith's children were:

- Edith, 1679–1691
- Emma, 1680–1691

---

[232] *Immigrant Ancestors: A List of 2,500 Immigrants to America before 1750*, Virkus, Frederick A., editor. Baltimore: Genealogical Publishing Co., 1964, reproduced 1986. This shows that Christopher arrived in Baltimore in 1679.

[233] *Maryland Genealogies: A Consolidation of Articles from the Maryland Historical Magazine in Two Volumes*, Genealogical Publishing Company, Inc., Baltimore, 1980, 1997. Page 349 reports the lineage of Edith Cromwell. Pages 504–512 present the genealogy of the early Baltimore Gist family.

[234] "Gist Family of Baltimore County," Christopher Johnston, *Maryland Historical Magazine,* vol. VIII, no. 4. Page 373 gives an early history of Christopher Richard Gist family in Baltimore.

[235] *Colonial Families of the USA 1607–1775*, Mackenzie, George Norbury, and Nelson Osgood Rhoades, editors. Reprinted, Baltimore: Genealogical Publishing Co., Inc., 1966, 1995. Page 235 gives the name of Edith's father as Sir Oliver Cromwell.

- Captain Richard Jr., 1683–1741. See story below.
- Mary Polly, 1684–1739

He is my eighth great-grandfather. The lineage starting with his son is:

Captain Richard Christopher Gist, my seventh great-grandfather
William Gist Sr., my sixth great-grandfather
Major Joseph Gist, my fifth great-grandfather
Cornelius Howard Gist, my fourth great-grandfather
Elizabeth Pamelia Jones, my third great-grandmother
Eliza Pamelia Plummer, my second great-grandmother
Sarah "Sally" Younger, my great-grandmother
Blanche Betrand Raines, my grandmother
V. Elwood (Pat) Raines, my father

It is important to point out the Patriot connections discussed throughout this book with the Cornelius Gist, the Elizabeth Jones, the Pamelia Plummer, and the Sally Younger family lines.

## The Second Generation of American Gists

**Captain Richard Christopher Gist Jr. (son of Christopher Richard)**
Born: 1683, Baltimore, Maryland
Died: 28 August 1741
Wife: Zipporah Murray (1745–1760)

Richard was a surveyor of the western shore of Maryland. He was one of the seven commissioners in 1729 responsible for laying out Baltimore town and was commissioned in 1727 as one of the justices of Baltimore County, a position that he held for the rest of his life. He served as a presiding magistrate in 1736, and he represented his county in the Provisional Assembly in 1740 and 1741. He held extensive tracts of land, which he willed to his children. In 1737 and 1741 he was styled a captain, and he also held the rank of captain in the county militia during the French and Indian War. I found records indicating that he and his wife Zipporah were members of the Society of Friends, a Quaker organization, and that they were married in the Quaker Meeting Hall of Baltimore. They also were members of the Baltimore Saint Mary's Episcopal Church. [236] Their marriage was on 7 December 1704.

Richard and Zipporah had nine children—four daughters and five sons. All the sons served in the French and Indian War. Two had patriotic service during the Revolutionary War, and one made history. Their children were:

- Captain Christopher, 1705–1759. Although not a Revolutionary War Patriot, his story is told below with the third-generation Patriots.
- Captain Nathaniel, 1707–1787. Served in the French and Indian War.

---

[236] *Maryland Genealogies: A Consolidation of Articles from the Maryland Historical Magazine in Two Volumes,* Genealogical Publishing Company Inc., Baltimore, Maryland, 1980, 1997. Pages 505–507 give an accounting of the Christopher Richard Gist family.

- Edith, 1709–1770
- William, 1711–1794. Performed patriotic service during the Revolutionary War.
- Captain Thomas Sr., 1712–1787. Served in the French and Indian War and performed patriotic service during the Revolutionary War.
- Jemima, 1714–1784
- Ruth, 1716–1748
- John, 1722–1778. A Patriot and soldier in the Revolutionary War.
- Sarah, 1724–1770

Their children are listed in *Colonial Families of the USA.*[237]

The following are the stories of the five sons of Captain Richard Christopher Gist Jr. and Zipporah Murray.

## The Third Generation of American Gists

### 1. Captain Christopher Gist II
Born: 12 May 1705, Baltimore, Maryland
Died: July 1759, somewhere between Richmond, Virginia, and Winchester, Virginia
Wife: Sarah Howard (1711–1757)

While Christopher's birth, early life, marriage, and business affairs are well recorded in Baltimore church records and other official records, he quickly became a frontiersman in Pennsylvania and the Ohio territory before record-keeping institutions were established there. Although his life was short, many of his important activities occurred on the frontier. Below are some of the references I relied upon to construct his life and accomplishments after leaving Baltimore. He made history!

- "Christopher Gist and his Sons," Lawrence A. Orrill. Taken from a paper read at a meeting of the Historical Society of Western Pennsylvania on 26 January 1932. This is a twenty-eight-page, well-documented story of Christopher and his sons from around 1750 until his death in 1759.
- "The Journal of Christopher Gist, 1750–1751," Lewis P. Summers. *Annals of Southwest Virginia, 1769–1800*, Arlington, Virginia.
- *Annosanah: A Novel Based on the Life of Christopher Gist,* Christian Wig, Heritage Books, November 2015. This book remains in print.
- *Colonial Families of the USA 1607–1775,* Volume I, George Norbury Mackenzie and Nelson Osgood Rhoades, editors. Genealogical Publishing Company, Inc., Baltimore, Maryland, 1966, 1995. Pages 239 to 265 give an insight into his and his sons' lives.
- *Christopher Gist of Maryland and Some of His Descendants, 1679–1957,* Jean Muir Dorsey and Maxwell Jay Dorsey, Hassel Street Press, 2021. This is a recently published, well-documented book.

---

[237] *Colonial Families of the USA 1607–1775,* Volume VI, Mackenzie, George Norbury, and Nelson Osgood Rhoades, editors. Reprinted, Baltimore: Genealogical Publishing Co., Inc., 1966, 1995. Page 236 lists the children of Christopher Richard Gist Jr.

Christopher married Sarah Howard in 1728 in Baltimore. She was the daughter of Joshua Howard, a British military officer. Her two sisters also married Gist brothers (Nathaniel and William). Christopher is my sixth great-granduncle.

He had inherited land and other business holdings from his father and seemed to be set for life. His problem was that he was not well educated and was a poor businessman and, consequently, was not successful at that line of work. On 6 June 1745, he sold his business to the firm of Cromwell and Standsbury and then in 1750 he stated he was a resident of Virginia when he sold the Gist lime pits formerly owned by his father to Tobias Stansbury.[238] I have also seen accounts of his early business career in which he was operating a fur trading business in Baltimore and that his warehouse burned. The warehouse contained furs he had sold to an English fur company, and his company was held liable for the loss. He may have departed Baltimore to escape this legal claim. He spent several years exploring the Ohio River Valley and building relationships with Indian leaders in that region; thusly, he became a well-known explorer respected by colonial military leaders, politicians, and Native American tribal leaders alike. The name of the book referenced above, *Annosanah*, is reported to be an Indian word for "He who speaks the truth."

Before 1750, Gist had settled his family in the northern part of North Carolina County, then a Virginia county, near the Yadkin River, where he met Daniel Boone's father, a neighbor. The current river drainage area is now in the state of North Carolina, but it was recognized as part of the Virginia colony before the Revolutionary War. This was near what is now Wilkesboro in Wilkes County, North Carolina. It is not difficult to compare his activities with those of Daniel Boone, with a couple of notable exceptions. Christopher could read and write quite well and was successful in finding someone to pay for his exploration and mapping skills. Later in 1750, the Ohio Company chose Gist to explore the country surrounding the Ohio River as far west as what was to become Louisville. That winter, he mapped the Ohio country from Pittsburgh west to the Ohio River. He then crossed the Ohio River into Kentucky and returned to North Carolina along the Yadkin River. It is important to note that Gist was exploring and traversing the Kentucky territory sixteen years earlier than the famed Daniel Boone in 1765. Upon his return to North Carolina County, he found that his family had returned to Roanoke, Virginia, because of Indian attacks. He rejoined them there, and again in the summer of 1751, he returned to explore Pennsylvania and western Virginia. During his exploratory campaigns, he obtained a large tract of land in what is now Pittsburg, Pennsylvania, and built improvements on it. It is important to know that the Ohio Company was formed to explore lands west of Virginia and had as employees Robert Dinwiddie, the governor, and George Washington.

In 1753, he again returned to the Ohio country, after which he met a new and inept Virginia colonial major and the governor of Virginia. Governor Robert Dinwiddie hired him to lead the major to Fort LeBoeuf, near Lake Erie, so that they might deliver a message from the governor to the French commander of that fort, telling him to leave the area. They were successful in locating the fort, but the French commander ignored their request. During their return trip, the major elected to outpace their soldier guard detail to speed their trip back to Richmond and was attacked by

---

[238] *Maryland Genealogies: A Consolidation of Articles from the Maryland Historical Magazine in Two Volumes*, Genealogical Publishing Company Inc., Baltimore, Maryland, 1980, 1997. Pages 505–507 give an accounting of the Christopher Richard Gist family.

Indians. Gist prevented the Indians from killing the major in a hand-to-hand encounter, and they escaped certain death. The major was about to be scalped before Christopher intervened. Christopher was about to kill the Indian for his misdeeds, but the major insisted he be let go. They continued their journey, and that night while crossing the freezing Allegheny River, Christopher saved the major from drowning. They had hurriedly built a raft, as they were being pursued by Indians, and the major fell into the ice-clogged river. Again Christopher saved him, pulling him to the safety of the raft. As they were unable to proceed in the ice-filled river, they spent the night on an island, but by morning, the river had frozen, and they could finish the river crossing by waking on the ice. The major was George Washington. Gist had saved Washington's life twice in one day. I have seen an Oliver Stone television special featuring the life of George Washington, in which Gist was recognized for his acts. As mentioned in the Ashby family story above, Washington knew how to cross the Alleghenies, as he had led survey crews through the Ashby Gap a few years earlier. But he had not ventured much farther beyond. He would have been lost without Gist as a guide.

In 1754, Washington (now a colonel)—with Gist as a guide and a detachment of Virginia Militia—attempted to drive the French from that region. The French soundly defeated Washington and the detachment at the Battle of Fort Necessity on 3 July 1754, and this was the beginning of the French and Indian War. Even though Washington lost that battle, he returned to Richmond as a hero. He would get another chance, as he said he knew where to go now.

Gist was also acting as a guide, now as an army captain, for Washington in 1755 during the Braddock Campaign. Washington was a colonel and regimental commander by then. Remember, we discussed the role of Captain John Ashby and his brother Nimrod Ashby in that campaign in the "Nothing There but Indians and Ashbys" chapter of this book. Christopher was also a company commander during this campaign, and his company payroll on 25 January 1756 consisted of about twenty-eight men, two of which died that month.[239] I will note that his youngest son, Thomas, also served in the campaign and was taken prisoner by Indians and held for a year before he could escape in Canada and make it to safety in New York. His story is told below with the fourth-generation Gist family stories.

After the Braddock Expedition, at Washington's request he traveled to Tennessee to meet with native tribes in seeking support for the war. In 1759, it is told, he contracted smallpox and died. The exact location of his death is unknown, but *Christopher Gist of Maryland and Some of His Descendants*, noted above, maintains that he died on 29 July 1759 while traveling from Richmond to Winchester, Virginia. I have seen other accounts asserting that he died in either Tennessee or South Carolina after meeting with the Tennessee tribes. I believe his wife Sarah preceded him in death.

Early in his exploration of the western Pennsylvania area he obtained a large tract of land there, and it soon became a stopover point for those headed west. There are roadside historical markers identifying his plantation holdings in what is now Fayette County near Pittsburg, Pennsylvania. His son later settled on that land. Christopher had acquired that land during his first trip to

---

[239] *Virginia's Colonial Soldiers*, Lloyd DeWitt Bockstruck, Genealogical Publishing Company, Inc., Baltimore, Maryland, 1998. Page 55 contains a roster of the names of the men assigned to Gist's company dated 25 January 1756.

Pennsylvania and built structures on it. The Indians destroyed his buildings when they were chasing him and George Washington out of the Northwest Territory.

Christopher and Sarah had seven children. His four sons served in both the French and Indian War and the Revolution, and their stories follow with the fourth-generation stories. Their children were:[240]

- Richard, 1729–by 1780
- Violetta, 1731–1768
- Colonel Nathaniel, 1733–1796. Served in the Revolutionary War and was captured at the Siege of Charleston.
- Anne Nancy, 1734–1795
- Captain Thomas, 1735–1785. Served in both the French and Indian War and the Revolutionary War and was held prisoner by Indians for a year.
- Nancy, 1737–1802

## 2. Captain Nathaniel Gist

Born: 1707, Baltimore, Maryland
Died: 7 October 1784, Sevierville, Tennessee
Wife: Mary Howard (1713–1755), daughter of Joshua Howard and Joanna O'Carroll and sister to Sarah, wife of Christopher Gist above
DAR: No
SAR: No

Nathaniel was the second son of Richard Gist and Zipporah Murray and was born in Baltimore. He was a brother of Christopher, discussed above. He married Mary Howard in 1729 in St. Paul's Church in Baltimore.

He lived in Baltimore until 1745 and moved to Lunenburg County, Virginia. Part of this county later became Halifax County in 1752. He moved to Dan River, Rowan County, North Carolina, in 1754, where he served as lieutenant of the militia during the French and Indian War. It appears he followed his brother to North Carolina, as he served with his brother Christopher's company as a lieutenant under the command of Colonel George Washington in 1756.[241] He was present at the Battle of Fort Necessity, which George Washington lost in grand style. He was serving as a captain for George Washington in the First Virginia Regiment.[242] I am uncertain how long he served, but a reasonable assumption is that he did not serve after the Braddock Campaign ended, as his brother did not serve after the war but continued working for the governor and George Washington.

---

[240] *Maryland Genealogies: A Consolidation of Articles from the Maryland Historical Magazine in Two Volumes*, Genealogical Publishing Company Inc., Baltimore, Maryland, 1980, 1997. Pages 505–507 give an accounting of the Christopher Richard Gist family.

[241] *Virginia Genealogical Society Quarterly*, vol. 31, no. 2. Page 28 states that Nathaniel served as a lieutenant in his brother Christopher's company in Colonel Washington's First Regiment in 1766.

[242] Ibid. Page 90 shows he served as a captain in Washington's regiment directly under George Washington.

He returned to North Carolina, and in 1767 he is shown on the Cumberland County tax list. He received a land grant in Cumberland County for 156 acres on 18 April 1770 (grant number 17), which was for his service in the French and Indian War. I found no evidence of his service in the Revolutionary War. He may have lived in Virginia in 1782 when he made a claim for the rifles lost by his sons Nathaniel and Richard, who were killed in the 1780 Kings Mountain battle. This claim was filed on 18 September 1782 in Washington County, where his sons had enlisted in the Washington County Militia commanded by Colonel Campbell. Their stories are told below. In 1784, he lived with his son Joshua in western North Carolina, which later became eastern Tennessee. He died in Sevierville, Tennessee, in 1784.

Nathaniel and Mary had seven children. His six sons all served in the Revolutionary War, with two being killed in the same battle. Their children were born in Baltimore, and their births are recorded there.

- Captain Benjamin, 1730–1810. Patriot of the Revolutionary War
- Zipporah, 1732–Unknown death date
- Captain Christopher, 1734–1794. Patriot of the Revolutionary War
- Ensign Nathaniel, 1736–1780. Killed in the Revolutionary War
- Captain Joshua, 1739–1819. Served in the Revolutionary War
- Richard, 1742–1780. Killed in the Revolutionary War

### 3. William Gist Sr.

Born: September 1711, Baltimore, Maryland
Died: 19 November 1794, Baltimore, Maryland
Wife: Violetta Howard, sister to Sarah Howard, wife of Christopher Gist
DAR: A045549
SAR: No

William is a Patriot and my sixth great-grandfather. He never served in the military but is recognized by the DAR as a Patriot for signing the Oath of Allegiance in 1778. His story was told in chapter four and is presented here to document his children. William and Violetta had nine children.[243] They are:

- Major Joseph, 1736–1803. A Patriot discussed earlier in this book. He is my fifth great-grandfather.
- William Jr., 1743–1802
- Ann Calhoun, 1745–1799. Married Joseph Calhoun, first mayor of Baltimore.
- Sarah McClure, 1747–1819
- Elizabeth McGee, 1750–1794
- Captain Thomas, 1750–1808. A Patriot of the Revolutionary War.
- Captain John, 1752–1782. A Patriot of the Revolutionary War.
- Violetta Lewis, 1755–1783
- Ellen Barnes, 1757–1799

---

[243] *Baltimore County Families 1659–1759,* Robert W. Barnes, reprinted for Clearfield Publishing Company, Inc. by Genealogical Publishing Company, Inc., Baltimore, Maryland, 1996. Page 258 records the names of the children of William Gist Sr.

In 1750, he owned fifty acres at Wolf Den and fifty acres at Gist's enlargement and another sixty acres at the same enlargement.[244] He is a brother to Christopher and Nathaniel Gist, discussed above.

### 4. Captain Thomas Gist Sr.

Born: 13 July 1712, Baltimore, Maryland
Died: 24 May 1787, Baltimore, Maryland
Wife: Susannah Cockey (1715–1834), married 1735
DAR: A134216
SAR: No

Thomas is the son of Richard Christopher Gist Jr. and Zipporah Murray of Baltimore and a brother to Christopher, Nathaniel, and William, discussed above, and John, discussed next. He is my sixth great-granduncle. His birth records are recorded at Saint's Paul Episcopal Church in Baltimore.

He spent his life in the Baltimore area and served in the Baltimore Militia as a captain during the French and Indian War. He did not serve in the Revolution but is recognized by the DAR as a Patriot for patriotic service, as he signed the Oath of Allegiance and served on the Baltimore Committee of Safety.[245] He married Susannah Cockey on 2 July 1735, and they had nine children—three daughters and six sons, five of which served in the Revolutionary War. His children and his wife are named in *Baltimore County Families 1659–1759*.[246] Their children are:

- Elizabeth Bramblett, 1736–1826
- Captain John, 1738–1800. Served in the Revolutionary War
- Colonel Thomas Jr., 1741–1813. Served in the Revolutionary War
- General Mordecai, 1742–1792. Served in the Revolutionary War
- Richard, 1745–1746. Died as an infant
- Colonel Joshua, 1747–1821. Served in the Revolutionary War
- Rachael, 1750–1825
- Captain David, 1753–1820. Served in the Revolutionary War
- Violetta, 1755–1783

The stories of his Patriot sons are told with the fourth-generation stories below. He owned 216 acres of land named "The Adventure."

### 5. Captain John Gist

Born: 1722, Baltimore, Maryland
Died: 5 June 1778, Loudoun County, Virginia
Wife: Mary Lewis (1722–1795), married in 1742 in Fairfax, Virginia

---

[244] Ibid.
[245] *Colonial Families of the USA, 1607–1775*, database online, Lehi, UT: Ancestry.com Operations, Inc., 2016. Pages 238 and 239 give that he served on the Baltimore Committee of Safety in 1776 and also give the names of his children.
[246] *Baltimore County Families 1659–1759*, Robert W. Barnes, Genealogical Publishing Company, Inc., for Clearfield Publishing Company, Inc., Baltimore, Maryland, 1996. Page 193 lists the names and birth dates of his children and the name of his wife.

DAR: No
SAR: No

While I have for some time known of this John Gist who lived in Loudoun County, Virginia, I had been unable to assign him to the line of Baltimore Gists, as his birth does not appear in the Baltimore church records or the several records I have used to document this great family. Also, neither the DAR nor SAR had records of membership applications submitted by his descendants. Therefore, I had decided not to include his family in this book. However, after obtaining a recently published book documenting the Baltimore Gist family, I discovered mention of this John as a son of Christopher the explorer. Then, after close examination of his difficult-to-read last will and testament, I discovered that in 1778 he named his brother Thomas as the executor of his estate. This Thomas, discussed above, is the documented son of Richard Christopher Gist Jr. and Zipporah Murray of Baltimore and the brother of Christopher, Nathaniel, and William, also discussed above.[247] I have a copy of John's Loudoun County, Virginia, will of 5 June 1778 that lists his brother Thomas as executor of his will. He married Mary Lewis (1722–1795) in 1742 in Fairfax, Virginia. Mary is named in this will; however, her family name is not given.

I believe you will see in this story that in spite of the lack of solid birth records, John was closely associated with his Baltimore brothers and nephews and also shared a close relationship with George Washington, as did his kinsmen. In fact, you saw earlier in this book that Washington owed a great deal of his success as a regimental commander in the French and Indian War to Christopher. Given that Christopher died unexpectedly as a young man, Washington was unable to pass his appreciation on to him. Maybe General George Washington went the extra mile for his brother Captain John Gist.

He moved to Loudoun County, Virginia, probably following his marriage. He was a tobacco planter and rented land from fellow farmer and neighbor George Washington. I found two rent receipts from George Washington in which he paid rent for land on Hunting Creek with tobacco he had grown on that land.[248] He paid his rent in 1760 with 920 pounds of tobacco and in 1761 with 729 pounds of tobacco. John also owned a plantation and was a slaveholder.

John joined the Continental Army on 1 June 1778 as a captain in Colonel Nathaniel Gist's Additional Regiment. He served in that regiment until March 1779, when he was transferred to the Third Maryland Regiment under the command of General Mordecai Gist's First Maryland Brigade. Both Nathaniel and Mordecai Gist were his nephews. As discussed later in this chapter, soldiers were reassigned to the Maryland regiment when General Washington understood that the Indians were not a viable part of the regiment and most of the remaining soldiers were from Maryland. The Gist Regiment was then reformed with ten companies of Virginia men and moved to the southern theater of operations, where they were captured by the British. Nathaniel Gist and his Virginia regiment remained prisoners until the end of the war. Gist was eventually promoted to general. The Maryland regiments had a distinguished combat record in both the northern and southern theaters of operation. Several other family Patriots outlined in this book

---

[247] *Christopher Gist of Maryland and Some of His Descendants, 1679–1957,* Jean Muir Dorsey and Maxwell Jay Dorsey, Hassel Street Press, 2021. Pages 5 and 164 establish that John was a son of Richard and Zipporah Murray.
[248] *The Diaries of George Washington,* edited by J.C. Fitzpatrick, 9 July 1760 and July 1761.

also served in one of those regiments. See the following chapters about the Kings Mountain and Guilford Courthouse battles. These were hard-fighting professional units.

John was retired on 1 August 1780, most likely from combat injuries encountered with the Maryland regiment, which had fought in numerous battles in the northern theater before being moved to the southern theater in January 1780. It is important to note that John was not a young man and was at least fifty-eight years of age at the time of retirement. It is one thing to be assigned to a militia regiment at that age, but it is entirely another matter to serve in a front-line combat unit such as the Maryland Continental Line units. His final pay settlement voucher reflected full pay as a captain from 1 June 1778 until 1 August 1780. That final settlement also included five years of full captain's pay in lieu of half-pay for life. His total settlement amounted to more than $2,500 current Virginia money. He was retired before the unit's transfer to the southern theater of operations, and he no doubt knew he did not belong there. I have a copy of an approval of his separation agreement signed by George Washington. I am simply unsure of the reason for his discharge; however, I am not aware of other such large settlements for any other reason. He also received a three-hundred-acre Maryland land grant (number 857) for his service. General Washington made a written statement that he owed John the chance to return to his plantation.

I have a nearly complete copy of his military records documenting his two years of service as well as his final payment statement. Neither he nor his wife lived long enough to file for a pension. I am uncertain of his death date, but he probably did not live long after being retired from the army. His wife Mary outlived him by nearly fifteen years.

He wrote his will on 5 June 1778 in Loudoun County, Virginia, prior to departing for service and named his wife and ten children. He was a slave owner and left slaves to each of his children and several grandchildren. His proposed son John, shown below, was not named in this will. His children are:

- Mary Keene, 1743–1821. Married Francis Keene (1744–1818), and they settled in Lexington, Fayette County, Kentucky.
- Henson Lewis, 1745–1792. Remained in Loudoun County.
- Thomas, 1747–1806. Settled in West Virginia.
- Nancy, 1748–Unknown death date. Died in Y, Somme, France.
- Nathaniel, 1750–1818. Settled in Lexington, Fayette County, Kentucky.
- John Jr., 1753–After 1820. Remained in Loudoun County.
- Violet Lewis, 1766–1817. Remained in Virginia.
- Elizabeth, 1757–Unknown death date.
- Sarah, 1763–Unknown death date. Died in Y, Somme, France.
- Constant Scott, 1765–1834. Died in Washington D.C.
- William, 1769–1834. Settled in Lexington, Fayette County, Kentucky.

## The Fourth Generation of American Gists

**Third-generation explorer Captain Christopher and Sarah Howard (stories above) had three sons: Richard, Nathaniel, and Thomas.**

## 1. Richard Gist

Born: 2 September 1729
Died: Before 1780
Wife: Unknown
DAR: No
SAR: No

Richard was born in Baltimore to the explorer Captain Christopher Gist and Sarah Howard. His birth records are at Saint Paul's Episcopal Church, and these records establish him as the son of Christopher and Sarah. I and other researchers have strived to not confuse this Richard with the Richard (son of Nathaniel born in 1742) who was killed at the Battle of Kings Mountain, as this Richard was about fifteen years older. They are clearly different men.

Richard was about sixteen years old when his family left Baltimore. He was with his father when he started the settlement with the Ohio Company in 1753. That year, he claimed his rights to 357 acres under an allowance of a settlement made by his father Christopher earlier that year. He later assigned that land to his brother Thomas in August 1771 for a sum of 50 pounds. On 3 April 1769 he was in Bedford County, Pennsylvania, later Fayette County, with his brother Thomas. At this time, he applied at the land office in Pennsylvania for land. A tract of 322 acres was surveyed for him on 18 October 1770. (Land Office Bureau, Department of Internal Affairs, Harrisburg, Pennsylvania, survey No. 180, Fayette County, Pennsylvania.) He later sold this land to his brother Thomas on 13 August 1771. (Fayette County Pennsylvania Deeds C, Deed Book 1, page 452.) The information concerning these land transactions was furnished by Sean Perkins on 21 December 2021. Mr. Perkins also determined that Richard, son of Christopher, was not alive by 1 January 1780, as his younger brother Nathaniel was deemed by the county of Kentucky to be the lawful heir to his father's grant for his service in the French and Indian War (his father was also deceased by this time). (Grant Book B, page 279, Commonwealth of Virginia.) Remember that at this time, Kentucky was a Virginia county.

I could find no evidence that he served with his father Christopher in the French and Indian War, but I did find him enlisted in his brother's regiment for the Revolution. He enlisted in brother Colonel Nathaniel Gist's Continental (Additional) Regiment by 1777. The intent of this regiment was to contain at least five hundred Comanche fighters, but it never attained that level of manning. It did consist of maybe four companies of Maryland soldiers, and Richard served in one. We found records showing that Richard was transferred to the Maryland Third Continental Line Regiment then commanded by Richard's cousin Colonel Mordecai Gist. Mordecai soon was promoted to general and assumed command of the Second Maryland Brigade of the Continental Line. This regiment and brigade transferred from the northern theater to the southern theater in late 1779, and it fought in some of the most important battles of that phase of the war, including the Guilford Courthouse battle and Cowpens.

His cousin Mordecai was a fighter, and his units always held and never retreated. They were depended upon for that strength. I was unable to track Richard Gist to that point of the war, but some researchers have claimed to have done so. It is alleged that he fought at the Battle of Kings Mountain and was killed on 7 November 1780 and is buried at the national cemetery at that battlefield, a national historic site. As I mentioned above, I challenge that assertion—it is true that a Private Richard Gist was killed at the Kings Mountain battle and is buried at that national cemetery, but it is not this Private Richard Gist. The facts are that the Second Maryland Regiment did not fight at the Kings Mountain battle, but they were nearby. I believe that the Richard Gist killed at Kings Mountain was the son of Captain Nathaniel Gist and the brother of Ensign Nathaniel Gist, who was also killed at that battle. Richard, son of Nathaniel, will be recognized later in this chapter. I will also provide some detail of that important battle and how it relates to several Patriots of this book in the later chapter on the Battle of Kings Mountain.

Unfortunately, I have been unable to track Richard Gist's life beyond his transfer to the Third Maryland Continental Line Regiment. Perhaps he was killed in one of the many battles in which that historic regiment fought. Maybe he served his term of enlistment, but my research has not solved that mystery. I found records that seemed to indicate he returned to Fayette County, Pennsylvania, following the war and owned property there near his brother Thomas, but I was unable to document that story. He was probably dead by 1780, and I have found no records of a marriage or children, and he almost certainly died intestate, probably in Pennsylvania.

## 2. Colonel Nathaniel Gist

Born: 15 October 1733
Died: 30 October 1796 (this date is questioned)
Wife: Judith Cary Bell (1750–1833)
DAR: A045442
SAR: P-1667578

Nathaniel was born in Baltimore, Maryland, and was the son of explorer Captain Christopher Gist and Sarah Howard. He would be my first cousin, seven times removed. His birth records are at Saint Paul's Episcopal Church, and he would have been twenty-two years old when he served as a captain with his father in the French and Indian War at the Battle of Fort Necessity. He later served in the Braddock Expedition and the Forbes Expedition and served in western Virginia (now West Virginia), North Carolina, and what is now Tennessee. Late in the Forbes Expedition in 1760, he recruited Indian tribes to support the colonies in defeating the French. During this expedition, he married a Cherokee Indian lady named Wurteh Wu he Eagle (1742–1814) and had a son. This son is reputed to be the famous Cherokee Sequoyah. Sequoyah went by the English name George Gist (Guess) and was credited with being the first to write and record the Cherokee alphabet in 1820.[249] This reference certainly fails to prove who the father of Sequoyah might have been, but it is known that Sequoyah used the last name of "Gist" and Nathaniel was unmarried and serving as a recruiting officer in the Kentucky and Tennessee territory at the right time prior to the Revolutionary War. Sequoyah claims to have been born in 1760, but some sources give a later date.

Nathaniel was well known by General George Washington, who offered him a commission as a colonel in command of Gist's Additional Continental Line Regiment during the Revolutionary War. This unit was to be four companies of southern frontier rangers and five hundred

---

[249] "The Father of Sequoyah: Nathaniel Gist," *Chronicles of Oklahoma*, Samuel C. Williams, 25 May 1937. This article makes a claim that Nathaniel was the father of Sequoyah and that Sequoyah later visited the Gist Family in Kentucky.

Cherokees; however, only three companies were formed from Virginians and Marylanders. Instead, the companies of John Gist (his brother) and Joseph Smith were attached to the Third Maryland Regiment, while the company of Samuel Lapsley served with the Eleventh Virginia Regiment. In April 1779, Gist's regiment absorbed eight companies from two other regiments and marched to Charleston in December and arrived there in April 1780. Gist and his regiment were captured on 12 May 1780 during the Siege of Charleston. He and his unit remained prisoners until the end of the war. He retired from the army on 1 January 1783 as a general. I have a copy of his National Archives Revolutionary War records.

He received seven thousand acres in Kentucky for his services in the war, and he moved there in 1793 with a large contingent of slaves and built an estate called "Canewood." He is said to have died there around 1812. Historians have established his death in 1796, but there is evidence to suspect that he survived until the War of 1812. The book *Colonial Families of the USA* gives an excellent account of his life and career, including the names of his children.[250]

After the war, he married Judith Cary Bell (1750–1833), and they had seven children:[251]

- Henry Cary, 1784–1833
- Sarah Howard Bledsoe, 1785–1849. Her son became a U.S. senator from Kentucky.
- Judith Bell Boswell, 1788–1843
- Dr. Thomas Nathaniel, 1790–1856. Became a War of 1812 surgeon.
- Anna Maria Hart, 1791–1818
- Eliza Violet Blair, 1791–1877. Her son became a U.S. senator from Missouri and an ancestor of a twentieth-century Missouri governor.
- Maria Cecil Gratz, 1797–1841

I think it likely that George Sequoyah Gist (1740–1842) was his son, as I have read multiple accounts claiming this relationship. George was a remarkable man, being a native silversmith and later the writer of the Cherokee/English dictionary. It is said he later regretted writing that dictionary when he learned that it was being used to teach tribal members to read the bible. George served in the Kentucky Militia during the War of 1812, and his wife claimed a pension based on that service. George may have died in Mexico while searching for tribal members that had been removed from Tennessee and Kentucky.

### 3. Lieutenant Thomas Gist
Born: 1735
Died: After 1786
Wife: Elizabeth (last name unproven) (1720–1810)
DAR: No
SAR: No

---

[250] *Colonial Families of the USA 1607–1775,* Volume I, Mackenzie, George Norbury, and Nelson Osgood Rhoades, editors, Genealogical Publishing Company, Inc., Baltimore, Maryland, 1966, 1995. Page 240 gives an excellent account of Nathaniel's life and career, including the names of his children.

[251] *Colonial Families of the USA, 1607–1775,* database online, Lehi, UT: Ancestry.com Operations, Inc., 2016. Page 240 lists the children of Colonel Nathaniel and Judith Cary Gist.

There were five Thomas Gists from the Baltimore Gist line, all serving during the Revolutionary War. Researchers have confused these men, and that is easily done. This Thomas was born in Baltimore in 1735, and the Saint Paul's church records establish the date and that his father was Christopher Gist the explorer and his mother Sarah Howard. He is the brother of Nathaniel and Richard, discussed above. His life quickly led him to the frontier with his father and mother. He moved to Virginia with his family and likely to North Carolina and Pennsylvania. However, most of his early life took place in Virginia, except for the short North Carolina experience, and his later life was lived in Fayette County, Pennsylvania.

At about the age of twenty, he joined the Colonial Virginia forces with his father Christopher and was commissioned as a lieutenant during the French and Indian War, serving under George Washington. He fought in some major battles and was present for the Braddock Expedition. He was awarded a land grant from the king for his services, but he probably did not claim that land. Stories of his life vary as they are not well documented, but it is clear he was captured by the Wyandot Indians near Fort Duquesne on 14 September 1758.[252] He was taken near to what is now Detroit, where he was adopted by an Indian family and treated well. The tribe later moved north into Canada, and in September 1759, he and two other prisoners walked out of camp and headed east. They made it to Fort Niagara in three weeks, where he made a written report to General Gage concerning the strengths and plans of the tribe.

As described in his older brother Richard's story above, he was back in Fayette County, Pennsylvania, later in 1759 and involved in land transactions with him in 1759 and 1760.

I have seen stories of his life claiming that he served during the Revolutionary War in his brother Nathaniel's regiment; however, I was not able to document service in that regiment. Colonel Nathaniel Gist's Regiment was captured in Charleston, South Carolina, in 1780 and remained prisoners until 1782. I am confident Thomas was not in that regiment when it was captured. I found records of his enlistment as a private in the Tenth Virginia Line Regiment for three years. His National Archives records show he was assigned to the Second Virginia Regiment, but this unit was consolidated with the Tenth Regiment after his enlistment. As this was a Virginia Line Regiment, it was not captured. However, I believe the regiment was present at the Battle of Kings Mountain. I have an unpublished roster with his name on it along with four other Gists that I will discuss later.

He probably served until later in 1780 and then returned to Virginia, where I found a civil court case in which a former Virginia store owner filed a lawsuit against Thomas for money owed by his father, Christopher. His father had purchased supplies amounting to more than 110 pounds and paid only 30 pounds, leaving an 80-pound debt. As his father was deceased (1759), his son was be held liable. I am unsure of the verdict, but Thomas soon moved to Fayette County, Pennsylvania, where he probably still owned land he had purchased from his brother. He remained there until his death after 1786, in which year he was listed on the Fayette County tax list, as well as in a Pennsylvania special census.

---

[252] "Thomas Gist's Indian Captivity, 1758-1759," Howard H. Peckham, *Pennsylvania Magazine of History and Biography*, Number 80, July 1956, pp. 310–311.

I was unable to discover the name of his wife or the names of his children.

---

> **Third-generation Captain Nathaniel Gist and Mary Howard (stories above) had five sons: Captain Benjamin, Captain Christopher, Ensign Nathaniel, Captain Joshua, and Richard.**

**1. Captain Benjamin Gist**
Born: 1730
Died: 1810
Wife: Mary Jarret (1732–1810)
DAR: A045394
SAR: No

Benjamin was the son of Captain Nathaniel Gist and Mary Howard and was born in Baltimore, Maryland. As with his brothers, his birth is recorded in the only church in Baltimore at that time. He moved to Lunenburg County, Virginia, with his parents by 1750, where he married Mary Jarrett on 6 November 1752. Her parents, Thomas and Rebecca Jarrett, gave them one hundred acres of land after the marriage. They later sold the land back to her parents in March 1756 and soon moved to Orange County, North Carolina. His father had already moved to North Carolina and joined his brother Christopher's company to fight in the French and Indian War. Benjamin operated a grist mill there and served as a road overseer. By 1767 he sold land obtained by a grant and moved to Union County, South Carolina. He received a five-hundred-acre land grant there but sold that land in 1776. He then moved to Washington County, now Greene County, Tennessee.

He was appointed justice of the peace upon formation of Greene County and served as captain of the militia under Colonel John Carter, and later under Colonel John Sevier.[253] Soon after the battle of Kings Mountain, his company was given credit for thwarting an attack on the frontier settlements by the Cherokees. He did not serve in the battle of Kings Mountain, as did his brothers Nathaniel and Robert who were killed in that battle, but he did serve in the Battle of Boyd's Creek. John Sevier was a noted fighter and became the first governor of Tennessee. Sevierville, Tennessee, is named after him.

Benjamin also served as a captain in the Chickamauga Expedition in April 1779 under Colonels Shelby and Montgomery. While this was arguably a Revolutionary War campaign, it had little to do with the Revolution and more to do with dealing with the Cherokee Indian tribes who were making life difficult for the Tennessee and North Carolina settlers. This conflict was paid for by the colonies of Virginia and North Carolina, and few records were kept of participants, except for the officers, and that included Benjamin.[254]

---

[253] *Roster of Soldiers from North Carolina in the American Revolution*, published by the North Carolina Daughters of the American Revolution, Seeman Press, Durham, North Carolina, 1932. Page 421, Appendix, states that Captain Benjamin Gist was a justice of Washington County and in 1780 was a captain in its militia.

[254] *The History of Hamilton County and Chattanooga, Tennessee*, Volume I, Zella Armstrong, The Lookout Publishing Company, 1931. Page 167 lists Captain Benjamin Gist as a militia leader in this expedition.

He received several land grants, most of which fell within the borders of Greene County when it was organized in 1783. He received his first Greene County grant (number 193) on 22 October 1783. On 20 September 1787, he received an additional four hundred acres in Greene County. That land lay on the north side of the Nolichucky River on Gist's Branch. This information was obtained from research of land, tax, and court records of Washington and Greene Counties by Jane Kay Buchanan of Oak Ridge, Tennessee.

He was again appointed justice of the peace in August 1785 and served as a grand juror several times. In 1784, he was elected as a delegate to the second convention called to organize the state of "Franklin," and in 1787 he signed a petition of inhabitants of the "Western Country" to establish a new state. He continued to buy and sell land in Washington County, and by 1800, he and several other families from Greene County moved to Barren County, Kentucky, and Smith County, Tennessee, border counties on those state lines. He received a Barren County land grant of fifty acres on 20 January 1804 (Kentucky Land Grant Book 6). I believe he also purchased land there from the land sales in Tennessee. While these several moves may seem confusing, the boundaries between Tennessee and Kentucky moved several times before these states were created. I do not believe he moved very far.

He and Mary Jarrett had eight children. Three fought in the Revolutionary War and two in post-war military service. Their births are recorded in the Gist family bible documented in *Christopher Gist of Maryland and Some of His Descendants*.[255]

- Joseph, 1751–1844. Married (1) Hannah Breed and (2) Elizabeth (Belew) Springer and served in the Revolutionary War as an Indian spy for Colonel Sevier. His story is later in the book with the next generation Gists.
- Mary Stevenson/Stinson, 1755–1822. Married James Stinson, a Revolutionary War Patriot.
- John, 1757–1820. Married Hannah Geron and served in the Revolutionary War in the Washington County Militia. His story is later in the book with the next Gist generation.
- William, 1759–1828. Served in the Knox County, Ohio, militia in 1792.
- Thomas, 1764–1837. Patriot in the Revolutionary War. Married Elizabeth Russell and served as an Indian spy for Colonel John Sevier. Adjutant in the Kentucky volunteers in 1794. His story is later in the book with the next generation of Gists.
- Amie Lowry, 1767–1846. Married Alexander Lowery.
- Ann McLain, 1771–Unknown death date. Married James McLain.
- Captain Benjamin Jr., 1773–1846. Married (1) Rebecca Hinds and (2) Rebecca Chism. Served in the Tennessee Forty-Eighth Regiment in the War of 1812

His burial location is not known.

---

[255] *Christopher Gist of Maryland and Some of His Descendants, 1679–1957,* Jean Muir Dorsey and Maxwell Jay Dorsey, Hassel Street Press. 2021.

## 2. Captain Christopher Gist
Born: 21 September 1734
Died: May 1794
Wife: Lucy McNeil (1738–1799)
DAR: No
SAR: No

Christopher's birth records are at the St. Paul's Church of Baltimore and establish that he was the son of Captain Nathaniel Gist and Mary Howard. His wife Lucy McNeil was also born in Baltimore, and her birth records are located at the same church.

I found no records that Christopher was a soldier in the Revolutionary War. He was a soldier in the French and Indian War, as we found payroll records showing he was a captain in 1755. I have discounted the possibility that those records were of his uncle Christopher, a third-generation Patriot who also fought in that war and whose story is told above. There are no DAR or SAR records reflecting his service in the Revolution. What I did find, however, was that he received a North Carolina land grant for his service in the French and Indian War and that he was in Cumberland County, North Carolina, by 1771 with his wife Lucy. That grant was for 287 acres. In fact, he was probably in North Carolina well prior to 1771. His only son, Joseph, was born in 1755 in North Carolina. Christopher probably departed Virginia immediately following discharge from the army and headed to North Carolina. This makes sense since his uncle Christopher was also there at that time.

The fact that he was in North Carolina by the time of the Revolution did not prohibit him from serving, so future research will focus on his belonging to a North Carolina militia.

His will was proved in 1795 in Cumberland County, North Carolina, which supports a May 1794 death. He owned 365 acres of land, eleven slaves, and normal farming implements and tools. His wife wrote her will that year, and she lived until 1799.

## 3. Ensign Nathaniel Gist Jr.
Born: 15 October 1733
Died: 7 October 1780
Wife: Dinah Van Hook (1738–1778)
DAR: A045438
SAR: P-1667565

Nathaniel was the son of Captain Nathaniel Gist and Nancy Howard. He was born in 1733 in Baltimore, and his birth records are found at St. Paul's Church there. Some researchers have confused this Nathaniel Gist with his cousin Colonel Nathaniel Gist, son of the explorer Christopher Gist, discussed above. That is easy to do.

Ensign Nathaniel grew to adulthood in Virginia, as his father and his family had moved to Lunenburg County, Virginia, by 1745. His father moved to North Carolina by 1754 and fought in the French and Indian War, and I believe Nathaniel and his wife Dinah also moved there. I am unsure of Nathaniel's activities in North Carolina prior to the Revolutionary War, but it is likely that he had some interactions with his uncle Christopher following the French and Indian War, as I found undocumented family stories to that effect. Nathanial and Dinah's sons were born there, and following the war, sons John and Aaron became early settlers in Lawrence County, Tennessee. His oldest son, Nathaniel III, remained in Washington County, Virginia, for the remainder of his life.

While I have displayed his DAR and SAR Patriot numbers, I will add that both organizations have credited his service to an incorrect unit. They have credited his service to the unit of his cousin Nathaniel Gist, who was the son of explorer Christopher Gist. The unit credited for his service never fought at Kings Mountain.

This Nathaniel joined the Washington County, Virginia, militia commanded by Colonel William Campbell. I previously discussed this regiment in the story of Patriot Richard Lee. This regiment was a very active Virginia Line Regiment with a motivated commander who was aggressive and knew how to fight. By summer 1780 the regiment was assigned to North Carolina to counter the British advances toward Virginia from the Charleston area. Their previous assignments involved protection of the valuable lead mines in Washington County. Colonel Campbell had gained a reputation as a no-nonsense and brutal commander. He was now needed to protect his colony from the coming British invasion from the south. When they arrived in South Carolina, the various commanders agreed that Colonels Campbell and Sevier should lead the attack.

The stage was set for this battle when British Major Patrick Ferguson of the General Cornwallis army announced to the Overmountain Men of eastern Tennessee and North Carolina that they should stay home and take care of their children as he advanced north toward Virginia. Those were fighting words for the mountain men, and they, in conjunction with the Virginia Line units, cornered Major Ferguson and his Tory fighters on the crest of Kings Mountain, South Carolina, on 7 October 1780. They made quick work of the British officer and his Tory fighters, as the battle lasted no more than two hours. A total of 225 Tories were killed, as well as Major Ferguson. There were 716 Tory soldiers captured, so this was a major setback for the British army and a sad day for the Gist family of Baltimore. Nathaniel was killed in that battle and is buried in the national cemetery at Kings Mountain National Military Park.

Ensign Nathaniel Gist's name is on one of the monuments at the battlefield memorial. He is listed with the incorrect rank of second lieutenant. The source of his name and rank was provided by the author of a credible book on that battle, but the author later attributed the mistake to an error of his.[256] The rank of second lieutenant was not a militia rank but a Continental rank, and this was a state unit. Nathaniel served under the command of Captain Edmonson, who was also killed in that battle. See my chapter on the Kings Mountain battle later in the book for more details and references on this important battle.

I further confirmed that this Nathaniel Jr. was the son of Nathaniel by the fact that his father of North Carolina made a claim with the Washington County, Virginia, court for a lost rifle about a year following the battle, stating he was the legal heir. His father was in fact living in North

---

[256] *King's Mountain and Its Heroes: History of the Battle of King's Mountain,* Lyman C. Draper, Peter Thompson, publisher, Cincinnati, 1881. Page 304 lists Nathaniel Gist as being among those killed at that battle.

Carolina then. Father Nathaniel also made a similar claim for his other son Richard's rifle. He received 4 pounds and 10 shillings for the claim.[257]

I also discovered evidence of a letter filed with the Second Continental Congress (second session, journal page 278) containing a claim for service for Nathaniel. The status was "Laid on the table." I am not sure who made the claim, as his wife's death occurred before that of Nathaniel's, but likely it was his father who made the claim.

Nathaniel Gist and Dinah Van Hook had four children, but I have been unable to document either his wife or his children. Their proposed children were:

- Nathaniel III, 1762–1781
- John, 1764–1817
- Aron, 1766–1818
- George, 1768–1843

## 4. Captain Joshua Gist

Born: 7 July 1739
Died: 22 December 1819
Wife: Elizabeth Kellam (1749–1818)
DAR: A045432
SAR: P-166753

Joshua was the son of Captain Nathaniel Gist and Mary Howard (third-generation Gists) and was born in Baltimore in 1739. He married Elizabeth Kellam on 26 November 1766. He was probably named after his maternal grandfather Joshua Howard. He was a small boy when his parents moved from Maryland to Virginia and later to North Carolina. By 1763, he served on a jury in Cumberland County, North Carolina, and bought and sold several tracts of land in that county over the next ten years. In 1772, he applied for and received a license to run a tavern in his house, and in 1777, he was appointed as a captain in the county militia and served in Colonel Thomas Brown's Brigade.

Joshua was an Overmountain Man. This term was applied to those men that crossed from west to east from Tennessee and North Carolina to fight the British on their final campaign from South Carolina to Virginia.[258] They were feared by the Tories, who knew they did not waste many bullets on the Tories when a rope was cheaper and just as effective. They were greatly respected by the British, who would have preferred to return to Virginia without interference from the Overmountain Men. I was inclined to identify Ensign Nathaniel Gist, discussed above, with this term, but his residency in Washington County, Virginia, would probably rule him out. You will later see additional Gists being assigned this identifier.

His brigade is credited with serving in the Battles of Cowpens and Kings Mountain. I have noted other Gists serving in the Kings Mountain battle but have been unable to confirm that his militia fought there. However, nearly 1/3 of the militia at that battle were Overmountain Men from

---

[257] *Annals of Southwest Virginia 1769–1800,* Lewis Preston Summers, 1930. Page 1117 shows that Nathaniel Gist claimed to be heir-at-law.
[258] *The Overmountain Men,* Pat Alderman, Overmountain Press, 1970, pp. 81–96.

North Carolina. I could not find a Colonel Thomas Brown, so it is likely that his regiment was small and combined with the unit of Colonel John Sevier. His regiment was present, and he commanded most of the North Carolina soldiers in that battle. I have a Kings Mountain roster containing the names of the four Gists participating in the battle.[259]

He received a 1,800-acre land grant in Cumberland County for his service and quickly sold that land. He served in the North Carolina General Assembly in 1784 and was appointed lieutenant colonel of Greene County, North Carolina, that year. He served on several boards and commissions that took part in the attempt to form the state of "Franklin." That was an unsuccessful attempt, as the state of Tennessee was soon formed from that part of North Carolina. His large plantation soon was in what is now Sevier County, Tennessee. He was appointed by John Sevier as assistant judge of the superior court of the proposed new state of Franklin. Once Tennessee became a state in 1795, he became a full magistrate of the court in 1796.[260]

On 10 June 1785, Gist, along with John Sevier, finalized an agreement with the Cherokee Indian tribe over the territory lying within the proposed state of Franklin. The Treaty of Dumplin Creek was signed by John Sevier, Joshua Gist, and Ebenezer Alexander. Figure 8-1 below is a Tennessee historical roadside marker recognizing that agreement. More than thirty Cherokee chiefs signed that treaty with a state that never existed, as Congress did not approve its entry into the union. Tennessee soon became a state, with John Sevier becoming its first governor.[261]

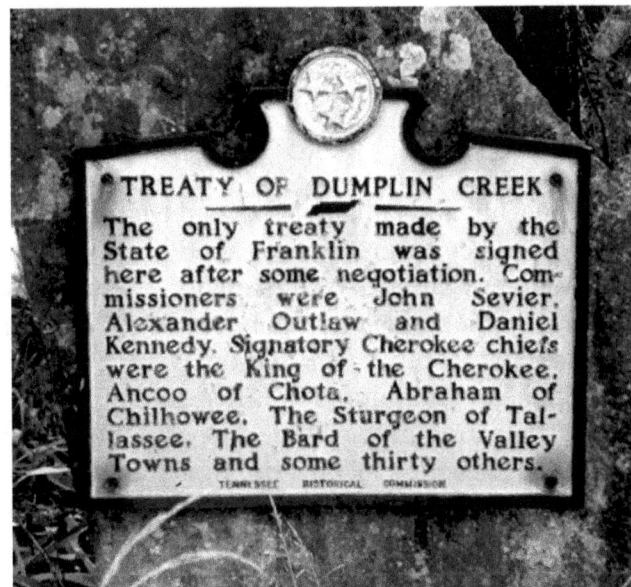

Figure 8-1: The Treaty of Dumplin Creek
Roadside Marker in Tennessee
**Provided by the Historical Marker Database. Hmdb.org**

---

[259] "Battle of King's Mountain, October 1780," British Battles, archived from the original on 29 October 2010, p 121.
[260] Unpublished transcribed article for *Echoes Magazine* written by Jean Muir Dorsey, who was the author of *Christopher Gist of Maryland and Some of His Descendants, 1679–1957.*
[261] Ibid.

By 1810 he had probably moved to Henderson, Kentucky, and is shown living with his son Nathaniel in the 1810 census there.

Joshua and Elizabeth had ten children that I verified from the Bomar family bible:[262]

- Mary Smith, 1769–1828
- Richard, 1770–1789
- William, 1770–1790
- Sarah Brown, 1772–1801
- Elizabeth, 1774–1818
- Mary Rachel Porter/Smith/Loudermilk, 1777–1828
- William, 1780–1800
- Jane Yell, 1780–1850
- Mordecai, 1782–1855
- Nathaniel, 1784–1843
- Naomi, 1785–Unknown death date

## 5. Richard Gist
Born: 1742
Died: 7 October 1780
Wife: Unknown
DAR: No
SAR: P-1666747

Richard was born in Baltimore to Captain Nathaniel Gist and Mary Howard. Church records support that birth data. As with his brothers, he grew to adulthood in Virginia, and as with brother Nathaniel, he joined Colonel William Campbell's Washington County Militia. He was assigned to a mounted detachment of that regiment, which might account for his participation in the Battle of Kings Mountain. I later discuss the fact that foot soldiers were left behind for this attack. This seems to account for the fact that nearly all injured or killed soldiers were officers, who owned horses. The conjecture of his participation in this battle is speculation, but the facts of that battle seem to bear this theory out. He nevertheless lost his life in that battle and is buried at the cemetery there with his brother Nathaniel. His name is not listed on the first monument at the battlefield park but was added to a later monument.

His father made a claim for Richard's lost rifle and stated he was his legal heir. I unfortunately found little else about this Patriot's life. There has been disagreement as to his age, but his birth records in Baltimore appear to settle that issue.

---

[262] Loose pages from the Bible of Elijah Bomar and Fannie McGee contain the names and partial birth dates of Joshua Gist and Elizabeth Kellam's children.

> **Third-generation William Gist Sr. and Violetta Howard (stories above) had four sons: Major Joseph, William Jr., Thomas, and John.**

## 1. Major Joseph Gist
Born: 1738
Died: 1803
Wife: Elizabeth Elder

Joseph's story is told earlier in this book as a Raines Patriot.

## 2. William Gist Jr.
Born: 1743
Died: 1802
Wife: Sarah Fincher

William did not serve in the Revolution.

## 3. Captain Thomas Gist
Born: 19 May 1750
Died: 1808, Baltimore, Maryland
Wife: Ruth Bond (1744–1812), married in 1785
DAR: No
SAR: No

Thomas served in the Baltimore Regiment as a captain. This regiment was commanded by his cousin Colonel Thomas Gist. This was the Soldiers Delight Regiment in which his older brother Major Joseph Gist and cousin Major Joshua Gist served. I will discuss Patriot Colonel Thomas Gist and Major Joshua Gist later in this chapter. Thomas spent his entire life in the Baltimore area as a farmer and businessman.

Captain Thomas Gist married Ruth Bond, and they had three children:

- William B., 1800–Unknown death date
- Ruth, 1798–Unknown death date
- Thomas Bond, 1800–1843

## 4. Captain John Gist
Born: 26 July 1752
Died: 1782, Baltimore, Maryland
Wife: None
DAR: No
SAR: No

Captain John Gist was the son of William Gist and Violeta Howard and was born in Baltimore, Maryland. He served as a captain in his cousin Colonel Thomas Gist's Soldiers Delight Regiment of the Baltimore Militia.

John spent his life in the Baltimore area, never married, and had no children.

---

**Third-generation Thomas Gist Sr. and Susan Cockey (stories above) had six sons: Captain John, Colonel Thomas Jr., General Mordecai, Colonel Joshua, Captain David, and Richard.**

---

**1. Captain John Gist**
Born: 22 November 1738
Died: 16 July 1800, Virginia
Wife: Elizabeth Norton (1737–Unknown death date)
DAR: No
SAR: No

John was the son of Captain Thomas Gist and Susannah Cockey of Baltimore, Maryland. His birth and parents' names are recorded at St. Paul's Protestant Episcopal Church in Baltimore. It is easy to confuse this John Gist with the John Gist who was the son of Christopher the explorer, discussed above, but they are clearly different men. Both men were born in Baltimore and served in the Revolutionary War with the Virginia Continental Army in Gist's Additional Regiment, so the confusion is understandable.

He served as a captain in Captain Stanbury's Company in the colonial war in 1767. ("Colonial Muster and Payrolls," page 81, Rolls of Records, Annapolis.) It is likely that this represented Maryland's resistance to the Stamp Act. I find no records of actual fighting at this time, but the future was becoming clear—there was trouble brewing in Baltimore, and the Gist's were ready for a fight.

The dates of his military service in the Revolutionary War are not known. He enlisted as a captain in Colonel Nathaniel Gist's Continental Line unit (identified as Gist's Additional Regiment). I have a 1778 payroll for the regiment that included his name. This unit is discussed elsewhere in this book and consisted of three or four companies of Maryland soldiers and several companies of Indians from Virginia. This regiment was clearly a Virginia regiment, but by 1780 General Washington reassigned all the American soldiers to the Maryland Continental Line and reconstituted the unit with Virginia soldiers. It is my belief that John, if he was still in the service in 1780, should have been assigned to the Maryland regiment. However, if he remained in his nephew Nathaniel Gist's Regiment, he would have been relocated that year with the Virginia regiment to South Carolina and soon captured by the British. The unit remained prisoners until late 1782. I believe he remained in the Virginia Continental Line unit he enlisted in and served in South Carolina until released in 1782 for three reasons. First, he was authorized a four-thousand-acre land grant for his service. Maryland soldiers did not receive such grants. This grant was the sole reason for his heirs' 1820 court claim (see the next paragraph). Second, I am unable to discover records supporting his serving in a Maryland unit that received most of the Virginia soldiers. Third, Major General Smallwood, who was the Maryland Third Brigade commander, signed a document attesting that Captain John Gist was amongst Maryland officers assigned to Colonel Nathaniel Gist's Virginia Regiment.[263] It is easy to confuse this John with the John (1722–1778) who was the son of Christopher, discussed above. They both served in the same Virginia regiment until John, son of Christopher, was assigned to the Maryland regiment.

This John's last will and testament of 1790 was presented in 1820 Baltimore court proceedings in which his heirs requested that the state of Virginia award land grants earned from his service during the Revolution.[264] It is important to remember that thirty years had elapsed between the writing of the 1790 will and the filing of the 1820 probate case. John had died in 1800, and his surviving wife, Elizabeth, had filed a will in 1803. She died prior to 1820, and there were no surviving children by the 1820 court case. His children were named in the 1790 will.

The Baltimore 1790 census shows ten persons residing in his home: one male over sixteen, two males under sixteen, five females, and two slaves. *Virginia Soldiers of 1776,* noted above, states that in the 1820 court case, he had no surviving wife or children. I believe his wife Elizabeth was born in England and might have returned to England shortly after his death. His children were not named in that court case; however, his mother and siblings were named.

John had considerable Maryland landholdings that were listed in his will:

- Land in Rock Springs in Frederick County, Maryland, on Pipes Creek
- Land on Lady's Manor in Baltimore County
- "Nicholson's Manor," containing 360 acres, including the plantation dwelling
- The "Final Settlement," containing 3½ acres
- Tract called "Mount Pleasant," containing 19¼ acres
- A lot in the city of Baltimore on Steward Street adjoining Walker's Tavern
- A tract of land called "Deer Creek" containing 313 acres in Baltimore County
- A 100-acre tract of land, part of "Lady's Manor," called Lot 92

These real-estate holdings were divided amongst his surviving children according to the 1803 will of his wife. The 4,000-acre land grant was assigned by share basis to his surviving nephews.

John and Elizabeth had four children. Their birth and death dates are not known, except that all were deceased prior to 1820. These children were named in his will:

- Charles Norton Gist, 1769–prior to 1820
- Jessie Seabrooke, 1790–prior to 1820
- Charolette, Unknown birth date–prior to 1820
- Harriet, Unknown birth date–prior to 1820

---

[263] *Bailey-Britton History and Genealogy,* T.H. Bailey, Kingsport, Tennessee, 1961, vol. 18, p. 366. Officers of Maryland who are part of Nathaniel Gist's regiment. Signed by Major General Smallwood.
[264] *Virginia Soldiers of 1776,* Vol. 1, Burgess, Louis Alexander, Richmond, Virginia: Richmond Press, 1927, pp. 52–55.

### 2. Colonel Thomas Gist Jr.
Born: 30 March 1741
Died: 22 November 1813
Wife: Penelope Dye Cockey (1757–1820)
DAR: A045446
SAR: P177760

Thomas was the second son of Captain Thomas Gist and Susannah Cockey of Baltimore, Maryland. His birth date and parents are recorded at St. Paul's Protestant Episcopal Church in Baltimore, Maryland. Land and court records show he used the suffix of Jr. with these records. He married Penelope Dye Cockey late in his life on 6 May 1792 in Baltimore, Maryland. The 1790 census shows two males over the age of sixteen in his home and no females. That census also reflects six slaves. I found no records of an earlier marriage, and some DAR records also support the contention that he had only one wife.[265] I will note that there are some DAR records naming Mary Noland as his wife and stating that he had one son, but the public records I have reviewed reveal only one wife: Penelope Dye Cockey.

He lived on a tract of 360 acres of land called "Nicholson's Manor" that had been bought by his father in 1775. This land is in Baltimore County about a mile east of Shawn, which is about seven miles northeast of the St. Thomas Church.[266] I have a photo of his home on that land, and it is impressive.

Thomas was commissioned as a captain in the newly formed Baltimore Militia in early 1777. He was quickly recommended for promotion to colonel to the Baltimore Committee of Safety, and they approved that promotion. The fact that his father served on that committee may or may not have played a role in his quick promotion, given the Gist family's reputation for public service. All of Thomas Gist Sr.'s sons became very successful military leaders, and I doubt if their father's influence directly affected that success. Read General Mordecai, Colonel Joshua, and David Gist's stories below, as well as his brother's story above.

Thomas commanded the Soldiers Delight Regiment of Baltimore for the duration of the war. Other Gist family members served as officers in that regiment, and their service is discussed in their stories elsewhere in this chapter. Thomas commanded the regiment in which my SAR Patriot, Joseph Gist, served. I found no evidence that this regiment faced any conflict, and that is probably fact, as I could find no records of any battles of significance being fought in Maryland.

On 12 December 1783, he received a military warrant for ten thousand acres of land in Fayette County, Kentucky, and in 1784 he received a warrant for another three thousand acres. Later he received three more tracts of land there for a total of ten thousand acres. I believe he soon sold those warrants and purchased several more tracts of land in Baltimore County.[267] His will of 15 January 1807, proven on 12 December 1813, left the home, plantation, and slaves to his wife

---

[265] *Colonial Families of the USA 1607–1775*, Mackenzie, George Norbury, and Nelson Osgood Rhoades, editors. Reprinted, Baltimore: Genealogical Publishing Co., Inc., 1966, 1995. Page 114 lists the family of his father John as well as John Jr.
[266] *Christopher Gist of Maryland and Some of His Descendants, 1679–1957*, Jean Muir Dorsey and Maxwell Jay Dorsey, Hassel Street Press, 2021. Page 139 gives an account of his land holdings in Maryland and Kentucky.
[267] Ibid., p. 139.

Penelope. The remainder of his holdings were left to his nephews, sons of his brother Mordecai, David, and John. Again, he seems to have had no surviving children.

## 3. General Mordecai Gist
Born: 22 February 1742
Died: 2 August 1792
Wife: (1) Cecil Carman (1742–1770) and (2) Mary Poly Sterrett. (1763-1779) and (3) Mary McCall (1749-1812)
DAR: A045436
SAR: P-166754

Mordecai, the third son of Captain Thomas Gist Sr. and Susannah Cockey, was born at their Baltimore estate "Stone Hall." His birth date and parents are recorded at St. Paul's Protestant Episcopal Church in Baltimore, Maryland. He received an education sufficient to be a businessman, and he was said to be at least six feet tall as an adult.

He married Cecil Carman of Baltimore in 1768, but she died giving birth to their daughter, also named Cecil, in 1770. He worked as a businessman mainly on Gay Street in Baltimore, and his business activities required that he travel abroad. He did so in 1771, buying a large quantity of goods such as textiles, cooking utensils, and guns. I have a copy of a Baltimore 24 April 1772 newspaper advertisement announcing that he had moved his retail and wholesale business and that he had a fresh supply of English clothing and household goods. He had likely moved to a larger store in a better location. He also announced that all past credits were due and needed to be settled.

He never inherited any of his father's estate, as his father lived a long life, nearly outliving Mordecai. But he did buy and sell land his entire life, so his business activities were profitable, and he had land holdings in Baltimore, Pennsylvania, and South Carolina. He was a slave owner, and I found advertisements he posted looking for escaped slaves in a 15 October 1778 New Jersey paper stating that a female slave and her son had taken leave of his camp. Later this slave had apparently been apprehended by the Fifth Maryland Regiment, but she was released due to her claim that she was free and married to a soldier. He had stated in the ad that she was a mulatto. When discovering this event, he ran another ad in the same paper on 19 November of that year increasing the reward.

He was a radical supporter of the American independence movement, and in 1774, he supported an event known as the "Annapolis Tea Party." He was a member of the Baltimore Independent Cadets by 1774, which he formed at his own expense. By late 1774, the Independent Cadets had ceased to exist. On 1 January 1776, he was made a second major of General Smallwood's First Maryland Regiment. The colony authorized Smallwood's Regiment to support the Revolution and leave the state in support of the war by July 1776. The regiment then became a Continental Line unit. They marched to New York in support of Washington's campaign to defend New York from British invasion. The invasion came on 27 August when Colonel Smallwood and deputy commander Lieutenant Colonel Ware were attending a court martial ordered by General Washington. They left Major Gist in charge of the regiment. That was a fateful decision for the war.

The British force under the command of General Howe marched around the American left, fooling the Americans, who thought that this was the main attack. They then engaged the Americans from their front. The Americans were ordered to retreat, and the Maryland Second Regiment, now commanded by Gist, was ordered to guard the retreat. He guarded the retreat very successfully, risking his life on several occasions despite being hopelessly outnumbered. The regiment did eventually retreat, but the British did not capitalize on this opportunity, as it was late in the day. He was recognized as a promising young leader after this battle, despite the fact of the campaign being a failure. One might say he saved the Revolution, as Washington was certainly at risk of capture if the defense of his retreat had failed. Washington was well aware of this risk and knew who had saved the day. Gist was soon promoted and given command of the regiment, and Colonel Smallwood was promoted to general. The Revolution might have ended that day if this retreat had not been so well protected. Sometimes there is honor in a "victorious retreat."

As a regimental commander, he participated in the Philadelphia Campaign and several battles, further distinguishing himself. By 1779, he was promoted to brigadier general. During the summer of 1780 he marched to South Carolina and linked with his former commander General Smallwood. They suffered a disastrous defeat at the Battle of Camden despite the great performance of the Maryland troops. The Maryland regulars had performed well and stood their ground, but the militia units retreated. Both Smallwood and Gist were later recognized by Congress for their bravery during this battle. The Maryland troops consisted of both the First, Second, and Third Regiments organized under the First Maryland Brigade commanded by Gist. He had earlier commanded the Second Regiment and served in the First Regiment as a major. These were tough regiments and were respected by the British. The Second Regiment fought at the Battle of Guilford Courthouse, which will be discussed in a later chapter in this book.

Gist served until the end of the war and was present at the Cornwallis surrender at Yorktown.

After the war Gist moved to Charleston, South Carolina, and purchased a plantation there. He did not seek public office but spent most of his time running the plantation. In the 1780s Gist married a third time in marrying Mary McCall. He died in the fall of 1792 at the age of forty-nine. The recorded versions of his death date vary from August to October of that year. His gravestone shows a date of 2 August 1792. He is buried at Saint Michael's Church Cemetery, Charleston, South Carolina.

It is worth noting that Mordecai was a Freemason, as was General Washington. He was also a grand master, as was Washington. This connection brought the two men together in many documented meetings throughout their lives. The last recorded meeting of these two men was in Charleston, South Carolina, when President Washington visited that town and Gist held a formal masonic ceremony honoring Washington. Gist did not live long following that meeting.

His will of 1 September 1792 named his children and sisters Elizabeth and Rachel and nephews Mordecai and William. Daughter Cecil was not named, as she died as an infant. His children were:

- Cecil Cernan, 1770–1771

- Independent, 1779–1821
- Susannah, 1784–1822
- States, 1787–1822

I found many Mordecai Gist stories and books, as he is an important historical figure. Most contained significant errors concerning his family, military service, and business activities. The Boston Archives were used extensively to validate this story, and I feel it best represents his life and contribution to history. As a note, the term "Yankee Doodle Dandy" can be attributed to this Gist. Check it out. I'll leave that research up to the reader.

## 4. Richard Gist

Born: 1 November 1745
Died: 17 November 1746

Richard was the son of Captain Thomas Gist Sr. and Susannah Cockey. He died in infancy and is buried in the St. Thomas Episcopal Church Cemetery in Owings Mills, Baltimore County, Maryland.

## 5. Colonel Joshua Gist

Born: 17 October 1747
Died: 17 November 1839
Wife: Sarah Harvey
DAR: A45434
SAR: P-166753

Joshua Gist was the son of Captain Thomas Gist and Susannah Cockey and was born in Baltimore, Maryland. His birth date and parents are recorded at St. Paul's Protestant Episcopal Church in Baltimore, Maryland. He married Sarah Harvey of Baltimore, and they spent most of their lives in Maryland. I have their marriage records. His brothers Captain John, Colonel Thomas, General Mordecai, and Captain David also served in the Revolution.

After their marriage they moved to a tract of land named "Falls Dale" in Baltimore County, where his father Thomas and brother John Jr. also owned land. When Frederick County was formed, his land lay in the new county.[268]

Joshua served in the Baltimore County Soldiers Delight Militia as a second major under the command of his brother Colonel Thomas Gist. He also took the Oath of Allegiance in 1778. His cousin Major Joseph Gist, a family Patriot discussed earlier in this book, also served in that regiment. As a colonel he later commanded the Twentieth Regiment of the Maryland Militia when Maryland was threatened with an invasion of British forces in May 1779.[269]

---

[268] *Christopher Gist of Maryland and Some of His Descendants, 1679–1957*, Jean Muir Dorsey and Maxwell Jay Dorsey, Hassel Street Press, 2021. Page 151 gives an account of his service and land holdings.
[269] *History of Western Maryland*, Volume 2, J. Thomas Scharf, 1968. Pages 920–921 give a sketch of Colonel Joshua Gist's Revolutionary War accomplishments as well as his brother General Mordecai Gist. It also lists the names of Joshua and Sarah Harvey's children who are buried in the Gist Cemetery in Carroll County, Maryland.

He remained in command of the Twentieth Regiment of the Maryland Militia until the time of the Whiskey Rebellion. I found an article describing a local uprising in support of the Whiskey Rebellion in which the colonel merely appeared riding his horse with no troops or weapons except for his sword, and the crowd dispersed out of respect for him. He actually cut the cords to an illegal liberty pole erected by local townspeople. He lived to the age of ninety-three, and his grave is marked by a DAR grave marker.[270]

He owned a large plantation named the "Long Farm" and is buried in a cemetery across the road from his still-standing home. His wife and several of his children, as well as some of the children of his brother General Mordecai, are buried there also.

His will, which was written on 21 November 1837 and proven on 21 November 1839, lists four of his children: Harriot, Federal Ann, John, and Thomas. John was named as executor. The names of the remainder of his children were obtained from Mary Sterrett Gist's bible in the possession of Mrs. Robert Gist of Westminster, Maryland.

He and his wife Sarah had twelve children:

- Anna, 1774–1790
- James Harvey, 1775–1823. Married Mary Elliot.
- Susannah Jones, 1778–1817. Married Joshua Jones and is buried in the Gist Cemetery.
- Rachel, 1780–1830. Married Independent Gist, a first cousin and son of General Mordecai Gist. They are buried in the Gist Cemetery.
- Mordecai, 1782–1835. Executed on 14 December 1835 after being taken prisoner in Tampico, Mexico, while serving on General Mexia's expedition into Mexico. This poorly planned expedition infuriated General Santa Anna to the point that he issued a "no quarter" policy that may explain the severity of the later Alamo battle.
- Polly Julia Poulson, 1784–1804. Married Samuel Poulson.
- Thomas, 1786–1846. Married Harriot Poulson.
- Sarah Harvey, 1788–1818. Buried in the Gist Cemetery.
- Harriet Dorsey, 1790–1864. Buried in the Gist Cemetery.
- Joshua Cockey, 1792–1878
- General George Washington Gist, 1795–1854. He died in Platte County, Missouri. The 1850 census indicates he was a surveyor and magistrate. I did not confirm the military rank.
- Federal Anne Bonaparte Gist, 1797–1890. Never married and is buried in the Gist Cemetery.

Joshua was buried with military honors at the Gist Cemetery on 20 November 1839.

---

[270] Ibid.

### 6. Lieutenant David Gist

Born: 29 April 1753
Died: 3 August 1820
Wife: Rebecca Hammond
DAR: A045400
SAR: P-332638

David was the youngest son of Captain Thomas Gist and Susannah Cockey of Baltimore, Maryland. His birth date and parents are recorded at St. Paul's Protestant Episcopal Church in Baltimore, Maryland. His brothers John, Joshua, Mordecai, and Thomas were also Patriots and are discussed above.

David served in the Baltimore Militia as a lieutenant under Captain Murray. This was the Soldiers Delight Battalion under the command of his brother Colonel Thomas Gist. He served with his brother Major Joshua Gist and cousin Major Joseph Gist. I note that this unit is sometimes referred to as a battalion, but most historical references seem to recognize the regiment status, especially given that the commander was a colonel, not a lieutenant colonel—a rank which would have commanded a battalion.

Following the war, he soon moved to Fort Boonesborough, Kentucky, where he became one of the original trustees, along with Daniel Boone, in 1779.[271]

By 1785, he had returned to Baltimore, where he married Rebecca Hammond (1767–1827) on 5 June 1785. The remained in Baltimore, where we find him for the 1790 census with a wife and a son under the age of sixteen, as well as seven slaves.

By 1800, we find him in Clark County, Kentucky, on the Compiled Census Substitute Index and the tax list for that county. He had bought land on Stones Creek there from his cousin Nathaniel Gist. He soon built a large home on that land, of which I have a later photo.

David and Rebecca had three sons, which I have not proven:

- Razin Hammond, 1787–1845
- Thomas Hammond, 1789–1832
- David Richard, 1791–1848

David is buried in the Mount Sterling Cemetery in Montgomery County, Kentucky, as are his three sons.

---

[271] *Boonesborough: Its Founding, Pioneer Struggles, Indian Experiences, Transylvania Days, and Revolutionary Annals*, Ranck, George Washington, Louisville, Kentucky: J.P. Morton and Co., 1901. Page 111 lists David Gist as an original town trustee.

# The Fifth Generation of American Gists

**Captain Benjamin Gist, a fourth-generation Gist, son of Captain Nathaniel Gist (their stories above), had three sons: Joseph, John, and Thomas.**

### 1. Joseph Gist

Born: 27 August 1751
Died: 31 August 1844
Rank: Private
Wife: (1) Hannah Breed (1755–1815) and (2) Elizabeth (Betsy) Springer/Belew (1787–1866)
DAR: A045429
SAR: P-166752

Joseph was born in Lunenburg, Virginia, to Captain Benjamin Gist and Mary Jarret. He moved with his family, including both his and his wife's parents, to the Fairforest Creek settlement in Union County, South Carolina. He and his extended family then moved to Washington County, North Carolina in 1777.[272] Hannah's parents remained in South Carolina. As a fourth-generation Gist, he would be my first cousin seven times removed. Hannah died in 1814, and Joseph married Elizabeth Belew, who had been widowed, in 1816.

He clearly meets the description of an Overmountain Man, as he enlisted in a North Carolina Militia unit commanded by Colonel John Sevier in 1777 and served several enlistments as an Indian spy, serving until 1780.[273] This source lists Joseph as a Kentucky soldier, however Kentucky was a Virginia terrritoy during the revolution with part of the territory becoming Tennessee. He was in several skirmishes with the Indians and served until at least March 1780. He served with the North Carolina Militia at the Battle of Kings Mountain. I have an unpublished list naming him along with Joshua, Nathaniel, Richard, and Thomas Gist. Colonel Sevier was a well-known Revolutionary War officer who later became the first governor of the new state of Tennessee. Sevierville, Tennessee, is named after him. On 23 August 1784 Joseph was a delegate from Greene County to a convention to consider the formation of a new state to be called the state of Franklin, which was to be organized from Washington, Sullivan, and Greene Counties.[274] Statements made by him at his pension hearing in 1835 also support these activities.

His second wife, Elizabeth, applied for a pension on 22 August 1835, and it was approved (W-7517).

---

[272] *History of the Lost State of Franklin*, Samuel C. Williams. Page 30 has the history of Benjamin and Joseph Gist and their families in South Carolina and North Carolina, including Joseph's Revolutionary service as an Indian spy under Colonel John Sevier.
[273] *Historical Register of Virginians in the Revolution: Soldiers, Sailors, Marines, 1775–1783*, John H. Gwalthney, Genealogical Publishing Company, Inc., Baltimore, Maryland. Page 310 lists Joseph as a Kentucky soldier.
[274] *History of the Lost State of Franklin*, Samuel C. Williams.

The term "Indian spy" deserves some explanation, as that term is probably unique to the Revolutionary War in the southern theater of operations, maybe unique to this unit. In today's army, this job might be called long-range reconnaissance patrol (LRRP) or cavalry screening operations. Colonel Sevier wisely used these mountain frontiersmen to keep an eye on the various Indian tribes for obvious reasons. They were a threat to the frontier families, and there was a constant threat that they would become supportive of the British forces. This was his early warning "trip wire" for that threat.

I am not aware of any published records about the Indian spies related to the Revolution. I reviewed the pension applications of several Patriots claiming such service, and some gave considerable detail concerning their activities. They used the term "ranger" when describing their duties, meaning they "ranged" in their area of responsibility. They usually enlisted for three-month periods, summer only, under the command of Colonel Shelby and one of his company commanders. Their responsibilities initially were to protect the remote families in the woods (frontier) by attacking the Indian villages. As the Revolutionary War developed in the Carolinas, they performed, as I alluded to above, as trip wires for protection of the flanks of the regular forces. More than one pension statement mentioned that they received little supervision and that the leaders rarely visited them in the woods. I read two pension statements in which the claimants fought in the Battle of Kings Mountain under Colonel Sevier.

Gist owned several tracts of land in Greene County (now Tennessee), some of which he sold in 1795 and 1796. In about 1801, he and his family moved to Barren County, Kentucky. He was married twice. First to Hannah Breed, then to Elizabeth (Betsy) Springer/Belew. Betsy had previously been married.

He had eight children with Hannah Breed and three with Elizabeth Springer/Belew. These are the unproven children I have found:

- Sarah Hardin, 1773–1858
- William Breed, 1775–1820. Soldier in the Tennessee Militia during the War of 1812.
- Mary Thompson, 1777–1850
- Christopher H., 1779–1850. Soldier in the Tennessee Militia during the War of 1812.
- Joseph Jr., 1783–1835
- Marinda "Mary" Hansford, 1785–1822
- Phobe Pricilla "Prisey" Mercer, 1785–1860
- Anna Harlan, 1791–1872
- Belew, 1818–1896
- Marinda Eubank, 1824–1858
- Son Gist, 1826–1826

The last three children's mother was Elizabeth. I used several sources to discover the names of Joseph's children to include his July 1844 pension application. I did not find his will.

He is buried in the Old Mulkey Cemetery in Tompkinsville, Monroe County, Kentucky. His headstone is inscribed "Indian Spy, Revolutionary War." There is a DAR plaque attached to the stone.

## 2. John Gist

Born: 23 November 1757
Died: 9 June 1820, Monroe County, Kentucky
Rank: Private
Wife: Hannah Guerian (1761–1794)
DAR: No
SAR: P-166762

John, brother of Joseph Gist above, was also born in Lunenburg County, Virginia, to Captain Benjamin Gist and Mary Jarret. As with his brothers, his birth is recorded in the Gist family bible and is referenced in the Christopher Gist family book.[275] He also moved to North Carolina with his family and then married Hannah Guerian in South Carolina. He enlisted as a private in the Washington County, Virginia, militia under the command of Colonel John Campbell. This regiment was based in the southwest corner of Virginia near the North Carolina line.[276] Following the war he moved to Kentucky and is listed in a Kentucky roster of soldiers and pensioners serving in the Revolution.[277] He is listed on an unpublished roster of those serving in the Battle of Kings Mountain in October 1780, and in fact his unit did participate in that battle, as did several other Patriots discussed in this book. His participation in the Kings Mountain battle is somewhat easier to document than that of his brother Joseph, the Indian spy discussed above, in that his regiment was clearly directly involved in the fighting. See the Kings Mountain chapter later in this book.

He no doubt received a Kentucky land grant for this service, and we see him enlisting in the Knox County Regiment on 11 September 1792 as a private for a term of five days. The enlistment was for protecting the frontier south of the Ohio River. He was paid the sum of $3.52 for this short service. I have a copy of his military records for that period showing he served under the command of Captain John Menefee.

I have a copy of early Kentucky land records in which was recorded his purchase of fifty acres of land in Hawkins County on 18 July 1793. He paid cash for that land.

John and Hannah had the following unproven children:

- John M. Jr., 1792–1863
- Benjamin, 1794–1844
- Thomas, 1797–1852
- Hiram, 1800–1875
- Lillie Bayless, 1804–1881
- George, 1805–1859
- John Jarrett, 1811–1853

[275] *Christopher Gist of Maryland and Some of His Descendants, 1679–1957,* Jean Muir Dorsey and Maxwell Jay Dorsey, Hassel Street Press, 2021. Page 139 lists the birth of John Gist.
[276] *Annals of Southwest Virginia, 1769–1800,* Summers, Lewis Preston. Baltimore, Maryland: Genealogical Publishing Co., 1996. Page 1391 reflects that John served in the Washington County, Virginia, militia.
[277] *Roster of Soldiers in Kentucky,* reissued by the Genealogical Publishing Company, Inc., Baltimore, Maryland, 1968. This contains a list of pensioners and soldiers, including Virginia soldiers who served in the Revolutionary War. Page 4 lists John Gist as a soldier.

He is buried in the Old Mulkey Cemetery in Tompkinsville, Monroe County, Kentucky, as are his father and brother Joseph.

### 3. Thomas Gist

Born: 10 October 1764, Washington County, Virginia
Died: 22 March 1837, Spartanburg, South Carolina
Rank: Private
Wife: Elizabeth Russel (1769–1836)
DAR: A05447
SAR: P-166762

Thomas, brother to John and Joseph Gist above, was also born in Lunenburg County, Virginia, to Captain Benjamin Gist and Mary Jarret. As with his brothers, his birth is recorded in the Gist family bible and is referenced in the Christopher Gist family book.[278]

As with his brother Joseph above, Thomas was an Overmountain Man while serving in the Revolutionary War under the command of Colonel John Sevier. He served for sixteen months and twenty-one days as a private, with three enlistments within that regiment. The details of his service taken from his August 1832 pension application are as follows:

- Spring of 1778. One year as an Indian spy under the command of Captain John Newman in Colonel John Sevier's Regiment of what was then North Carolina.
- 1779. Three months as a private in Captain James Stinson's Company in Sevier's Regiment. Participated in an engagement against the Cherokee Indians at Boyd's Creek.
- Spring of 1781. Served three months in Captain Samuel Wallace's Company in Sevier's Regiment. Fought in the Battle of Monck's Corner and several other engagements not mentioned by name.

Unlike his brothers John and Joseph, I found no evidence that he served in the battle of Kings Mountain. I cannot rule out his participation in that battle, as I found an application for pension filed by Abel Pearson in which Thomas Gist testified to Pearson's participation in that battle.[279] One could infer from that statement that Thomas was present at Kings Mountain at that time. I also found evidence that his rifle served in that battle, as he later made a claim for reimbursement for a rifle taken by Captain Nathan Reid's Company of regulars.[280]

He was awarded a pension on 21 August 1832 and was a resident of White County, Tennessee, at that time. The pension (number S1172) amounted to $56 a year. No other claims have been made by others regarding his service. The year 1832 would have been the earliest that he could have made this claim, as this unit was regarded as a militia or state unit.

---

[278] *Christopher Gist of Maryland and Some of His Descendants, 1679–1957*, Jean Muir Dorsey and Maxwell Jay Dorsey, Hassel Street Press, 2021. Page 139 lists the birth of Thomas Gist.

[279] *Some Tennessee Heroes of the Revolution*, Zella Armstrong, reprinted for the Clearfield Publishing Company Inc. by Genealogical Publishing Corporation, Inc., Baltimore, Maryland, 1989, 1996. Page 55 lists John Gist as testifying that Abel Pearson fought at the Battle of Kings Mountain.

[280] *Calendar of the Tennessee and King's Mountain Papers of the Draper Collection of Manuscripts*, Madison: State Historical Society of Wisconsin, 1929. Page 163 of Volume III records his claim for reimbursement for the rifle taken from him.

The 1830 federal census records him as being in White County, Tennessee, with four persons and no slaves in his household. That count probably involved him and his wife and a male and female under the age of sixteen.

Thomas and Elizabeth had twelve children; however, their births are unproven:

- William, 1784–1870
- Benjamin, 1785–1857
- John, 1791–1853
- Polly, 1794–1804
- Russell, 1797–1830
- Thomas Jr., 1800–1897
- George Newton, 1803–1853
- Christopher Columbus, 1804–1830
- Andrew, 1805–1860
- Aaron, 1807–1872
- Mary, 1809–1839
- Jarrett, 1811–1853

Thomas is buried in the Cantrell Gilliand Memorial Garden in Spartanburg, Spartanburg, County, South Carolina.

**"Three things prompt men to a regular discharge of their duty in time of action: mutual bravery, hope of reward, and a fear of punishment."**

*—George Washington's letter to the president of Congress, 9 February 1776*

### Chapter Nine: The New England Perrigo Family of Patriots

I am descended from the Perrigo Patriots David and James Sr., discussed earlier in chapter four. There has been a family mystery about the identification of the father of my third great-grandfather Justus Perrigo Sr. for as long as I can remember. Other family researchers have also struggled with that question for years. One of those researchers was quite dedicated to research of the Perrigo family and published a family newsletter for several years.[281] He addressed the question more than once but was unable to offer an acceptable answer to the mystery. I tackled that mystery in 2022, and my research resulted in my book *The Problem of the Perrigo Patriots of Pownal,* published in 2024.

It is not my intention to reprint that book in this chapter, but I am compelled and maybe even proud to address the stories of the Perrigo Patriots in this book. After all, this is a Patriot book. I think their stories deserve to be told amongst those of other family Patriots.

First, it is important to see where these Patriots fit into the Perrigo family tree. The modified family tree in figure 9-1 on the following page will aid in visualizing those relationships as you read their stories.

---

[281] The Perrigo Papers, compiled by Prof. Robert E. Bishop of Bradenton, Florida, Volume I and II, from 1980 to 1982. Digitized and paper copies of all the issues are in my possession. This is an unpublished, public domain record.

# Figure 9-1: Five Generations of the Perrigo Family Tree

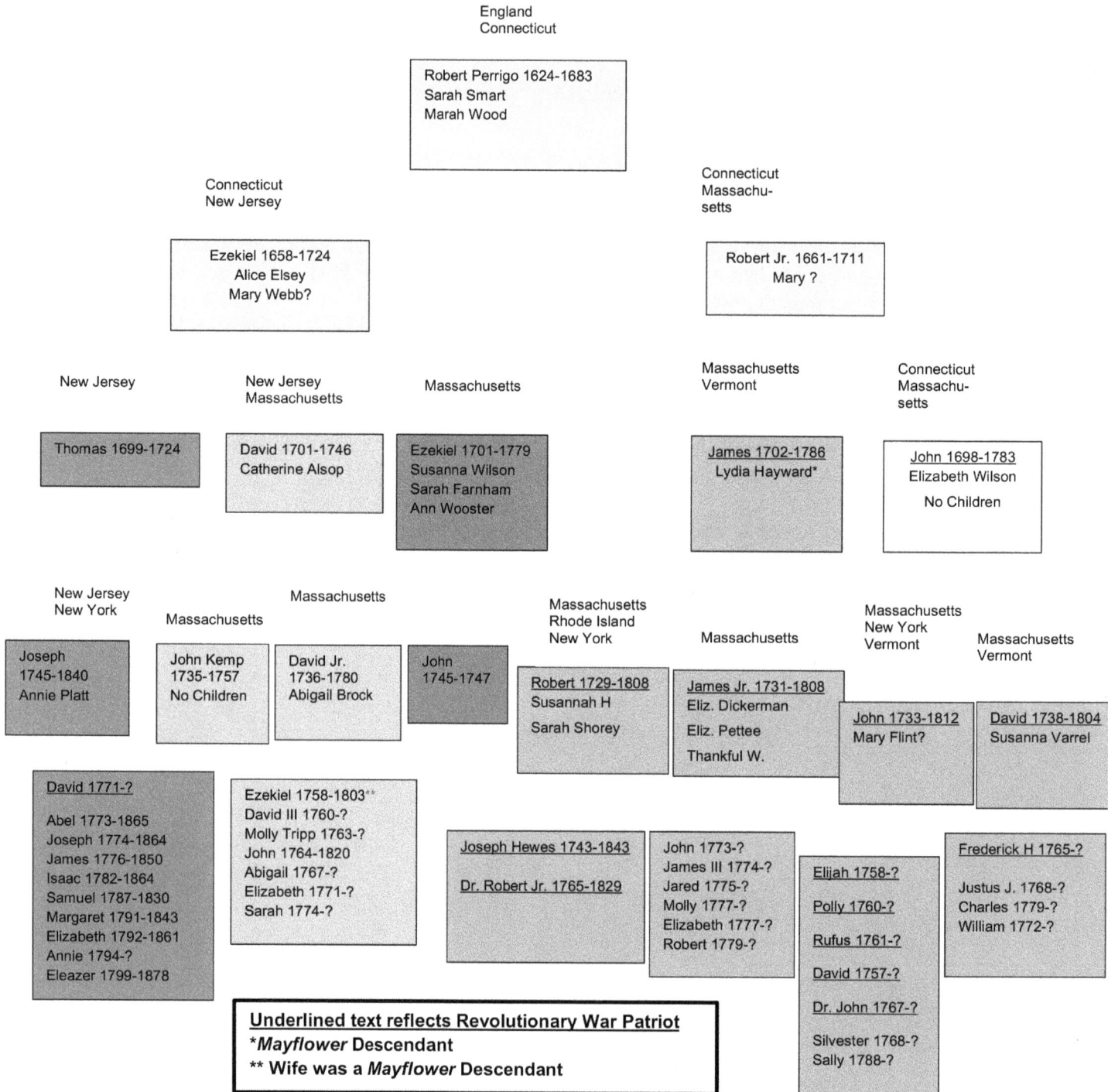

England
Connecticut

Robert Perrigo 1624-1683
Sarah Smart
Marah Wood

Connecticut
New Jersey

Ezekiel 1658-1724
Alice Elsey
Mary Webb?

Connecticut
Massachu-
setts

Robert Jr. 1661-1711
Mary ?

New Jersey

Thomas 1699-1724

New Jersey
Massachusetts

David 1701-1746
Catherine Alsop

Massachusetts

Ezekiel 1701-1779
Susanna Wilson
Sarah Farnham
Ann Wooster

Massachusetts
Vermont

James 1702-1786
Lydia Hayward*

Connecticut
Massachu-
setts

John 1698-1783
Elizabeth Wilson

No Children

New Jersey
New York

Joseph
1745-1840
Annie Platt

Massachusetts

John Kemp
1735-1757
No Children

Massachusetts

David Jr.
1736-1780
Abigail Brock

John
1745-1747

Massachusetts
Rhode Island
New York

Robert 1729-1808
Susannah H

Sarah Shorey

Massachusetts

James Jr. 1731-1808
Eliz. Dickerman

Eliz. Pettee

Thankful W.

Massachusetts
New York
Vermont

John 1733-1812
Mary Flint?

Massachusetts
Vermont

David 1738-1804
Susanna Varrel

David 1771-?

Abel 1773-1865
Joseph 1774-1864
James 1776-1850
Isaac 1782-1864
Samuel 1787-1830
Margaret 1791-1843
Elizabeth 1792-1861
Annie 1794-?
Eleazer 1799-1878

Ezekiel 1758-1803**
David III 1760-?
Molly Tripp 1763-?
John 1764-1820
Abigail 1767-?
Elizabeth 1771-?
Sarah 1774-?

Joseph Hewes 1743-1843

Dr. Robert Jr. 1765-1829

John 1773-?
James III 1774-?
Jared 1775-?
Molly 1777-?
Elizabeth 1777-?
Robert 1779-?

Elijah 1758-?

Polly 1760-?

Rufus 1761-?

David 1757-?

Dr. John 1767-?

Silvester 1768-?
Sally 1788-?

Frederick H 1765-?

Justus J. 1768-?
Charles 1779-?
William 1772-?

**Underlined text reflects Revolutionary War Patriot**
*Mayflower* Descendant
** Wife was a *Mayflower* Descendant

I have told the stories of my fifth and sixth great-grandfathers David Perrigo and his father James Perrigo Sr. in chapter four of this book, so I'll not repeat those stories, but I will begin with third-generation John and continue with the remaining ten Patriots of the fourth and fifth generation. Keep in mind that the given name of David appears five times over the three generations discussed. I recommend that you refer to the family tree as you study these stories.

**John Perrigo**
Born: 1698, Lyme, New London County, Connecticut
Died: 1783, Boston, Massachusetts
Burial: Unknown location
Service: Revolutionary War
Wife: Eliza or Elizabeth Wilson, married on 4 January 1729 in Roxbury, Suffolk County, Massachusetts
DAR: No
SAR: No

John is a third-generation Perrigo, a son of Robert Perrigo Jr. and Mary, and a brother to James above. He is my sixth great-granduncle. He was born in Lyme, New London County, Connecticut, and married Eliza or Elizabeth Wilson (1702–1783) in Roxbury, Suffolk County, Massachusetts. He is named in his grandfather's estate court summons of 1717, as were his brothers Ezekiel and James.[282] His wife Elizabeth was a sister of his brother Ezekiel's wife and was mentioned in his father-in-law Henry Wilson's March 1747 will, of which I have a copy.

It appears that John, as with his brother Ezekiel, spent most of his adult life in Boston. He was born in Connecticut, as were his brothers James and Ezekiel, and married in Roxbury. His marriage is recorded in the Old North Church records, and that is a historical church associated with the Paul Revere midnight ride. He can be found listed in the Boston tax assessor's list of 1780, although his address is not given, but I believe he lived near that church.

I first considered the possibility that he served in the French and Indian War in Connecticut, but I believe the records I found belonged to his relative John Kemp Perrigo, also of Massachusetts. John Kemp was a fourth-generation Perrigo who lost his life in the French and Indian War, and that story is told in my Perrigo book. This John would have been at least fifty-six years old for that war, but not too old to fight.

I have been compelled to give serious consideration to the possibility that he was a Revolutionary War Patriot having served in the Connecticut Third Regiment. I have his National Archives records, but they describe nothing of his later life. Again, his enlistment in a Connecticut regiment requires explanation. My research of this family line has not identified another John Perrigo of this generation who was located close to Connecticut, except for the son of brother James. That John lived in Vermont at the time of that war and also served in the war in Vermont. His story follows. If we quickly note that he was approaching his eightieth birthday, that would be

---

[282] 1719 court summons to Henry Peterson regarding the probate of the will of Robert Perrigo. New London County court records, held in the Connecticut State Library in Hartford. Used to establish the children of Robert and their locations, as well as several grandchildren.

correct. I have researched more than one eighty-year-old Patriot, and they existed—just go back and read his brother James's story. Different unit but about the same age!

The Connecticut Third Regiment was initially a Massachusetts Regiment that was approved for assignment to the Continental Line. This does not explain the fact that a man the age of John Perrigo was serving when he was not expected to do so; however, his records reflect that he served for only ten days in 1781 near the end of the war. After careful consideration, I will give John Patriot credit, as I have those records and simply cannot attribute that service to another John Perrigo. He had no descendants, so no one has used his service for membership in either the DAR or SAR.

He and his wife Eliza or Elizabeth had no children. We found that he, in his will of 14 January 1779, left 1/3 of his assets to Susanna, the daughter of his brother Ezekiel. It is interesting to note that niece Susanna was dead by the time of his will execution in 1783. He had simply not updated his will; however, the will stipulated that the proceeds also be divided amongst her two children.

## Robert Perrigo
Born: 18 April 1729, Stoughton, Norfolk County, Massachusetts
Died: 18 December 1808, Kingsbury, Washington County, New York
Burial: Unknown location in New York
Service: Two enlistments in the French and Indian War; Revolutionary War in the Second Rhode Island Regiment
Service Dates: In 1759 and fifteen days in 1762; at least three months ending in September 1779
Wife: (1) Susannah Holmes, married in 1754 and (2) Sarah Shorey, married in 1760

Robert is a fourth-generation Perrigo and the son of James Perrigo and Lydia Hayward, making him my fifth great-granduncle. Stoughton city birth records prove this relationship. His younger brothers James Jr., John, and David are all Revolutionary War Patriots.

Robert was born and married in Massachusetts. Stoughton is located about seventeen miles from Boston and thirty miles from Providence, so he did not stray far from this area until later in his life. He married his first wife, Susannah Holmes (1726–1759), in Plymouth, Massachusetts, which is south of Boston. She died within five years of their marriage. I have records of his being warned out of Plymouth in 1754, the year of their marriage.[283] As with his father in Bridgeport in 1739, the warning out was a notice that public assistance was not available and that it was time to move on. He then married Sarah Shorey (1740–1820) in 1760 in Bristol, Massachusetts. It is fair to say this area was settled by those seeking religious freedom, and history is filled with stories of those who wanted to practice a pure religion. It was hard to fit in if you were not an ardent and strict religious follower. We are not sure how the Perrigo family fit into this community that supported religious freedom only as long as it was of the correct variety. Salem was just on the

---

[283] *An Index to Plymouth County, Massachusetts, Warnings Out: From the Plymouth County Court Records, 1686–1859*, Ruth Wilder Sherman F.A.S.G., Robert M. Sherman F.A.S.G., and Robert S. Wakefield F.A.S.G., Society of *Mayflower* Descendants, 2003. Page 44 lists Robert Perrigo being warned out in 1754.

other side of the town, and only sixty years had elapsed since the witch trials there. If you were warned out of town, it was time to leave on a good horse.

I found Plymouth County probate records showing that Robert and his new wife Sarah received a legacy "inheritance" from her father's estate in November 1760. Her father's name was Miles Shorey. This court transaction was witnessed by his father James, who may have lived nearby at that time, as he moved to Pownal by 1765. James's location in 1760 is useful for discussions concerning his descendants James Jr. and James III later in the book. It is also useful in determining where his father lived after being warned out of Bridgewater in Plymouth County in 1739.

We find Robert in Providence, Rhode Island, in 1765 and 1766, where he operated a shop in which he served as a "cordwainer." A cordwainer made shoes from new leather, as opposed to a cobbler, who relied on previously used leather. His shop was identified by the "sign of a boot," and he also sold butter in small amounts. It is likely that his shop was in Newport, but I found two distinct records attributing a boot shop to him, one in Providence[284] and one in Newport. Having lived in Newport, I can relate that, while these towns are near to each other, Newport is located on Aquidneck Island. They are separated by Narragansett Bay, and there were no bridges in the 1700s. A trip between these towns would not have been a daily trip for a busy cordwainer, so we are left to wonder about his shops and if there were one or two. What is clear is that he had come a long way from being warned out of Plymouth, Massachusetts, just a few years earlier and thirty miles down the road. This information was provided by Oscar Perrigo of New York who documented this occupation from the Rhode Island Historical Tracts No. 15, Pg. 214.

He served in the French and Indian War in Connecticut in 1759, serving in the company commanded by Captain (later Colonel) Wooster.[285] Then again in 1762 he served as a sergeant in the Rhode Island Army in the French and Indian War in Captain Hawkins's Company.[286] He served in the French and Indian War in 1759 with his brother David Perrigo Jr., to be discussed below.

He remained in Rhode Island, and we again find him in the Second Company of the Second Rhode Island Militia Regiment commanded by Colonel Cook in the Revolutionary War. He served at least 3½ months in 1779 in Captain Hawkins's company. This was a local militia, so it probably saw little action, but one should not underestimate the importance of local security in this area, being just a few miles from Boston and near the main north/south business corridor from Boston to New York. This was a strategically important piece of real estate, and equally important waterways surrounded them. It was a hotbed of activity, and I have read accounts of city selectmen and safety committees discussing the importance of security in the area. Robert was likely more interested in the security of his family and business than earning a little cash, as was probably his priority during the French and Indian War ten years prior to the Revolution. I have his National Archives records reflecting his service.

---

[284] *The Planting and Growth of Providence*, Henry C. Dorr, S.S. Rider, 1862. Page 214 states that Robert Perrigo at the "sign of the boot" also sold butter in small quantities.

[285] *Rolls of Connecticut Men in the French and Indian War, 1755–1762*, Volume II, Connecticut Historical Society, Clearfield Publishing Company. Pages 74 and 75 list Robert Perrigo as serving in Captain Wooster's company. They also show that he was in the Albany, New York, hospital from 27 May until 31 October 1759.

[286] *Rhode Island in the Colonial Wars: A List of Rhode Island Soldiers and Sailors in the Old French Indian War, 1755–1762*, Howard M. Chapin, Rhode Island Historical Society, 1822. Page 110 lists Robert Perrigo as having served as a sergeant in Captain Hawkins's company in 1762.

Robert moved to New York possibly around 1782, about the time his brothers and cousins moved there following the Revolutionary War. His son Dr. Robert Jr. later served as an officer in the New York Militia in the War of 1812. He is shown on the 1790 census as living in Washington County, New York, and is shown owning land in that county on the Washington County Tax Rolls, as was his son Robert Jr. until after 1800.

He had two children by his second wife, Sarah Shorey. I can document this relationship with a pension request by his son Joseph Hewes in which he mentions his father and brother Dr. Robert Perrigo. His children were:

- Joseph Hewes, 1763–1843. Patriot of the Revolutionary War.
- Dr. Robert Jr., 1765–1829. Patriot of the Revolutionary War and veteran of the War of 1812.

Robert died on 18 December 1808 in Kingsbury, Washington County, New York.

## James Perrigo Jr.
Born: 27 April 1731, Stoughton, Norfolk County, Massachusetts
Died: 20 December 1808, Norfolk County, Massachusetts
Service: He served in the French and Indian War. He also served with Colonel Marshall's Regiment in the Massachusetts Second Militia Regiment under Captain Fisher in the Revolutionary War.
Wife: (1) Elizabeth Dickerman, married on September 1756 in Massachusetts (she died in 1767) and (2) Elizabeth Petee, married in 1768 (she died in 1798) and (3) Thankful Wright, married in 1799
DAR: A 089021
SAR: P-268708

James Jr.'s parents were James Perrigo and Lydia Hayward of Stoughton, Massachusetts, so he is a fourth-generation Perrigo. We believe he spent his entire life in Massachusetts. The Perrigo Papers mistakenly place him in Pownal, Vermont, by 1790, but it was his father who had moved to Pownal, probably by 1765. We see his father in a 1771 Vermont census that establishes his being there by 1765. It is reasonable to assume that the son would migrate to unsettled territory and the father remain in the hometown, but that was not the case in this instance. The "Old Man" moved to the frontier. This reference also lists James Jr.'s intentions to marry his first wife, Elizabeth Dickerman, in 1756. She died in 1767. He married Elizabeth Petee in Stoughton on 30 December 1758. His second wife died in 1798, and he married Thankful Wright on 23 September 1799 in Wrentham, Norfolk County, Massachusetts.

He was a clockmaker in Wrentham, and a picture of one of his clocks is shown below in figure 9-2. These clocks are truly works of art and are sometimes sold in modern antique auctions, bringing high prices. He is recognized as possibly the first Massachusetts clockmaker. His early clocks were constructed of wood works with painted faces and cabinets made by other craftsmen. His son James III was also a Massachusetts clockmaker, and I presented pictures of clocks made by both men in my Perrigo family book. He was also a member of the Masonic lodge. I have a copy of his membership card. Records of modern sales of his clocks can be found by internet searches. They remain popular items for collectors.

Figure 9-2: James Perrigo Jr. Clock

A close observer should note that this clock face photo attributes the clock to J. Perrigo, not James Jr. I have photos of clocks made by his son James III, and those photos show the maker's name as James Perrigo Jr. For some unknown reason, both James Jr. and James III did not recognize James Sr. Both James Jr. and James III held clockmaker licenses in Massachusetts. This situation is not unusual in genealogy research. There were in fact three James Perrigos from Norfolk County, Massachusetts, and the records establish them as father, son, and grandson, even if they did not use the correct suffixes with their names. Two made clocks, and one did not.

James Jr. served as a sergeant in the French and Indian War in Massachusetts with his brother John in Thatcher's Regiment.[287] These records reflect he was from Plymouth, Massachusetts. The Plymouth location may be a hint that his father and family remained in Plymouth County somehow after being warned out of Bridgewater. The time served during this enlistment is not certain, as men enlisted for campaigns, not necessarily for a set period. Thatcher's Regiment was assigned to the Crown Point and the Bay of Fundy Expeditions. They likely served some of their

---

[287] *Massachusetts Officers and Soldiers in the French and Indian Wars, 1755–1756*, edited by K. David Goss and David Zarowin. Page 298 reflects that Sergeant James Perrigo, age twenty-five, and his brother John, age twenty-three, were hired in Thomas Doty's Company of Colonel Thatcher's Regiment in Plymouth County in 1756.

enlistments in New York and probably saw some action. They did get to see New York, with John possibly remaining there or returning soon after his service.

James paid Ebenezer Howe to serve on 19 April 1776 for 10½ days on a minuteman call-up. I first thought this record should be attributed to his son James III, but he was only two years old. This call-up on 19 April was for the battle of Lexington, the first battle of the Revolutionary War. He later paid Ebenezer to serve three years in the Continental Army.[288] This transaction seems to fly in the face of his next action.

He later enlisted in the Massachusetts Second Regiment.[289] The enlistment date was 27 January 1777, and the enlistment period was three years. I will mention that while the DAR has approved memberships based on his service, the unit attributed to his service differs from the above reference. It is important to discuss the fact that his brother John also served in the Second Massachusetts Regiment. That fact is a little confusing, as brother John's regiment was a Continental Line unit that was also designated as a state militia and then back to a Continental Line unit more than once during the war. It was commanded by Colonel Bailey for most of the war. They were different units. I believe that James Jr. served his entire enlistment in the colony of Massachusetts. I have National Archives records supporting his service, but they are incomplete. The roster card reflects the Second Regiment but does not give the regimental commander's name. These records contain a single company roster but do not show the dates of service. The suggestion that there were two Massachusetts Second Regiments is not unusual. One was a Continental Line unit a few times as well as a state militia unit a few times. The Second Regiment in which James Jr. belonged was a Boston Militia unit supervised by the Boston Committee of Safety. This duplication of unit designations is common and occurred in Maryland and Virginia and other colonies also. This seems to be supported by the fact that he paid Ebenezer Howe to serve in the Continental Army. He was about to be drafted, so he contracted for Ebenezer to serve for him. He remained in Massachusetts while serving in a local militia.

He had a daughter with his first wife, Elizabeth Dickerman:

- Waitstill, 1759–1794

He had six children with his second wife, Elizabeth Pettee:

- John, 1774–1834 (twin)
- James III, 1774–1834 (twin)
- Jared, 1775–1865
- Molly Mann, 1777–1811 (twin)
- Elizabeth "Betty," 1777–1805 (twin)
- Robert, 1779–1834

---

[288] *Massachusetts Soldiers and Sailors of the Revolutionary War,* Volume 8, Boston, Massachusetts, Secretary of the Commonwealth, Wright and Potter Printing, 1896–1908. Page 384 reflects that James Perrigo paid Ebenezer Howe to serve three years for him in the Continental Army.
[289] Ibid., vol. 12. Page 141 reflects that James Perrigo served in the Massachusetts Second Regiment commanded by Colonel Reed Hawes.

His daughter Waitstill and son Robert were not listed in his will of 1805. Waitstill died in 1794, and we have her death records listing her father and mother. I have the birth records of Robert, but I am unsure why he was not listed in the will.

James Jr. died on 20 December 1808 at the age of seventy-seven. I have confirmed that he is buried in the old Norfolk County cemetery with his wife Elizabeth and daughter Waitstill.

## John Perrigo

Born: 1733, Stoughton, Norfolk County, Massachusetts
Died: 31 October 1811, Essex, Chittenden County, Vermont
Service: French and Indian War and Revolutionary War
Service Dates: 1755–1756 in the French and Indian War. 11 to 21 October 1780 in the Revolutionary War
Wife: Mary (last name unknown, but possibly Flint), unknown marriage date.
DAR: A089023
SAR: P-268709

John was the son of James Perrigo Sr. and Lydia Hayward of Stoughton, Norfolk County, Massachusetts. He was born in Stoughton, where his parents had lived for several years, before he relocated to New York and later Pownal, Vermont. His father was the son of Robert Perrigo Jr. (1661–1711), also of Massachusetts. We know father James was the son of Robert Jr. from court records involving a lawsuit over property in Massachusetts naming the children of Robert. We know John was the son of James from several sources, including the Stoughton vital birth records[290] and *Genealogical and Family History of Northern New York* by Richard Cutter.[291]

I am unsure of the family name of his wife Mary, named in his 1805 will. I suspect that she might have been Mary Flint of New York, but that is not proven. Bob Bishop stated in the Perrigo Papers that John Perrigo and Mary Flint were the parents of David Perrigo, who was a drummer in the Revolutionary War. I must risk adding confusion to this family line by stating that Bob Bishop also claimed that David the drummer's father was Joseph Perrigo. I have been unable to document that claim, as John's will clearly establishes that he was the father of this David. That will also documents the name of his wife as Mary.

He enlisted in the Massachusetts Militia during the French and Indian War with his brother James Jr. under Captain Thomas Doty in the Thatcher Regiment.[292] See my description of that service in the James Jr. story above. I have always assumed that John returned to Stoughton or Plymouth County, Massachusetts, after the war and later moved to Pownal. That assumption may have been wrong given that his sons David and Rufus made sworn statements for their military

[290] *The Record of Births, Marriages and Deaths and Intentions of Marriage in the Town of Stoughton and the Town of Canton from 1727–1845*, Canton, Massachusetts, printed by William Bense, 1896. This book contains the town vital records of the James Perrigo family, including James and Lydia's marriage, the births of sons Robert, James Jr., and John, as well as son James Jr.'s marriage intention toward Elizabeth Dickerman.
[291] *Genealogical and Family History of Northern New York*, Volume I, William Richard Cutter, p. 1169. Note: I refer to this as the "Cutter Account" in this book.
[292] *Massachusetts Officers and Soldiers in the French and Indian Wars, 1755–1756*, edited by K. David Goss and David Zarowin. Page 298 reflects that Sergeant James Perrigo age twenty-five, and his brother John, age twenty-three, of were hired in Thomas Doty's company of Colonel Thatcher's regiment in Plymouth County in 1756.

pension hearings that they were born in Dover, New York, in the late 1750s and early 1760s. Dover, New York, is across the Connecticut state line, due north of New York City, and lies in the Hudson River Valley. He probably got to see the valley in the 1755–1756 enlistment and perhaps remained there. That may have been where the work was. He was, however, in Pownal by 1765. If Mary Flint was his wife, then he likely married in New York, as I have records of Mary Flint of New York and of her marriage to a Perrigo, but I have been unable to determine if her husband was John Perrigo.

John lived for a time in Pownal, Vermont, prior to and following the Revolution, as we see several petitions signed by him and sons David and Rufus.[293] They were shown on the 1790 census there also.

During the Revolution, he served in the Vermont Militia under Captain Nathaniel Seely; the regiment was commanded by Colonel Samuel Herrick. Both the DAR and SAR recognize his service, though he did not live long enough to file for a pension for his Revolutionary War service. His service was for just ten days in October 1780, and this is recorded in a National Archives roster as well as *Soldiers, Sailors, and Patriots of the Revolutionary War, Vermont*.[294] Colonel Herrick's Regiment of militia was a large regiment whose purpose was maintaining local security within the southeast section of the state, including Pownal. While they probably saw no heavy combat, they did have combat losses and performed an important role. The regiment consisted of several basic infantry companies as well as at least one company of rangers. Most of these companies were called up as needed, sometimes for only ten or twenty days, as was the case with this call-up. I noticed that at least three companies were called up on 10 October, so the safety committee must have seen a threat in that area. He was paid for seventy miles of travel, so the threat must have been within a thirty-five-mile radius of Pownal.

I found that in Vermont prior to the Revolution, he sold land to a man named Beloved Carpenter and that he held a note for 33 pounds for that debt. In 1776, Carpenter joined the King's Army, and the colony quickly confiscated that land. In October 1779, John requested that he be reimbursed for his loss from that confiscation, as Beloved Carpenter still owed John for the land. He submitted a petition signed by several other men supporting that claim. The colony then paid John 30 pounds for the money owed him.[295]

In 1782, he and his sons David and Rufus signed a petition requesting that a bridge be built over the Hoosack River. That request was not approved by the Vermont colony. The town of Hoosack was just across the river from Pownal and had a population of Puritans from New York. One can imagine that the Puritans wanted little to do with the rowdy Baptists, and a bridge would only complicate that situation. Thus, the Puritans rejected the "Bridge to Nowhere," as Pownal was certainly not a destination in their point of view.[296]

---

[293] *The State Papers of Vermont,* Volume Eight, General Petitions 1778–1787, Edward Hoyt, editor, Montpelier, Vermont, 1952, pp. 67–77. The signatures of John and his sons David and Rufus are included.

[294] *Soldiers, Sailors, and Patriots of the Revolutionary War, Vermont,* Major General Carleton Edward Fisher and Sue Fisher, Picton Press, Camden, Maine.

[295] *State Papers of Vermont,* Volume Six, Sequestration, Confiscation and Sales of Estates, edited by Mary Green Nye, published by Rawson C. Myrick, Secretary of State, 1951. Page 107 describes the petition of John Perrigo concerning the estate of Beloved Carpenter.

[296] *The State Papers of Vermont,* Volume Eight, General Petitions 1778–1787, Edward Hoyt, editor, Montpelier, Vermont, 1952. Page 67 contains the petition for a bridge in Pownal. John and sons David and Rufus also signed that petition.

John had the following children I documented from his final will, written in 1805 and read in court in December 1812. He left each of his children $1. A grandson Salrava was left $108.

- David, 1757–1826. Revolutionary War Patriot (drummer)
- Elijah, 1758–1796
- Poly Wilson, 1760–1812
- Rufus, 1761–1833. Revolutionary War Patriot
- Dr. John, 1767–1820. Revolutionary War Patriot
- Sylvester, 1768–1820
- Sally Clark, 1788–Unknown death date

Several researchers attribute the parentage of these children to David Perrigo Jr. and Abigail Brock, David being a cousin of John. That seems to be an incorrect assignment, as four sons and two daughters are named in the will of John. Additionally, son Rufus claimed in his Revolutionary War pension application that he was born in New York. John had apparently lived there following his service in the French and Indian War. I do not believe that this David Perrigo Jr. ever lived in New York but spent most of his life in Massachusetts. Although not poof of relationship, the DAR has awarded memberships based on John and his sons' Revolutionary War service.

I sometimes wish I could sit around the dinner table with this family and listen to the rich stories that might have been told. Think of it! Father served in both the French and Indian War and the Revolutionary War and was a very early settler in Vermont. Three sons served in the Revolutionary War. One son was a doctor and a surgeon in the war, and one was a storied legend of that war. A third son was also a noted fighter and changed units to stay in the fight. This was a family of Patriots, and they would fight. I can also imagine that cousin Justus J.—who lived nearby and was about ten to twelve years of age during the later stages of the war—wanted badly to make his mark in the world. It is clear that he did just that, but in a later war.

We are uncertain of John's burial location, but it was likely in Chittenden. We will tell the stories of his Patriot sons later in the book. His probate case is interesting for the fact that, after the inventory of his belongings and the listing of his assets, it was determined his estate was insolvent and that he owed more than could be paid to creditors.

### David J. Perrigo

Born: About 1771, probably Monmouth County, New Jersey
Died: After 1855
Burial: Unknown location
Service: Revolutionary War, Fourth Regiment of the New Jersey Militia
Wife: Unknown
DAR: No
SAR: No

David is the proposed son of Thomas Perrigo and Anne Platt of Sussex County, New Jersey, and is a fifth-generation family member. He is the fourth David to be discussed in my Perrigo book and is not discussed in either the Cutter Account or the Bishop Perrigo Papers. I consider this to be an unproven relationship with his father and mother.

I found David in a New Jersey state census of 1855 and in the 1850 federal census in Sussex County, New Jersey. The federal census shows him at an age consistent with a birth year of 1771, hence that is his assigned birth year shown above. This birth year is the year following the marriage of his mother and father. He was listed in his brother Abel's family bible, which I used to document much of the New Jersey Perrigo family, but later family members had apparently added his name.[297]

He served in the New Jersey Fourth Regiment during the Revolutionary War, with his service beginning on 10 March 1778 and lasting for nine months. He was discharged in September 1779. He certainly did not serve at the age of nine, so was there a second David Perrigo of Sussex County, New Jersey? I have a copy of his military records.

I found no records of a marriage, but the 1830 federal census shows him in Sussex County with a man and woman of the appropriate ages, with one other female family member, so he was possibly married.

The documentation I found that places him in Sussex County is as follows:

- The Sussex County tax list for June 1793
- The New Jersey 1855 census
- The federal 1830 census for Sussex County
- The federal 1840 census for Sussex County
- The federal 1850 census for Sussex County
- The New Jersey 1855 census for Sussex County
- The National Archives Revolutionary War rolls

The date or location of his death is not known. The state 1855 census is the latest public record I found for him. My research of the Sussex County, New Jersey, Perrigo family found only proven descendants of Thomas Perrigo and Anne Platt except for this David. I cannot assume the late entry of his name in his brother Abel's family bible as proof of relationship.

### Joseph Hewes Perrigo

Born: 7 October 1763, Providence, Rhode Island
Died: 29 August 1843, Granby, Oswego County, New York
Burial: Unknown location
Service: Rhode Island Line in the Continental Army from 6 March 1781 to 25 December 1783
Wife: Meriam Maxwell, married 17 November 1794 in Plainfield, Windham County, Connecticut
DAR: No
SAR: No

---

[297] His brother Abel Perrigo's family bible contains the name of brother David. That name was added later by unknown family members for an unknown reason. The bible is in the possession of Greta Olsen and George Sweeney.

Joseph is a fifth-generation Perrigo and the son of Robert Perrigo and Sarah Shorey of Providence, Rhode Island. He is the fifth Joseph we have featured in this book. He was born in Providence, Rhode Island, and resided there until he was eighteen years old and joined the Rhode Island regiment commanded by Colonel Olney on 2 March 1781 for the duration of the war. He joined in Providence, Rhode Island. His company commander was Captain William Allen. We know he is the son of Robert and Sarah Perrigo because of statements made by him pertaining to his military pension in 1824, and this location is consistent with the location of his parents at the time of his birth. Remember, his father also served in the Revolutionary War in a local militia, as did his brother Dr. Robert, who will be discussed below.

He served as a regimental fifer during his service in this Continental Line Army unit. After enlistment, he soon marched to Virginia and later participated in the Siege of Yorktown, the final campaign of the war. After the end of the war, his unit moved to Oswego, New York, where he stated he was injured by frostbite on his hands and legs. He was discharged on 25 December 1783 at Saratoga, New York. The *Regimental Book*[298] gives his occupation at the time of enlistment as laborer and states that he had dark hair and stood five feet seven inches tall. This book gives his enlistment date as 5 April 1781, and other records, including statements made by him in sworn affidavits, show either 2 or 6 March of that year.

Following the war, he returned to Exeter, Rhode Island (note that Exeter is not a Rhode Island County, but a town), and was married about one year later to Meriam Maxwell of Plainfield, Windham County, Connecticut. They were married by a justice of the peace in Plainfield and lived with her family for about one year after their marriage. I have those marriage records. They then moved to Salem, Washington County, New York, where he was able to borrow the money to buy a farm. He farmed the remainder of his life until he could no longer work. One can speculate that he became familiar with New York while serving in the military and chose to return there to farm. His father Robert had also moved to Washington County and died there in 1808. He and Meriam had one son. His son confirmed this fact in a sworn statement in his 1832 pension request. Joseph and Meriam's son was:

- Robert 1785–1865. Remained in New York and had nine children

He filed for a pension in Washington County, New York, claiming he was sixty-seven years of age and that neither he nor his wife were able to work and that they had no sources of income. It appears that his initial pension request was not approved because of lack of documentation of some sort. He reapplied in 1824 in Washington County, and his request was held until he could explain why he had waited so long to make the claim. The pension act was passed in 1818, and he would have been eligible after that date. While there was no disability requirement to make a pension claim, it was common practice for the claimant to make a needs statement. One can only guess why he waited. He was not married when he served, so his wife Meriam would not have been eligible for a pension on his behalf until the 1833 Pension Act. She did make such a claim

---

[298] *Regimental Book: Rhode Island Regiment for 1781 &c.*, Bruce C. MacGunnigle, Rhode Island Society of the Sons of the American Revolution, 2011. Pages 103 and 104 list Joseph Hewes Perrigo and give his enlistment date, height, and the color of his hair, as well as identifying him as a fifer.

in 1834, and it was approved. It appears he lived with his only son later in his life. He died on 29 August 1843 in Granby, Oswego County, New York.

### Dr. Robert Perrigo Jr.

Born: 4 November 1765, Providence County, Rhode Island
Died: 13 August 1829, Erie County, Pennsylvania
Burial: Old Bristol Farm Cemetery, Girard, Erie County, Pennsylvania
Service: Rhode Island Militia during the Revolutionary War and the New York Militia during the War of 1812
Wife: Anna Nancy Rock
DAR: No
SAR: No

Robert Jr. is the fifth-generation son of Robert Perrigo and Sarah Shorey of Providence, Rhode Island. He was born in Providence County, Rhode Island, and at the age of sixteen joined the Rhode Island Regiment for the Revolutionary War in 1782. His length of enlistment was nine months, and he was discharged on 20 December 1782. Unlike his older brother Joseph Hewes, who joined the Continental Army, Robert joined the militia. It is likely the Continental Army could not enlist a sixteen-year-old man, but the militia was more than willing to accommodate him.

I did not find proof of his birth to father Robert Sr., but I found a statement on the pension application of his brother Joseph Hewes in which Joseph mentioned a business dealing with his brother Robert, who was then deceased. This application was dated in 1832, and Robert Jr. died in 1829. The Perrigo Papers are supportive of this relationship.

Robert Jr. married Anna Nancy Rock—daughter of John Rock and Anna Nancy of Argyle, New York—at an unknown date, but probably after having moved from Rhode Island, as did his father and brother. He and Anna Nancy had one son:

- Dr. James Rock Perrigo, 1795–1860. Married Drusilla Babcock and later moved to Lafayette County, Wisconsin. Children settled in Illinois and Iowa. He is the third Perrigo doctor I have discovered of this era.

Robert Jr. served in the New York Militia as a lieutenant during the War of 1812 period and later moved to Erie County, Pennsylvania. At some point in his career he became a doctor, and his headstone in Pennsylvania is so marked. He is buried in the Old Bristol Farm Cemetery in Girard, Pennsylvania. I will discuss what we know of his medical career later in this chapter.

I found a claim presented by Dr. Robert Perrigo of Rhode Island for reimbursement for medical supplies that he had used while serving as a medical doctor during the Revolutionary War. That claim was approved and paid. The Perrigo Papers briefly mention a Dr. Perrigo who served in that war, and I speculated the author was referring to the son of Robert. I simply cannot attribute medical practice to Robert Jr., the son of Robert, during the Revolution, because of his age of sixteen and because of his military records, which I have. There was almost certainly another Dr. Robert Perrigo of Rhode Island who was a Patriot, and I doubt if he was related to this Perrigo line.

**Sergeant David Perrigo**
Born: 1757, Skenesboro, now Whitehall, New York
Died: 27 May 1826, Highgate, Vermont
Burial: Unknown but probably Georgia Township, Franklin County, Vermont
Service: Continental Army, Green Mountain Boys
Rank: Sergeant/Drummer
Service Dates: 26 December 1776 to December 1779
Wife: (1) Susan Hayward and (2) Eunice Hurlburt
DAR: AO89011
SAR: No

David is a fifth-generation Perrigo and the son of John Perrigo and Mary (possibly Flint) of Vermont. While I could find no birth records, he stated in his 1814 pension hearing that he was fifty-seven years old. Statements made by his wife at later pension hearings following is death seem to support that date, so his birth year is attributed to those statements. He is listed in his father's 1810 will. While there is some confusion about his birthplace with regard to military enlistments and pension requests, he was certainly born in or close to Pownal, Vermont, or in New York only a few miles from Pownal. That is where his father spent several years, and David is the proven son of John. He signed at least one petition in Pownal along with his father, and that is shown with his father's story above. That petition was the "Bridge to Nowhere" petition of 1780, and it also contained the signature of his brother Rufus, as they both remained in Pownal for a few years following the war.

This David is the fifth David Perrigo I have presented in this book, and he is discussed in the Perrigo Papers as well as in the Cutter Account. Both those resources incorrectly attribute his birth to a different father. In fairness to Bob Bishop, author of the Perrigo Papers, he asserts that this David was the son of a lady with the family name Flint and that her husband and the father of David was Joseph Perrigo. I believe this statement was probably based on New York marriage documents claiming Joseph Perrigo married a Flint. I have been unable to locate those documents. Moreover, I have not documented a fourth-generation Joseph Perrigo, except the Joseph of the New Jersey line. This Joseph Perrigo line was discussed at length in my Perrigo book, and I do not believe they ventured from New Jersey until after 1800. The fifth-generation Joseph Hewes Perrigo discussed above was clearly not the father of this David, as they were brothers. I recommend that readers review the family tree in figure 9-1 above to visualize this issue. I maintain that the mother of David was probably Mary Flint, based on the will of John, but that is speculation. I believe that the will of John Perrigo sets this issue to rest, and the petition signed by John, David, and Rufus, seemingly of the same household, reinforces that position. I will risk further confusion by asserting that the Joseph Perrigo of New Jersey also had a son David! He was also a Revolutionary War Patriot. They are certainly different David Perrigos.

David enlisted in Captain Simeon Smith's Company of Seth Warner's Regiment of the New York Line on 26 December 1776 for three years as a sergeant and drummer.[299] It should be noted that Vermont was not a colony but was considered territory of New York. David was living in Vermont and was possibly a logger by trade. (Bishop Perrigo Papers.) He was discharged at Ft. George, New York, in December 1779 and applied for a pension on 24 April 1818, and it was approved (pension certificate 12886 and pension number W19981). His pension was for $8 per month, and he stated he was wounded several times in combat. His service as a regimental drummer probably led to one or more injuries, as they were not armed and were good targets for the enemy. Vermont records also show that he enlisted in the Vermont Militia in December 1776 but only served for eight days. He was discharged and then joined the Continental Army on 26 December 1776. I have his National Archives records as well as his pension request.

David stated in his pension hearing that he had been a farmer and that he was unable to work and support his family, which consisted of his wife and a daughter who had a child and had lost her husband.

David saw a lot of action and fought with some historical figures of the war. Colonel Seth Warner's Regiment was originally known as the Green Mountain Boys. This unit was initially established by Ethan Allen prior to the Revolution. They became well known for their role in protecting early Vermonters from land encroachments from New York land speculators. They were also well respected by General Washington for their role in protecting Quebec. During the winter of 1775–1776, the regiment was involved in the Siege of Quebec after Benedict Arnold was wounded in an attack by the British, who were attempting to regain control of the Quebec fortress. The army at Quebec was hit by an epidemic of smallpox and lost many men. Colonel Warner was not a doctor, but he had a great deal of practical knowledge of remedies he had learned from his father. He encouraged his men to inoculate themselves by making an incision and exposing themselves to the disease. This would give them a mild form of the disease that they could survive, but they would infect those around them that had not been inoculated.[300] This practice was prohibited by George Washington, but it worked for them, as they suffered far fewer casualties from the disease than other units in the campaign. In the spring, British warships came to Quebec, and Warner's Regiment abandoned the fort to return to New York. Colonel Warner served not only as commander of the retreat, he also served in the rear party and helped tend to the sick. They were being pursued by the British, and he saved their backside as they retreated. They lived to fight again. I will add that David was not a member of the regiment for that campaign.

On 5 July 1776, Congress authorized New York to raise a regiment consisting of the Green Mountain Boys. This act was "suggested" by General Washington and was controversial in the colony, as the Green Mountain Boys had been engaged in some fighting against the colony when they attempted to redraw the line between the colony and the territory of Vermont. New York lost in that attempt, and the Green Mountain Boys were outlawed by the colony. The Green Mountain Boys were also responsible for preventing the Vermont territory from seceding from the colonies and joining with Quebec prior to the Revolution. David lived in Vermont at the

---

[299] *The State of Vermont: Rolls of the Soldiers in the Revolutionary War, 1775 to 1783*, John E. Goodrich, Tuttle, Rutland, Vermont, 1904. Page 111 shows that David enlisted on 26 December 1776 and was discharged on 26 December 1779.
[300] "Reminiscences of Colonel Warner," David S. Broadmore, *Historical Magazine*, July 1860.

time. Congress could not authorize a territory to raise a unit, so New York was directed to authorize this regiment and reluctantly did so, assuming Ethan Allen would be elected the commander. The regiment was authorized as Warner's Additional Regiment.[301] Colonel Warner was again elected as commander of the reorganized (now Continental Line) unit by his men, probably because of his skill in taking care of them and because he was a good leader. This surprised Ethan Allen, who assumed he would be elected. David Perrigo joined the unit in December of 1776 as the newly authorized regiment was recruiting in Vermont. I have no way of determining if he previously fought with the original Green Mountain Boys prior to the war, as they did not keep good records, but it is certain that he would have been aware of their history and may have served with the regiment prior to his enlistment in the Continental Army.

In January 1777, the regiment was quartered on Mount Independence. That summer, they were involved in countering Burgoyne's invasion and retreat, which resulted in several battles: Ticonderoga, Hubbardton, and Bennington. Their losses were heavy, with both disease and combat injuries. In his obituary, a New York newspaper gave an account of David's actions at the Battle of Bennington.[302] His drum was destroyed by a bullet, and it tumbled down a hill. He immediately grabbed the rifle of a fallen comrade, charged the enemy line, captured an enemy drum, and returned to the battle. Later after the war, he used that drum at the funeral of his friend Ethan Allen. The regiment performed well and was praised by General Gates. I maintain that they were the key unit in cutting off General Burgoyne's retreat at Bennington, which was a major early victory for the Continental Army. This victory probably convinced the king of France to support the colonies, and without this support we might not have won the war. This victory also motivated the Continental Congress to provide additional support to the army, as they were close to abandoning the Revolution due to several recent losses by General Washington. The regiment was recognized for their unusual tactics. These tactics are not unlike current army ranger tactics, which consist of unconventional movements as opposed to frontal assaults. They could be very effective with few troops. I have read accounts that claimed Colonel Warner abandoned his troops during the Battle of Bennington when it appeared they were losing the battle. That is a true claim, but the Colonel returned to the battle with additional troops he had quickly raised in the neighborhood. This was his neighborhood, and he was well known. They then won that battle as daylight was fading.[303] The losses of opposing troops were quite heavy, with American losses being relatively low. While this was a very large battle and many other American units were committed, it was an early turning point for the war. General Gates praised Colonel Warner on their contributions to the outcome of this important battle.[304] They made a difference, and maybe that drum was important.

I have read an account that Benjamin Franklin—who was then based in Paris, France, as the American ambassador—used the victory at Bennington and subsequent surrender of General Burgoyne as a selling point for French assistance. That request was approved, and that assistance could probably be credited as a turning point for the Revolution. Few would argue that point.

The regiment was disbanded in December 1779, and David was discharged at that time. I can think of few Revolutionary regiments that contributed more to the American victory than the

---

[301] 5 July 1776 Journals of the Continental Congress, Library of Congress, American Memory.
[302] *Collections of the Vermont Historical Society*, Volume I.
[303] Ibid.
[304] Ibid.

Green Mountain Boys. While this is a debatable assertion, it does make for interesting conversation, and I believe the facts support this stance. I believe the Perrigos were true fighting men. The Perrigo Papers allege that, prior to the war in Vermont, if they could not find a worthy opponent to fight, they would fight amongst themselves for entertainment.

We do not know where David is buried, but it is likely in Georgia Township in Franklin County, Vermont, near Highgate, Vermont, the location of his death. Accounts of his life show that, except for his military service, he never strayed farther than twenty miles from the Lake Champlain area of western Vermont. He was born in New York, but that location is only a few miles from Pownal and across Lake Champlain.

I believe the drum used by David may be on exhibit in a Bennington County Historical Society museum, as I have seen a picture of that exhibit.

### Dr. John Perrigo Jr.

Born: 1767, unknown location, but probably New York or Pownal, Vermont
Died: 7 March 1820, Burlington, Chittenden County, Vermont
Burial: Elmwood Cemetery, Burlington, Vermont
Service: Vermont Militia in the company of Nathaniel Seeley's alarm men in the regiment commanded by Colonel Samuel Herrick beginning 11 October 1780
Wife: Almira Hitchcock, married in 1796 in Kingsbury, Washington County, New York
DAR: A089023
SAR: P-268709

Dr. John Perrigo Jr. is a fifth-generation Perrigo and the son of John Perrigo and his wife Mary (possibly Flint) of Pownal and then Clarendon, Rutland County, Vermont. He is a brother of Rufus and David, discussed above. The birthplace of Dr. John is not certain; he was possibly born in New York, but probably it was in Pownal, Vermont. His brothers David and Rufus gave New York as their birth state in their pension hearings, but his father had been a citizen of Pownal for several years prior to the war and signed a petition there in 1782 for the bridge discussed above. I believe Dr. John was born soon after his father and uncle David arrived in 1765. The DAR records his birthplace as New York but offers no evidence of that location except his marriage there. The 1790 census for his father shows him in Clarendon, Vermont. We know he is the son of John because of being listed in his father's will of 1811 and the fact that he signed a petition with his father in Pownal.

He married Almira Hitchcock in Kingsbury, Washington County, New York, in 1796, and they had six children. The children were listed in John's probate case. They were:

- Charles Herbert, 1796–1862. Became a lawyer and settled in Julien Township, Dubuque County, Iowa.
- Mary Ann van Duzee, 1797–1867. Married and settled in Hastings, Minnesota.
- John Dean, 1801–1832. Married and remained in Burlington.
- Charlotte Smith White, 1804–1866. Married and settled in Viroqua, Vernon County, Wisconsin.

- Isaac Hitchcock, 1807–1875. Married and settled in Lockport, Niagara County, New York.
- Minerva Martindale Goodrich, 1811–1862. Married and settled in Dubuque, Dubuque County, Iowa.

Dr. John served in the Revolutionary War for six months, in the Vermont Militia. His unit was a unit of alarm men that was called to Burlington for a ten-day call-up in October 1780. I have his National Archives records. I believe this call-up might have been the only active duty he served in the war.

He died on 7 March 1820 in Burlington at the age of fifty-three, and he is buried in the Elmwood Cemetery in Burlington. His probate case is interesting as his oldest son, Charles, was appointed administrator and was directed to quickly inventory the estate. Charles was about twenty-four years old, and the youngest child was about nine years old. After the inventory, it was discovered his estate was insolvent and the many bills could not be paid. The list of debts is many pages in length, with most amounts being under $10 and some several hundred. The probate judge directed that Charles make a list of what he recommended be paid to each person holding the debt. After one year, Charles discovered five acres of land owned by Dr. John, but that small parcel did not adequately cover the many debts. It is unclear how many dollars remained to support his wife and children after the estate was settled. I will add that Charles was or soon became a lawyer.

Medical practice in the early 1700s was no guarantee of financial success, as patients often did not or could not pay for services rendered. Country doctors often needed a source of income to support their medical practice. Land speculation was sometimes the solution.

Bob Bishop elaborated on these debts in the Perrigo Papers, and he was probably correct in asserting that many individuals were indebted to Dr. John for various medical services he had delivered over his many years of practice. I noticed numerous debts owed to him in his son's accounting of his assets, but there were no descriptions of those amounts owed him. Those bills would never be collected. Bishop also discussed the land speculation activities of Dr. John, and there seemed to be many. These activities would be interesting research for future projects, but I will not pursue those now.

The fact that two fifth-generation Perrigos have presented themselves as doctors in early New England poses some questions. Dr. Robert Perrigo Jr., son of Robert discussed above, was born in Rhode Island, moved to Argyle, New York, shortly after the Revolution, and eventually moved to Pennsylvania. Dr. John Perrigo discussed here remained in the Chittenden, Rutland County, Vermont, area for most of his remaining life. He did not stray far from Pownal. How did they obtain their medical training? We may never know the answer to this question, but this question bears some research. Bob Bishop in the Perrigo Papers posed a similar question about Dr. John, who seemingly served as a doctor during the Revolutionary War. Bishop's response to his own question was that there was a medical college located not far from Pownal in Vermont and that maybe he attended that college. The following is the result of some cursory research by me on that subject.

The book *The First Medical College in Vermont: Castleton, 1818–1862*[305] gives the history of this college in Castleton, Vermont. The college did not graduate its first doctors until around 1822 and was closed by 1862. The college had about 2,500 total students, with maybe 1,400 completing the instruction. The list of graduates does not include anyone with the name of Perrigo, and I did not expect to find them on that list, given that Dr. John was dead in 1820 and Dr. Robert was in New York. Castleton is near the western border of Vermont, as is Pownal, which is several miles to the south near the Massachusetts border. The medical training received by Dr. John was soon after the Revolution, and Castleton College did not exist until forty years after that war. Dartmouth College in New York and the several colleges in Massachusetts were the only choices. However, there were other options for a young man of that era and location to obtain medical training and education. The book referenced above explains that many doctors in the frontier regions were prepared for their careers through the "preceptor system." This was essentially an OJT process. There were no entrance requirements, except one can imagine that being able to read and write would be useful. Some prospective doctors already held a four-year degree in the arts. The referenced book explained that most students at this college in the early 1800s did not graduate before beginning their practice. Some attended only one term. Many did, however, possess a four-year general education degree before beginning training at the medical school. In the preceptor system, the student doctor paid the licensed doctor for training, and I expect this was the route taken by both Robert and John Perrigo. The colonies did not issue licenses or standards for qualification to practice for several years.

Dr. John Perrigo, contrary to family legend, almost certainly did not serve as a doctor during his ten-day call-up in 1780 in Burlington. He may well have been a practicing doctor at that time, but I found no records supporting that idea. In fact, the only evidence of his being a doctor is on his 1820 death certificate generated by the city of Burlington giving his name as Dr. John Perrigo Jr. In fairness, descendants of Dr. John seem to hold that he had a long medical career, and I have no reason to doubt that claim. More research is in order, as this is an interesting story. He was certainly a Patriot.

If Dr. Robert Perrigo received medical training at the college level, it was likely received in New York, as he was less than twenty years old when he left Rhode Island. There were several medical colleges in New York at that time, and maybe he attended there, or perhaps he studied under another doctor. Again, he was a Patriot, and we owe both him and Dr. John Perrigo much.

I think these were intelligent and brave men, and I believe their lives deserve more research in order to document their contributions. They just did what they could.

---

[305] *The First Medical College in Vermont: Castleton, 1818–1862*, Frederick Clayton Waite, Vermont Historical Society, Vermont Printing Company, Brattleboro, Vermont, 1919.

**Frederick Howard Perrigo**
Born: 10 April 1765, Pownal, Bennington County, Vermont
Died: 26 December 1850, Ellenburg, Clinton County, New York
Burial: Unknown location
Service: Revolutionary War, 1 July 1781 to 26 November 1781 in Fletcher's Regiment of the Vermont Militia as a private. He also served in the New York Twenty-Ninth Infantry during the War of 1812.
Wife: Mary "Polly" Van Ornam, married on 16 April 1791 in Charlotte, Chittenden County, Vermont
DAR: A 089012
SAR: No

Frederick is a fifth-generation Perrigo and the son of David Perrigo and Susan Varrel of Pownal, Bennington County, Vermont. This is an unproven relationship, as with his brother Justus Sr. As has been previously discussed, their Pownal connection is strong for several reasons, and they certainly do not fit into the John Perrigo family group of Pownal. I believe that his father lived with him when the 1800 Vermont census was taken, with Justus Sr. living nearby. Statements made by him during his pension hearings seem to prove he was born in Pownal.

Frederick married Mary "Polly" Van Ornam on 16 April 1791 in Chittenden County, Vermont. This marriage took place after he had served in the Revolutionary War in the Vermont Militia under the command of Colonel Fletcher. I did not find their marriage records; however, they both testified for one of his pension hearings that they had been married by a justice of the peace in Charlotte, Vermont, in 1791. I noticed from the pension hearings that Frederick could read and write, but Mary could not.

He served in the same Revolutionary War unit as his cousin Rufus. He served about ten months and was discharged in November 1781. The dates of service shown above are recovered from his records, which I have. The claim of ten months comes from many sworn statements from Frederick and fellow soldiers during his pension hearings.

He joined the New York Twenty-Ninth Infantry Regiment in 1813 and served about six months. During this service he was severely injured by a fall from a horse while spreading an alert notice at night. He was discharged about four months later because of his inability to perform his duties. This injury severely affected his ability to work for the remainder of his life and was the justification for applications for pension submitted by him and by his wife after his death.

His National Archives files for pension claims are extensive, with more than two hundred pages that I discovered. The New York Militia apparently never declared that Frederick had been disabled, as with his brother Justus Sr., who had been injured in combat and declared disabled.

It appears that he filed for disability in early 1830, but after several requests for additional information, the application was rejected. He obtained a doctor's certification that he was truly disabled, and several witness statements were included, attesting to the fact that he had been injured while performing his duties.

After his death, his wife applied for a pension and for a land bounty. She was quickly awarded a $30-per-year pension (number W-26858) for the remainder of her life, as well as a 160-acre land grant. It appears that she obtained the services of a lawyer in this instance, as she left written instructions for the land grant to be forwarded to her attorney when it was granted. I could find no record of where this grant was to be awarded.

During the several hearings pertaining to his Revolutionary War claims, he provided some interesting information about where he spent his life until 1823. He said he was born in Pownal on 10 April 1765 and that after the Revolutionary War he remained in Pownal until 1785, when he moved to a town in Massachusetts until 1788. He then moved to Willsboro, New York, until 1805 and then moved to Peru, New York, until 1810. He then moved back to Willsboro until 1813, when he enlisted, and then he moved back to Peru until 1823. It appears that he later moved to Ellenburg in Clinton County, New York, and remained there until his death. The claim of being in Willsboro from 1788 until 1805 is consistent with the tax records of 1802 and 1803 and the 1800 federal census. I believe his father David lived with him until his death in 1803. I will add that his 1765 birth date in Pownal is consistent with his father's arrival there that year. The only other Perrigo living in Pownal in 1765 was his grandfather James Sr. This point was crucial in my establishing his relationship with Justus Sr., my fourth great-grandfather.

Frederick may have kept his own written records, as during the pension hearings he relayed the names of all eleven of his children and the dates and times of their birth, along with the weather conditions. This was useful in researching their family histories, since there is a lack of birth records in Vermont. His children were:

- Dorcus Brownson/Ames, 1791–1879. She married Brownson, first name unknown, and later Edward Ames. She had five children and remained in Willsboro the remainder of her life.
- Nancy, 1793–Unknown death date
- Clara "Clarey," 1795–Unknown death date
- Mary, 1797–1803. Died as a youth.
- Sarah A. (Sally) Moore, 1800–1864. Married Elias Moore and lived in Clinton, New York.
- William Alexander, 1802–1873. Married Mary Ann Shepard. They had eight children and remained in Clinton County, New York. He was a day laborer, but his son William became a doctor.
- James Drake, 1803–1833. Married Sarah Ann French, and they had ten children and remained in Clinton County, New York. He was a farm laborer.
- Robert Adair Bell, 1806–1861. Moved to Montreal, Canada, in 1825. Married Laura Julia Dunning, and they had five children. He remained in Canada.
- Charles Jefferson, 1808–1904. Married Mina Manzer, with one son, Ernest, found. He remained in Clinton County.
- Fredrick Howard Jr., 1810–1884. Married Charlotte Temple Ash. They had ten children and settled in Montcalm County, Michigan.
- Marian, 1813–1813. Died as an infant.

I could find no will or probate records for Frederick, and his burial location in unknown. I think it was quite unfortunate that his injuries consisted mainly of a rupture in his stomach area—these injuries are today very treatable, sometimes on an outpatient basis.

"A soldier above all others prays for peace, for it is the soldier who must suffer and bear the deepest wounds and scars of war."

*—Douglas MacArthur*

## Chapter Ten: The Overmountain Men and the Battle of Kings Mountain

The term "Overmountain Men," as related to this period of the war, was used to describe the men of Lieutenant Colonel John Sevier's unit, composed mainly of men from the part of North Carolina that soon became the state of Tennessee. Of course, there was a mountain range between them and the Kings Mountain area in South Carolina. British Major Ferguson had made public comments directed to the men of Sevier's unit for them to stay home and take care of their wives rather than suffer defeat from their greatly superior force. Ferguson's unit was covering the western flank of the British main force as it was making its way back to Virginia to win the war. This message traveled quickly, and the Overmountain Men accepted the challenge. The game was on!

This battle occurred on 7 October 1780 in South Carolina. Of this we are certain; other proposed facts are less certain. I have studied this battle over the years, and in spite of the efforts of many respected historians and authors, we may never know all the names of the Patriots who participated in this battle. It is beyond the scope of this book to recount the battle, but I have mentioned several family Patriots who have been recognized for their participation. I choose not to attempt to alter history by documenting family Patriots that had some claim to being at that battle, but I have mentioned two Gist Patriots who were killed there—Private Richard Gist and Ensign Nathaniel Gist. I believe Richard succumbed to his battle injuries a following day. Mistakes were made on the 1890 monument at the national historical site, and names were omitted or errors made with spelling. This is easy to understand, and there is confusion about both Richard Gist and Nathaniel Gist. They were both killed, but the monument and Draper's book *King's Mountain and Its Heros* adds to this confusion.[306] Richard was not named initially, but later corrected lists show his name being added. Nathaniel's rank was listed as second lieutenant, but he was an ensign. Several historians have attempted to set the record straight, but many facts about the battle remain elusive.

Various historical accounts state there were between 1,127 and 1,661 men, 14 regiments, 14 detachments, and 234 companies present on or around that mountain. Given the fact that the fighting militias were from the colonies of Virginia, North Carolina, and what was soon to be the state of Tennessee, it is easy to understand the weaknesses of command and control in such an operation.[307] There were more militia soldiers available for the fight than space available on the mountain top!

Colonel William Campbell of the Washington County, Virginia, Militia was generally in charge of the battle for the top of the mountain. He was discussed earlier in this book in the stories of Patriots George Lee, Nathaniel, and Richard Gist. Campbell was chosen by his peers to lead the

---

[306] *King's Mountain and its Heroes: History of the Battle of King's Mountain,* Lyman C. Draper. Peter G. Thompson, publisher, Cincinnati, 1881. Reprinted by Forgotten Books, 16 November 2016. London, England.
[307] Ibid.

attack, and he did that well.[308] Remember he was inclined to start a battle quickly and found it difficult to detune operations once victory was assured. Lieutenant Colonel John Sevier of Washington County in North Carolina, the future governor of Tennessee, was there with his unit. Of course, there were units present not affiliated with these two units, but these were the largest. Two Gist brothers—Joseph and John—who were Indian spies were there. General Mordecai Gist and Captain Benjamin Gist of the Maryland Brigade may have been near, but they were with the Continental Line forces, and this was a militia-led battle. They did not participate.

I have found claims that Colonel Nathaniel Gist, son of Captain Christopher Gist, participated, but he was a prisoner with his Virginia Continental Army regiment at Charleston. Nathaniel Gist made a claim for payment for both Ensign Nathaniel and Richard Gist's rifles a year following the battle. This was the father of both men—he lived in North Carolina and was still alive. He claimed to be "heir at law." Remember, there were three Nathaniel Gists, as discussed in the Gist chapter.

The "fog of war" was thick at this battle. Here are some thoughts of mine concerning the conduct of that battle:

- The militia leaders decided to leave the infantry behind and ride horses into battle. This was not a cavalry battle, but horses were good bullet shields.
- Nearly all officers had good horses.
- Many militia captains had few men, sometimes no men, under their command during the actual battle on the mountain (their men did not have horses). There were more officers engaged than enlisted militiamen, and this is normally not an assurance of victory.
- Majors led as few as two captains with no enlisted men. Those companies with enlisted men had an average of five men.

These facts lead us to consider that we may never know the exact "order of battle," that is, which officers led specific men at a specific location and time of the battle? Stories of the battle relate that the militiamen would be driven back, regroup, and charge the hill again and again. I doubt if all 1,200 men would have been engaged simultaneously, but replacements were readily available. British Major Ferguson was killed early in the battle, and that quickly drew activities to an end. Many prisoners were taken.

I read a soldier's pension claim in which he said he was there because he could hear the guns. That pension was approved, as it should have been. [309]

I salute those Patriots, and I wish I knew all the names, especially those losing their lives, as their efforts helped turn the tide of the Revolutionary War.

---

[308] *King's Mountain: The Defeat of the Loyalists, October 7, 1780,* J. David Dameron, DaCapo Press, 1 October 2003.
[309] Ibid.

These are the soldiers featured in this book that are proven to have been in the Battle of Kings Mountain:

- Joshua Gist served in the North Carolina Militia under John Sevier.
- John Gist served in the North Carolina Militia under Sevier and was an Indian spy.
- Joseph Gist was an Indian spy who served in Sevier's North Carolina Militia.
- Richard Gist served in the Washington County, Virginia, Militia under Colonel Campbell and was killed in the battle.
- Ensign Nathaniel Gist served in the Washington County Militia under Colonel Campbell and was killed in the battle
- Thomas Gist served in the Tenth Virginia Line at the battle. Thomas had also served in the French and Indian War and had been captured by Indians.
- George Lee served under Colonel Campbell in the Washington County Militia. He also soon fought in the Guilford Courthouse battle, discussed next.

> **"The tree of liberty must be refreshed from time to time with the blood of Patriots and tyrants."**
>
> —*Thomas Jefferson*

## Chapter Eleven: The Guilford Courthouse Battle

I did not initially intend to focus on individual battles involving Patriots presented earlier in the book, but through further research, the Battle of Guilford Courthouse distinguished itself for two reasons. First, it was arguably the beginning of the end for General Cornwallis and his British army in the southern area of operations. Second, at least seven of the Patriots presented earlier in the book almost certainly participated in that battle. Additionally, I have studied that battle as one of the first true cavalry battles for the colonies and for the soon-to-be United States. It was a landmark battle for many reasons and truly deserves a chapter in this book honoring those soldiers. These Patriots were there, and they gave a good account of themselves.

Sergeant Joshua Pearce Sr. served in the First Maryland Regiment. This was a battle-hardened unit that General Nathanael Greene relied on to hold their line against the professional British soldiers. This Continental Line regiment under Colonel Smallwood had never fought in its home colony but had served in eight major battles, including the recent Cowpens battle. This unit and the Lee and Washington cavalry units were as close as they could get to being professional army fighting units. The British would have their hands full with these three units.

The Rains brothers Anthony, Lawrence, and John were close to home, maybe within fifteen miles, and knew what they were fighting for. John, the youngest brother, was a fighter, and his brothers probably stuck close to him. General Allen put the North Carolina Militia regiments on the front line, and when the cavalry units of Lee and Washington moved latterly out of their firing fields just prior to the central battle, the North Carolina soldiers were the shooters. They held as long as possible, but General Greene knew they would quickly be pushed back, and he was correct. When they retreated, the First Maryland and Seventh Maryland Regiments were dug in and prevented the British from pursuing them. Remember, these regiments never retreated during the war—Mordecai Gist had taught that trait to them at the Battle of Long Island years earlier.

William Webb II of the Maryland Seventh Regiment served alongside the Maryland First Regiment discussed above. Again, along with the First Regiment, these were hard-fighting units.

The army of the southern theater commanded by Major General Nathanael Greene was camped at the Guilford Courthouse on 1 March 1781 with between four thousand and five thousand soldiers. This force consisted of North Carolina Militia, reinforcements from the Virginia Militia consisting of three thousand men, and two regiments from Maryland. The Hillsborough District Brigade—consisting of both the Randolph and Chatham County Regiments—was present as well as the Virginia regiment from Patrick Henry County.[310] After all, Greensboro is but a few miles

---

[310] *Long, Obstinate, and Bloody: The Battle of Guilford Courthouse,* Lawrence E. Babits and Joshua B. Howard, University of North Carolina Press, 2009. Page 122 relates that the British had a force of about 2,100 men, while Greene's force numbered at least 4,500 men.

from those counties. Two independent Continental units are worthy of note. The presence of Lieutenant Colonel Henry Lee's "Lee's Legends" and Colonel William Washington's First and Second Continental Light Dragoons made this a cavalry battle, one of the first true cavalry battles of the war. Also, several of the North Carolina Militia regiments were mounted, as I read several pension requests in which the soldier stated he was in a militia cavalry unit for that battle. However, I would consider them mounted infantry as opposed to true cavalry units.

The British forces commanded by Lieutenant General Cornwallis, consisting of 1,900 men, were camped at Hillsborough, North Carolina. The Cornwallis force consisted of Tory and freed slave forces as well as British regulars. They had just recently met in battle at the Battle of Cowpens, with the British suffering losses of their light infantry and most of their logistics supplies being burned by themselves to prevent capture by the rebels. Their intent was to destroy the Nathanael Greene army and proceed to Yorktown, then catch a ride with the British navy to New York and win the war. Ethan Allen stood in their way at Greensboro, and his forces outnumbered the British forces by more than two to one.

When General Cornwallis learned of Allen's forces at Greensboro, he quickly decided to give battle. At about 2:00 pm on 15 March, advance forces consisting of British Dragoons and Lighthorse Lee's Dragoons met about four miles west of the courthouse.[311] [312] There was a brief skirmish, and Lee's forces withdrew to Allen's defense perimeter around the courthouse. Allen's defensive line was made up of three lines, the first consisting of the North Carolina Militia regiments. The Rains brothers—Anthony, Lawrence, and John—would have been in that first line of defense. The second defensive line consisted of Virginia militia in which Colonel Abraham Penn was positioned with the Patrick Henry Regiment.[313] Colonel William Campbell's Regiment was on the left center of the second line, and George Lee was certainly in that unit. Lieutenant Colonel Lighthorse Lee fully expected the North Carolina Militia to quickly retreat through the second line, and they did just that, but only after delivering several volleys of very destructive fire against the British.[314] Later British accounts of the battle mentioned that they did not expect such destructive fire that early in the battle.

The battle lasted no longer than ninety minutes, with the British controlling most of the action. The Americans were quick to retreat, but the British did not pursue them and consolidate their victory. Most historians consider this a British victory, but they lost a quarter of their men. The British newspapers later stated that another such victory would ruin the British army. Allen's colonial army lost less than one hundred men, with over one hundred wounded. Their losses would have certainly been greater, but the cavalry forces were effective in preventing the British forces from pursuing the retreating Americans.

---

[311] *The Road to Guilford Courthouse: The American Revolution in the Carolinas,* John Buchanan. John Wiley and Sons Ltd., New York, 1997. Pages 369–371 describe the first contact between the forces of Lee and Campbell with the British about four miles west of the Guilford Courthouse.

[312] "New Garden, Battle of," Lindley S. Butler, *NCpedia,* 2006. This gives additional information about the first contact.

[313] *The Road to Guilford Courthouse: The American Revolution in the Carolinas,* John Buchanan. John Wiley and Sons Ltd., New York, 1997. Pages 372–373 describe positioning of the forces at the main battle at the courthouse.

[314] *Long, Obstinate, and Bloody: The Battle of Guilford Courthouse,* Lawrence E. Babits and Joshua B. Howard, University of North Carolina Press, 2009. Page 175 relates that the North Carolina militiamen performed somewhat better than expected and proved themselves useful in this battle.

After the battle, it was reported that more than five hundred North Carolina men were missing, greatly exaggerating the losses incurred. It was later determined that most simply went home soon following the battle.[315] Colonel Campbell's Regiment held the line and may have lost more than one hundred men and suffered the brunt of the losses. Lighthorse Lee later notified the Virginia legislature of the heroic action of Campbell and his men. Campbell openly claimed that Lee had sacrificed his unit. Colonel Campbell died of a heart attack later that year after being promoted to general.

I can say with confidence that the Americans were not poor fighters, as Ethan Allen's operational strategy had been similar in recent battles: cause the British to deploy, kill as many of them as possible, then retreat to fight another day. That was an effective strategy. It would not have been possible without skilled cavalry to help shape the battlefield, provide intelligence, and exploit weaknesses. That is what cavalry should do, and that is what it has done in subsequent wars. As for as the individual accounts of mounted militia soldiers, I think they were just that: mounted soldiers. They were probably not trained cavalry soldiers or accustomed to that manner of fighting.

Following the Guilford battle, the Cornwallis forces retreated south to South Carolina to rebuild and restock, with Ethan Allen's forces in pursuit. Remember, Cornwallis's forces had burned their trains following the earlier Battle of Cowpens, so they badly needed to forage and reorganize. Their destination was Yorktown, Virginia, and the British fleet, but the Dismal Swamp was between them and their destination. General Washington and the southern army leaders were keenly aware of this barrier and used it to their advantage. George Washington knew that swamp quite well, as he had personally surveyed it prior to the French and Indian War with the intent of making an investment there. That swamp was many times larger during the colonial period than it is today. That barrier made the advancement of the British forces a slow one, which allowed General Washington sufficient time to prepare for the coming battle at Yorktown that ended the war. It also permitted Ethan Allen's forces to push their advancement and restrict the British from effectively foraging and reconstituting their forces with freed slaves and Tories.

The Guilford battle did not win the war, but it was likely the beginning of the end. Sergeant Joshua Pearce Sr., the Rains brothers, George Lee, William Webb II, and perhaps Richard Gist played their part and were witnesses to a landmark battle. They also protected their homes and families, which I am sure was their first objective.

---

[315] *A Guide to the Battles of the American Revolution,* Theodore P. Savas and J. David Dameron, Beatie LLC, 2010. Page 175 relates that many of the North Carolina militiamen returned home after the battle.

As mentioned above, I believe there were at least seven family Patriots featured in this book who participated in this important battle. They were:

- Joshua Pearce—He was assigned in the First Maryland Continental Line Regiment and was probably positioned on the second line of defense.
- Anthony Rains—North Carolina militia.
- Lawrence Rains—North Carolina militia.
- John Rains—North Carolina militia.
- William Webb—Seventh Maryland Regiment and First Maryland Brigade.
- Richard Gist—Third Maryland Continental Line Regiment of the First Brigade. I am simply unsure if he was still alive by the time of this battle.
- George Lee—He was in Colonel William Campbell's Montgomery County, Virginia, Regiment, which took severe losses.

I must temper this claim with the fact that I have few records definitively proving these men were in the fight. First, their units were present, and that was not difficult to establish. Second, these men were serving in those units the day of the fight, but that alone does not establish the claim. Maybe they had other duties, maybe they were sick, or maybe they were late in arriving. One may have been deceased by the time of the battle. Richard Gist (1729–1780) served in more than one regiment, but his last assignment was in the Maryland Third Continental Line Regiment, and that unit was positioned in the second line of defense. His death date and location have never been determined, as he simply cannot be accounted for after 1780. He was the son of Christopher the explorer, and his records are easily confused with his cousin Richard, who lost his life in the Kings Mountain battle in October 1780.

A final note regarding this landmark battle and the Rains family participants that should spark an interesting question or two: What about the rifle formally belonging to young Ambrose Rains? That rifle was appropriated by a Randolph County Militia officer, with a voucher being presented to Ambrose or his father. Ambrose was reimbursed by the Randolph County Court for the rifle following the war. Did that rifle find its way to the Battle of Guilford Courthouse? Did it help defend that first line of defense?

**"It must be laid down as a primary position, and the basis of our system, that every Citizen who enjoys the protection of a free Government, owes not only a proportion of his property, but even his personal service to the defense of it."**

*—George Washington's letter to Alexander Hamilton, Friday, 2 May 1783*

## Chapter Twelve: The Untold Family Patriot Stories

Research continues of the following possible family Patriots. Their stories did not make the deadline for publication of this book, and I am sure there are more to be discovered. While most of the men I continue to research are confirmed Patriots, their ties to a Raines/Painter line must be proven. Additionally, their stories must be developed with extensive research and documentation.

I expect these stories and others to be the centerpiece of a future edition of this book.

1. Charles Jones, father of Patriot Ellis Jones. I have not proven him to be the father of Ellis, but family histories of Ellis written by his descendants have made that assertion. I also have SAR records reflecting Ellis as a son of Charles, but that is not proof. Charles was a Patriot, and the details of his life make him a likely father of Ellis. Charles's proven father was a slave trader who died in Africa, so this story will be intriguing when I make the Ellis/Charles Jones connection.

2. Father of Davis Scott of the Scott/Painter line. Emma Jo and I believe that Davis Scott's father, name unknown, probably fought in the Revolution, and I have identified nine Virginia Revolutionary War Scott Patriots who settled in Kentucky where Davis was born in 1795. He was born in Lincoln County, and most early settlers in that county were there because of Revolutionary War land grants. It may take years to complete this family history and to document a Patriot. Davis Scott was a very interesting and colorful settler, and even though we have not yet identified his father, his story will be worth the effort. Davis Scott was Jo's second great-grandfather, a very early settler in Monroe County, Missouri, and a War of 1812 veteran.

3. George Rains Sr. If his brother Ishmael and mother Mary sold materials and services to the Revolutionary soldiers, it is possible that George did likewise, as they were neighbors. I am reviewing Randolph County, North Carolina, court records for such a sale. It is also possible that Randolph County Militia records will establish him as a Patriot, but the condition of these records may prohibit that. While I am not a direct descendant of George, this will add to the Rains story told in a previous chapter.

4. James Crooks III (1745–1823). He is a Patriot for patriotic service because of a supply tax being paid by him. His proven son James IV (1786–1813) is a possible father of Joseph Morris Crooks (1814–1866), who is Emma Jo's second great-grandfather on the Scott line. I have been unable to prove the relationship of James IV and Joseph Morris, as his father was killed in the War of 1812, with Joseph Morris being born soon after his

father's death. Joseph III's father, James Alexander Crooks, is also a Patriot, and this father/son relationship is proven.

5. John Bennett Hawkins (1744–1806). He was the father of Francis (1776–1850), who married John Johnston (1774–1827) of the Painter line. His father, Martin Johnston, served in the Virginia Third Continental Line Regiment and is featured in this book. I am confident that I will be able to prove the relationship of John to his daughter Francis, as I have a copy of John's wife Sarah Elizabeth Moulton's will that mentions Francis. John served in the Virginia Third Continental Line Regiment and is Emma Jo's possible fifth great-grandfather.

6. John Allen (1744–1804). John is the father of George Allen, who married Barbary Myers, daughter of Patriot Henry Myers discussed earlier in the book. John served in the New Hampshire Militia during the Revolutionary War and died in Montgomery County, Kentucky. John is also a *Mayflower* Descendant. I have proven his proposed son George's relationship with his wife Barbary and their family, as well as their connection to their daughter Melinda, who married Joseph Morris Crooks (see number 4 above for their connections to Emma Jo's Scott family line). Further proof of George being the son of John is needed.

7. Benjamin Taylor Jr. (1745–1815). Benjamin is the possible grandfather of Mildred (Millie) Taylor, who married Milton Toney Younger, the father of Charles Lee Younger, whose photo is shown earlier in this book. Charles Lee is my second great-grandfather, making Benjamin Jr. my fifth great-grandfather. Benjamin was born in Virginia and died in Pulaski County, Kentucky, and served in the Virginia Line during the Revolutionary War under the command of General George Rogers Clark. His son William (1775–1867) was born in Virginia and lived in Madison County, Kentucky, and died in Blackwater, Cooper County, Missouri. William's daughter Mildred (1801–1875) was born in Kentucky. She outlived her husband Milton Toney Younger by twenty-three years and is buried in the Millers Chapel Cemetery in Heath Creek Township in Pettis County, Missouri. Several generations of the Younger and Raines families are also buried in that cemetery. This will add one more Younger family Patriot story when I fully document the relationships of Benjamin Taylor Jr. to his possible son William and his possible granddaughter Millie.

A future edition of this book has begun with a research project in the search for women Patriots. These women usually did not fight in organized regiments as did their husbands and fathers but served the Revolution in logistics roles with their material and financial support. Imagine if you will that, in the absence of the male of the house, finances were likely tight. All the Revolutionary units subsisted not from an organized supply system but from foraging within the local economy. Company officers would issue vouchers for food and supplies they obtained, and the seller would make claims for reimbursement to their county government well after the conclusion of the war. Many of these records still exist. Both the SAR and the DAR recognize these women as Patriots and will grant membership based on such validated claims.

I believe this research will yield recognition of some additional family Patriots. Remember, the Revolution was a divisive war, with communities comprised of revolutionaries, Tories, and anti-war religious zealots. Any woman who supported the colonial militias put herself at the mercy of those who disagreed with the undisciplined revolutionaries and was placing herself and her family at risk. I also cannot discount the possibility that some women served in medical capacities and even fired shots in anger. Remember, in the introduction I stated that these Patriots placed their lives, fortunes, and sacred honor at risk in this great gamble. They knew the risks, as did their families. This line of research is relatively new, and I have documented Mary Rains, mother of Ishmael, as a Patriot, but her kinship must be proven. There are more to come. Ann Scott, Sarah Rains, Eve Catherine Painter, and Elizabeth Triplett are candidates for this honor. Those will be great stories.

**"If there be trouble, let it be in my day, that my child may have peace."**

*—Tom Paine*

## Chapter Thirteen: Final Muster Call

This book featured the life stories and family relationships of forty-five Patriots from which Emma Jo and I are directly descended. Four additional chapters featured the stories of sixty-two additional Patriots related to our direct ancestors. They were either brothers, sons, or grandsons of the featured forty-five Patriots. It's worthwhile to ponder the implications of the actions of these men and their families. The following summations will be of some assistance.

These Patriots hailed from eight of the thirteen colonies and one territory. Pennsylvania, New York, Massachusetts, Maryland, Virginia, North Carolina, New Jersey, Connecticut, and the Vermont territory were their homes. They fought not only for an idea, but for their homes, colonies, and families. I am unsure if any fought for the idea of a "United States," as the concept of united colonies just did not take on any significance in the minds of the common man until a few years after the Constitution was finalized and approved. Most fought to preserve the freedoms that had eluded previous generations in a European setting. One can also consider that incentives offered by the various colonies were a source of motivation. Many of these men and their families received land grants and subsequently followed those incentives in the westward movement to Kentucky and beyond. Within fifty years many of their children were living in Texas, Missouri, Iowa, and Oregon, making history in those states.

The term "family commitment" takes on added dimensions when one considers the fact that father, son, and grandson involvement in the Revolution was not unusual. I documented more than twelve father and son Patriots and four three-generation family teams in support of a war that lasted about seven years. Several Patriots were married, and their wives either stayed behind living in a frontier settlement or moved to support their husbands. This war was a family affair.

At least three of these men were born in Europe and became citizen soldiers or political leaders within a few years of arriving on the eastern seaboard. Three families were among the first residents of early Massachusetts and had been colonial citizens for four generations prior to the Revolution. Several of these Patriots were first-generation Americans. They all had a reason to fight, whether it was freedom of religion, land ownership, or preservation of their status quo. Four family lines can claim first-family *Mayflower* descendance.

They were all volunteers. A sharp reader may point out that Pennsylvania had a conscription law, but they were still volunteers. Several Patriots served their initial enlistment obligation, were discharged, and subsequently volunteered in a second unit.

They fought in all thirteen colonies and frontier territories in dozens of major Revolutionary War battles. Their voluntary service in the military and in political leadership was instrumental in the colonies' victory. Most fought in combat units and were wounded more than once. Several were taken prisoner of war during their service. None of these soldiers were professional solders, so they returned to their rural way of life following the war. I believe most were farmers or became farmers or plantation owners following the war.

The statement I made in chapter one that **each Patriot placed their life, sacred honor, and fortune at great risk for their family's freedom and the freedoms we enjoy today** was at least partially prophetic. I discovered that none of our direct relatives lost their lives in the Revolution, but we could make the case based on pension claims that some believed their lives were shortened due to combat or accidental injuries. It was a brutal war.

Their sacred honor has been preserved, no doubt. This book hopefully serves to enhance that honor. There are renewed efforts to locate and document the graves of Revolutionary War Patriots, and that effort continues with both the DAR and SAR and other organizations. We will continue our efforts in search of the unknown burial sites of these Patriots and ensure those sites are appropriately recognized and marked.

Finally, maybe one of these Patriots could be considered wealthy by any measure—historical or current—but most were of meager means. Discussions of the wealth of any of the two Lee lines conjures up images of European noble wealth, but that is probably inaccurate. The Lees were probably wealthy in terms of land but held little cash. Within a generation of the war, that family's wealth had been well-diluted. The same could be said of the Whipple and Reinecker wealth. Many of these Patriots died with few assets, as attested by their claims for pension. It is easy to imagine that some of them passed their estates, however small, to their children prior to their death. What can be said about these forty-five Americans is they all became landowners much more quickly than might have been otherwise possible, and their descendants prospered in the westward expansion. Their successful Revolution set the stage for the later growth of this nation in ways that simply would not otherwise have been possible. They became landowners and citizens with a stake in history. They were Patriots!

# Directory of Figures

# Bibliography

## Primary Sources

Official Military Records of all soldiers, National Archives

Missouri Digital Heritage: www.sos.mo.gov

Ipswich, Massachusetts, Town and Vital Records, 1620–1988

Official Military Records of Pennsylvania Soldiers of the Revolution, Pennsylvania Archives

Cumberland Association Records

Federal Census Reports for various states, counties, and census years, National Archives files

Kentucky County tax lists, internet-based Kentucky files

Randolph County, North Carolina, tax lists

Scott Family of Missouri Bible. Beginning with Davis Scott through Cerra Scott, documenting the Scott, Murphy, and Roney families of Missouri. In possession of the Scott family.


## Secondary Sources, Published

*Cavaliers and Pioneers: Abstracts of Virginia Land Patents and Grants.* Abstracted by Nell Marion Nugent. Volume Three, 1695–1732. Virginia Book Company, Serryville, Virginia, 1979.

*Roster of Soldiers From North Carolina in the American Revolution.* Genealogical Publishing Co., Inc., 1977.

"List of Revolutionary War Soldiers of Virginia." Special Report of the Department of Archives and History for 1912. H.J. Eckendorf, Archivist. David Bottom, Superintendent of Public Printing, 1913. Virginia State Library.

*Historical Register of Virginians in the Revolution: Soldiers, Sailors, Marines, 1775–1783.* John H. Gwathmey. Richmond, Virginia, 1938. Reprinted by Genealogical Publishing Company Inc., Baltimore, Maryland.

*Valley Forge Soldiers.* Society of the Descendants of Washington's Army at Valley Forge.

*Colonial Families of the Southern States of America: A History and Genealogy of Colonial Families Who Settled in the Colonies Prior to the Revolution.* Stella Pickett Hardy. Tobias A. Wright, Printer and Publisher, 1911.

*Younger/Plummer Families in Missouri.* Bob Younger. Morningside Press, Dayton, OH.

*Massachusetts Soldiers and Sailors of the Revolutionary War: A Compilation from the Archives.* Volume I. Massachusetts Secretary of the Commonwealth. Wright & Potter Printing, 1896–1908.

*History and Genealogy of "Elder" John Whipple of Ipswich, Massachusetts: His English Ancestors and American Descendants.* Blane Whipple. Whipple Development Corporation, Victoria, British Columbia, 2003.

*Dear Brother: Letters of William Clark to Johnathan Clark.* James J. Holmberg. Yale University Press, New Haven and London.

*Thomas Jefferson Encyclopedia,* Based on J.R. McGrew, Monticello Research Report. Hanover, Pennsylvania, May 1991.

*Revolutionary War Bounty Land Grants Awarded by State Governments.* Lloyd DeWitt Bockstruck. Genealogical Publishing Co., Baltimore, Maryland, 1997, 1998.

*North Carolina Revolutionary War Accounts.* Weynette Parks Haun. W.P. Haun, Durham, N.C.

*Colonial Caroline: A History of Caroline County, Virginia.* T.E. Campbell. The Dietz Press, Inc., Richmond, Virginia, third printing 1989.

*Virginia Militia in the Revolutionary War: McAllister's Data (1913).* Place of publication unknown. J.T. McAllister.

*The Compendium of American Genealogy: First Families of America.* Vol VII. Frederick Adams Virkus. A.N. Marquis and Company.

*Virginia's Colonial Soldiers.* Lloyd DeWitt Bockstruck. Genealogical Publishing Co. Inc., Baltimore, Maryland, 1988.

*Virginia Northern Neck Land Grants, 1694–1742.* Gertrude E. Gray, compiler. Genealogy Publishing Company Inc., Baltimore, Maryland, 1987.

*Revolutionary War Records: Virginia Army and Navy Forces with Bounty Land Warrants for Virginia Military District of Ohio and Virginia Military Scrip from Federal and State Records.* Gaius Marcus Brumbaugh. Genealogical Publishing Company, Baltimore, Maryland.

*Shenandoah Valley Pioneers and their Descendants: A History of Frederick County, Virginia.* T.K Cartmell, 1909.

*Virginia Soldiers of 1776.* Volume II. Compiled by Louis Burgess. Richmond Press, Richmond, Virginia, 1927.

*Encyclopedia of Virginia Biography.* Volume IV. Lyon Gardiner Tyler, LLD. Lewis Historical Publishing Co., New York, 1915.

*Colonial Records of North Carolina.* Vol X, 1775–1776. William Saunders.

*A History of Henry County, Virginia.* Judith Parks America Hill. Heritage Books Inc., 2003.

*History of Patrick and Henry Counties, Virginia.* Virginia G. Pedigo and Lewis G. Pedigo. Genealogical Publishing Co. Inc., Roanoke, Virginia, 1933.

*The Maryland Militia in the Revolutionary War.* S. Eugene Clements and F. Edward Wright. Heritage Books Inc., 2008.

*New York in the Revolution as Colony and State.* James A. Roberts. The Press of Brandow Printing Company, Albany, New York.

*A Calendar of the Warrants for Land in Kentucky, Granted for Service in the French and Indian War.* Abstracted by Philip Fall Taylor. Clearfield Company, Inc., Baltimore, Maryland.

*The History of Tuscarawas County, Ohio.* Warner, Beers and Company, 1884.

*Patriots of the Upcountry: Orange Country, Virginia, in the Revolution.* William H.B. Thomas. Orange County Bicentennial Commission, 1976.

## Unpublished Sources

Daughters of the American Revolution (DAR) Website: Records of Ancestors and Patriots. Internet resource.

Sons of the American Revolution (SAR) Website of Patriots. Internet source.

Letter from Town of Ipswich, Massachusetts, dated 2 May 1978 naming the parents of Samuel Adams and his marriage to Jemima Whipple. Located with the city and in our files.

The Perrigo Papers. Family research papers submitted by many Perrigo family members and distributed for family review. Contained in our files.

Letter of J.M. Jones relating Ellis Jones's family history dated 27 April 1892. Located in our files.

"Richard Henry Lee of Virginia: A Biography." Mary Elizabeth Virginia. An unpublished dissertation submitted to the faculty of the graduate school of the State University of New York at Buffalo, 1992. Contained in university files.

"The Little Wells Family in North America: Alexander Wells, 1727–1813." Harold and Nadine Hull Arnold, 1969. Edited and reorganized by Harold Hull Arnold, 1998. Located in our files.

www.ingramcontent.com/pod-product-compliance
Lightning Source LLC
Chambersburg PA
CBHW050353110426
42812CB00008B/2448